INSEPARABLE

❊ INSEPARABLE ❊

The Original Siamese Twins
and Their Rendezvous with
American History

Yunte Huang

LIVERIGHT PUBLISHING CORPORATION

A Division of W. W. Norton & Company

Independent Publishers Since 1923

New York | London

For information about permission to reproduce selections from this book, write to
Permissions, Liveright Publishing Corporation, a division of W. W. Norton & Company, Inc.,
500 Fifth Avenue, New York, NY 10110

For information about special discounts for bulk purchases, please contact
W. W. Norton Special Sales at specialsales@wwnorton.com or 800-233-4830

Manufacturing by LSC Communications Harrisonburg
Book design by Chris Welch
Production manager: Lauren Abbate

Library of Congress Cataloging-in-Publication Data

Names: Huang, Yunte, author.
Title: Inseparable : the original Siamese twins and their rendezvous
with American history / Yunte Huang.
Description: First edition. | New York : Liveright Publishing Corporation, a Division
of W.W. Norton & Company, [2018] | Includes bibliographical references and index.
Identifiers: LCCN 2017055799 | ISBN 9780871404473 (hardcover)
Subjects: LCSH: Bunker, Chang, 1811–1874. | Bunker, Eng, 1811–1874. | Conjoined twins—
United States—History—19th century. | Conjoined twins—United States—Biography.
Classification: LCC QM691.B86 H83 2018 | DDC 616/.043092 [B] —dc23
LC record available at https://lccn.loc.gov/2017055799

Liveright Publishing Corporation, 500 Fifth Avenue, New York, N.Y. 10110
www.wwnorton.com

W. W. Norton & Company Ltd., 15 Carlisle Street, London W1D 3BS

1 2 3 4 5 6 7 8 9 0

Contents

List of Illustrations   ix

Preface   xi

Prologue: A Game on the High Seas   xv

PART ONE ❊ IN SIAM

  1. Siam   3

  2. The Chinese Twins   6

  3. Cholera   15

  4. The King and Us   20

  5. Departure   26

PART TWO ❊ FIRST YEARS

  6. A Curiosity in Boston   39

  7. The Monster, or Not   51

  8. Gotham City   57

  9. The City of Brotherly Love   66

  10. Knocking at the Gate   70

  11. Racial Freaks   80

  12. Sentimental Education   89

PART THREE ❖ AMERICA ON THE ROAD

13. The Great Eclipse   97
14. A Satirical Tale   102
15. The Lynnfield Battle   108
16. An Intimate Rebellion   117
17. Old Dominion   125
18. Emancipation   131
19. A Parable   138
20. America on the Road   146
21. The Deep South   163
22. Head Bumps   170

PART FOUR ❖ LOOK HOMEWARD, ANGEL

23. Wilkesboro   187
24. Traphill   197
25. A Universal Truth   206
26. Foursome   225
27. Mount Airy, or Monticello   235
28. The Age of Humbugs   252
29. Minstrel Freaks   268

PART FIVE ❖ THE CIVIL WAR AND BEYOND

30. Seeing the Elephant   283
31. Reconstruction   297
32. The Last Radiance of the Setting Sun   306
33. Afterlife   317

Epilogue: Mayberry, USA   327
Acknowledgments   349
Notes   351
Selected Bibliography   373
Index   381

List of Illustrations

Frontispiece: Chang and Eng *(Courtesy of Wellcome Library, London)*

page xv: Cunard Steamer *Palmyra (Courtesy of the Osher Map Library Collection, University of Southern Maine)*

page xxiii: Passenger List of the *Palmyra (Courtesy of the National Archives, Washington, DC)*

page 1: A Siamese Canal *(Courtesy of New York Public Library)*

page 29: Robert Hunter's House, Bangkok *(Courtesy of Ira Hsiao)*

page 33: Contract between Siamese Twins and Robert Hunter/Abel Coffin, 1829 *(Courtesy of Surry County Historical Society, North Carolina)*

page 37: Chang and Eng, Lithograph *(Courtesy of Wilson Library, University of North Carolina at Chapel Hill)*

page 39: Passenger List of the *Sachem (Courtesy of the National Archives, Washington, DC)*

page 52: Chang and Eng in an Oriental Setting, Lithograph, 1829 *(Courtesy of Wellcome Library, London)*

page 57: Advertising Poster *(Courtesy of Wilson Library, University of North Carolina at Chapel Hill)*

page 70: Chang and Eng, Lithograph *(Courtesy of Wellcome Library, London)*

page 84: Chang and Eng Playing Badminton, 1830 *(Courtesy of Wellcome Library, London)*

page 95: Account Book of Chang and Eng *(Courtesy of Wilson Library, University of North Carolina at Chapel Hill)*

page 137: Signatures of Chang and Eng *(Courtesy of State Archives of North Carolina)* page 185: Chang and Eng's House, Traphill *(Courtesy of Wilson Library, University of North Carolina at Chapel Hill)*

page 239: Grace ("Aunt Grace") Gates, First Slave Owned by Chang and Eng Bunker *(Courtesy of Wilson Library, University of North Carolina at Chapel Hill)*

page 240: Bill of Sale for Two Slaves Sold to Chang and Eng Bunker *(Courtesy of Wilson Library, University of North Carolina at Chapel Hill)*

page 256: P. T. Barnum and General Tom Thumb *(Courtesy of New York Public Library)*

page 269: Chang and Eng Bunker and Their Children *(Courtesy of Wilson Library, University of North Carolina at Chapel Hill)*

page 281: Union and Confederate Dead, Gettysburg Battlefield, Pennsylvania, July 1863 *(Courtesy of the National Archives, Washington, DC)*

page 298: Chang and Eng Bunker Families, 1870 *(Courtesy of Special Collections Research Center, Syracuse University Libraries)*

page 301: Chang and Eng Bunker and Their Wives and Children *(Courtesy of Special Collections Research Center, Syracuse University Libraries)*

page 307: Eng's House, Where the Twins Died *(Courtesy of Wilson Library, University of North Carolina at Chapel Hill)*

page 331: Statue of Andy and Opie Taylor, Mount Airy, North Carolina *(Photo by author)*

page 334: Chang and Eng Bunker's Grave, White Plains, North Carolina *(Photo by author)*

page 335: White Plains Baptist Church, North Carolina *(Photo by author)*

page 339: Sign for Mayberry Campground, Mount Airy, North Carolina *(Photo by author)*

Preface

The focus of *Inseparable* is the extraordinary life of Chang and Eng Bunker, the original Siamese Twins, who, by virtue of their physical anomaly, were seen as freaks, subhuman, or, as Victor Hugo so devastatingly couched it in *The Hunchback of Notre Dame*, "an almost." An odd pair, they beat impossible odds—touring the world, making money, getting married, and having children. Better yet, they did all of this with grit and gusto.

It feels like a cliché to say that their story is an example of the triumphant human spirit. This is the kind of trope you might find in a high school primer, for their experience actually not only questions what it means to be *a* human but also examines the outer limits of living one's own life and dying one's own death. As the cornerstone of liberal democracy, individualism is not capable of defining or, conversely, confining the conjoined life of the Siamese Twins. To them, being human meant being more than one, inseparable from the other—never alone in life, death, happiness, pain, procreation, or even in answering the call of nature. They defy what Leslie Fiedler once called "the tyranny of the normal," a cultural malaise the eminent literary critic cogently denounced.

Writing this book at a historical moment when we see, once again, a rising tide of human disqualification, of looking at others as less than human or normal, has given me an acute sense of urgency. My concern has much less to do with partisan kibitzing (yes, a very *un*Chinese word) than with the disquieting fact that, in the words of the great Yogi Berra, "It's like *déjà vu* all over again."

The fact that this remarkable story commences in the age of Jacksonian democracy and gathers steam at the apex of American humbuggery is not an insignificant aspect of my book. Although P. T. Barnum, much to his chagrin, did not play a key role in Chang and Eng's career, the Prince of Humbugs was, in fact, a mover and shaker of American popular culture in his time, the progenitor of an industry that entertained and exploited and made money out of displaying curiosities, be they freaks, wonders, beauties, or beasts. Even the glitzy beauty pageant today has its origin in the nineteenth-century freak show as niftily orchestrated by Barnum. Or, for that matter, the film industry also began in the freak show before making the transition to projecting beautiful faces or beautified illusions, and part of the cinema's power persists with shock and awe. As history reveals, the success of the freak show, indubitably the birthplace of American mass entertainment, relied not only on the ingenuity and sacrifice of superb showmen like the Siamese Twins but also on the braggadocio and charlatanism of impresarios, or carnival barkers, who enticed crowds via sales puffery and manipulation of public opinion. Barnum once said to the effect that the American people loved to be entertained and humbugged—or, more bluntly, according to some, "There's a sucker born every minute."

As I relate in *Inseparable*, it would contribute very little to our understanding of American culture if we were simply to dismiss Barnum and his ilk as conniving charlatans or Yankee peddlers. We need to recognize a humbug as a trickster, a confidence man who is not necessarily the Devil, even though he often traffics in devilish ways. Being tricked by a con man, as Herman Melville reminded us long ago in *The Confidence-Man*, is a price we pay in the confidence game called Democracy. It is worth noting, then, that the boom of the freak show as humbuggery coincided with the rise of the common man during the Jacksonian Age, an era that nowadays some see as approximate to our own. When everyone feels entitled to an opinion but cannot, by virtue of ignorance or innocence, tell the difference between a gag and a gem, between what showbiz calls "gaffed freaks" and "born freaks," the confidence man swoops in to make you feel better while he takes your money, or outright steals your soul. In this sense, the freak show, which lies at the heart of Chang and Eng's story, is not just about looking at others as less human. To borrow a concept from the eminent anthropologist Clifford Geertz, a freak show is a "deep play." Or, in the streetwise lingo of a humbug, it is "the long game."

Brushing against the grain of American individualism, democracy, and humbuggery, the story of Chang and Eng is also complicated by their imbroglio with the institution of chattel slavery, miscegenation, and a host of other incendiary issues that roiled nineteenth-century America. Virtually sold into slavery, they would later own and trade slaves themselves. Having married two white sisters—an unusual union denigrated as "bestial" by some penny-press editors—they might also have fathered children with their own slave women. As slaveholding Southern gentry, they stood staunchly with the Confederacy in the epic fight against the Yankees, who once exploited them. All these narrative strands, in varying shades of verity and plausibility, make their biography more complex even than the short, fleshy band that so famously connected them.

The legacy of Chang and Eng, not surprisingly, survives far beyond their death. I don't just mean the longevity of their brand name, which now applies to every pair of conjoined twins; or the thriving Bunker clan, their proud descendants numbering more than 1,500 today; or their shared liver on permanent display as an anatomical curio at the Mütter Museum in Philadelphia. As I will show at the conclusion of the book, after their story seems over (and, no, I'm not giving away anything), we are surprised to find what we can call their "Mayberry connection." Most fans of *The Andy Griffith Show* would know that Mayberry, the fictional setting for that most popular 1960s American rubecom, was based on Griffith's actual birthplace, Mount Airy, North Carolina. But, unknown to most, Mount Airy was also the adopted hometown of Chang and Eng, the place where they lived and died. It is fair to say that *The Andy Griffith Show* is supposedly about the "American normal," Mayberry being a sleepy hamlet where everyone is kith or kin, an Arcadia where no trouble is too big for the amiable sheriff and his bungling deputy. The fortuitous coexistence of Andy Griffith and the Siamese Twins—one representing the "normal" and the other the "freakish"—is a case of cultural symbiosis. It is a condition often forgotten or willfully ignored, as were any racial themes in what, in fact, appeared like Jim Crow–era Mayberry, which featured virtually no black character in its folksy haven. The norm, to paraphrase Fiedler, continues to tyrannize the abnormal, burying it deep underground, into the granite foundation of America. Chang and Eng revolted against that tyranny, in part by mimicking it, and, in the course of their incredible life and beyond, revealed the inseparable tie between what's accepted as human and what's rejected as freakish—that is the story of the Siamese Twins I want to tell.

A Game on the High Seas

CUNARD STEAMER *PALMYRA*

I t was supposed to be a routine voyage. The Cunard Royal Mail steamer *Palmyra* left Liverpool on July 30, 1870, setting sail for New York City.

Only five years earlier, the American Civil War had come to a close, with a loss of more than 600,000 lives. Not only had it ineradicably changed the nation and its way of being, it also had abolished the brutal institution of slavery and ended that tragic crossing known as the Middle Passage, a few thousand nautical miles to the south of the *Palmyra's* route. The burning embers that had erupted in the wake of General Sherman's March to the Sea had long since cooled off, but the South remained bitter and defiant, mired in the slow and painful process known as Reconstruction. At the same time, the North, along with the rest of the country, was hurtling along at almost unchecked speed toward

the future. Few seemed to heed the backwoodsman Henry David Thoreau's contrarian wisdom: "Why the hurry?" America was, in fact, in an
existential hurry, with the iron horse—the train—leading the charge of
economic expansion. The 1869 completion of the transcontinental railroad, built on the backs and lives of Irish and Chinese coolie laborers,
had brought the nation together, at least spatially. New towns sprouted
along newly laid railroad tracks like bamboo shoots after a spring rain.
Cattle kingdoms arose like tumbleweed in Texas and the plains states.
The dizzying pace of urban expansion and frenetic economic development had ushered in a new era in America: the Gilded Age.

The *Palmyra*, built in 1866 to keep abreast of the exponential increase
in transatlantic traffic, was a medium-size steamship—2,044 in ton-
nage, 260 in nominal horsepower, and a passenger capacity of forty-six
in cabin class and 650 in steerage.[1] On this particular westward voyage,
the *Palmyra*, under the command of Captain William Watson, carried
29 passengers in cabin class and 377 in steerage.[2]

A steamer like the *Palmyra* was a major improvement on a sailing
ship, cutting the length of the transatlantic journey from an almost
insufferable eight weeks down to two. However, these were the early
days of cruise voyages, with conditions aboard still crude, if not primitive. Cabins were as small as a so-called cat's ear, dimly lit by a single
candle. Passengers had to wash their own dishes. To get fresh milk—
before the age of electricity and refrigerators—the company actually
carried live cows aboard. To control rats, cats—which, of course, were
oblivious to the class divisions of cabin and steerage—were taken along
for the cruise.[3] Charles Dickens, who had crossed the Atlantic nearly
three decades earlier on the SS *Britannia* to visit the United States,
complained bitterly of tasteless food, inebriated cooks, and cramped
cabins, about which the famous novelist wrote, "nothing smaller for
sleeping in was ever made except coffins."[4] Mark Twain, the globetrotter
who coined the term *Gilded Age*, blessed these newfangled steamships
with an even more withering remark in his travelogues, characterizing
the meals as "plenty of good food furnished by the Deity and cooked by
the devil."[5] Colorful derision aside, the customary seagoing fare was a

far cry from what the steamship companies had advertised as the luxury of "a cheerful, hospitable, and elegant Floating Hotel."[6]

On her second day at sea, as land faded on the horizon, the *Palmyra* glided toward the deep waters of the blue Sargasso Sea. The ship's strong prow sliced through the water like a cheese-cutting knife, spewing fierce foam into the air. After breakfast, cabin passengers began to mingle or disperse. Those who felt queasy went to their cabins, while others lingered behind, engaging in all sorts of trivial pursuits to while away their time. Mr. John H. Slatt, a middle-aged English businessman, strolled on deck with his cane and stared at the vast monotony of the ocean, reminiscing about his first trip to America on the *Europa* more than twenty years earlier. Mr. Jacob Cigrange, a redheaded merchant, native of Luxembourg and now a proud resident of Fredonia, Wisconsin, lounged on a weatherworn deck chair, watching the vagaries of the clouds. Mrs. Rosa Prang, a Swiss blonde in her early forties, took her six-year-old nephew John to the stern rails to look for whales, porpoises, and sharks, which often frequented this part of the ocean. The boy was especially excited about seeing what the sailors called the Portuguese man-of-war, or Nautilus, that might appear in the ocean in days ahead. Those mystical sea snails, of light violet color under the sun, would ascend to the surface, putting up small "sails" and using their tails as navigating rudders. But there was nothing to see that day under a gray sky, except for scattered whitecaps that could easily be mistaken for sightings of something else.

In her earlier years, Mrs. Prang (née Gerber) had followed the footsteps of her brother and immigrated to America. On that trip from her native Switzerland to Paris, she had met a lanky young Prussian named Louis, whose deep-blue eyes had followed her across the aisle as the crowded four-wheeled diligence rumbled through Alpine mountain roads and flat French countryside. She had not thought much of him at the time, although she had been impressed by his story—he was running away from the Prussian police because he was a revolutionary radical. They went separate ways in Paris, and she set sail for America. Five years later, when one day she was milking cows on her brother's farm in Ohio, she received a letter from Louis asking her to meet him in Boston and marry him. At the time, she had been entertaining a marriage proposal from a neighboring young farmer. Maybe it was Louis's piercing blue eyes, or maybe it was his radical ideas and foolish ways, but the letter tantalized her with a future that was at least more appealing than the certain monotony of being a farmer's wife. Without further reflection, Rosa sold her cows to pay for her fare and headed for Boston.

The first few years of their marriage were hard financially. Louis had tried his hand at manufacturing stationery and leather goods, but he finally found his calling in wood engraving. In 1860, he founded L. Prang and Company, a brand that would soon become recognizable all over the world, for during the Civil War, the company sold millions of battleground maps and pictures of soldier heroes, living or dead. Unknown to Rosa, Louis's bigger reputation would still lie in the future. After the printing of greeting cards during the 1873 Christmas season, the man Rosa had chosen to marry in a leap of faith would become known in history as the "Father of the American Christmas Card."[7]

Aboard the *Palmyra*, when little John became bored from watching the ocean, Rosa took him to the saloon on the quarterdeck. As they entered, she saw a strange scene unfolding, almost like a stage play. Though the windows were open to let in the fresh air, the saloon door had remained shut to avoid sudden drafts. Without thorough ventilation, the strong smell of tobacco mixed with the ocean's salty tang. Mr. and Mrs. Herman and Honersia Ohly and their cousin were playing whist at a table with Mr. James Berrisford, an English merchant now living in Ohio. Earlier at breakfast, Rosa had chatted with Berrisford and his wife, Elizabeth, about the midwestern state where she had once milked cows.

The unacknowledged center of attention in the room, however, was a quiet chess game being played at another table. One player, a comely black man in his fifties, wearing a black suit and a bowtie, looked dignified, almost regal. The other player—or, strictly speaking, the other two—looked Asian. Wiry men getting on in years, with salt-and-pepper hair, they had deeply wrinkled faces that resembled maps of Asia. They wore identical, elegantly tailored suits, and, most surprising of all, they appeared to have been sewn together.

The distinguished black man, as hard as he tried to focus on the game, could not help but steal sidelong glances at the conjoined pair sitting across the chessboard. His attention was secretly drawn to the fleshy cord that connected the twins, an object of curiosity that had, in fact, tantalized millions worldwide who had flocked to exhibition halls, museums, ballrooms, pitched tents, or county fairgrounds to witness the famously proclaimed *lusus naturae* (freak of nature). The twins, who had withstood all probing gazes over the years, whether from queens or councilors, princes or paupers, did not particularly heed the black man's stealthy stare, nor did they mind the curious looks from fellow passengers who all seemed to be absorbed in their own business of distilling boredom drop by drop.

Before the Cunard Steamship Company had adopted strict policies regarding passenger conduct, the saloon on the quarterdeck used to be much noisier. Musicians, theatrical troupes, and minstrels on tour would perform loudly and freely. Itinerant preachers and other evangelizing speakers would also take the opportunity to deliver speeches, trying to save some souls or change a few minds. According to company records, all this changed after a "memorable disturbance" had occurred in 1846. That year, as the Cunard company record shows,

> One Frederick Douglass, a man of color, came from America in the *Cambria*, then commanded by Captain Judkins, for the purpose of speaking and lecturing in England on the abolition of slavery. . . . Being a second-cabin passenger, he had not the privilege of the quarterdeck; but on the last day, after the saloon dinner, he went aft among the first-class passengers, and delivered himself of a bitter discourse on abolition. . . . A large circle of his supporters gathered round him to hear his speech; those who differed from him also listened with great patience for some time. . . . A New Orleans man, the master of a ship in the China trade, and who had been during the greater part of the voyage, and was more particularly

on this occasion, very much intoxicated, poked himself into the
circle, walked up to the speaker, with his hands in his pockets and
a "quid" of tobacco in his mouth, looked at him steadily for a minute, and then said, "I guess you're a liar!" The negro replied with
something equally complimentary, and a loud altercation ensued
between them.

Pretty soon a melee broke out between enraged supporters of the
opposing sides, who were "scattered into a dozen stormy groups about
the deck." The chaos lasted for almost an hour, until the captain, with
the aid of military officers aboard, finally "lulled the tempest and separated the contending parties." In the middle of the tumult, as the anonymous company record-keeper noted, referring to Douglass, "this demon
of discord had vanished." Thereafter, the Cunard Steamship Company
issued strict regulations on passenger conduct, "to prevent the possible
recurrence of such an affair."[8]

Since then, the saloon and quarterdeck had become much quieter,
and indeed boring, as typified by this moment on the *Palmyra*. One of
the twins—unfortunately, we don't know which one—was absorbed in
the game against the gentleman. He took a long, satisfying pull on a
cigar after thoughtfully moving a piece on the board, while the other
turned his face away, almost instinctively, as he had done all his life,
allowing his twin brother to have his fun. Both twins were said to be
excellent at chess, a game they had learned on their first voyage to the
New World almost a lifetime earlier. But they did not like playing in
opposition to each other, because it would be, as they put it, no more fun
than "playing with the right hand against the left."[9] Over the years, they
had made a pact: If one plays chess, the other will stay quiet and mind
his own business. In fact, due to their unique physical condition—even a
simple call of nature would have to be answered in the brotherly presence
of the other—they had a pact for everything they did: eating, drinking,
sleeping, dressing, washing, conversing, traveling, performing, fighting,
hunting, and, yes, lovemaking. Doctors even suspected that they might
dream similar dreams, or versions of the same, like musical variations.

Their suave opponent turned out to be none other than Edward James Roye, newly elected president of Liberia. Born on February 3, 1815, in the small town of Newark, Ohio, Roye was the son of a fugitive slave who had escaped from Kentucky and ended up managing a ferry service on the Wabash River in Indiana. As a child, Roye was fortunate to be among the few "colored" kids admitted to the local schools in Ohio. According to one biographer, when Roye gained admittance to Newark High School, his teacher was Salmon Portland Chase, who by 1870 became chief justice of the United States.[10] Despite his decent education, Roye began work after high school as a barber, considered a most "suitable" occupation for a black man at the time (Newark would not have its first white barber until 1856). He then attended Ohio University in Athens. A few years later, Roye followed in his father's footsteps and set out westward, settling down also in Terre Haute, where he bought properties, operated a barbershop, and established the first bathhouse in town.[11] Although his business prospered, Roye was disheartened to find that nineteenth-century America was not, if it ever would be, a great place for a free black man. When fortunate enough to be unencumbered by chattel slavery, free blacks were not lucky enough to be free from discrimination, segregation, violence, and the malicious suspicion that their presence posed a threat to the purity of white blood and a temptation to those still bound in slavery.

Ever since the birth of the Republic, the question of what to do with free blacks mingling with white populations had puzzled the Founding Fathers. In 1782, Thomas Jefferson, a hearty worrier over miscegenation but hardly a warrior fighting it, suggested a solution that would gain increasing support in the country: removing free blacks beyond the reach of mixture. Slavery is evil, so reasoned this champion of the natural rights of man and an unapologetic owner of slaves, but abolishing human bondage would pose a greater danger of racial commingling. This fear coincided with the other worry shared by slaveholders: The existence of free blacks would have a corrupting influence on those still in chains. Removing free (and freed) blacks from the United States, as Jefferson suggested, became a magic bullet. Spearheaded by the American Colonization Society (ACS), a movement to plant a colony in West Africa gained traction, leading to the birth of Liberia—first as a colony for American settlers in 1822 and then as a new nation in 1847.[12]

Unnerved by the worsening race relations in America and lured by the promise of a new start in a free land, Roye joined thousands of African Americans sponsored by the ACS to settle in Liberia. After his arrival there in 1846, Roye, a man of considerable acumen, enjoyed a meteoric rise in the newly founded Republic of Liberia. He first made a fortune in shipping and brokerage, then turned to law and politics, winning election to the Supreme Court. After two years, he was advanced to chief justice. A few months prior to his *Palmyra* voyage to New York, Roye had been elected president of Liberia. He had just traveled to England, trying to negotiate a loan from London bankers, and now he was on his way to the United States, his native land, to raise funds for building a railroad in his adopted country. But as he would soon find out upon landing, the America of 1870, basking in the glow of the Gilded Age, was still no place for a black man, presidential or not. As the *New York Daily Tribune* reported on August 17, 1870, Roye and his secretary of state, Hilary R. W. Johnson, who would himself become president of Liberia fourteen years later, had trouble finding a hotel room: "Both gentlemen express themselves much pleased with their visits to the United States, but are not partial to the exclusiveness of a hotel proprietor."[13]

The Asian twins, with whom Roye was now playing chess, were likewise no strangers to racism. Like Roye, Chang and Eng Bunker were also, against all odds, self-made men. Born on a riverboat in a fishing village in Siam on May 11, 1811, Chang and Eng had from birth been joined at the sternum by a piece of cartilage with a fused liver. At age seventeen, they were taken by British businessman Robert Hunter and American ship captain Abel Coffin to the West for a touring exhibition as freaks of nature. Displaying entrepreneurial talent, the twins later managed to free themselves from their owners and operate the tour on their own. Within a decade, they had made enough money to repair comfortably to rural North Carolina, where they purchased land and

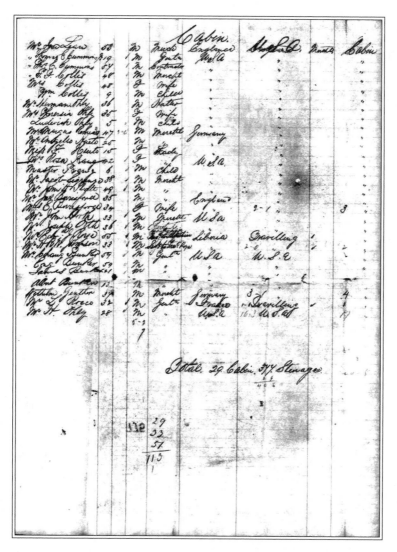

PASSENGER LIST OF THE *PALMYRA*

bought black slaves. Even worse in the eyes of republican patriarchs like Jefferson, they married two white sisters and fathered twenty-one children, two of whom, James and Albert, age twenty-one and thirteen, were now aboard the *Palmyra*. If Liberia was a solution to white America's fear of miscegenation, the Siamese Twins and their boys were the living embodiment of that racial nightmare.

In some ways, the leisurely chess game aboard the *Palmyra*—a welcome interruption in a monotonous ocean voyage—was indeed an intermission in a large historical drama unfolding in nineteenth-century America. The chain of events, the twists and turns, the jostles and lurches that had brought these three men together for a relaxing game in a newfangled steamship saloon would take more than a book's worth of narration. The immediate event that had placed the twins aboard at this moment was the recently concluded Civil War—or, as the twins would prefer to call it, the War of Northern Aggression. After the Southern Secession in 1861, the twins had stood staunchly with the Confederacy and sent their two adult sons, Christopher and Stephen, to the battlegrounds to fight the Yankees. Both sons were wounded and captured by the Union Army. Chang and Eng remembered those agonizing days and months during the war. When the news of their sons' capture came, they sat up by spermaceti candles long into the night and pored over those Prang maps of battlefields—almost as if, by tracing that popular Boston lithographer's prints, they could somehow track down and recover their lost progeny.

When the war ground to a bitter halt, the twins were thrilled to see their sons, though wounded, come home alive. Other Southerners were not so lucky: The 260,000 Confederate war dead would leave behind roughly 85,000 widows and 200,000 fatherless children. Out of the 111,000 Tar Heelers who went to war, 40,275 (or more than one-third) had died. It was the greatest loss of lives suffered by any Confederate state. Chang and Eng's anguish came in a different way—they were broke. The war had wiped out their patriotic investment in Confederate bonds, rendered worthless by the defeat of the South. It also decimated their major asset—thirty-two slaves worth about $26,550, according to county tax records of 1864. Under the circumstance, the twins had no choice but to resort to one asset they still possessed: their conjoined bodies.

And so they hit the road again as itinerant showmen. This time, they took along some of their children, occasionally even their wives, to show the world that however abnormal they might look, their double union with two white women, considered freakish and even bestial, was able to produce normal offspring.

Their journey had presently led them to this game of chess with the black man who was a symbol of the Emancipation. As the chess pieces moved across the board on the *Palmyra*, boatloads of freed blacks were traveling in the opposite direction toward Liberia, a presumed land of *liber*. In the ensuing months, the same American newspapers that would follow the peregrinations of the Siamese Twins and the Liberian president would also report on the continuing black diaspora to West Africa. The New York *Sun*, for instance, reported on November 14, 1870: "Two hundred colored men and women from different places in North Carolina sailed on Wednesday for Liberia, where they go to make their homes."[14] Between 1825 and 1893, out of the more than fourteen thousand black settlers who went to Liberia, North Carolina would contribute 2,030, a disproportionately high number,[15] though we do not know whether any of the freed slaves formerly owned by Chang and Eng were among those from the Tar Heel State.

Nor do we know who won the chess game, or whether they even finished the match, although the outcome of the bigger game, with human bondage and black emancipation at stake, had already been decided for them by the Civil War. The only thing we do know is that at some point during the game, Roye, the former midwestern small-town black barber-turned-president of a free nation, asked the twins, somewhat offhandedly, a delicate question—and the game ended right then. The twins started to rise. As Eng tried to stand up, he was suddenly pulled down by the fleshy string that tied him to his brother. Over the years, constant tugging had stretched the cord from its original four inches in length to five and a half. Something appeared terribly wrong with Chang; his face looked ashen, and he couldn't move the right side of his body, the side closer to Eng. According to the *New York Times*, Chang "was stricken by a paralytic shock." The twins—both the immobile Chang and the healthy Eng—had to be confined to their berth for the rest of the transatlantic journey.[16] The abrupt decline of Chang's health brought an end to the spectacular and unusual career of the twin brothers. They would never go on the road again.

To fathom the depth and complexity of the story of Chang and Eng, a life—to quote an awestruck and somewhat hyperbolic nineteenth-century newspaper editor—"commencing in a Siamese sampan, ending in the backwoods of North America—a life beginning in the utter obscurity of a fisherman's hut, passing out amid such noise and notoriety as falls to the lot of only one mortal in ten millions,"[17] we need to go back to the very beginning, to that humble houseboat, thatched with *attap*, afloat on the muddy Meklong River. . . .

❧ Part One ❧

IN SIAM

(1811–1829)

A SIAMESE CANAL

Siam

A dream-like scene, peculiar to this Venice of the East.
—Anna Leonowens, *The English Governess at the Siamese Court* (1870)

Siam, August 1824. A sweltering late afternoon rather like the inside of a steamer basket. After a torrential monsoon storm, Meklong, a fishing village about sixty miles west of Bangkok, showed signs of life again. The red-hot disk of the tropical sun blazed as it dipped into the Gulf of Siam, spilling a pool of liquid gold. Inside the sand bar, up the *paknam* (river mouth), where the water turned brown and muddy after a rain, the Meklong River came alive with Chinese junks, swift sampans, and tiny canoes, all sculled expertly by peddlers who screamed the praises of their wares in shrill, singsong voices. Uneven rows of floating houses, thatched with *nipa* leaves and grounded by bamboo poles drilled into the river bottom, wobbled on water like oversize matchboxes. Fronting many of these boathouses were single-table stalls that sold anything from dried fish, fresh vegetables, fruits, and utensils to other household items. Competing for attention with the peddlers zigzagging the river on their craft, the houseboat traders also bellowed as if in a yodeling match. It was the cacophony of a floating bazaar.

Amid the clang and din, a shiny 30-ton cutter, imperiously sporting an English nameboard, *The Friends*, nosed into this tableau like a haughty bird of prey alight in a chicken yard. Standing on the stern was a European man with a head of wild hair, a chiseled chin, a high nose, and penetrating eyes. He was the boat's owner, Robert Hunter, a British businessman hailing from Greenock, Scotland. His family had been tobacco traders in colonial Virginia until they were driven out by the Revolutionary War and began to dabble in the manufacture of glass, linen, and cotton. Adopting the family trade, Hunter had first gone to India. As soon as Singapore transformed itself, seemingly overnight, from an island of mangrove swamps to an international free port in 1819, Hunter ventured there and operated a few businesses, including Hunter-Watt & Company. Using Singapore as his base, Hunter traveled frequently to various parts of the Malay Archipelago and eventually arrived at Bangkok in the summer of 1824.[1]

In fact, that year was a time of uncertainty in the capital of Siam. King Rama II had died in July, leaving the throne to Phra Nangklao, widely believed to be a usurper because he was the king's son by a concubine. The more legitimate heir, Prince Mongkut, Rama II's son by a queen, was bundled off to a monastery to shield him from the perils of the power struggle. Ishmael was crowned while Isaac was exiled. In addition to palace intrigues, 1824 also witnessed the outbreak of the Anglo-Burmese War in March. Even though they were happy to see the defeat of the hostile neighbor who had invaded Siam many times, the Siamese were shocked by the technical superiority of the British and alarmed by rumors that their own country would be next in line for a British attack.[2]

The Siamese desperation made Hunter look like a godsend, for he came bearing a thousand muskets as a gift for the king. Rama III was so pleased that he awarded Hunter the honorary title of *Luang Avudh Viset* and ordered a dwelling place to be arranged for the smooth-talking Scotsman. Hunter would soon take a Siamese wife and become a partner in trade with the king and his ministers, who had enjoyed a virtual monopoly on commerce with other nations.[3] As a businessman, Hunter was said to be shrewd and hardheaded. Arrogant beneath his Scottish reserve, he was socially adaptable, "with a persuasive tongue and the useful ability of 'getting in' with the right people." In the words of Kay Hunter, one of the Hunter descendants who has tracked down the colorful stories of her illustrious ancestor: "In many ways he was typical of the Westerner who had adopted the East; he had money, he had power, and was thus inclined to throw his weight about, but he was without that bluff *bonhomie* so peculiar to the English abroad. Instead, he had the studied reserve of the Scot, unless he was roused, when a quick temper and an infuriating arrogance betrayed him. On the surface his ways were smooth and relaxed, but the fact remained that Robert Hunter never missed opportunities."[4]

Cruising down the Meklong on that steamy summer day in 1824, Hunter would stumble upon a so-called golden opportunity. A sportsman fond of sailing and hunting, Hunter often took his friends in his boat and went on shooting expeditions to the swamps along the bold, rocky coast of western Siam. On that day, after bagging enough ducks and snipes, Hunter and friends set sail for home in Bangkok.[5]

With the sun gone, dusk set in swiftly. A half-moon hove into view on the far horizon, faint as a partial thumbprint on a windowpane. One by one, lanterns appeared in front of the floating houses and torches blazed on junks, dappling the brackish river with flickering reflections. Standing by the gunwale, Hunter suddenly saw something moving in the water: Like a mysterious creature crawling out of Greek mythology, two bodies naked from the waist up, two heads and four arms, swam in perfect tandem like one body. Amazed, Hunter drew his boat closer to the two-headed, Hydra-like creature, which by now had effortlessly climbed into a little dinghy. In the dim light, against glimmering reflections, Hunter was astonished to find that the creature was not some amphibious reptile but in fact two teenage boys, connected by a band of flesh at the bases of their chests.[6]

Eighteenth-century Italian philosopher Giambattista Vico once said, "All barbarian histories have fabulous beginnings." The story of the Siamese Twins is not necessarily one that contains much barbarity, unless we believe, perhaps rightly so, that the nineteenth-century obsession with abnormality—that insatiable desire of humans looking at other humans as monsters—reveals something disturbingly barbaric. Nor does an adventurous, curio-seeking Scotsman's so-called discovery of a pair of conjoined twins rise to the level of a fable. But the chance encounter certainly set the stage for two of the most fabulous showmen the world would ever see.

⪰ 2 ⪯

The Chinese Twins

No place south of China is the rendezvous of so many Chinese junks as Siam.
—Charles Gutzlaff, *Journal of Three Voyages Along the Coast of China* (1834)

O n a rainy day in May 1811, Chang and Eng were born in a small houseboat at the fishing village of Meklong. Their father, Ti-eye, was a fisherman from southern China; their mother, Nok, was half Chinese and half Siamese. Like a neatly packed bundle, the twins came out of their mother's womb with the head of one between the legs of the other. Unwrapping the package, the midwife was shocked to discover that the babies were tied together by a piece of flesh at the sternum. Nok had borne four children previously and would produce three more in the coming years—a total of nine kids, all of whom, except the twins, had normal births.[1]

As the rain hissed in the palm fronds and waves rocked the boat gently, the newborn twins lay quietly on the bamboo mat, perhaps curious about the strange new world they had just entered. The year 1811, however, was not a peaceful one in world history: In January, an uprising of more than four hundred slaves, led by Charles Deslondes, was brutally put down in the newly American New Orleans, killing sixty-six blacks, whose heads were strung up along the roads of the city. In March, Ned Ludd led English workers in violent riots against industrial mechanization, a movement that gave birth to the word *Luddites*, and the British government responded with mass shootings, hangings, and deportations to the colonies. In July, Venezuela, after years of rebellion led by Simón Bolívar and others against colonial rule, became the first South American country to declare independence from Spain, while

in November, General William Henry Harrison fought an especially
bloody battle against the Shawnee Indians in Tippecanoe and put an
end to Tecumseh's dream of a pan-Indian confederation. In November
and December, two massive earthquakes hit Missouri at New Madrid,
among the most powerful in American history, causing the mighty Mississippi River to flow backward and church bells to ring as far away as
Philadelphia.

In the ancient Kingdom of Siam, however, 1811 was rather peaceful. In fact, the entire fifteen-year span of Rama II's reign (1809–24)
has been characterized by historians as "a breathing spell between
crises," a halcyon interlude between the First and Third Reigns of the
Chakri Dynasty.[2] Dubbed the "Poet King," Rama II devoted himself
to literature, art, and the construction of pleasure gardens filled with
artificial lakes, islands, and pavilions where his passion for poetry and
dance could be given free rein.[3] Rather than battling with neighboring
states, Rama II preferred spending his time rendering the Indian epic
Ramayana into Siamese, chanting lines such as "I should bathe you with
scented water/pervaded with the fragrance of flowers."[4] John Crawfurd,
the British envoy to Bangkok in 1822, reported that the reigning monarch was "one of the mildest sovereigns that had ruled Siam for at least
a century and a half."[5]

Such was the historical moment into which the Siamese Twins were
born. Only two years into Rama II's reign, the country was enjoying
the calm between storms, made possible by a benevolent king and a
lack of belligerence directed against Siam by such traditional enemies as
Burma. News about the conjoined twins created a small ripple and, in
fact, reached the ear of the king. A dabbler in the interpretation of symbols and signs—one day he would correctly predict his own impending demise after seeing the death of two white elephants—Rama II
regarded the abnormal birth as an omen portending something evil in
his kingdom. He issued a death warrant for the conjoined twins. But
the king's wish for removing a bad sign was merely a whim, like an
insignificant word on the scented scrolls of *Ramayana*, catching only his
momentary attention. Soon the king lost himself in the poetic tales of

Sita and forgot all about those baleful newborns of a Chinese fishmonger in Meklong.

In quick order, their parents named them "In" and "Chun," two words that caused no small amount of speculation as to their meanings. At first, some had thought that the words—or their later variants, "Eng" and "Chang"—simply meant "right" and "left," referring to their positions in relation to each other. This belief was discredited in 1874 by Dr. William H. Pancoast in his well-publicized autopsy report on the twins. As if scientific medical knowledge were not enough to reveal the anatomical mystery of the conjoined twins, the curious Philadelphia doctor consulted an authoritative dictionary of the Siamese language and found that the words *Eng* and *Chang* did not at all signify right and left. Instead, Pancoast found that, "In the Siamese language, words spelt exactly in the same way may have an entirely different signification according to the accompanying accent. Thus, by a different pronunciation, a word is made to do service for various meanings. Of all the different significations of the words Eng and Chang, those which give for Eng the meaning of 'strictly, to tie strongly,' and to Chang that of 'unsavory, tasteless,' seem applicable." Based on these findings, Pancoast supported another common belief that "the names were given them to express their natural characteristic. Eng was ever the stronger and healthier of the two, and of a pleasant disposition; Chang was irritable, and less amiable."[6]

A century later, Irving Wallace and Amy Wallace, the father–daughter team who coauthored a popular biography of the twins in the 1970s, supplied a different explanation by citing a Thai textbook that states: "Their mother called them 'In' and 'Jun.' . . . In and Jun were the names of a certain kind of local fruit growing on trees. When the fruit was raw, it was green, and we called it In fruit, and when the fruit was ripe it was yellow, and we called it Jun fruit. Since to Europeans the pronunciation of these two words was not familiar, they pronounced them Eng–Chang."[7]

All of these etymological speculations, colorful and plausible as they may sound, fail to consider the simple fact that the twins were ethnically Chinese. The family spoke a Chinese dialect at home and also wrote in Chinese. Hence it is reasonable to suggest that the origin of their names ought to be found in the Chinese language, not Siamese. As we shall see later, on a document they signed in 1829, the twins wrote their names in Chinese characters, which will solve the mystery for us. For now, let us continue with the story of their early life in the land of Bengal tigers and white elephants.

Although later known to the world as the "*Siamese* Twins," In and Chun were called the "*Chinese* Twins" by the locals in Meklong. So, in order to understand the larger framework of their journey, a brief tour of Chinese Siamese history is worthwhile. The twins' family belonged to a large, thriving Chinese community in Siam, a country that historically had always welcomed the Chinese. As early as the thirteenth century, the Chinese diplomat Zhou Daguan had found his countrymen doing business in places that would later become part of Siam. In the fifteenth century, the famous Ming Dynasty maritime expeditions led by the eunuch Zheng He brought Chinese to Ayudhya and other parts of Siam. That encounter, according to historians, may well have led to the first of Siam's *lukjin*—children of Chinese fathers and Siamese mothers. In the following century, Portuguese accounts described Chinese merchants as being "everywhere established" in Siam, and Chinese records showed that pirates from China ravaging the high seas headquartered in South Siam. Especially in the long period of Siam's isolation after the 1688 Ayudhya Revolution, which spelled the end of European trade, Siamese commerce was dominated by Chinese junks that brought goods and immigrants. When John Crawfurd visited in 1822, he estimated that there were about 440,000 Chinese out of a total population of 2,790,500 in Siam, more than 15 percent. The estimate made by D. E. Malloch during the Burney Mission in 1826 gave the Chinese an even bigger share, almost one-fourth of the population.[8]

These numbers tell the story: The Chinese were a welcome presence among the Siamese, a fact confirmed by most historical accounts. One of the officers on the Zheng He expedition in the fifteenth century wrote that, "whenever [a Siamese woman] meets a Chinese man, she is greatly pleased with him, and will invariably prepare wine to entertain

and show respect to him, merrily singing and keeping him overnight."[9]
Such an idyllic account may sound like a run-of-the-mill exaggeration by an explorer in faraway places. Early South Sea narratives, for
instance, were full of accounts of mermaidlike island maidens, *wahi-
nes*, who, upon a ship's arrival, jumped off beaches, swam, and climbed
aboard half naked, eager to entertain European men and cater to their
carnal cravings. But there seemed to be no question of the warm feelings that the Siamese historically harbored toward the Chinese. As a
seventeenth-century Chinese traveler stated, "The inhabitants [of Siam]
accept the Chinese very cordially, much better than do the natives of
any other country."[10]

In the early nineteenth century, the Chinese living in Siam enjoyed
special privileges, thanks to one heroic man whose story is still shrouded
in the mist of legend: Phraya Tak, often known as Taksin. Born in 1734
to a Chinese father and a Siamese mother, thus making him a *lukjin*,
Taksin had been adopted by a noble family. In 1767, when the Burmese
invaded Siam and captured the capital city of Ayudhya, Taksin rallied
the country to expel the invaders. He became king and ruled Siam for
more than fourteen years, until he was overthrown in 1782. He was said
to have met his end by being "tied up in a velvet sack and struck on the
back of the neck with a sandalwood club."[11] The seeming brutality was
merely a ritual for executing royalty by the rules of an ancient law, which
also dictated that Taksin be given a royal cremation by his successor,
Rama I. As homage to Taksin and his Chinese heritage, the new king
decreed that the Chinese would be "exempt from corvée [unpaid labor]
and from the requirement to attach themselves to a patron or government master."[12] Rather than fall victim to servitude or slavery, as did
most native Siamese and all other Asian foreigners, the Chinese would
only need to pay a triennial head tax.

Despite the special treatment accorded the Chinese, life was not easy
for a hard-scrabbling fisherman and his wife trying to raise a large family. Adding three more babies after the twins, the family of nine kids
and their parents lived in the crowded houseboat afloat on the Meklong,
a boat moored by bamboo poles driven into the river, its roof thatched

with leaves. In the front part of the vessel, a table was set up as a plat-form for selling the catch of the day and other items. Like other house-holds living on the river, they also had a dinghy tethered to their floating domicile, to be used as a convenient means of transportation.

The town of Meklong (today Samut Songkhram), where the twins spent their formative years, had a population of a few thousand souls, many of whom were Chinese. The earliest Western description of the town was given by Claude Céberet du Boullay, the French envoy sent by Louis XIV to Siam on the eve of the 1688 Revolution. As Céberet described in his journal: "This town . . . is situated on the banks of a stream also called the Meklong, a league from the sea. The water is good here. The town has no walls, but is defended by a small square fort with four very small brick bastions."[13] By the time the twins saw light, Meklong had emerged from a rustic village to become a bus-tling river town. Jean-Baptiste Pallegoix, bishop of Mallos, who spent decades doing missionary work and traveling extensively in Siam from 1830 to 1862, spoke of Meklong as "a populous and beautiful city, with its floating bazaars, fine pagodas and gardens, and a population of ten thousand, the largest proportion of which is Chinese. . . . The soil is remarkably fertile, and the salt-pits produce enough to supply the whole kingdom."[14] Sir John Bowring, governor of Hong Kong—who went to Siam in 1855 and later quoted extensively from Pallegoix in his classic *The Kingdom and People of Siam* (1857)—also mentioned an American missionary who had visited Meklong and had been impressed by the "villages of Chinese, with their floating houses and well-filled shops."[15]

Located conveniently by the river, about a mile from the sea and con-nected to Bangkok by canals, Meklong provided an easy access point for traders. Siam was rich in natural products, including sugar, sapan wood, bêche-de-mer (sea cucumber), birds' nests, shark fins, gamboge (yellow dye), indigo, cotton, ivory, and many other items that attracted Chinese traders, who had dominated Siamese commerce in the absence of European competition. Karl Gutzlaff, a German missionary who had diligently followed the Chinese to Siam to save their pagan souls, and who figures more prominently later in this narrative, noted in his jour-

nals dating from 1831 that every year in the months of February to
April, about eighty Chinese junks arrived from Hainan, Canton, Amoy,
Shanghai, and other ports, bringing various articles for the consumption of the Siamese and the Chinese.[16] Edmund Roberts, the American
envoy to Siam in 1833, marveled at these watercraft: "A true Chinese
junk is a great curiosity; the model must have been taken originally
from a bread-trough, being broad and square at both ends."[17] The live-
liest and most informative account of the annual fleet was provided
by Dan B. Bradley, an American missionary who arrived in Siam in
1835, brought the first Siamese printing press, and initiated vaccina-
tions against smallpox:

> Junks in the China trade would then as now make but one voy-
> age in a year, taking advantage of the favoring SW monsoon in
> June to sail from Bangkok, and of the NE monsoon to return the
> latter part of January and first part of February. From February
> to June there were annually from 60 to 80 of these *monsters of the
> deep* moored in the river, forming two lines, all heading down the
> stream, always ready as to position, to start on another voyage.
> These two long lines of junks were practically a great Bazaar for a
> period of two months or more from the time of their arrival. Each
> junk was freighted with the goods of several parties, each of whom
> occupied a part of the deck for the display of his wares until they
> were all sold out.[18]

As Bradley and others noted, these "monsters of the deep" brought from
China massive amounts of crockery, such as cups and dishes, plus teas,
silks, crapes, brassware, sugar candy, playing cards, dice, paper, dried
vegetables, Chinese trunks, chests, Japanese woodenware, mirrors, and
so on. Merchandise sold on these floating bazaars would be further distributed to smaller vendors, including the twins' mother, Nok.

Nok was said to be a capable trader who eked out a living by supple-
menting her husband's catch of the day with other sources of income.
Historically, it was quite common for Siamese women to marry Chinese

men due to a number of factors: First, very few Chinese women emigrated, forcing overseas Chinese men to either remain single or marry local women. Second, according to G. William Skinner, Siamese women, not their menfolk, were the traders in the indigenous population. These women had "a certain amount of business know-how and could appreciate the advantages of an industrious Chinese husband."[19] We do not know whether Nok had met her future husband, Ti-eye, through business dealings, perhaps haggling over prices at the local floating bazaar. Their ethnicities and professions would certainly make their marriage fit the sociological norm, except that Nok was half Chinese and half Siamese, making the union possibly a result of arranged marriage, also a common practice in the Chinese community. Either way, the parents raised the twins and their siblings as Chinese, speaking Chinese (possibly Cantonese) to them, and at some point letting them learn to read and write in Chinese as well. Judging by the incredible efficiency with which the twins would later learn to speak, read, and write in English, their elementary education might not have been rudimentary, despite their low station in life. However fantastically unreliable her tale was, Anna Leonowens, the famous English governess who taught the sixty-plus children and the entire harem of King Mongkut in the 1860s, made a keen observation in her autobiography that might shed some light on the state of literacy in Siam: "The fact is remarkable, that though education in its higher degrees is popularly neglected in Siam, there is scarcely a man or woman in the empire who cannot read and write."[20] Also, based on the fact that the twins in their early teens were able to do business on their own, we can be reasonably certain that they had also learned basic arithmetic. As for whether or not they knew how to use the *suan-pawn* (abacus), which Edmund Roberts in 1833 saw many Chinese use "as an assistant in making calculations," we do not know.[21]

While mentally the twins seemed to be two perfectly normal human beings, physical abnormality remained the story of their life and their daunting challenge. At birth, their connecting band had been only four inches in length, but through wear and tear, it stretched to five and a half inches, giving them a bit more flexibility. Learning to walk, a milestone for *Homo sapiens*, was particularly difficult for them because they had to cross the evolutionary marker together, which required extra coordination. One account described their initial efforts in pedestrianism as being like "two inebriated men, with locked arms, endeavoring to proceed in a fixed direction."[22] Swimming, a necessary skill for anyone living near water—a missed step in the gap, a sudden jerk of the boat, a leaking or capsized vessel could all lead to drowning—posed no small challenge to the conjoined twins. In addition to the difficulties of synchronizing their bodies, their parents must have warned them of the ghosts waiting underwater to pull them down—Chinese believed that drowned ghosts cannot enter the cycle of reincarnation until they have found replacements by drowning others. People living close to water were especially mindful of spirits hovering underwater, ready to wreak havoc in people's lives. Jacob Tomlin, a Protestant missionary from London, ridiculed the Chinese folly of trying to appease the watery spirits, as he wrote in his journal upon arrival in Bangkok in August 1828:

> The people are again turned to their folly, and the old man who was so busy on Tuesday is making his prostrations to the winds and waves, and an equally liberal oblation of bacon, fowls, eggs &c is brought out. Huge bundles of gilt and printed paper were successively cast into the sea in a blaze. Considering the labour and expense of gilding and printing, the quantity thus thrown away was quite astonishing. The whole, neatly cut, gilded, and printed, would have been a sufficient burden for a stout man! Several dollars were in this way wantonly squandered on the waters.[23]

After learning to swim in tandem, the twins also learned other skills, such as rowing and fishing. In fact, they were well on their way to maturing as a fisherman's children. Then, disaster struck.

☞ 3 ☜

Cholera

In the spring of 1819, just as Sir Thomas Stamford Raffles, governor general of Bencoolenand and representative of the British East India Company, had finished clearing out mangrove swamps in Singapore and had turned the island into an entrepôt, a virulent strain of cholera hit Siam. An acute diarrheal disease caused by food or water contamination, cholera had long been a scourge of South and Southeast Asia due to the region's humid climate, poor sanitation, and dense population. An epidemic had first started in India in 1817 and then reached Ceylon (now Sri Lanka) the following year, before spreading in all directions via trading vessels. It arrived in Siam that April, when the twins were about to turn eight.

The death toll was staggeringly high. Dead bodies arrived so fast and in such shocking numbers that the monasteries could not keep up with the cremations. Many corpses were just thrown in the river, further polluting the water and exacerbating the epidemic. In the dark hours, fear and rumor ran rampant. Some thought that the cholera was caused by the recent construction activities in the palace, where Rama II had been busy building his pleasure gardens. Large rocks had been taken from the sea to build a mound in the gardens, a move that might have angered the guardian spirits of the ocean. Prone to supernatural interpretation of human events, the Poet King held a special exorcism ceremony: "Sacred stanzas were chanted, all around the city large guns were fired, and a procession was held with the nation's most sacred objects," wrote historian B. J. Terwiel. "The king temporarily relieved all people of their duties and exhorted all to make merit, chant sacred mantras, and practice munificence. Even those on palace duty were requested to remain home and look after their families. . . . The king advised people to let the animals roam around freely in the markets, and prisoners were freed. The populace was asked not to kill any living being, thus avoiding harmful acts."[1]

And, miraculously, the epidemic subsided.

In the following years, every time the spasmodic cholera returned, or when it raged in neighboring countries, the king would again resort to neoromantic rituals, using potent spells to ward off the danger. John Crawfurd, who visited Bangkok during one of these epidemic episodes, duly noted in his journals:

> The re-appearance of the epidemic cholera spread great alarm amongst the people, a matter which was apparent enough from the precautions which they took against its attacks. The King, under some superstitious imagination, which I am unable to explain, directed the people to keep at home, and abstain from all work for seven days. . . . The secular superintendent of the great temple, which was the first we visited, called upon us in the course of the day, and said that he had no fear of the *cholera morbus*, as he made frequent prostrations before the idols, and wore a skein of cotton thread round his neck as a charm. As he spoke, he pointed at this potent amulet![2]

British condescension notwithstanding, Crawfurd might have had good reason to sneer at what he regarded as unscientific, superstitious practices, for they were ineffective; and he was informed by the Phra Khlang (principal minister) that the cholera had killed one-fifth of the Siamese population within only a few years.

Among these victims, six were from the twins' family. Three of their younger siblings had been the first to succumb to the epidemic, followed by their father, who fought a prolonged battle against what he regarded as the evil spirits, struggling in vomit, diarrhea, and pain till the tragic end. Soon thereafter, the Scourge of Southeastern Asia took the lives of two more siblings, leaving only an older brother named Noy, a sister, their mother, and the twins themselves.[3]

Widowed in her thirties, Nok now had to pick up the pieces and raise four young children on her own. According to Judge Jesse Franklin Graves of North Carolina, who in the 1870s wrote a biographical sketch based on the twins' recollections of their early life in Siam, Nok had at first tried to make oil from cocoa nuts, but the labor in that process was too hard for her and her children, who had to assist her in earning a living: "By very great industry and economy she finally collected a little stock of various notions with which she spread her table and again began to trade." A smart merchant, she soon made enough money to start a small business of raising ducks and selling eggs.[4]

At their tender age, the twins grew very fond of raising ducks. Harvesting eggs with bare hands, watching the eggs hatch into fuzzy ducklings, holding a fledgling whose feathers weren't yet dry—all these activities certainly delighted two curious boys. It was even said they had a pet duck with whom they could talk.[5] But this was, after all, a way of making a living, not a sidewalk sale of Girl Scout cookies. Every day, the twins got up at the crack of dawn, drove the ducks waddling out of the enclosure and onto the muddy bank, and let them paddle and feed in the river, while the two duck "fanciers" rowed their dinghy and kept close watch. To get more nutritious food for their ever-increasing brood, the boys would row down the river to the gulf to catch shellfish. Other lucky catches on those trips, such as *platoo*, a kind of sardine, a common dish after salting, would either bring a few more cowries to their mother or add more flavor to their bowls of rice. But it was preserved duck eggs that constituted the main source of their income, and they were quick to learn the ancient recipes.

For centuries, the Chinese have honed their skills for making preserved duck eggs, which are of two kinds: One is called Century Egg (*pidan*), and the other is just plain pickled egg (*xian yadan*). For the former, eggs are dipped into a pasty mix of salt, ashes, lime, and rice chaff.

The mixture will harden and preserve the eggs for as long as needed. When the coating is peeled off and served on a dish, the egg looks blackened like an aged mummy, giving out a pungent smell—hence the moniker Century Egg, or even Thousand-Year Egg.[6] For the plain pickled eggs, one simply dips eggs into a mix of salt and wet clay. Both methods can preserve eggs for a very long time, providing two reliable, delicious items for a Chinese dinner table.

In addition to preserved eggs, the sale of ducks also brought in considerable profit, for duck meat was another delicacy for Chinese and Siamese alike. Even at their young age, the twins were said to be shrewd hawkers who knew how to take advantage of their customers' curiosity about two conjoined boys plying their trade. It was not necessarily a confidence game, but it was a skill that would come in handy later, when their trade would be their own bodies.

While the twins prospered as small merchants, the ancient kingdom of Siam went through transformations under the peaceful reign of Rama II, whom John Crawfurd had characterized as "one of the mildest sovereigns that had ruled Siam for at least a century and a half." Crawfurd's time frame, "a century and a half," was significant because it referred to the length of time when Siam had remained in self-imposed isolation after the famous Ayudhya Revolution of 1688. Right at the center of that dramatic event was an enigmatic adventurer named Constant Phaulkon. Born Constantine Yeraki to Greek Orthodox parents in 1647, Phaulkon spent a wanderlust youth on English merchant ships and arrived in Ayudhya, the ancient capital of Siam, in 1678. His Greek name, "Yeraki," means a bird of prey, so he changed it to "Phaulkon" (falcon). And, true to that name, Phaulkon soared high as soon as he landed in the court of King Narai. He learned to speak fluent Siamese within two years, ingratiated himself into the service of the king, and rose rapidly from a humble position as interpreter and accountant to become the king's principal minister. A recent convert to Catholicism, Phaulkon used his influence to assist, openly as well as clandestinely, French Jesuit missionaries in their attempts to convert the king and his subjects, who were all considered Buddhist "idolaters." With Phaulkon's aid, the padres played such a deep game of conversion that two of them even shaved their heads, donned the robes of Siamese *talapoys* (monks), and infiltrated the Buddhist temples. The ruse backfired. When King Narai lay in his deathbed in 1688, the soaring falcon experienced not just a fall from grace but a final plunge—Phaulkon was arrested by his political enemies, charged with treason, and promptly executed. The French were expelled, and Siam shut its door to Europe.

For well over a century, except for maintaining her traditional ties to China and neighboring states, Siam survived in isolation. But things began to change, especially after 1785, when the British took possession of the island of Penang, followed by more territorial acquisitions in the region. When international trade was revived after the Napoleonic Wars, European powers began to mount pressure on Siam for improved commercial relations. Portugal, its empire already in decline, was the first to crack open the long-bolted door, procuring contracts from the Siamese in 1818 and then establishing a consulate two years later. An ascending Great Britain followed suit, first sending John Crawfurd on a failed mission in 1822, followed by Captain Henry Burney, who succeeded in obtaining a treaty from Bangkok in 1826. The United States also dispatched an envoy led by Edmund Roberts, who secured favorable terms from the Siamese in 1833.[7]

Siam was finally opening up—slowly at first, but steadily nonetheless.

This time, the global tides would wash ashore not a falcon but a hunter—Robert Hunter, who would scout the coast of the Andaman Sea, searching for opportunities and profits. He would soon be dubbed the Second Constant Phaulkon. In fact, Tan Puying Sap, the Siamese woman Hunter married, was a descendant of Phaulkon and his Japanese wife. Inevitably, Sap became a great asset to her husband—unlike Phaulkon, Hunter spoke very little Siamese. Through his wife and other assistants, Hunter would exert as much influence on Siam as he would on the conjoined twins, whom he would espy on a late summer day in August 1824. The twins had just wrapped up another day's duck business, and were dipping in the river to cool off after a monsoon storm, when the Scotsman burst into their world.

⊱ 4 ⊰

The King and Us

When he first laid eyes on the twins, Robert Hunter instantly knew he had found a most precious curio.

Conjoined twins were rare, and most of them would not grow to maturity. Back in Great Britain, Hunter had heard of the famous Biddenden Maids, Mary and Eliza Chulkhurst. Those twins, born in the twelfth century in Kent, England, allegedly were joined at the hips and shoulders. Even though some skeptics considered them to be a mere fable, the Biddenden Maids had been commemorated for centuries in Kent with a big celebration on Easter Sunday. The festival each year drew thousands of spectators, who would gobble up the special Biddenden cakes bearing impressions of the twins. Veracity be damned, the legend grew—the cakes were reputed to be a cure for stomachache, or great souvenirs that would engender luck.[1]

Or, closer to home, in Glasgow, Scotland, where the Hunter family business was based, there had been the Scottish Brothers, born in 1490, often referred to as the "Northumbrian Monster," for "the lower half of their bodies was fused," sharing "one set of genitals and two legs." They had been raised and educated at the court of King James IV of Scotland, became fluent in half a dozen languages, and learned to sing duets—"one a tenor and the other a treble bass." They "lived to the age of twenty-eight" and died a few days apart, with the survivor dragging along the corpse of his brother "before succumbing to infection from putrescence."[2]

In more recent times, there had been the Hungarian Sisters, Helen and Judith, who had visited England and created a stir. Born in Szony in 1701, they were joined back to back, with a single vulva but two vaginal tracts. After viewing them in London, Alexander Pope was so smitten that he was said to have immortalized the twins with a poem:

Two sisters wonderful to behold, who have thus grown as one,
That naught their bodies can divide, no power beneath the sun.
The town of Szoenii gave them birth, hard by far-famed Komorn,
Which noble fort may all the arts of Turkish sultans scorn.
Lucina, woman's gentle friend, did Helen first receive;
And Judith, when three hours had passed, her mother's womb did
      leave.

Unwilling to leave anything to the imagination, Pope continued:

One urine passage serves for both; one anus, so they tell;
The other parts their numbers keep, and serve their owners well.
Their parents poor did send them forth, the world to travel through,
That this great wonder of the age should not be hid from view.
The inner parts concealed do lie hid from our eyes, alas!
But all the body here you view erect in solid brass.[3]

Also inspired by the Hungarian Sisters, elite members of the Scriblerus Club, including Pope, Jonathan Swift, Robert Harley, and others, coauthored a satirical tract, *Memoirs of the Extraordinary Life, Works, and Discoveries of Martinus Scriblerus* (1741), in which interested parties carry on a heated debate over conjoined twins.

These were all sensational tales about "freaks" that tickled curious minds. And now, standing right in front of such a specimen of what Pope had called a "great wonder of the age," Hunter was not going to miss this opportunity. He approached the twin boys, and, with the aid of his servant Hattee—described in language typical of the period as "a fat good humored little Siamese-Chinese"[4]—Hunter made inquiries into their lives, asking about their birth, family, and other details. When he was done, he already had a plan. He promised to come back soon.

And he did, repeatedly, like the suitor returning again and again to serenade the girl he had first sighted at the bend of a country road. It did not take much for Hunter to convince both the twins and their mother to agree to his scheme of taking them on an exhibition tour to Europe and America. Sweet-tongued and persistent, he managed to tickle the prepubescent imaginations of the twins about the big, wide world out there. As for their mother, he lured her with lucre, more money than she would ever see in her life as a riverine merchant. Of course, he promised to bring them back, safe and sound, soon after the tour.

The obstacle, however, lay with the king. In Siam, the king owned everything within his dominion: land, wealth, products, people. No one was allowed to leave the country without the court's permission. The Chinese in Siam might have enjoyed special privileges of exemption from corvée labor and avoidance of exploitation by feudal lords, but they were still the king's subjects and his possessions. In China, ever since the Ming Dynasty of the fourteenth century, there had also been similar laws forbidding travel overseas without permission, as well as in Japan before the Meiji Reform in 1860.

Forced to approach the king, Hunter was disappointed when Rama III did not consent to let him take the twins. The honeymoon of the king and the British trader, sweetened by Hunter's dowry of a thousand muskets, had proved short-lived, and now he and Rama III were partners in trade. Unless Hunter could come up with an enticing offer, the king was unwilling to let go a prize possession as rare as the white elephants. Hunter would have to wait for a more opportune time.

In fact, Hunter's request piqued the king's curiosity. Realizing that he had not seen these wonders of the age born in his kingdom, the king ordered that they be brought to him for a personal viewing.

When the royal summons reached the humble boathouse in Meklong, it threw the family into a panic. The family scrambled to get the twins ready for this very special occasion: getting haircuts, mending clothes, and washing duck-yard mud off their bare feet. According to Graves, the twins soon "repaired to Bangkok accompanied by their mother and single sister, not forgetting to take along a cargo of their now famous eggs."[5] Meeting the king might be a big deal, but the twins, having acquired a keen business sense, would not want to miss the opportunity of plying their trade at the famous bazaar in the capital city.

It was their first trip to Bangkok, the "city of wild plums." With a population in the early nineteenth century of more than 400,000 souls, half of them perennially afloat, the city seemed to have risen from water like a *deus ex machina*. As the boat, rowed by eight muscular men garbed in the king's red livery, entered the serpentine Meinam River, the twins were overwhelmed by the splendor and magnificence of the scene: Under a blazing sun, against the sultry sky, a panorama of palaces, temples, pagodas, and floating houses spread out as far as their eyes could see. Single-plank bridges arched to a giddy height of thirty feet. Spidery canals were thronged with boats. A fleet of gaudy Chinese junks was anchored in the middle of the stream, surrounded by the pandemonium of haggling traders.

Upon arrival, the twins were hurried to a secluded location, where a eunuchlike courtier drilled them on the etiquette of being in the presence of the monarch. After a sleepless night, the twins were taken to the palace in a covered hammock—the king, exercising a variant of *droit de seigneur*, did not want anyone else to see them before he did. But at their curious age, the twins could not help prying open the curtain and peeking at the animated street scenes of the capital. After they entered the front gate guarded by musket-armed soldiers, they reached a courtyard where a white elephant was chained to poles. Newly caught in the wild, the pachyderm was yet to be tamed before she could join the team of royal white elephants, all supposedly animated by the transmigrated souls of deceased monarchs. Of course, the twins had no idea that one day they would share with those treasured creatures the distinction of being one of the three most famous Siamese exports, the other two being white elephants and Siamese cats.

Still concealed, the twins soon arrived at the Hall of Audience, where Rama III, a corpulent man approaching forty, sat cross-legged like a

Buddha on the ten-foot-high gold throne. In front of him, in a scene almost anticipating *The King and I*, hundreds of court officials groveled on stomachs and elbows like amphibious toads. A contemporary narrative captures the setting where the monarch viewed the twins:

> The extent of the audience-chamber is thirty-five by seventy feet. The middle of the floor, about one-half of the whole width, is raised eighteen inches above the rest, leaving a sort of lobby on each side, equal to one-fourth of the breadth of the whole room, and extending its entire length. A row of six pillars, three feet square, stood on each edge of the middle floor; and the walls, ceiling, and pillars were hung with red gilt paper, and the floors were carpeted. Chandeliers and lamps of various patterns were suspended from the ceiling, and numerous Chinese paintings and mirrors adorned the walls. From a central point, the floor gently rises in an inclined plane up to the throne, at the farthest end of the apartment.[6]

The twins were then let out of the hammock like animals released from a cage, and were told to crawl toward the throne. As they covered the distance, obviously in tandem, the king was amused by the rare, if not surreal, sight. His Majesty launched saliva into a golden spittoon and then renewed his quid of betel and areca-nut, a pastime shared by almost all of his subjects, a national habit that blackened their teeth and, as described in countless travelogues, dismayed foreign visitors in no small degree. When the twins scampered to about forty feet from the throne, they were told to stop. As instructed the previous night, they made three *salaams* by placing their palms against their foreheads. Again three times they knocked their heads on the ground. As they did so, the entire cohort of officials and courtiers present also bowed three times. The king then asked some questions about them and their family. All the queries were filtered in whispers through a line of courtiers, one of whom crouched by the throne, another by the twins, and yet another somewhere in the middle—Siamese court etiquette forbade any visitor to speak to the king directly. The answers were relayed back to the king in a way that resembled the modern-day children's game called the "Chinese Whispers"—except that here each answer with its relay was preceded by three *salaams* and a lengthy recitation of a string of the king's titles: "Phra, Putie, Chucka, Ka, Rap, Si, Klau, Si, Kla, Mom, Ka Prah Putie Chow."[7]

While this elaborate Siamese ritual was being performed, a few swallows flew in and out of the open court. Kneeling on the ground and stealing sidelong glances with their peripheral vision, the twins sensed the swift movement of the swallows alighting on the beams and chandeliers. The Chinese considered these migratory birds an auspicious sign because their annual return in spring coincided with the beginning of the sowing and planting season. Eschewing interest in the power and wealth—the king in his rich gold clothing, the officials in their silk sarongs—the twins, betraying their rural roots, were more interested in the swallows, which gave them much-needed distraction, or perhaps an ironic perspective. In the future, in faraway places, when hundreds of curious onlookers would gawk, scream, and taunt them as freaks on stage, they would remember this moment, when the birds flew over their heads, chirping their throaty notes, heeding neither kings nor queens with their pretensions. The birds taught the twins to free themselves, to take the wings of fancy, a momentary reverie, withdrawing deep into their inner selves, while the world looked on with contempt and disgust, awe and bemusement.

Suddenly, a loud clang of gongs, as if in a Siamese theater, emerged from an invisible place, followed by a flourish of music played on pipes and strings. Yellow silk curtains were pulled over the throne, shielding the godlike king from view. The entire court made the three obligatory *salaams* yet again and loud salutations in concert. Before the twins knew it, their viewing by the king was over.

⇒ 5 ⇐

Departure

For the twins, the trip to Bangkok was both eye-opening and remunerative. In addition to selling their duck eggs at the bazaar after the palace visit, they also peddled the king's gifts as soon as they got back home. Many years later, sitting in the cool breeze of their North Carolina front porch on summer days or by the warm fireplace on winter nights, the twins would often reminisce about that unforgettable trip to the Siamese capital. By then, retired comfortably from the world and seemingly without a thing to worry about, they would express regret about selling those royal gifts for what in retrospect must have been a paltry sum. But the family had needed the money then to survive and to expand their duck and egg business. Like lake water that settles down after a stone skiffs the surface, life soon returned to its peaceful norm for the twins in their small fishing village.

Robert Hunter, however, could not forget the "wonder boys" he had "discovered." A hardheaded Scotsman, he was not going to give up easily and let Rama III's refusal stand in the way of his golden dream. Since his arrival in 1824, Hunter had tried, not always successfully, to exert influence on Siamese affairs. Besides his trade partnership with the king and the nobles, Hunter also worked as an intermediary for newly arrived Westerners. Siam, slowly opening up to the outside world, rich in natural resources, and populated by four million pagan souls, attracted a new wave of both fortune seekers and God's soldiers, many of whom crossed paths with Hunter. During the 1826 Burney Mission, which opened British trade with Siam, Captain Henry Burney was eager to seek assistance from Hunter, who was indeed present, at the captain's personal request, when the mission was received in audience by Rama III.[1] Hunter was also there when the American envoy Edmund Roberts was negotiating treaty terms with the king in 1835, and, in fact, Hunter helped to correct an intentional mistranslation by a Siamese interpreter who tried to smooth over a potential conflict. According to William Ruschenberger, who accompanied Roberts, "The King stated that the Americans were on a footing with the English, which Mr. Roberts denied; saying that such was not the spirit of the Treaty. The secretary nearest the King translated the reply; that Mr. Roberts *admitted it, and was very much obliged to His Majesty.* Mr. Hunter, who was present, informed Mr. Roberts of the misinterpretation. He repeated what he had at first said, which was then correctly rendered."[2]

With no inns or hotels available, foreign visitors often had to rely on the hospitality of local hosts, such as Hunter, to put them up for a few nights or even weeks. Even as late as 1862, Anna Leonowens, for instance, still had trouble finding lodging upon her arrival in Bangkok and almost had to sleep under the stars until a gracious host rescued her from her plight. Hunter's house in Bangkok was a hub for these sojourners and a center of activity. When he first arrived, Hunter had lived in a floating house, "double the size of any of the others, very neatly painted, well furnished, with a nice little verandah in front." Not fond, however, of the dampness of a floating house, Hunter soon bought timbers and built a European-style grand mansion on the east bank of the Meinam. It was described as "a large white washed brick building two stories in height, and forming three sides of a square, the fourth being closed by a high brick wall. The ground floor was appropriated to warehouses, kitchen, and servants' quarters, the upper portion being occupied by the Europeans."[3] According to Frederick Arthur Neale, who served as a military officer in Siam, Hunter's new residence was "a very fine prominent house, opposite to which the British ensign proudly floated on feast days, and here every stranger found a home, for a very prince of hospitality was Mr. Hunter." Neale, who had stayed with Hunter for a long time, later recalled the leisurely fashion in which visitors conducted business and enjoyed hospitality at Hunter's:

> We breakfasted at ten and after that meal were wont to walk backwards and forwards on the splendid balcony Mr. Hunter had erected, as much for the sake of exercise as to enjoy an uninterrupted half hour's chat. Then Mr. Hunter betook himself to his counting house. . . . Occasionally we amused ourselves at Mr. Hunter's by playing Lagrace and we were once or twice guilty of a game at ringtaw. Night, however, brought with it its enlivening candle lights. The darker and more stormy the night, the more brilliantly illuminated the rooms used to be, and if the weather was particularly damp, we made ourselves comfortable with a good dinner and some fine old sherry, and then as a wind up, a drop of hot whisky toddy. . . . One hour before midnight, as indicated by the old clock at Mr. Hunter's house, was the signal for us to disperse for the night, and long before that time arrived, the whole city was hushed in deep repose.[4]

Given its reputation and importance, Hunter's house, known in Siamese as "*Hang Huntraa*," was dubbed the "British Factory."

Among the guests Hunter hosted were Jacob Tomlin and Karl Gutzlaff, who arrived in August 1828 as the earliest Protestant missionaries to Siam. Sent by the London Missionary Society, Tomlin was from Lancashire with a degree from Cambridge and nothing else to brag about, whereas Gutzlaff was a German whose colorful exploits would leave a large footprint in Asia.[5] Condemning Buddhism as a "system of the grossest lies," and claiming that all Asians were dishonest, Tomlin and Gutzlaff devoted themselves to saving these pagan souls. Unlike their Roman Catholic predecessors (and competitors), who had kept a low profile in Siam, Tomlin and Gutzlaff were carried away by their Protestant zealotry. They "freely distributed literature regarding the imminent eclipse of false doctrines such as Buddhism," a brazen act that immediately incurred the wrath of the king, who ordered the expulsion of the

ROBERT HUNTER'S HOUSE, BANGKOK

two missionaries. But Hunter intervened, protesting that "neither had broken any law and that their presence was allowed under the treaties of 1822 and 1826."[6] Permitted to stay, the Protestant duo went on to produce the first Siamese translation of the Bible, even though they managed to garner only a handful of conversions, chiefly among their Chinese servants and assistants. Ironically, a reverse conversion might have occurred: Before leaving Siam in 1831, Gutzlaff became a naturalized subject of China by being adopted into the clan of Kwo, taking the name Shih-lee and wearing Chinese garb. As described in his journals, he now had to "conform entirely to the customs of the Chinese, and even to dispense with the use of European books."[7] Whether Gutzlaff's Sinicization meant he truly went native or it was merely a scheme deployed by an overzealous missionary to get closer to the Chinese—it's more likely the latter—he felt, like many other transients in Bangkok at the time, deeply indebted to Hunter for assistance. This eccentric German, whose name still graces a busy street in Hong Kong, would later play a key role in the diplomatic negotiations during the First Opium War between China and Great Britain.

Despite his great influence, Hunter was not always successful in his interventions in the foreign affairs of Siam. One time, Hunter took a guest, Captain Wellar of the bark *Pyramus,* hunting in the fields. Wellar wandered off and found himself within the precincts of a Buddhist monastery, where evening prayers were being held. Unaware of the Buddhist taboo on taking lives, Wellar shot two pigeons, and soon all hell—whether Christian or Buddhist—broke loose. The monks, alarmed by the crackle of firearms on monastery grounds, rushed out to find Wellar nonchalantly collecting his kill. When the monks tried to wrest the pigeons from his hand and to take his gun, a scuffle ensued. Even though they were not the legendary Shaolin monks trained in martial arts, these sons of Muang Tai ganged up on the Westerner who had showed no respect for innocent lives. When Hunter finally caught up with his friend, Wellar had already been knocked out cold. Seething with anger, Hunter went to the Siamese officials and demanded justice, threatening that if the demand was not met, he would "take the *Pyramus* in front of the royal palace and let the King hear from the mouth of her guns." As if that was not enough, he further threatened to send for foreign troops and "establish British rule in Siam." But the king was unperturbed by the threats and rebuffed Hunter by stating that "the monks had their own ecclesiastical judiciary in which he could not meddle."[8] Incidents such as this indicated both the extraordinary position Hunter held at the court and the limits of his influence, which seemed not enough to sway the king's position on matters of justice or on allowing the conjoined twins to leave the country. For the latter, Hunter would need additional help, and it came in the form of a Bible-thumping American ship captain named Abel Coffin.

Like a character drawn from a Melville novel, Coffin hailed from the whaling port of Newburyport, Massachusetts. A seasoned mariner and shrewd Yankee trader, he had made many trips to Asia, dealing in tea from China and sugar from Siam. In Bangkok, he fell in with the two

Protestant missionaries, Tomlin and Gutzlaff, and befriended Hunter, the local business honcho. Coffin might not have cared much for the German chameleon in Chinese pantaloons, but he certainly spent a lot of time with Tomlin and often invited the English missionary to give sermons to his crew on the Sabbath. Tomlin's Bangkok journals from those years made constant references to Coffin, describing their field trips together and adventures in a "godless country." On October 13, 1828, Tomlin wrote in his journal, "At the request of Captain Coffin, commander of an American vessel, I went and delivered a short exhortation to his crew from the parable of 'the publican and the Pharisee.'" A few days later, he wrote, "In the afternoon accompanied Captain Coffin within the city walls to see the cavalry and elephants exercised, but were disappointed, none appearing except half a dozen long-tailed ponies mounted by half-naked Siamese, destitute of all martial accoutrements." Together they also witnessed the most inhuman torture of captives inside cages. As Hunter had done, Coffin went to Tomlin's rescue when the latter ran afoul of the Siamese for his missionary work. On January 23, 1829, a party of Siamese soldiers searched Tomlin's house under the pretense of looking for contraband opium, but Coffin put an end to the charade and forced the Phra Klang to apologize for the affront.[9]

What gave Coffin the unusual power in his dealings with the Siamese was the same thing that had once made Hunter the king's favorite: firearms. In late 1828 and early 1829, when Rama III was trying to put down a revolt in a vassal state in Laos, he badly needed guns for the military campaign. Coincidentally, Coffin arrived from India with several crates of muskets that he had acquired at an auction in Calcutta. He sold the firearms to the king for a handsome profit, and the king, now with more firepower in his arsenal, quickly quashed the revolt. When he captured the rebel leader, the king put him in a cage and invited Coffin, accompanied by Tomlin as indicated above, to witness the gruesome torture of the captive.

Knowing Coffin's warm relationship with the king, Hunter, who had looked for every opportunity to advance his interest in the conjoined twins, approached the American ship captain with a proposal: They could become partners if Coffin could persuade the king to let the twins out of the country. A proud son of Puritan forefathers well versed in rhetorical persuasion, Coffin knew just what buttons to push when he broached the topic to Rama III. He appealed to the king's vanity, suggesting that if he would allow the twins to depart, "the world might behold that the favored empire of Siam could alone produce, of all the nations of the earth, such a living wonder as the famous united brothers."[10] Still intoxicated by his recent military victory and most grateful to the Yankee's timely infusion of firearms, the king eventually acquiesced. Overjoyed, Hunter and Coffin, though not checking at first with the family, immediately made plans to take the twins out of the country for a world tour.

Like a sign from heaven, a lunar eclipse occurred on March 20, 1829. It was a spectacular view in the night sky over Siam, and there was countrywide commotion. As soon as the dark shadow of the earth crept onto the face of the moon, eating away the silvery disk like a Chinese moon pie, a boisterous cacophony of gongs, drums, cymbals, cooking pots, and washbasins resounded everywhere, mingled with the roar of cannons and muskets fired at irregular intervals. The Chinese and Siamese believed—and still believe to a degree—that a lunar eclipse is caused by a hungry sky dog trying to devour the moon, and that people need to prevent the disaster by scaring away the evil canine with loud noises.[11]

The waxing and waning of the moon also happens to be a metaphor for the reunion and separation of a family for the Chinese. One can imagine how loudly and passionately Nok, the mother of the twins, was banging her cooking pots during the two-hour lunar eclipse. They had celebrated the Chinese New Year not too long ago, and now her twin boys would leave her for a long journey to the other side of the globe. Her family would not be whole for some time, the eclipse appearing as an ominous sign.

Reluctant as she was to let her twin boys go—they were only seventeen and were the mainstay of the family business—the offer of $500 from Hunter and Coffin (in ways reminiscent of the transactional nature of slavery, though lacking the barbarity and oppression) and the prospect of more money in the future were too tempting to turn down. Besides, the white men had promised to bring back her boys within five years. To further alleviate her worry, an arrangement was made for a Chinese neighbor, a young man named Tieu, to travel with the twins as a companion and caretaker.

On the day of departure, April Fools' Day of 1829, the twins signed a contract, a document that has miraculously survived the passage of time to this day. In this contract, handwritten by Hunter and witnessed by Tieu, Chang and Eng agreed "to engage ourselves with our own

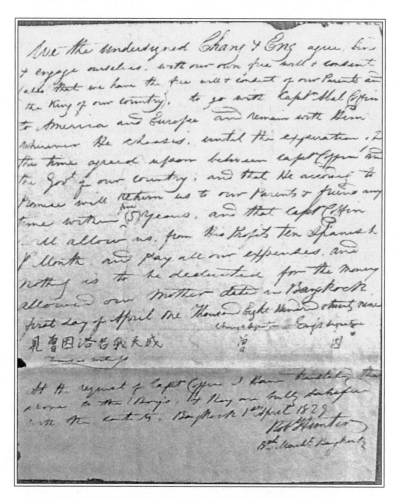

CONTRACT BETWEEN SIAMESE TWINS AND
ROBERT HUNTER/ABEL COFFIN, 1829

free will and consent (also that we have the free will & consent of our Parents and the King of our country) to go with Capt. Abel Coffin to America and Europe and remain with him wherever he chooses until the expiration of the time agreed upon between Capt. Coffin and the Govt. of our country, and that he according to promise will return us to our Parents and friends anytime within five (5) years, and that Capt. Coffin will allow us from his profits ten Spanish per month and pay all our expenses, and nothing is to be deducted from the money allowed our mother."

Although the contractual provisions were well documented, the physical existence of the contract had remained unknown to the world until 1977, when a descendant of Captain Coffin advertised the family heirloom for sale.[12] From this document, which is now in the collection of the Surry County Historical Society in North Carolina, we can shed light on a question that has long puzzled biographers and scholars: the names of the twins. Here we find the explanation of why the famous Siamese Twins came to be known as Chang and Eng. On the contract they signed, their names appear for the first and only time that we know in Chinese as 曾 and 因.

曾, which means "once" or "increase," is pronounced in Mandarin Chinese either as /zeng/ or /ceng/, and in Cantonese as /tsang/ or /zang/. 因, which means "cause," is pronounced in Mandarin Chinese as /yin/ and in Cantonese as /yen/. Therefore, Chang and Eng, an anglicized variation of the original "Chun" and "In," is a phonetic approximation of the Cantonese pronunciations of 曾 and 因.

Right next to their signatures is a Chinese sentence scribbled by their witness and travel companion, Tieu: 見曾因洛名我天成. The sentence can be translated as "I, Tian Cheng, witnessing Zeng and Yin signing their names." 天, the first Chinese character in Tieu's name 天成, is pronounced in Mandarin Chinese as /tian/ and in Cantonese as /tieu/, which explains why he is known as "Tieu." The Chinese word for "signing" is actually misspelled; it should have been 落 rather than 洛, indicating that Tieu probably had only a rudimentary level of education.

At the bottom of the contract, in a postscript, Hunter added: "At the request of Capt. Coffin I have translated the above to the Boys, and they are fully satisfied with the contract."

Carrying light luggage and their pet python in a cage, waving teary farewells to their mother and siblings, the "boys" stepped aboard the *Sachem*—a double-decked, three-masted, 387-ton ship—and sailed for the New World. Unbeknownst to them, they would never see Siam again.

❧ Part Two ❧

FIRST YEARS

(1829–1831)

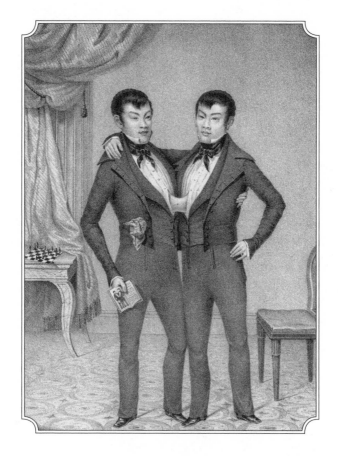

CHANG AND ENG, LITHOGRAPH

A Curiosity in Boston

"No! by the great Sachem, no!"

—Mark Twain, *The Adventures of Tom Sawyer*

PASSENGER LIST OF THE *SACHEM*

After what seemed like an infernal voyage lasting 138 days, the *Sachem* hove into Boston Harbor on August 16, 1829. In addition to a cargo of sugar, sapan wood, gamboge, buffalo horns, leopard skins, and tin, the Nantucket-based merchant ship declared only two passengers on board: Robert Hunter, male, age twenty-six, merchant from Scotland; Teene [i.e., Tieu], male, age seventeen, servant from Siam. It was odd that Chang and Eng were not listed as passengers on the ship manifest. Was it, perhaps, because they were seen as "monsters" and hence not human? Or was it because Captain Abel Coffin did not want anyone on the dock to have a free peek at the "rarity" he had acquired from a distant land? At least one historian has speculated that the twins were hidden under a tarp and smuggled into Boston in an enclosed carriage.[1] Like the monomaniacal Captain Ahab hiding his secret crew on the *Pequod* and saving those colored bodies of dubious origin for the ultimate goal of catching Moby-Dick, Captain Coffin also kept his stowaways under cover for maximum effect and profit. In a similar move, P. T. Barnum, the future impresario, when he took twenty-five-inch-tall General Tom Thumb to England in 1844, sneaked the midget past customs by camouflaging him as a suckling infant in a woman's arms.

Two months earlier, when the *Sachem* had approached St. Helena, a remote island where the dethroned Napoleon Bonaparte had died in isolation eight years earlier, Coffin could barely contain his enthusiasm. On June 28, he shot off a missive to his wife in Newburyport, Massachusetts: "Susan, I have two Chinese boys, 17 years old grown together they enjoy extraordinary health. I hope these will prove profitable as a curiosity."[2]

When Coffin penned this letter to his family, *curiosity* was a loaded term, a word that encapsulated the shifting, early nineteenth-century dynamics of cultural history and global geopolitics, reflecting Emerson's line that "Language is the archives of history." As an English word, *curiosity* originally refers to an intellectual inclination to inquire, a virtuous attribute that Thomas Hobbes believed to be lying at the foundation of the human institutions of language, science, and religion. David Hume identified it as "that love of truth, which [is] the first source of all our inquiries." But curiosity has also been depicted as "the cause of mankind's errors," that "lust of the eyes" sanctioned in the Bible: "Be not curious in unnecessary matters: for more things are shewed unto thee than men understand" (Ecclesiasticus 3:23).[3] From Eve's temptation by the forbidden fruit to Pandora's peeking into the box, curiosity has been regarded as a sign of impiety, a mark of discontent. Vladimir Nabokov once called curiosity "the purest form of insubordination."

This double connotation of curiosity—as a human desire to know more and as an onanistic peeping into the forbidden—remained with the word as it began to acquire a reference to new, exotic objects brought from distant shores in the Age of Discovery. Peter Coffin, the New England innkeeper in Herman Melville's *Moby-Dick* (1851), tells Ishmael that Pacific savage Queequeg has "a lot of 'balmed New Zealand heads (great curios, you know)."[4] The *Oxford English Dictionary*, in fact, cites the sentence spoken by Captain Abel Coffin's fictional cousin as the earliest recorded use of the word *curio*. Likewise, in Captain Coffin's family letter, by "curiosity" he most likely meant an odd, anomalous creature caged or staged in public spaces for profit. Variously called "monsters," "freaks," "*lusus naturae*," "freaks of nature," "rarities," "oddities," "eccentrics," "wonders," "marvels," "nature's mistakes," "strange people," "prodigies," and "very special people," these animal and human exhibitions had become a fad since the late eighteenth century and would continue throughout the nineteenth. Charles Dickens's *The Old Curiosity Shop* (1861), peopled by dwarfs, giants, misfits, waxworks, cheats, and performers, aptly captures the Zeitgeist of an age obsessed with human and nonhuman curiosities.[5] As Leslie Fiedler puts it, "Some authors of the nineteenth century, indeed, seem so freak-haunted that remembering them, we remember first of all the monsters they created. We can scarcely think of Victor Hugo, for instance, without recalling his grotesque Hunchback of Notre Dame, any more than we can recall Charles Dickens without thinking of his monstrous dwarf, Quilp, or our own Mark Twain without remembering 'Those Incredible Twins.'"[6]

The Americans Chang and Eng would meet upon their arrival in 1829 were certainly a curious bunch. A young nation with a bursting population of twelve million people, America was in the throes of an industrial revolution that would begin to chip away at the Jeffersonian agrarian republic. Andrew Jackson, "Old Hickory," a decorated general from the Far West (that being Tennessee) who had made his fame by decimating Native American tribes, had been sworn in as the seventh president, striking terror into the hearts of those who were still guided by the Founding Fathers' philosophy. Jackson had little patience for East

Coast nabobs and almost immediately sounded a bugle call of Manifest Destiny that would soon be heard as far off as the Pacific Slope.
Americans were busy building turnpikes, canals, railroads, transform-
ing a localized subsistence economy into a nationally integrated market
economy. In the midst of this industrial frenzy arose the political cry
of the common man, the staple of Jacksonian democracy. The Revolutionary War had already relocated the sources of political authority
from monarchy to "We, the People"; the Jacksonian Age further solidi-
fied the transfer of power, undermining credentials, coats of arms, or
university degrees as guarantees of what might pass for truth. Beyond
his daily clockwork toil at farms and emerging factories, the common
man needed not so much truth, virtue, or divine wisdom distilled from
lyceum podiums or church pulpits, but rather entertainment, diver-
sion, or, preferably, liquor distilled mostly at home but served in pubs
and saloons.

Despite the prevalence of moonshine, the deep roots of Puritanism
and broader Christianity, with their strict regulations against idleness
and exhortations for frugality, had not made America a particularly welcome place for popular entertainment. Foreign visitors could not help
but notice the contrast with Europe. In 1832, the British author Fanny
Trollope wrote in *Domestic Manners of the Americans*, "I never saw a population so totally divested of gayety; there is no trace of this feeling from
one end of the Union to the other. They have no fêtes, no fairs, no mer-
rimakings, no music in the streets, no Punch, no puppetshows. If they
see a comedy or a farce, they may laugh at it; but they can do very well
without it; and the consciousness of the number of cents that must be
paid to enter a theatre, I am very sure turns more steps from its door
than any religious feeling."[7] Though Trollope sounded a bit too censori-
ous in her put-down of penny-pinching, uncouth citizens of the New
World, France's Alexis de Tocqueville confirmed Trollope's observation
in *Democracy in America*, arguably the most prophetic book ever written about nineteenth-century American democracy: "The Americans
are both a Puritan and a trading nation. Therefore both their religious
beliefs and their industrial habits lead them to demand much abnega-

tion on the women's part and a continual sacrifice of pleasure for the sake of business, which is seldom expected in Europe."[8]

Despite an apparent Calvinistic creed of repression, American recreation grew nonetheless in the form of tavern sports, horse racing, cockfights, card playing, hunting, fishing, concerts, theater, and so on. The interests of America's early presidents reflected these activities. George Washington, for example, attended cockfights, as did Abraham Lincoln, whose presence at such an event was described vividly in a biography: "They formed a ring, and the time having arrived, Lincoln, with one hand on each hip and in a squatting position, cried, 'Ready.' Into the ring they toss their fowls, Bap's red rooster along with the rest. But no sooner had the little beauty discovered what was to be done than he dropped his tail and ran."[9] Andrew Jackson, as a young man in North Carolina, was known as "the most roaring, rollicking, game-cocking, horse-racing, card-playing, mischievous fellow, that ever lived in Salisbury." A president of the common folk and the frontiersmen, Jackson was also the living embodiment of popular American recreation, having left behind a note among his earliest personal effects that read: "How to feed a Cock before you have him fight Take and give him some Pickle Beef cut fine. . . ."[10]

Around the time of Chang and Eng's arrival, the minstrel show, which would become so popular in the 1840s that it gave birth to mass entertainment, had just emerged on the scene. Although cultural historians often cite the 1843 opening of Dan Emmett's Virginia Minstrels at the Chatham Theatre in New York as the landmark date, it was actually the comedian Thomas D. Rice who gave the earliest, most popular blackface performances in Louisville, Cincinnati, and Pittsburgh around 1829. And very much related to the Jim Crow show (more on that later) was the display of human anomalies. Or, to adopt the parlance of the day, the freak show.

Prior to Chang and Eng, America had seen at least two living human anomalies on display: Henry Moss and Martha Ann Honeywell. Moss, a black man from Virginia whose body was covered with white patches, was exhibited in Philadelphia in 1796, drawing great interest from across the social spectrum, especially among members of the prestigious American Philosophical Society. Honeywell, a young woman without limbs who could help herself to drink and do needlework, had a long run on display at the Peale Museum in New York, beginning in August 1828. While Moss was mostly a local attraction, Honeywell did have a national appeal and would, in ensuing years, be exhibited in "all the principal cities of the Union."[11] But, as Coffin expected, the Siamese Twins would easily top these exhibitions and take the freak show to a new level of sensation.

To prepare the twins for exhibition, Captain Coffin and Robert Hunter had to do some grooming, just as elephants and lions caught in the wild needed to be tamed before entering the circus ring. During the four-month-long voyage from Bangkok to Boston, Chang and Eng had taken English lessons from the crew members, familiarized themselves with Western manners, and learned to play checkers, chess, and other games that would later become part of their exhibition routines. Intelligent youths, they were quick learners. By the time they landed in Boston, "they were able to understand the language fairly well and to carry on simple conversations in broken English, as well as to do a limited amount of reading."[12] In chess and other board games, they also became excellent players, soon able to beat the men who had taught them.

Boston was then a robust city with more than sixty thousand residents. Perched on an island and accessible by roads built over water, it sported a magnificent three-story State House overlooking the scenic Boston Common, making it literally what the Puritan leader John Winthrop had imagined as "a city upon a hill." With its cobblestone streets, elegant Greek Revival mansions, and saltbox houses, the city, as many visitors from the Old World had observed, resembled an English town. Construction had just been completed on the Tremont House, a four-story, granite-faced hotel with a Greek portico, and it would begin to receive guests within a month. Often regarded as America's first modern hotel, Tremont House had unsurpassable luxuries and conveniences: indoor plumbing and running water, free soap (one wonders whether guests back then stole the soap), locked rooms, and bellboys. Charles Dickens, who stayed at the hotel during his 1842 visit and was much impressed by the grandeur, described the Tremont as having "more galleries, colonnades, piazzas, and passages than I can remember, or the reader would believe."[13]

To Chang and Eng, Boston was a far cry from Bangkok, a city of gilded palaces, tiered pagodas, spidery canals, and floating bazaars. One can easily imagine the awe with which the twins gazed at their first American city. It turned out, however, that the sense of wonder cut both ways, for the Bostonians were equally taken aback by the sight of the curiosity from Siam.

The day after their arrival, the Boston *Patriot* ran an article, the first ever in the Western Hemisphere, about the Siamese Twins:

> *Lusus Naturae*—The *Sachem*, arrived at this port yesterday, has on board two Siamese youths, males, eighteen years of age, their bodies connected from their birth. They appear to be in good health, and apparently contented with their confined situation. We have seen and examined this strange freak of nature. It is one of the greatest living curiosities we ever saw.

It seems that even though Coffin and Hunter had smuggled in the twins as stowaways, they certainly knew the importance of publicity and had invited a reporter for a sneak preview. The reporter's article, which would spawn countless reprints all over the country in the ensuing days, goes on with its description of the newly arrived "freak of nature":

> The two boys are about five feet in height, of well-proportioned frames, strong and active, good-natured, and of pleasant countenances, and withal intelligent and sensible—exhibiting the appearance of two well-made Siamese youths, with the exception that by a substance apparently bony or cartilaginous, about seven inches in circumference and four in length, proceeding from the umbilical region of each, they are firmly united together.

As though writing about the purebred dogs at the Westminster shows (which did not, in fact, begin until 1877), the reporter observed:

> They have a good appetite, appear lively, and run about the deck and cabin of the ship with the facility that any two healthy lads would do, with their arms over each other's shoulders, this being the position in which they move about. They will probably be exhibited to the public when proper arrangements have been made. They will be objects of great curiosity, particularly to the medical faculty. Their unnatural union is not more of a curiosity than the vigorous health they enjoy, and their apparent entire contentedness with their condition. One of the boys is named Chang, the other named Eng; together they are called Chang-Eng.[14]

The *Patriot* article also identified key players in the staging of exhibition—the medical doctors. The rise of medical science in the nineteenth century went hand in hand with the institution of the freak show as a business. In premodern times, human monstrosity, whether collected in a gentleman's cabinet of curiosities or displayed in taverns and on street corners, had been interpreted as evidence of God's design or wrath, woven into a narrative of wonder, suggestive of such mytho-logical figures as centaurs, griffins, sphinxes, mermaids, and cyclops. As medical science matured and eclipsed religion to become the authorita-tive cultural narrative, anomalous bodies began increasingly to be rep-resented as pathology cases, to be classified and studied by experts of teratology. Wonder turned into error, the marvelous into the deviant, and the stage for a freak show also became a medical theater, where the esteemed "lecturers" or "professors" would provide authoritative assess-ments of the displayed monstrosity.[15]

The first medical authority to put a stamp of approval on the Sia-mese Twins was a man keenly aware of medicine as public theater. John Collins Warren, hailing from an illustrious line of Boston doctors and trained in Edinburgh, was the face of medicine in nineteenth-century America. In 1815, Warren had inherited from his father the mantle of a chair professorship at Harvard, and the next year he became the first dean of Harvard Medical School. Soon he became the founding member of the Massachusetts General Hospital, and in 1824 he was appointed consulting physician of the city of Boston. When he was invited to examine the newly imported Siamese Twins, Warren was by all accounts at the peak of his career: He was a leading surgeon in New England, a champion of the temperance cause, and the founding editor of the *Boston Medical and Surgical Journal* (precursor of the prestigious *New England Journal of Medicine*).

Besides his pedigree and accomplishments, what distinguished Warren from his peers was his role as an impresario of staging medicine for public viewing. In 1823, someone donated an Egyptian mummy to the Massachusetts General Hospital. While his colleagues puzzled over what to do with a millennia-old corpse that seemed to have little to contribute to medical science, Warren took charge of installing the mummy as a museum piece at the hospital. A consummate scholar, he researched antiquities, consulted Diodorus and Herodotus, and published an article about the mummy in the *Boston Journal of Philosophy and the Arts*. With an eye on connecting with local readers, Warren alluded in his article to the curious case of Timothy Sprague, a local man in Malden who had died of a snake bite in 1765. Having lain in the ground for more than fifty years, Sprague's body was exhumed by accident in 1817 and found to be in surprisingly good condition: The skin was firm and strong, the flesh solid, and the cellular membrane resembled "the grain of the under surface of leather." The features of the corpse were so well preserved that "they were at once recognized by those who knew him when living." The connection between antiquity and local lore did the trick for Warren's first curatorial venture: The mummy exhibition was so successful that it brought in about $3,000 to the hospital's coffers in a single year.[16] Warren's most famous contribution to the medical theater would be his orchestration in 1846 of the first use of ether anesthesia in surgery, an operation staged publicly like a peep show, with a hired photographer in attendance. In fact, there was so much theatricality involved in that surgical amputa-

tion that Warren, mindful of chicanery pervasive in popular entertainment at the time, had to reassure his audience: "Gentlemen, this is
no Humbug."

While Warren was most rigorous in his research and practice, others were not. In fact, frauds were already prevalent in public entertainment. For instance, the so-called Feejee Mermaid, a carefully crafted
hoax that would be acquired by P. T. Barnum one day, had already
made its debut in 1817. Owners of genuine curiosities, or "born freaks,"
to be distinguished from "gaffed freaks," often looked to medical professionals for help in establishing credibility. In Dr. Warren, the owners
of Chang and Eng had certainly found the best authority.

Invited by Coffin and Hunter, Warren examined the twins several times and subsequently published two reports—one titled "Siamese Brothers" in the *Boston Medical and Surgical Journal* (September
1829) and the other titled "An Account of the Siamese Twin Brothers United Together from Their Birth" in the *American Journal of the
Medical Sciences* (November 1829). As Michel Foucault put it in *The
Birth of the Clinic*, "At the beginning of the nineteenth century, doctors described what for centuries had remained below the thresh-
old of the visible and the expressible. . . . A new alliance was forged
between words and things, enabling one to see and to say."[17] Sweeping
aside centuries of mythological fancies regarding abnormal bodies,
and looking at the conjoined twins through the clinical lens of physiology and pathology, Dr. Warren penned his findings in the prosaic
language of modern medicine: "The substance by which they are connected is a mass two inches long at its upper edge, and about five at
the lower. Its breadth from above downwards may be four inches; and
its thickness in a horizontal direction, two inches. Of course it is not
a rounded cord, but thicker in perpendicular than in the horizontal
direction."[18]

Warren seemed to have spent an inordinate amount of time on the
connecting band—the key to the twins' mystery—touching, feeling, and
holding it. He pressed the band forcibly between his fingers "before any
mark of pain was elicited." Unsatisfied, he did an experiment with a pin:

Being desirous of ascertaining if there was *any* point where both felt, we made an impression with the point of a pin in the exact vertical center of their connecting link; both said it hurt them. We then made other impressions, extending them very gradually further from this point: the result was, that within the distance of three-fourths of an inch from the center toward each boy, sensation was communicated to both by a single prick; beyond this it was excited in one only, the other perceiving it in no degree whatever.[19]

Warren concluded that there was nothing in the connecting band that would render surgical separation of the twins necessarily fatal, even though it might involve some danger because "it is not improbable that the peritoneum is continuous from the abdomen of one to that of the other."[20]

Besides examining the connecting cord, Warren also evaluated other physical aspects of the twins, including their pulses, heartbeats, respiration, and intervals of alvine and urinary evacuations. He observed their differing intellectual vigor and personalities, stating that Chang was more acute in perception and more irritable in temper than Eng.

A man given to fact and objectivity, Warren was not, however, immune from rumormongering; after all, an expert's testimony was part and parcel of freak shows, which thrived on the murky boundary between fact and fiction. Citing Captain Coffin, Warren stated that the twins' mother "had borne seventeen children. Once she had three at a birth, and never less than two, though none of her other children were in any way deformed."[21] Moreover, perhaps tempted by the theatricality of the occasion, Warren took a leap of faith. Referring to other documented "monsters" in history, such as the Hungarian Sisters, Warren made a bold prediction: "Their health is at present good; but it is probable that the change of their simple habits of living, for the luxuries they now obtain, together with the confinement their situation necessarily involves, will bring their lives to a close within a few years."[22]

In conclusion, Warren called the twins the "most remarkable case" of *lusus naturae* that had ever been known, a tagline that, along with his two reports, would become the blueprint for the promotional literature accompanying the twins' exhibitions. Carrying the full weight of "modern" medicine, these words by the former dean of Harvard Medical School put a stamp of legitimacy on the curiosity from Siam. Soon to be hailed as the "Eighth Wonder of the World," the Siamese Twins were now ready for their first American close-up.

The Monster, or Not

Curiously, the debut of the Siamese Twins in America was held at a ruined site. The Exchange Coffee House, a seven-story building clad in hammered granite and brick, had once been the pride of Boston. Funded by local financiers who had profited from the booming China trade, the building was completed in 1809. One of the largest and most imposing structures in the nation at the time it was built, the Exchange Coffee House combined a hotel, a café, and a public exchange. It boasted a giant dome, a portico of six Ionic columns, a spiral stairway, and about a hundred bedrooms scattered throughout the top floors. With a staggering construction cost of more than half a million dollars, this proud symbol of Boston's affluence and optimism had been the center of activities for about a decade until it burned to the ground in a spectacular fire on the evening of November 3, 1818. When the giant dome collapsed, the flames shot so high into the night sky that they were visible distinctly from sixty miles away.[1] Never to be rebuilt, the Exchange Coffee House had remained a ruined site, often compared to the Capitol in Washington after its destruction by the British army during the War of 1812. It would now provide the backdrop for the first display of the conjoined twins.

In the last week of August 1829, thousands of Bostonians, lured by a blizzard of publicity via newspaper reports, advertisements, handbills, and eye-catching posters, stood in long queues outside the tent at the Exchange, eager to get a peek at the curiosity from afar. Each of them would pay a stiff fifty-cent admission fee. In the promotional brochure for sale at ten cents, Bostonians saw an exotic scene: "An image of the young Chang and Eng presents them clad in pantaloons and tunics with ornate brocade. Their complexions are swarthy, even dark, and their slanted eyes and bulbous foreheads make them appear inextricably foreign. They stand against a backdrop that suggests a comfortable coexistence with what is presumed their natural habitat. Lush tropical vegetation graces the foreground. Behind them are palm trees and huts. Farther in the distance is domed architecture evoca-

CHANG AND ENG IN AN ORIENTAL SETTING,
LITHOGRAPH, 1829

tive of North Africa and West Asia, collapsing multiple Orients into one another."[2]

The twins in person did, in fact, shock the senses of the viewers, who thought they saw a monster. In the words of an Ohio visitor who later wrote about his experience, "The famous Siamese boys presented a sight, I admit, at first view a little revolting."[3] In fact, if the printer designing the poster had gotten his way, the headline would have been more provocative—"The Monster." But the owners objected, and the billing was later changed to a more benign "The Siamese Double Boys." Still, the "monster" idea certainly hovered in the minds of the crowds flocking into the tent. Mary Shelley's *Frankenstein*, first published in 1818, had been a hit in Boston. Even the honorable Dr. Warren would pepper his reports with such words as *monster* and *monstrosity*. To be fair, Warren's word choice was part of the standard scientific lexicon of the time. In 1755, the famous Swedish botanist Carl Linnaeus had already drawn a distinction among *Homo sapiens*, *Homo monstrosus* (monster man), and *Homo ferus* (wild man). According to Linnaeus and his followers, there was a descending hierarchy, a pecking order of sorts, which made up a "great chain of being." In *On the Origin of Species*, which appeared a few decades later, Charles Darwin would also suggest the existence of *Homo monstrosus* as a product of crossbreeding between *Homo sapiens* and other species in the great scheme of evolution.[4]

Science aside, the idea of a human monster, or freak, had had a long-lasting appeal in the popular imagination ever since Aristotle deemed a freak a *lusus naturae*, an aberration of the Natural Ladder. As Leslie Fiedler puts it in his trailblazing 1978 study, *Freaks*, "The myth of monsters is twice-born in the psyche." Fiedler believed that while the concept of the monster originates in the deep fears of our childhood, it is reinforced in adolescence by the young adult's awareness of his or her own sex and that of others. In the case of a young male, "his penis disconcertingly continues to rise and fall, swell and shrink—at times an imperious giant, at others a timid dwarf." For girls at puberty, the growth of breasts is also traumatic. "It is a rare young woman who in the crisis of adolescent shamefacedness does not feel herself either too flat-chested or too generously endowed, and in either case a Freak."[5] In other words, it is our own secret fear or self-image that draws us toward human anomalies on display. As Robert Bogdan maintains in a more recent study, "Dwarfs, for example, confront us with our phobia that we will never grow up." Bogdan emphasizes that the term *monster* or *freak* "is not a quality that belongs to the person on display. It is something that we created: a perspective, a set of practices—a social construction."[6]

To construct such a perspective, to tantalize the audience's deep psychic complex without turning them off, was a delicate balancing act, a lucrative art that P. T. Barnum and his ilk would practice to perfection in the coming decades. Captain Coffin might not have been Barnum, but he and James Hale, a twenty-eight-year-old Bostonian hired as the manager of the twins, understood well the art of showbiz. They widely publicized a version of Dr. Warren's report, which ends with a reassurance to the viewing public: "Let me add that there is nothing unpleasant in the aspect of these boys. On the contrary, they must be viewed as presenting one of the most interesting objects of natural history, which have ever been known to scientific men."[7] According to the *Boston Bulletin*, the twins "are taught no tricks to enhance the foolish part of an exhibition, but are allowed to conduct as they please, naturally and easily, according to the momentary dictates of their feelings."[8] Their exotic and abnormal appearance was shocking enough, and letting the twins act like a "normal" human being further intensified the sense of the uncanny: The monster is just like us, and yet so different.

After their sensational debut in Boston, the twins were then taken to Providence, only fifty miles to the south. New to the country and still struggling with the English language—newspapers reported that the twins would "master three or four English words every day"—they knew little about American geography.[9] Traveling in an enclosed carriage, the twins arrived in Providence, a city of about seventeen thousand people, where they were greeted by thousands of curious gawkers attracted by the advance publicity that Hale had arranged in the local papers, such as this one in the *Rhode Island American*: "The Siamese Twins, who have excited so much wonder in Boston, by their extraordinary union, will visit this town, and remain here only on Friday and Saturday next."[10] By this time, the twins had added new routines—somersaults in tandem, quick backflips, and occasional challenges to members of the audience for a game of checkers or chess. Once, to amuse the spectators, the twins, weighing together no more than two hundred pounds, carried a 280-pound man around the exhibition hall.[11]

Barely a month into their debut, the twins had already provoked intense debates over matters of religion, soul, and individuality. The fact that they were simultaneously two and one had provided not only a rare specimen for the medical professionals, but also ample food for thought for theologians, philosophers, and amateur thinkers. On the last day of the twins' exhibition in Boston, an article appeared in a local newspaper posing a series of "knotty questions." Playing on the Shakespearean line, "Double, double, toil and trouble," the author asked: What would happen if one brother converted to Christianity while the other remained a disciple "of the great Buddha"? "Would both souls be saved since one twin was a 'heathen'?"[12]

These questions about soul and salvation recalled a much earlier incident, in the sixteenth century, when an autopsy—supposedly the first by white men in the Americas—had been performed in 1533 after the birth of two conjoined sisters on the island of Hispaniola. The priest performing the baptism was, in fact, befuddled by the question of whether the girls had one soul or two. When the twins died eight days later, an autopsy was conducted, and, based on the findings, the girls were deemed as possessing two separate souls.[13] Given such a precedent, it was taken for granted that Chang and Eng had two separate souls, but the question of salvation remained. Moreover, the Boston author went on to ask: What if one of them committed a crime? "Would ye indict two men as an individual? Dare ye send Chang and his brother to jail when only Chang shall happen to break the peace? Or, if Chang and Eng should fall out together, tell us, we beseech ye, could Chang have his action for being assaulted by his other half, that is by himself?"[14]

Not everyone, however, thought the twins were worthy of the unusual attention they were getting. On September 15, the *Rhode Island American*, the same newspaper that had advertised their show in Providence, published an article by a David B. Slack, dismissing the brouhaha. "The world has profited but little by wonders of any kind, either in story or in fact," wrote the author, who insisted that the conjoined twins, as tricks of nature, were "sources of amusement that depressed and weakened the mind, not models for enlightenment." As such, Slack concluded, these boys "held no more significance for human society than did a double-yolked egg."[15]

Double-yolked egg or not, the twins were nonetheless able to hatch a sizable profit for their owners. Their alluring monstrosity in the age of American spectacle and minstrelsy ensured that there would be much more money to be made in days and years to come. After an extended stay in Providence, they took a steamboat and headed for New York City.

Gotham City

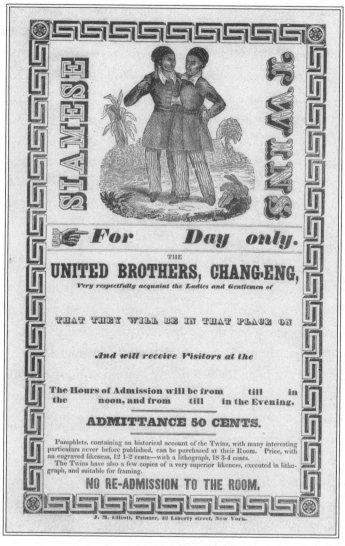

ADVERTISING POSTER

"**W**ent this morning to see the Siamese boys. This astonishing freak of nature is exceedingly interesting and the sight of it is not disagreeable, as I expected it to be," were the words jotted down in his diary by Philip Hone, the former mayor of New York City.[1] Born to a German immigrant carpenter in 1780, Hone was a self-made man. At seventeen, he partnered with his brother and launched an auction business, which made him a fortune. Retiring from business at forty-one, he successfully ran for mayor and assumed office in 1825. Widely known as a precentor of fashion, politics, and New York's intellectual life, Hone was a diligent chronicler of his native city, keeping detailed journals about his own daily life as well as the affairs of the city.

The twins arrived in New York on September 18, 1829, after an eighteen-hour journey by sea from Providence. Sailing between Connecticut and Long Island, looking at the low-lying, vanishing coastlines of New England, the twins must have recalled their memorable trip to Bangkok to see the king, or the journey down the Meinam when they left Siam only a few months earlier.

The steamer line between Providence and New York had first opened in 1822. Alexis de Tocqueville, who would travel the same route in 1831, spoke fondly of the sixty-league journey on one of these newfangled steamboats with a spacious interior and several large saloons providing comfortable sleeping and dining quarters for as many as eight hundred men and women. Entering New York by way of Long Island Sound, one could, in the words of Tocqueville, "picture a sea dotted with sails, a lovely sweep of notched shoreline, blossoming trees on greensward sloping down to the water, a multitude of small, artfully embellished candy-box houses in the background."[2]

There were, however, no Chinese junks here, or fishmongers' swift sampans, all of which would have made the twins feel at home. Instead, they saw a spectacle full of hum and buzz, clanking and ringing, a city fast becoming the greatest metropolis in the world.

As it turned out, 1829 was a relatively quiet year in New York, a fact borne out by Philip Hone's journals. In January, when the social season opened, a few bored residents on Bowling Green cleared an opening between their houses to host a swank fancy-dress ball, the first of its kind in this former Dutch settlement with a population soaring to two hundred thousand. It was soon followed by a masked ball at the Park Theatre, attended by the social swells, including the Hones. The Park had dominated in entertainment that year partly due to the success of new shows, partly because its major competitors, the American Opera House and the Lafayette, had either gone out of business or gone up in flames. The masquerades drew outcries from the city's more conservative citizens, who lobbied the legislature to outlaw them. In May, two steam locomotives arrived from England for use on the railroad belonging to the newly founded Delaware and Hudson Canal Company. Hone, a partner in the company, went to the foundry to see the first steam locomotives ever used in America—only to find that they were too heavy for the wooden rails with thin iron straps and had to be refitted. The quiet of January 1829 was shattered by June, however, when the steam frigate *Fulton*, built during the War of 1812, exploded at the Brooklyn Navy Yard, killing more than twenty-five men.[3]

The greatest thoroughfare in the city, Broadway, stretching for fifteen miles from the Battery in the south to Spuyten Duyvil Creek in the very north, bustled day and night with carts, hackney coaches, and horsemen. Along the street stood fine residences with graceful wooden porticos and pillars, in addition to the sylvan campus of Columbia College and the majestic American Hotel and Park Theatre. In certain sections, one could catch a glimpse of the Hudson's sparkling water. But most distinct of all, in the midst of all this glamour and splendor, was a sight that rarely escaped observant visitors: the pigs that waddled freely up and down the promenade, their noses always in search of offal. Dickens, in his *American Notes*, describes for us the stark contrast between the gaudy human scene and the scavenging swine: "Here are the same ladies in bright colours, walking to and fro, in pairs and singly; yonder the very same light blue parasol which passed and repassed the hotel-window here. Take care of the pigs. Two portly sows are trotting up

behind this carriage, and a select party of half-a-dozen gentlemen-hogs
have just now turned the corner."[4]

Beyond Manhattan, a brand new state prison, Sing Sing, named after
an Indian tribe, began receiving inmates transferred from Newgate
Prison in Greenwich Village, thus freeing up a prime real estate spot for
future developments. On Long Island, the Mosquito Cove revival, part
of the nationwide religious fervor known as the Second Great Awakening (more on that later), drew thousands of Methodists from hundreds
of miles around, who descended on the campground like mosquitoes.
On Staten Island, a young man by the name of Cornelius Vanderbilt
was managing a seven-vessel Gibbons Line, ferrying between Staten
Island and Manhattan. One day, this young man would pick up the
epithet "Commodore," for having built a shipping and railroad empire.

Back in the city, the biggest news prior to the Siamese Twins' arrival
was in the foreign sections of the newspapers—namely, the execution
of William Burke in Edinburgh, Scotland. An Irish-born peddler comb-
ing the streets of Edinburgh, Burke had partnered with boardinghouse
owner William Hare in pursuit of dead bodies. The beginning of their
deadly trade was innocent enough: One of the elderly tenants at the
flophouse had died while still owing four pounds in rent. To collect the
debt, Hare enlisted Burke's help in hauling the body to a local surgeon who gave dissection lessons to medical students. The surgeon paid
seven pounds ten shillings for the corpse, an impressive amount that
piqued the entrepreneurial spirits of Hare and Burke. The duo would
soon sell the surgeon another sixteen bodies of the newly departed,
mostly women. "Newly-departed that is at the hands of the two men,"
as the historian David Minor sardonically puts it. "When their lethal
venture was discovered and the two arrested, Hare agreed to a plea bargain offer and was spirited away to protect him against mob violence.
Burke's more violent and final departure delighted the huge crowds—
some estimates put the number at close to 40,000—gathered for the
public execution." Even after his hanging, Burke still had one more service to perform for the medical profession. In a case of poetic justice,
his body was taken to the medical school, where the students watched

doctors remove the top of his head for a lesson on the human brain. According to Minor, "Other young fans of the anatomical arts, kept out of the building for lack of space, began attacking the police and it wasn't until the town council intervened and promised everyone a good look that order was restored."[5] Although Burke's execution had taken place in January, the violence of his crime and death had put the otherwise hard-nosed New Yorkers on edge. There was widespread terror among women that copycats might commit the same heinous acts in the city by "Burking" them, which was Burke's modus operandi for producing fresh corpses—smothering.

The morbid curiosity of the Edinburgh mob was relevant in light of the twins' visit to New York, where the citizens' ongoing obsession with macabre news and human anatomy had drawn them to the spectacle of the "Canadian Giant," a man by the name of Modeste Maltacle, who weighed 619 pounds. Philip Hone, not one to miss anything happening in his city, went to see the show with measuring tape in hand. He later confided to his diary that one of the giant's ankles was three feet five inches in circumference.[6] Of course, New Yorkers would have more to chatter about when the steamer *Chancellor Livingston* arrived from Providence, bearing the spectacle of the United Siamese Brothers.

On September 20, 1829, Chang and Eng's show in New York opened at the Grand Saloon, Masonic Hall, on Broadway. As the *Evening Post* reported, the twins presented "a spectacle of great interest, alloyed, however, by those feelings of commiseration which human deformity must ever occasion." Every day (except Sunday) from 9 to 2, and then from 6 to 9, people flooded into the Masonic Hall to get a peek at what had been advertised as a "wonderful natural curiosity."

By now the twins had performed in America for more than a month, giving them enough time to polish their repertoire and hone their skills in interacting with an audience. With their English steadily improving, they gained more confidence in improvisation, entertaining the audience with their good-natured country boys' shrewd, simple wit. According to one report, when a one-eyed man attended their show, the twins insisted that he should be refunded half his admission fee, "since he could not see as much as others." When they saw a legless person in the audience, they generously offered a refund and a cigar, putatively "to atone for the fact that they had four arms and legs between them."[7] When a proselytizing priest approached them and tested these "pagan" boys' knowledge of salvation, the twins knew exactly how to return the favor. The priest asked them, "Do you know where you would go if you were to die?" Chang and Eng pointed their fingers upward. "Yes, yes, up dere," they said. "Do you know where I should go if I were to die?" The twins nodded and pointed their fingers downward. "Yes, yes, down dere," they replied.[8]

It was not entirely inconceivable that among the visitors who thronged the Masonic Hall would be a young man by the name of Herman Melville. Born in the city, the future author of *Moby-Dick* had just turned ten in the fall of 1829. Living beyond his means on borrowed money and mindful of the city's way of defining a person by his address, Melville's father, Allan, had just moved the family to a large house in a posh neighborhood on Broadway. Melville and his brother Gansevoort were sent to the nearby Columbia Grammar School. Herman was a troubled kid, slow in comprehension and suffering from a speech impediment, a disability shared by Billy Budd, the stuttering protagonist in Melville's last story. Even though we have no record of the teenage Melville visiting the Siamese Twins, his orbit lay in the proximity of the Masonic Hall. Those were the best years of Melville's childhood, when he was still spelling his last name as "Melvill." Pretty soon, his father would go bankrupt and die a broken man, leaving behind a widow with four kids and a sizable debt and putting an end to Melville's formal education. Self-taught thereafter, Melville became a sailor and then an author who would people his fiction with all sorts of human abnormality— one-legged Captain Ahab, fully tattooed Queequeg, stammering Billy Budd, to name just a few. References to the Siamese Twins actually abound in Melville's oeuvre. In *Moby-Dick*, Ishmael imagines that he and Queequeg are "united" by an "elongated Siamese ligature" and that the South Sea giant was his own "inseparable twin brother." In *The Confidence-Man*, the narrator describes a scene where "the two stood

together; the old miser leaning against the herb-doctor with something
of that air of trustful fraternity with which, when standing, the less
strong of the Siamese Twins habitually leans against the other." Melville
once told fellow author Richard Henry Dana Jr. that they were "tied
& welded" by a "Siamese link of affectionate sympathy." And in *Billy
Budd*, a novella left unfinished at his death, Melville described con-
trasting emotions by invoking the names of the Siamese Twins: "Now
envy and antipathy, passions irreconcilable in reason nevertheless may
spring conjoined like Chang and Eng in one birth. Is Envy then such a
monster?" Here, Melville, who had given up on fiction for twenty years
and worked quietly as a customs officer and a poet, might have been
struck by the poetic proximity of *Envy* and *Eng*, and the acoustic echo
between *Antipathy* and *Chang*.[9] Anyway, some of these colorful descriptions could not have been made by someone who had not observed the
twins closely or with much fascination.

While the twins' popularity soared, a story, possibly apocryphal, made
the rounds and later was picked up by a few biographers. Unhappy with
their hotel arrangements in New York and wishing for privacy and independence, Chang and Eng wanted to find lodgings for themselves. But
it proved to be a difficult task. No stranger to human varieties in what
was often regarded as a morally polluted city, most landlords would be
willing, if the price was right, to rent a room to almost anyone. A pair
of conjoined twins, however, made prospective landlords feel as if they
were harboring some indecent beasts. As a result, the twins were turned
away again and again as they tramped up and down busy streets and
quiet alleys, looking for a room. They finally got a break when they came
to a large house on John Street. The look on the face of the landlady as
she opened the door convinced the twins that their effort would be in
vain again, but they were wrong. The woman, quickly recovering from
her initial shock at the sight of the double men, went on to welcome
them inside and showed them a room on the first floor. This was probably the first time they had set foot inside an American domestic space.

Looking around the sparsely furnished room, they felt strangely
at home and were eager to take it when they suddenly heard move-

ment over their heads. Alarmed, they asked the landlady what it was. She assured them that it was just a tenant in the room above. With that explanation, their interest in the room immediately vanished, and they asked whether she had any room on a higher floor. The perplexed woman showed them the attic, which they found to be quite to their liking. Even though they had to climb three flights of stairs to get there, it was private, and, most important of all, no one would be walking over their heads. As they later explained to their landlady, in Siam it was considered bad luck to have anyone walk over one's head; hence, most houses there had only a single floor. This explanation was quite in keeping with some of the ethnographic descriptions of Siam at the time. When the British envoy visited Bangkok in 1822, he stayed on the second story of a house. According to William S. W. Ruschenberger, "To avoid the ill luck and disgrace of having any body for a moment actually over his head, the worthy Phra Klang (a man of some three or four hundred pounds substance) was in the habit of entering the Ambassador's apartments through a window, by a ladder placed against the outside of the building."[10] For the same reason, even today in many parts of Asia, it is considered a taboo or bad luck to walk beneath underwear or pants hanging outside on laundry lines. An undergarment is a synecdoche for a walking body.

After they moved in, Chang and Eng proved to be excellent tenants—quiet, considerate, and never in arrears for their rent. But the trouble of having to climb the stairs day in and day out eventually got to them. After a long day of work, performing before thousands of noisy viewers and standing at the center of attention for hours—perhaps reminiscent of Archibald MacLeish's poetic description of Vasserot, the armless ambidextrian performing before "those thousands of white faces, those dazed eyes"—they were often too tired to drag their conjoined bodies up the steep and narrow stairs. They eventually gave in to pragmatism and convenience and begged the landlady to let them move to the ground-floor room. Superstition be damned; the Siamese Twins were well on their way to becoming pragmatic Americans.[11]

Just as the twins were eager to imbibe the nation's fresh vapors,

America was also quick to absorb new elements landing on its shores. Less than two months after their arrival, the Siamese Twins had already entered the lexicon of the American language. The twins might have arrived too late for inclusion in the first edition of Noah Webster's *An American Dictionary of the English Language* (1828)—a monumental effort to assert America's linguistic and cultural independence from Mother England—but the ever-changing American English soon adopted the "Siamese Twins" as a metaphor for inseparable unions. On October 16, 1829, two months after the twins' arrival, the *Rhode Island American* reported on a cattle show in Worcester, Massachusetts, a festive occasion where a toast was given: "Worcester County and Rhode Island—Like the Siamese Twins united by a cord that cannot be severed with safety to either."[12] This quote predates the earliest citation of "Siamese Twins" in the *Oxford English Dictionary* by about a month. Soon afterward, the term entered common household usage and made it into the subsequent editions of Webster's dictionary. One day, on the brink of the American Civil War, "Siamese Twins," by then deeply ingrained in the national psyche, would be invoked again as a metaphor for a bond that might be cut only at the peril of both sides of the Union.

The City of Brotherly Love

C/all it love at first sight. Philadelphia—the city that still has Chang and Eng's fused liver in a tub of preservative liquid inside a museum, where a visitor can see a section of the brain of President Garfield's assassin as well as millions of other medical oddities and pathological specimens—first saw the conjoined twins in October 1829. After they had taken New York City by storm, Chang and Eng proceeded by steamboat and stage to the birthplace of the Declaration of Independence.

Foreign visitors to Philadelphia often complained about its dull physical layout, a rigidly rectangular grid of streets distinguished from one another, as Tocqueville put it, "by number rather than name . . . of a saint, a famous man, an event." Fanny Trollope hated its "extreme and almost wearisome regularity," and so did Dickens, who visited the city and said, "I would have given the world for a crooked street." The dreary city planning made Tocqueville believe that "these people know nothing but arithmetic."[1] However, what Philadelphia lacked in physical variety, it made up for in spiritual diversity. Founded by William Penn in 1681, this town on the Delaware River had attracted Anglicans, Presbyterians, Baptists, and especially Quakers, who were drawn by Penn's policy of religious tolerance. Literally meaning the "City of Brotherly Love," Philadelphia in the early nineteenth century had become a bustling mix of diverse communities and the third-largest port on the Atlantic seaboard, after Boston and New York.[2]

In some ways, Philadelphians, more than a hundred thousand strong in 1829, were ideal viewers who could best appreciate the kind of exoticism brought by the "wonder boys" from Siam. As early as 1784, the same year that the *Empress of China*, refitted from a gunboat during the Revolutionary War, had docked in Canton and opened the China Trade route, Peale's Museum in Philadelphia, the first of its kind in the young republic, had displayed Chinese curiosities among its collection of objects from Africa and India. The legendary founder of the museum, Charles Willson Peale, had started out as a portrait painter, capturing the profiles of many American notables at the time of the Revolutionary War. Peale had developed a strong interest in natural history and had collected artifacts and specimens and displayed them in his own home in Philadelphia before moving them to what would become the nation's first public museum in 1786. Among the items Peale had displayed, "what attracted the greatest curiosity was the collection of wrappings used to bind the feet of Chinese women and the tiny shoes and slippers that fit bound feet." By the time the Siamese Twins arrived, Peale's, now renamed the Philadelphia Museum, had assembled a sizable collection of Chinese artifacts that included wax models of "Chinese Laborers and Gentlemen," standing side by side with models of Native Americans and other "exotic" people.[3] But neither life-groups in dioramas nor life-size wax figures came close to sparking the electrifying sensation that two conjoined bodies in flesh and blood would generate.

On October 9, the *Aurora and Pennsylvania Gazette* told its readers, who had for years benefited from the curatorial wisdom and knowledge of Mr. Peale: "We had the pleasure, yesterday, of viewing the Siamese boys, and were much gratified to find that their intimate union is attended with but little bodily embarrassment, and does not in the least interfere with their happiness."[4] Excited by such reports and other advertisements, the curious came in droves, quickly filling up the exhibition rooms as well as the pockets of the twins' owners. By one account, the one-week exhibition grossed about $1,000, then a very handsome sum.

The extraordinary success of the show might have had to do with the fact that Philadelphia was not only the birthplace of the first public museum in the United States but also the national center of the medical profession. In the spirit of the Quaker tradition of philanthropy, the city had been a leader in the development of medicine since the eighteenth century. America's first public hospital was established in 1752 and the first medical school in 1765. The College of Physicians of Philadelphia, the oldest private medical society in the United States, was formed in 1787. The college later sponsored the Mütter Museum, which would play a vital role in the twins' autopsy in the future. Like their colleagues in Boston, the fellows of the college were much fascinated by the conjoined twins as a rare specimen of pathology. A physical examination of the twins by the city's leading doctors was set up, and among these physicians was Philip Syng Physick.

Dr. Physick (a corruption of Fishwick), widely regarded as the "Father of American Surgery," was a Philadelphia native who trained at the Royal College of Surgeons in London and the School of Medicine in Edinburgh. At the time, he was president of the Philadelphia Medical Society. In 1812, he invented a stomach pump made of a pewter syringe with a flexible tube. The first time he used the pump, he saved the lives of black twins suffering from an overdose of laudanum. Among his other achievements was the invention of the artificial anus in 1826.[5] And, because of his involvement in the making of carbonated water for the relief of gastric disorders—a recipe later improved by the enterprising pharmacist Townsend Speakman, who added fruit syrup to the concoction to make it more palatable—Physick was sometimes also called "Soda's Pop."[6] Given his deep interest in autopsy as a regular means of observation and discovery, Physick would not want to miss the opportunity of examining these conjoined twins, alive or dead.

By this time, Harvard surgeon John Warren's report, reprinted in newspapers throughout the country, must have been quite familiar to his colleagues in Philadelphia. Therefore, the new report that resulted from the examination by Physick and others, published in the *Aurora and Pennsylvania Gazette*, did not try to shed any new light on the anatomy of the twins' connecting band. Instead, it focused on the psychological effects of the unusual connection on the twins and their prospects for the future. The doctors found the twins' voices "disagreeable, coarse, and unmusical," a factor attributed to the influence of puberty. They observed that the twins did not like to talk to each other; rather than agree with the common belief that the twins' reticence toward each other might be "ascribed to an indifference to each other," the doctors maintained that "it is simply they have no information to communicate to each other."

As for the nagging question everyone was asking—the eternal what-if scenario that would dog every pair of conjoined twins in the future—the Philadelphia doctors, like modern-day stock analysts posting a mixed recommendation on a company, addressed the possibility of surgically separating the twins: "The separation I think may be practical, though not unattended with danger. If it were, who would urge it where there is such perfect union of feeling and concert of action; whilst they are healthy and active; happy and gay; and withal quite contented with their lot. At present I would be unwilling to disunite them, even if it could be accomplished without pain and without danger."[7]

As many biographers have pointed out, this talk of separating the twins was a marketing ploy, mere fodder contrived for publicity, because this connecting band was the moneymaker, without which there would be no Siamese Twins or their lucrative attraction. Decades later, when the twins had to partner with P. T. Barnum and go on the road again, the Prince of Humbugs successfully exploited the prospect of separating the twins as an eye-catching headline. As Barnum bragged in his autobiography, the popularity of the twins' European tour in the late 1860s was "much enhanced, if not actually caused, by extensive announcement in advance that the main purpose of Chang-Eng's visit to Europe was to consult the most eminent medical and surgical talent with regard to the safety of separating the twins."

Like Dr. John Warren's report, which became a key endorsement, the article by Physick, the eminent Philadelphia surgeon, also boosted the promotion of the twins to the world at large. The advancing medical science and the time-honored freak show became, like the bodies of Chang and Eng, intertwined.

Knocking at the Gate

CHANG AND ENG, LITHOGRAPH (1830)

"**S**outhern Asia, in general, is the seat of awful images and associations," Thomas de Quincey declared in his *Confessions of an English Opium-Eater* (1822), and he soon expanded that geography to include the entire continent of Asia, or wherever the mighty British Empire had flexed its colonial muscles in that part of the world. A prose master and inveterate opium addict, de Quincey was haunted by his exotic hallucinations—drug-induced nightmares in which he was surrounded by monstrous creatures, tortured by outlandish imageries: "I was stared at, hooted at, grinned at, chattered at, by monkeys, by paroquets, by cockatoos. I ran into pagodas: and was fixed, for centuries, at the summit, or in secret rooms. . . . I was kissed, with cancerous kisses, by crocodiles; and laid, confounded with all unutterable slimy things, amongst reeds and Nilotic mud." Like a ghost traveling in endless catacombs, he occasionally managed to escape, but then he found it was merely to transition to a different, but equally horrific, dream scene: "I escaped sometimes, and found myself in Chinese houses, with cane tables, &c. All the feet of the tables, sophas, &c. soon became instinct with life: the abominable head of the crocodile, and his leering eyes, looking out at me, multiplied into a thousand repetitions: and I stood loathing and fascinated."[1]

Unlike his predecessor Samuel Coleridge, whose opiate-induced reverie took him on an exhilarating time travel to Kublai Khan's Xanadu, de Quincey seemed to be cursed with sinister nightmares, an existential dilemma he blamed on a roaming Malay who had once knocked on his cottage door. A few years earlier, de Quincey claimed, a turbaned, "ferocious looking" Malay man happened by his mountain cottage, gesticulating in a foreign tongue, failing to communicate anything sensible to the baffled British writer. Like that fated knock at the gate in *Macbeth*, which de Quincey masterfully interpreted in an essay widely regarded as the paragon of English prose, the chance encounter with the mysterious Malay ushered in an unstoppable torrent of bad dreams: "The Malay has been a fearful enemy for months. I have been every night, through his means, transported into Asiatic scenes."[2]

Even a run-of-the-mill literary critic with rudimentary knowledge of cultural psychology can see through the smoke screen put up by de Quincey here. He called Asia, where the British Empire had been inexorably expanding, the "great *officina gentium*" (workshop of people). It is, as he put it, "the part of the earth most swarming with human life," a jungle where "man is a weed."[3] In other words, de Quincey's nightmare was really a symptom of the British guilt over colonial conquest of Asia, an expression of a collective unconscious torn between arrogance and fear, fascination and revulsion. Later, de Quincey would lose his son Horace in the First Opium War with China (1839–42), consequently turning the former guilt-ridden opium-eater into a most vocal, saber-rattling cheerleader for the opium trade and British pride. For now, however, de Quincey's candid confession, that he "stood loathing and fascinated," not only was a self-description but also aptly captured the British sentiment toward the exotic land of Asia, which now sent a representative not in the form of de Quincey's quaint, turbaned Malay, but rather the conjoined Siamese Twins.

After a whirlwind of successful and profitable debuts in major northeastern cities, Captain Abel Coffin and Robert Hunter decided to take the twins to the British Isles and Europe. On October 17, 1829, they boarded the packet ship *Robert Edwards*, bound from New York Harbor for England. Before their departure—perhaps minding Dr. Warren's warning about the potential early demise of the twins in a new climate and environment—Coffin took out a $10,000 life-insurance policy on his prized curiosity to cover any possible loss as well as the costs of shipping the bodies, should they die aboard, to the port of destination. He also packed for the journey an ample supply of embalming materials: molasses and corrosive sublimate (mercuric chloride). Live or dead, the twins would make money for their owners. In the long history of displaying human oddities, dead bodies were often just as lucrative for impresarios as live ones. As Susan Stewart puts it in her profound meditation on the abnormal, for curiosity seekers, "it does not matter whether the freak is alive or dead."[4] In Philadelphia, Charles Peale was known for staging spectacles of death at his museum. Just a few years down the road, P. T. Barnum would turn the corpse of Joice Heth, allegedly a 161-year-old slave and former nurse of baby George Washington, into an exhibition as profitable as when the woman was still alive.

Comforted by the large sum of insurance, and by the knowledge that even dead twins would be a cash cow, Coffin went ahead and did something that would plant a seed of resentment in the twins' mind. For the journey to England, Coffin had booked first-class tickets for himself, his wife Susan, and manager James Hale, while the twins and their companion Tieu had to travel in steerage. As the twins recalled later, while the first-class passengers wined and dined on fresh luxuries, Chang and Eng had to stay in cramped quarters and to "set down day after day to eat salt beef and potatoes." To make matters worse, when they protested the glaringly unfair treatment, Coffin blamed it on the ship captain, claiming that first-class tickets had been purchased for the twins but the cabins were overbooked. But the fact is, as the twins would later find out and describe angrily in a letter, Coffin had "screwed a hard bargain for our passage to England, in the steerage of the ship and having us under the denomination of his servants—all for the paltry savings of $100 and yet wishing to keep us in good temper and wishing moreover to make us believe that he spared no expense for our comfort."[5] Regarded as freaks, the twins would always have to fight to be treated as humans. The battle had merely begun, and the odds were against them, as England awaited their arrival.

After a month of rough autumn sailing across the icy-cold Atlantic, the *Robert Edwards* docked in Southampton on November 19, 1829. The twins were immediately taken to London, where Coffin had reserved rooms at the North and South American Coffee House on Threadneedle Street. Adjacent to the commercial epicenter of the Royal Exchange, the inn was a popular spot for ship captains and business representatives of American and European firms, who could get access there to American newspapers and obtain information about "the arrival and departure of the fleet of steamers, packets, and masters engaged in the commerce of America."[6]

As it happened, 1829 was the penultimate year of the reign of the ailing King George IV. Soon assuming the title of "the empire on which the sun never sets," Great Britain was on the verge of a spectacular ascent as a global power. Having defeated Napoleon in the previous decade, Britain saw its Royal Navy rule supreme in all parts of the world. When the Caribbean sugar economy declined due to competition and the abhorrence of goods derived from slave labor, the focus of the British colonial interest shifted to Asia, with the East India Company fast expanding its reach in India and China. The Industrial Revolution gave Britain the technological advantage over these Asian countries mired in millennia-old feudalism. In Siam, the 1826 Burney Treaty had given the British a colonial foothold. Domestically, the year 1829 also saw the passage of the Roman Catholic Relief Act, which for the first time allowed Catholic MPs to sit in Parliament. And after Parliament passed the Metropolitan Police Act, sponsored by Sir Robert Peel, the first thousand police officers, dressed in blue tailcoats and top hats, began to patrol the streets of London on September 29. These sartorially enhanced police were first nicknamed "Peelers," and then dubbed "Bobbies," both in honor of the minister who had pushed the bill through Parliament.

Arriving in London, then housing a staggering population of more than one and a half million, the twins were impressed not only by the newly minted Peelers on foot patrol, but also by the dense fog that had historically given the city its unique reputation. Ever since the eighteenth century, the smoke and soot from coal burning in the full-throttled engines of the Industrial Revolution led to a climatic menace. On long winter days, yellow, sulfurous smog blanketed the city and blocked the sun. In the famous opening of *Bleak House* (1853), Charles Dickens gave us a vivid description of how his native city suffered in the hoary grip of the demonic veil: "Fog everywhere. . . . Fog in the eyes and throats of ancient Greenwich pensioners, wheezing by the firesides of their wards; fog in the stem and bowl of the afternoon pipe of the wrathful skipper, down in his close cabin; fog cruelly pinching the toes and fingers of his shivering little 'prentice boy on deck. Chance people on the bridges peeping over the parapets into a nether sky of fog, with fog all 'round them, as if they were up in a balloon, and hanging in the misty clouds."[7]

On the day of the twins' arrival, *The Times* reported that what Dickens called a nether sky of fog had covered the metropolis and its vicinity: "In Westminster-road, at 11 o'clock in the morning, the opposite side was not visible. At 12 o'clock you could discern objects at a distance of 300 yards, and this continued for an hour or more, but at the same time the neighborhood of the Royal Exchange was nearly in midnight gloom."[8] Inured to the natural surroundings of a Siamese river town, Chang and Eng at first did not know what to make of the strange sights of a densely populated city rendered ghostly by smog. According to James Hale, "the day after their arrival there, it being necessary to have lighted candles in the drawing room at noon, in consequence of the fog and smoke, they went to bed, insisting that it was not possible it could be day-time." Moreover, the damp weather did not agree with the twins, who both immediately fell ill, suffering from colds and coughs. Despite their discomfort, these young fellows tried to keep up their spirits through wisecracking, a character trait that would stand them in good stead on and off stage. Taking a deadened coal from the grate and holding it up, they called it "the London sun." Seeing snowfall for the first time in their lives, they asked, perhaps mockingly, "whether it was sugar or salt."[9]

The reporters invited by Coffin for a sneak preview were smitten with what they saw. Their published reports soon filled the pages of newspapers distributed all over the British Isles. A lengthy article in the *Times* described the physical features of these wonder boys, playing up on the theme that the twins were at once strikingly normal, just like each one of us, and freakishly abnormal:

They are two distinct and perfect youths, about 18 years of age, possessing all the faculties and powers usually possessed at that period of life, united together by a short band at the pit of the stomach. . . . Their arms and legs are perfectly free to move. . . . In their ordinary motions they resemble two persons waltzing more than anything else we know of. In a room they seem to roll about, as it were, but when they walk to any distance, they proceed straight forward with a gait like other people. As they rose up or sat down, or stooped, their movements reminded us occasionally of two playful kittens with their legs round each other; they were, though strange, not ungraceful, and without the appearance of constraint and irksomeness.

The reporters drew attention to the twins' racial, or specifically Chinese, features, at a time when Chinese were still a rare sight in London. This was still a few decades before a large influx of Chinese immigrants would turn a part of the East End into the infamous Limehouse District, depicted in popular literature as a warren of opium dens, gambling parlors, and brothels:

In the colour of their skins, in the form of the nose, lips, and eyes, they resemble the Chinese, whom our readers may probably have seen occasionally about the streets of London, but they have not that broad and flat face which is characteristic of the Mongol race. Their foreheads are higher and narrower than those of the majority of their countrymen. The expression of their countenance is cheerful and pleasing rather than otherwise, and they seem much delighted with any attention paid to them.

In conclusion, the reporters reiterated their opening thesis, tantalizing the readers with a promise of wonder without impropriety: "Without being in the least disgusting or unpleasant, like almost all monstrosities, these youths are certainly one of the most extraordinary freaks of nature that has ever been witnessed."[10]

On November 24, after the twins had recovered, a private viewing party was held at the Egyptian Hall in Piccadilly, setting the stage for the public exhibition later. As in all previous previews in American cities, Coffin and Hunter, the proud co-owners, invited a most distinguished group of doctors and other social elites to this event. The guests were a roll call of the upper echelons of London in the fields of medicine, science, and politics: Leigh Thomas, president of the Royal College of Surgeons; Sir Astley Cooper, indisputably the most eminent surgeon and anatomist of the time and an authority on vascular surgery; Sir Benjamin Collins Brodie, a physiologist and surgeon who pioneered research into bone and joint disease and to whom Henry Gray would dedicate his famous book *Gray's Anatomy* in 1858; Sir Charles Locock, an obstetrician to the future Queen Victoria; William Reid Clanny, doctor and inventor of the safety lamp for coal mines; Henry Halford, physician extraordinary to King George III; George Birkbeck, doctor, academic, and philanthropist, who founded Birkbeck College (now part of the University of London); John Harrison Curtis, aurist (otologist) who treated deafness and wrote the most authoritative book in the field, *A Treatise on the Physiology and Diseases of the Ear* (1817); and other distinguished guests.

Equally as prominent as the guests was the venue chosen for this soirée. Situated in the heart of Piccadilly, the Egyptian Hall had an imposing façade resembling the ancient Temple of Tentyra (Dendera). It was founded in 1812 by William Bullock, a Pickwickian entrepreneur, showman, naturalist, antiquarian, silversmith, jeweler, taxidermist, botanist, zoologist, and traveler. The museum housed Bullock's vast collection of artifacts, ranging from curiosities brought back from the South Seas by Captain Cook to Napoleon's carriage captured at Waterloo. In 1824, Bullock had staged Britain's first exhibition of Mexican artifacts and natural fauna—a show that featured stone and pottery figures, indigenous deities, a jade Quetzalcóatl, an obsidian mirror, an Aztec calendar stone, forty-three glass cases of flora and fruits (melon, avocado, tomato, banana, breadfruit, prickly pear, etc.), and exotic birds, such as flamingos and hummingbirds.[11] In fact, the Egyptian Hall had played such an important part in seizing and inspiring the British colonial imagination about the world that Dickens, as the most studious chronicler of London, would one day immortalize the venue in his oeuvre.[12] In 1829, however, seventeen-year-old Dickens had just learned shorthand and was walking the foggy city streets as a freelance journalist.

And Bullock had already auctioned off his prize collections, sold the museum to his nephew George Lackington, and left for Mexico in the midst of a British frenzy of investing in Mexican silver mines.

On the bone-chilling evening of November 24, as Piccadilly's cobble-stoned street became a canal of thick fog and the gas lamps blinked their ghostly yellow eyes, the distinguished guests arrived one after another in crested carriages for the private levée. The twins, dressed in short green jackets and loose pantaloons, their long queues wrapped around their heads, made themselves presentable to the bigwigs garbed in swallow-tailed suits and bowties. As much as they would have liked to waltz freely across the ballroom, the way they used to swim in the Meklong, Chang and Eng had become more like caged animals—one of the many on the long list of curiosities that had or would come before this elite crowd, to be inspected, poked, tested, and, most important of all, verified. As the lead surgeon, Sir Astley was the first to approach the singular spectacle. After examining the band, its dimensions and appearance, Astley pronounced it "to be cartilaginous and not cutaneous only." His opinion was confirmed by the other doctors who took turns feeling the band. Although earlier in Boston, Dr. Warren had already made the discovery, the British physicians were astonished to find that the twins had but one navel, situated at the center of the connecting band, thus rendering the proverbial term *navel gazing* kind of moot. It was a parlor joke that would not be lost among the distinguished crowd steeped in wry British humor.[13]

Before the evening was over, thirty-four guests signed a statement testifying, as only the English could, to both the authenticity of the unusual union and the appropriateness of a public exhibition. "The public may be assured," the statement read, "that the projected exhibition of these remarkable and interesting youths is in no respect deceptive; and further that there is nothing whatever, offensive to delicacy in the said exhibition." As if one certificate were not enough, Dr. Joshua Brooks, an anatomist, drafted and signed a separate testimonial: "Having seen and examined the two Siamese Youths, Chang and Eng, I have great pleasure in affirming they constitute a most extraordinary *Lusus*

Naturae, the first instance I have ever seen of a living double child; they being totally devoid of deception, afford a very interesting spectacle, and they are highly deserved of public patronage."[14]

Both certificates would be reproduced verbatim in the promotional pamphlet for sale at future exhibitions of the twins, according the conjoined bodies an indisputable legitimacy and increasing their cultural capital in the eyes of the viewing public. Soon these "Siamese Youths" were the talk of the town in London and, in fact, the entire British Isles.

Racial Freaks

U nlike the United States, where puritanical blue laws held sway and sideshows had a hard time breaking into business, Britain enjoyed a long history of exhibiting human oddities and celebrating monsters of all sorts. The carnival spirit of Elizabethan bearbaiting survived well into the nineteenth century before finally falling victim to Victorian morality and middle-class decorum. The medieval fabliaux, saturated in scatological aesthetics and unbridled eroticism, applying a billingsgate language of abuse, curse, oath, and exaggeration, did much to propagate what Mikhail Bakhtin called "the grotesque concept of the body."[1] Bowdlerizing the fabliaux and watering down the salacity and vulgarity, authors such as Chaucer, Boccaccio, and Rabelais channeled a profound appreciation and an unabashed celebration of the grotesque body—denuded, debauched, and debased. Especially during the decadent reign of Charles II (1660–1685), who had both stuffed and staffed his court with freaks, dwarfs, and jesters, a resurgence of the popular interest in monsters swept through England. In the words of historian Henry Morley, "the taste for Monsters became a disease" after the Restoration.[2]

In the eighteenth century, explorers to "newly discovered" parts of the world brought back a bonanza of exotic species that had once existed only in the wildest imaginations. A partial list of grotesque and fantastic bodies on display at the so-called monster shows in England included a Man-Tiger from the East Indies, "from the Head downwards resembling a Man, its fore parts clear, and his hinder parts all Hairy"; a monster from the "Coast of Brazil, having a Head like a Child, Legs and Arms very wonderful, with a Long Tail like a Serpent, wherewith he feeds himself, as an Elephant doth with his Trunk"; a woman with three breasts; a boneless child; and a freak with one body, two heads, four arms, and four legs. In 1726, when Jonathan Swift published *Gulliver's Travels*, a satirical novel peopled by the likes of Lilliputians, Brobdingnagians, Houyhnhnms, and Yahoos, he both captured and parodied the era's obsession with dwarfs, giants, hermaphrodites, and other fantastical and monstrous beings. It was a Zeitgeist best represented by the Bartholomew Fair, a carnival celebration that lasted for three days each year in West Smithfield, beyond the Alder Gate outside the city wall of London.

Originally founded in 1133 by a monk who had been a court jester to Henry I, the Bartholomew Fair by the turn of the nineteenth century had become a shrine for the grotesque, a monumental assemblage of the strange and exotic that William Wordsworth called the "Parliament of Monsters." Henry Morley described the scene: "cripples about the altar, miracles of saints, mummings of sinners, monks with their fingers in the flesh-pot, ladies astride on the high saddles of their palfreys, knights, nobles, citizens and peasants, the toilers of idleness and industry, the stories that were most in request, lax morality, the grotesque images which gave delight to an uncultivated people." It was a carnival site that mixed miracle plays with circus freaks, where the devil emerged dramatically from a Hell-mouth, surrounded by satyrs, fauns, griffins, goblins, rope dancers, puppeteers, fire-eaters, and animal trainers.[3] Beginning as a tribute to a saint and held near the city gallows and a public burial ground, the fair was a perfect example of what Bakhtin termed "grotesque realism," of which the essential principle is degradation, "the lowering of all that is high, spiritual, ideal, abstract; it is a transfer to the material level, to the sphere of earth and body in their indissoluble unity."[4]

In November 1829, when the Siamese Twins opened to public view in London about a week after the private levée, the crowds that streamed

into the Egyptian Hall were certainly familiar with the carnival spirit
and aesthetics of the grotesque embodied by the Bartholomew Fair,
which would continue to thrive until 1855, when Victorian morality
finally won the day. But the twins also brought something different to
the otherwise-familiar variety of the freak show, something that would
redefine monstrosity and change the course of the Victorian sideshow
business in England and America: racial freaks.

As described earlier, Thomas de Quincey was not haunted by ordinary nightmares; he was disturbed by dreams of the Orient. And, as
he claimed, what triggered his torment was not a visit by any ordinary
goblin or devilish messenger from the beyond, but rather a turbaned
and inarticulate Malay—or, in other words, a "racial other." By the time
de Quincey wrote his *Confessions* and the twins were brought from
Siam, the presentation of exotic bodies belonging to "inferior races"
was about to become a staple of freak shows. The Age of Discovery
had already brought ample specimens from all corners of the world,
specimens that would fill up cabinets of wonders and museum collections or be installed as solo exhibitions. While most of those curiosities
were inanimate objects, as in Bullock's collection of items from Captain
Cook's voyages, increasingly more "live" samples were being brought
back, including the aforementioned Man-Tiger from the East Indies and
the serpentine monster from Brazil. Pretty soon, any exotic body of the
racial other, with or without traces of disability, would become objects
of curiosity. Especially with the rise of ethnology, phrenology, and other
scientific or pseudoscientific fields and fads that all looked at "primitive
races" as unevolved humans or "missing links," the borderline between
physical anomaly and the racial other became blurred, leading to the
construction of racial freaks.[5] Aborigines from Oceania, Asia, Africa,
Australia, South America, or any part of the non-Western world were
brought to be displayed in freak shows. In the candid words of a sideshow agent, "The fact they were different put them in the category of
human oddities."[6]

Take, for example, John Rutherford, a white mariner who had jumped

ship in the Pacific, taken up with a Maori woman, and had his body tattooed. A year before the twins' arrival in England, Britons were treated
to the sensational exhibition of Rutherford. In this case, mere adoption
of primitive, barbaric practices, such as tattooing, would turn even a
white man into a freak. It was a grim prospect that frightened Tommo,
Melville's alter ego in his first novel, *Typee*, when the Polynesians tried to
tattoo his face and make a convert of him. Or, when the Siamese Twins
returned to the United States after this trip to England, they would
make a museum appearance in New York next to Afong Moy, billed
simply as the "Chinese Lady." An otherwise perfectly ordinary woman,
she was exotically Chinese and had "monstrous" bound feet, thus rel-
egating her to the freak category.

Racial freaks, it seems, were everywhere, but few were as extraordinary as the Siamese Twins, who combined a rare physical anomaly
with racial exotica—the best type of specimen, as the *Times* put it,
"to gratify the curiosity of John Bull."[7] As soon as the door opened,
Britons from all walks of life hurried inside the Egyptian Hall, each
paying a half-crown. With their coiled queues and Eastern costumes,
the twins entertained hundreds of visitors each day, answering questions and performing acrobatic acts. At this point, they had mastered
the game of battledore and shuttlecock, a predecessor of badminton,
usually played by two people standing several feet apart. Since their
band could stretch no more than a few inches, the shuttlecock traveled between their rackets like a bouncing bullet, evidence of their
amazing dexterity.[8]

Mere viewing, however, was not enough to quench the curiosity or
skepticism of some visitors, who proceeded to poke or feel the twins'
fleshy band. One such curious John Bull, who signed his name "M. R.,"
arrived on the first day of the exhibition and then wrote to the editor of
the *Times* about his own examination of the connecting cord: "Immediately on my applying my hand, one of the boys exclaimed, 'Your hand is
cold, Sir'; and I have indeed no doubt that it is quite as sensitive as any
other part of the body."[9]

CHANG AND ENG PLAYING BADMINTON, 1830

Other letters poured in, and the newspaper editors were more than happy to print them, capitalizing on the door-busting frenzy at the Egyptian Hall. Some letter writers drew comparisons between the twins and the Biddenden Maids, while others dug up the history of the Scottish Brothers. In late November, when a two-headed Sardinian girl on display in Paris died, a newspaper article speculated that an invitation to the Siamese Twins would soon come from France. Sir Anthony Carlisle, an eminent physician who had attended the private preview, also chimed in and published an account of his own encounter with the wonder boys, opining with authority and ending on a note of dry, strained humor: "If, indeed, Nature had not carefully provided against its frequency to the human race, the occasional appearance of united twins would give rise to many legal perplexities."[10] Everyone, highbrow or lowbrow, seemed to be having fun with the twins. As in carnivals where the crowds celebrated, worshipped, mocked, and ridiculed the clowns who reigned over the festivities, Chang and Eng were poked, pinched, probed, and later even punched by gawkers.

In their perennial fascination with a rare specimen, the medical professionals continued to run tests on the twins. Dr. Peter Mark Roget, secretary of the Royal Society of London, came up with an experiment on the fleshy band: "A silver spoon was placed on the tongue of one of the twins, and a disk of zinc on the tongue of his brother: when the metals thus placed were brought into contact, the youths both cried out 'Sour, sour.' This experiment was repeated several times with the same result, and was reversed by exchanging the positions of the metals, when a similar effect was produced." According to Dr. George Buckley Bolton, who chose April Fools' Day in 1830 to present a report on the twins at the Royal College of Surgeons, Roget's experiment proved "that the galvanic influence passes from one individual to the other, through the band which connects their bodies, and thus establishes a galvanic circuit with the metals when these are brought into contact."[11] Perhaps what's even more remarkable is that the galvanic influence found to exist between two conjoined twins might have added fuel to one of Roget's lifetime obsessions, a work that earned him a name in history—the compilation of *Roget's Thesaurus of English Words and Phrases* (1852). A dictionary of synonyms, or words having the same or nearly the same meanings, *Roget's Thesaurus* was a landmark of English lexicography. Its countless reprints and new editions have graced the bookshelves and desks of every educated person working in the English language. Roget had started cataloguing words in 1805 but didn't publish the *Thesaurus* until 1852.

In another test, asparagus was served to Chang only, and the doctors checked their urine four hours later, only to find that Chang's had a distinct asparagus smell, but Eng's urine was not affected. Based on that, the doctors determined that "the sanguineous communication between the united twins is very limited."[12]

The asparagus experiment apparently not being enough, the twins were also stripped naked and had their genitalia examined. The doctors found their sexual organs to be "regularly formed," although they noticed that "the youths are naturally modest, and evince a strong repugnance to any close investigation on this subject."[13] As much as the doctors wanted to investigate thoroughly what they called "so curious an object of philosophical inquiry," they at least refrained from some of the more dangerous or even deadly experiments, such as the use of mercury. As Bolton, who had been hired as a personal doctor for the boys, acknowledged, "Because I am averse to the administration of mercury, unless it be imperatively demanded, I have not had an opportunity of knowing whether the mercurial influence would pervade the one youth, if applied exclusively to the other."[14]

Dr. Bolton recorded an incident that he found fascinating:

On the 9th of December they were both attacked with bronchial catarrhs, became pale and languid, coughed severely, and complained of pain in their throats; each of them had also slight pains during strong inspirations. Their skins were dry and cold, respirations hurried, pulses ninety beats in a minute, rather hard and small; the tongue of Eng was glazed and pallid as usual, Chang's became furred and dry. The bowels of both had been naturally relieved the day previous, and each was directed to take such medicines as experience had shown to be proper in the malady now common to both. Under this discipline and suitable diet, together with the additional clothing of leather waistcoats, and a leather coverlet for their bed, then considered to be required on account of the inclement winter, they both regained their ordinary state of health.

What fascinated Bolton was, he wrote, that "they have been treated as two distinct persons, although from the very unusual circumstance of their conjunction, the same causes of disorder are presented to both, and similar consequences have thence ensued."[15] In other words, are they really one or two? As all these experiments and records showed, the twins were actually both—they constituted one inseparable unit, yet they were two unique individuals. Such an ambiguity, the centerpiece of their attraction as a displayed object and a pathological specimen, challenged the corporeal limits of subjectivity. They defied the norm that had been the bedrock underlying the definition of a human being as an individual. *Individual*, as the *Oxford English Dictionary* defines it, is "a single human being, as distinct from a particular group, or from society in general." As a result, like a hermaphrodite, whose sexual identity is fluid, the Siamese Twins evoked fascination and horror. In an insightful essay, Elizabeth Grosz points out that the twins made for an object of prurient speculation while at the same time threatening the definitions that viewers had long used for classification of humans and identities. Echoing Fiedler, Grosz believed that "the perverse pleasure of voyeurism and identification is counterbalanced by horror at the blurring of identities (sexual, corporeal, personal) that witness our chaotic and insecure identities."[16]

Here we have finally discovered the root cause of Thomas de Quincey's nightmares: the fear of being incorporated into an alien other, what Grosz defines as an "intolerable ambiguity." Since that fated day when a turbaned Malay knocked on his cottage door, the English opium-eater had never recovered from the shock at the sight of a figure that was so outlandish and yet human just like himself. In his magisterial essay "On the Knocking at the Gate in *Macbeth*," de Quincey brooded over his initial inability to comprehend the significance of the heart-pounding knock in the Shakespearean drama, which broke up the deathlike stillness after Duncan's murder in the bedroom. "However obstinately I endeavored with my understanding to comprehend this, for many years I never could see why it should produce such an effect." A first-rate essayist, de Quincey was able to write his way out of the hermeneutical conundrum by arguing brilliantly that the spine-chilling knock forced us to "throw the interest on the murderer"—or, in other words, to feel the fragile and fallible humanity of the murderer who panics at the sound. "Our sympathy must be with *him*," he insisted. "Of course I mean a sympathy of comprehension, a sympathy by which we enter into his feelings, and are made to understand them—not a sympathy of pity or approbation." In an elaborate footnote, de Quincey further drew a distinction between "sympathy with the other" and "sympathy for the other," emphasizing that the interpretation of *Macbeth* relied on the former.[17] But in the case of a knock on his own door, de Quincey was never able to reach a moment of sympathy with or for "the other." For their unimaginable ambiguity and unassimilable difference, the Siamese Twins were racial freaks to Britons as much as the exotic Malay was to de Quincey.

"Macbeth: Whence is that knocking?"

Sentimental Education

*Indeed, Quasimodo, one-eyed, hunchbacked, bowlegged, could
hardly be considered as anything more than an almost.*
—Victor Hugo, *The Hunchback of Notre Dame* (1831)

L ove conquers all. Almost.

We do not know who she really was, or whether the story is apocryphal, merely another publicity ploy to drum up excitement over the "freaks." But it seemed that Victor Hugo, who, hounded by his publisher, was trying desperately to finish up *The Hunchback of Notre Dame* on the other side of the English Channel in the remaining months of 1830, was not alone in feeling the pull of a haunting attraction between a human monster and *la femme fatale.*

Sophonia Robinson, who went by Sophia, was a young and beautiful London socialite who delighted in poetry and exotica. After meeting the Siamese Twins, Sophia was smitten and fell violently in love with both of them. According to a promotional pamphlet, this enamored English Esmeralda took to the quill and wrote poetic epistolaries to the twins. Though not Shakespearean in literary quality, her expressed yearning was as strong as Elizabeth Barrett Browning's *Sonnets from the Portuguese*, poems of passionate love so scandalous that the poet had to pretend they were translations from another country. Sophia lamented the improbability of having both twins:

How happy could I be with either,
Were the other dear charmer away.

. . .

Thy love, thy fate dear youths to share
May never be my happy lot
But thou may'st grant this humble plea
Forget me not! Forget me not!

It seemed that this love affair was more doomed than the affection
between the gypsy dancer and the Hunchback of Notre Dame. Monstrous as he was, Quasimodo was one, or almost one, as the novelist
phrased it, whereas Chang and Eng were two, or two in one, making it
legally and morally prohibitive for Sophia to pursue the matter of heart
any further. Cursing Fate, she finally had to give up, at which point she
married, in the mocking words of a rumor columnist, "a commercial
gent of promising prospects and unexceptional whiskers."[1]

This romantic episode, though short-lived, opened the eyes of the
twins, who had just turned nineteen. Despite their abnormal physicality, the twins had reached sexual maturity just like any other men. Never
shy with the fair sex, they had flirted innocently with chambermaids and
other working-class women. On the day they had arrived in London, as
the *Times* reported, the chambermaid at the hotel "tapped their heads,
and told them they should be her sweethearts, at which they laughed,
and in a playful and boyish manner they at one and the same time kissed
each side of her cheek. On being jocularly told of this, they said it was
Mary that wanted to have them for a sweetheart, not they that wanted
to have Mary."[2] But with Sophia, it was the first time that one of Cupid's
arrows had been shot from the direction of a popular fair lady. Even
though they did not fall for her, they were taken by the possibility that
they could love or be loved just like any other human being. As Bolton
observed, love had now "become a very common subject of discourse
between them." The good doctor was concerned that "it is not an unreasonable conjecture, that some female attachment, at a future period, may
occur to destroy their harmony, and induce a mutual and paramount
wish to be separated."[3] Bolton was only partially right in his prediction.
One day, the twins would turn that glimmer of hope for love into reality,
but they would do it in a manner that would scandalize the world.

The sentimental education of these two Siamese youths went hand in hand with their study of other subjects. During their first voyage to the New World, they had already learned some spoken English from the ship's crew, but they had never taken language lessons with a tutor. Now a gentleman visitor, intrigued by the unusual sight, volunteered to teach them to read and write, perhaps as an experiment to try to correct Nature's error. The pupils, however, quickly outsmarted the master: The gentleman marked a large A on a card and then pronounced the letter. The boys imitated the sound exactly. He then formed a B and a C. While he was doing this, "Chang interrupted him, wishing to obtain the pencil; and both not only repeated the sounds of the three letters, but imitated their forms, Chang even making a pun on the letter C; for on being asked if he knew its form and pronunciation, he replied, laughing, 'Yes, I *see* you.'"[4]

Their quick progress in the English lessons was amply documented in the family correspondence of the Coffins. In a letter from London to her son and daughter in America on March 6, 1830, Susan Coffin wrote that Chang and Eng "have learnt to speak very good English they can converse very well."[5] In July, Abel Coffin wrote to his children that "the boys Chang and Eng are quite well and are very good they wish to be remembered to you they can speak English quite well."[6] In September, Abel wrote again to his children, telling them that "Chang and Eng send their love to you they can write almost as well as you and if you do not pay great attention to your writing they will soon write better as they are quick to learn."[7]

In November 1830, an English gentleman named John Layley gave the twins a copy of the newly published *A Dictionary of General Knowledge; Or, An Explanation of Words and Things Connected with All the Arts and Sciences.* Edited by the English lawyer and miscellanea writer George Crabb, the dictionary was modeled after Denis Diderot's *Encyclopedia,* sort of the "Wikipedia of the Enlightenment." Challenging religious authority and aiming to "change the way people think," Diderot's vast compendium of knowledge was credited with fermenting radical thoughts leading to the French Revolution. Crabb's dictionary was much smaller in scale and more modest in intellectual ambition. Although it incorporated general knowledge in the various fields of arts and sciences, the dictionary was a reconfirmation and repackaging of Christian interpretations of history and events as cited in the Bible and skewed by religious biases. For instance, Paradise was defined in the book as "The garden of Eden, where Adam and Eve dwelt in their state of innocence." Or, the History of Agriculture began with Abel and Cain, followed by Noah. Or, Gypsies were defined as "A wandering tribe, who are to be found in different countries of Europe, and are supposed to be of Egyptian origin."[8]

Inquisitive souls, the twins clung on to this compendium of knowledge. Even though the language of the book was still a bit too sophisticated for their level of English, they certainly enjoyed looking at the illustrations of things they used to know in their native language, such as elephant, buffalo, bridge, goose, pagoda, tiger, tortoise, rice, spider, and so on. They must have been surprised to see the entries for Pomona, Venus, and other Roman goddesses accompanied by images of half-naked or scantily dressed female bodies. This was no pornography, but it would be hard to underestimate the shock to the pubescent youths as they laid their eyes on illustrations of nude women for the first time.

From this book, the twins also learned the meanings of words and concepts that would define their unusual lives: exhibition, liberty, Negroes, phrenology, elopement, polygamy, etc. Throughout their lives, they would continue to mine the book's vast supply of knowledge, and they would pack it in their luggage for every trip. In 2012, when I visited the Mount Airy Museum of Regional History, I saw a tattered copy of Crabb's dictionary, apparently an heirloom in the twins' family, which contained John Layley's inscription and dedication to Chang and Eng. If Diderot's *Encyclopedia* had changed the way people think, Crabb's dictionary, conservative as it was in its intellectual outlook, supplied the twins with the necessary knowledge about the world that looked at them differently, a world where they fought hard to belong.

With London as their base, the twins were exhibited widely in Great Britain during their thirteen-month stay. According to James Hale, who had kept a detailed record of their itineraries, they had traveled "upwards of 2,500 miles in the kingdom, and received the visits of about 300,000 individuals in London, Edinburgh, Dublin, Liverpool, Manchester, Bath, Leeds, York, Sheffield, Bristol, Birmingham, and most of the principal cities and towns in the kingdom. They were honored by visits from her Majesty, Queen Adelaide, and others of the Royal family, the foreign ambassadors, nobility, and by most of the philosophers and scientific men of the age."[9] When in Liverpool, Charles X, the ex-king of France, visited the twins and left them "a present of a piece of gold," rather than paying the usual admission fee of half a crown. The twins wisecracked that perhaps the reason "why he gave them gold, was because he had no crown."[10]

As popular as they were in Great Britain, the twins failed to be impressed. Neither the climate nor the food sat well with them. As Susan Coffin told her children in a letter, "They are made very much of by all that see them though the boys do not like here as they did in Boston they say Boston the best." Having been away from Siam for about a year, they were also getting homesick. Again, as described in Coffin's motherly words to her own children: "Your mother very often says to Chang Eng I want to see my dear Abel and Susan they say me want to see my Mother Brother Sister Chang Eng is very good boys indeed they say that they love your mother much I tell them some times I am going home to America they say No No I shall cry mamah if you go home and leave me your Abel and Susan got one good mother and Uncle in America Chang Eng got none." For unknown reasons, the twins' travel companion, Tieu, was found to be misbehaving—"a very bad boy indeed," as Susan Coffin put it.[11] Robert Hunter, who was about to leave for Asia, had decided to take Tieu back to Siam, a move that further saddened the twins. Like the string of a kite flying higher and higher into the sky, the tie to their faraway home threatened to snap at any moment.

According to Captain Coffin's plan, Chang and Eng would be taken from Great Britain to France, the native land of Rabelaisian giants and freaks: Gargantua, Pantagruel, and other carnivalesque creatures of grotesque realism.[12] But French officials refused to grant them permission to cross the English Channel for fear of "maternal impressions," a time-honored belief that a pregnant woman seeing a monster would lead to deformation of her unborn baby. The superstition survived well into the twentieth century: When film became popular, many pregnant women in rural China were forbidden to go to a movie—either because movies often showcase monsters and freaks or because film itself is a freakish and frightening technology. The Chinese call film "the electric shadows." Parisians, thus deprived of an opportunity of peeking at "the wonder of nature," would have to make do, within a few months, with a fictional figure who was "almost human"—Quasimodo, the bell-ringing Hunchback of Notre Dame.

The French rejection brought the twins' European tour to an early close. In January 1831, just as Hugo's timeless classic was released onto the streets of Paris, and another popular book featuring the twins was coming off the press at a print shop in London, Chang and Eng boarded the *Cambria* and returned to America.

≈ Part Three ≈

AMERICA ON THE ROAD

(1831–1839)

ACCOUNT BOOK OF CHANG AND ENG

≽ 13 ≼

The Great Eclipse

In America, 1831 was dubbed the "Year of the Great Eclipse."

In the lead-up to the solar event, doomsayers predicted that the end of the world was coming. As one almanac peddler warned, the darkness would be such that domestic fowl would retire to roost, the moon would ride unsteadily in its orbit, and Earth would tremble on its axis. When the solar eclipse finally occurred on February 12—lasting one minute and fifty-seven seconds and covering a path up to sixty miles wide, America became a nation of anxious stargazers. From bleary-eyed elders to bright-eyed infants, everyone looked up to the darkening heavens through a piece of smoked glass and dreaded the worst. However, the highly anticipated apocalypse ended with a whimper, not a bang. The spectacle was quite a letdown, with the darkness fleeing, as one observer snorted, like "a thunder gust." The stargazers felt bamboozled by advertising quacks who had promised an exhibition of "fireworks or phantasmagoria."[1]

Anticlimactic as the celestial event was, it did launch a year of chaos and cataclysm that would decisively change the destiny of the United States. On January 1, William Lloyd Garrison published the first issue of *The Liberator*, igniting a spark that would soon turn into the wildfire of the abolitionist movement. In March, the Supreme Court, led by Chief Justice John Marshall, handed down a decision in *Cherokee Nation v. Georgia*, legitimizing the genocidal removal of Indians, blazing the infamous Trail of Tears. In August, Nat Turner led a violent insurrection of slaves in Virginia that shook the nation to its core. If the disappointed heaven-gazers in February had blamed doomsayers for their superstitious exaggerations that fizzled, they would now have to think again when Turner's band of rebels roamed and rampaged, spilling the blood of white masters, mistresses, and innocent children in the swampland of southeastern Virginia. In fact, Turner, a self-taught, literate preacher, had regarded the February eclipse as a divine signal for action. "I had a vision," as he confessed later in jail. "I saw white spirits and black spirits engaged in battle, and the sun was darkened—the thunder rolled in the Heavens, and blood flowed in streams."[2] After Turner was hanged, the nation had scarcely any time to recover from the shock before another calamity loomed on the horizon: cholera. It was the same epidemic that had begun in India in 1817 and taken the lives of Chang and Eng's father and siblings in 1819, reaching China by 1820, and then crossing the border into Siberia. After that, the epidemic ravaged Europe much as Genghis Khan's Mongol hordes had done. It made its appearance in Liverpool in September 1831, and, given the direct trading routes between Liverpool and the United States, would hit the nation with force by year's end, causing thousands of deaths.

When Chang and Eng watched the darkening sun from the decks of the *Cambria* on February 12, they probably recalled scenes of the lunar eclipse on the eve of their departure from Siam, when the locals, following custom, banged gongs, beat pots and pans, and screamed at the tops of their lungs to scare away the sky dog trying to swallow the moon.

On this return trip across the Atlantic, they made certain not to travel in steerage. Perhaps their protest the previous time had paid off; or perhaps Susan Coffin, who now alone managed the twins with the help of James Hale, had finally realized the importance of keeping the twins comfortable and contented so that she could milk more cash out of them. Now that Robert Hunter, prior to his departure for Asia, had sold his share in the twins to the Coffins, she and her husband had become sole owners of Chang and Eng. As Mrs. Coffin told her children in a letter, "Your Father has got these boys to earn money to send you both to school with."[3] Abel Coffin, traveling on the other side of the world, also wrote to tell his wife to "be kind to Chang Eng," although he immediately added, "but you must not let them have too much their own head it is necessary to have them mind you." Coffin acknowledged that he might have been harsh in his treatment of the twins, but he was also quick to defend himself. He asked his wife to tell Chang and Eng that, "although they might think I was hard with them I think their own good sense will convince them that I have never done anything but what is for their good. . . . I shall always do by them as by my own children."[4] These words of reluctant admission and ready self-exoneration revealed a relationship fraught with tension. In his self-righteous way, Coffin might have thought that he had been treating the twins like his children. Ahab might have thought that his harshness toward the *Pequod*'s crew was merely typical behavior of a strict patriarch, but Ishmael knew well, as did Melville in real life on the whaler *Acushnet*, that the condition aboard was no better than chattel slavery. Likewise, even though Chang and Eng now enjoyed traveling in cabin class rather than the dreaded steerage, they knew that the improved treatment did not originate from Mrs. Coffin's kindness. As they would put it bitterly one day in a letter, referring to themselves in the third person because the letter was written by an intermediary, "As to Mrs. Coffin doing all she could for their comfort & loving them & liking them—they say, they have no doubt that the number of thousands of hard shining dollars which they have enabled her to spend have made her like them—but let Mrs. C. look into her own heart & they feel confident she will discover that the great loving & liking was not for their own sakes—but for the sake of the said Dollars."[5]

The twins arrived back in New York on March 7. They had left the United States as two eighteen-year-old greenhorns, little known to the world. Fifteen months later, after an extended, profitable tour in Great Britain, they were now famous. Besides a vaunted reputation, they had also gained forty pounds, making their total weight 240 pounds, an increase that was facetiously ascribed by a newspaper reporter to "their eating so much of the roast beef of old England." Their height was now 5 feet 2 inches.[6]

A week after their return, on March 15, while the nine Supreme Court justices were still deliberating the fate of millions of Native Americans after William Wirt's passionate plea on the previous day in the case of *Cherokee Nation v. Georgia*, the twins were put on display again in New York City. Their success in England had served to stimulate further the curiosity of the American public. The ex-mayor and tireless diarist Philip Hone, who had missed the twins last time, eagerly went to the show on the opening day. That night, when he retired back to his Park Place mansion after a feast of eyes, he penned an elaborate entry in his journal:

> March 15.—Went this morning to see the Siamese boys, who returned last week from England. I did not see them when they were exhibited formerly in this city. This astonishing freak of nature is exceedingly interesting, and the sight of it is not disagreeable, as I expected to find it. They are now nearly twenty years old, kind, good-tempered, and playful; their limbs are well proportioned and strong, but their faces are devoid of intelligence, and have that stupid expression which is characteristic of the natives of the East. They are united by a strong ligament of flesh or gristle, without bone, about three inches in breadth and five in length. Their movements are, of course, simultaneous. They walk, sit down, play, eat and drink, and perform all the functions of nature in unison; their dispositions and their very thoughts are alike; when one is sick the other partakes of his illness, and the stroke of death will, no doubt, lay them both in the same grave; and yet their bodies, heads, and limbs are all perfect and distinct. They speak English tolerably well, and appear fond of talking.[7]

His condescension and racism notwithstanding, Hone shared with his contemporaries a guarded fascination with the exotic twins. In a few years, he would become an enthusiast of P. T. Barnum's exhibitions, being one of the first to visit the Joice Heth show and subsequently a frequenter to almost anything the Prince of Humbugs would care to put on display. In 1840, Hone would spend a few days in Philadelphia, visiting the famous Chinese Museum, mesmerized by what he described in his diary as "an immense collection of curious things collected by a Mr. Dunn during a residence of twenty years in China."[8] Seeing the twins, Hone had expected to experience revulsion, yet he felt a freakish fascination.

We do not know whether Edgar Allan Poe, drenched in sorrow at drinking holes in the city after his recent court martial and dismissal from West Point, visited the twins on Broadway. Newspapers carried daily reports and advertisements about the exhibition; handbills and posters were plastered all over the city. Judging by the nature of Poe's literary work, which shows a clear obsession with twins and all forms of human abnormality, it is not unreasonable to assume that Poe would have enjoyed watching the conjoined twins and appreciated their embodiment of the aesthetics of the grotesque. In Poe's story "The Fall of the House of Usher," Roderick and Madeline, two residents in that house of doom and gloom, were twins. Not only did they bear a striking resemblance, but also "sympathies of a scarcely intelligent nature had always existed between them." When one died, the other quickly dissipated. The story ends with the sister's spectral return, taking her brother away to the land of Nevermore: "with a low moaning cry, [she] fell heavily inward upon the person of her brother, and in her violent and now final death-agonies, bore him to the floor a corpse, and a victim to the terrors he had anticipated." In "Hop-Frog," the eponymous dwarf-cripple teamed up with Trippetta, a young female midget, and exacted revenge on the king and his seven councilors who had abused and mocked them. Hop-Frog tricked the king and his men into disguising themselves as ourang-outangs with tar and feathers, hanged them all from a chandelier, and burned them into "a fetid, blackened, hideous, and indistinguishable mass." In this dark tale of vengeance, Poe clearly identified with the freaks, the outwardly subhuman. "There is no exquisite beauty," Poe said, echoing Francis Bacon, "without some strangeness in the proportion." The connoisseur of the grotesque would certainly have appreciated the Siamese Twins.[9]

The first publication about Chang and Eng by a major writer, however, did not come from Poe but rather from Edward Bulwer Lytton, lionized in the British and American literary worlds at the time.

⊱ 14 ⊰

A Satirical Tale

A flamboyant dandy virtually forgotten by history, Edward Bulwer Lytton was once a towering figure in British letters. Before the outbreak of the Great War in 1914 turned public tastes against almost everything Victorian, the sales of Lord Lytton's books had rivaled those of his friend Charles Dickens. Born in 1803 at No. 31 Baker Street in London, just a few doors down the street from the fictional residence of the future Sherlock Holmes, Lytton was educated at Cambridge. Supported by his heiress mother's allowance, he had lived a playboy's life of extravagance and notoriety before storming into the London literary scene with the 1828 publication of his novel *Pelham, or the Adventures of a Gentleman*. Featuring a hero who was the epitome of wit and dandyism, *Pelham* was a huge commercial smash, enabling Lytton to receive enormous sums in advance for his future books. Riding the wave of success, Lytton went on to write a book of verse about the exotic sensation that was the rage of London, the Siamese boys.[1]

Prior to the publication of Lytton's book, Chang and Eng, though the talk of the town everywhere they went, had inspired only bits of doggerel as ephemeral as the reputation of their obscure authors, such as this one that had appeared in the *Berkshire Chronicle* in 1829:

> My yellow friends! and are you come,
>   As some have done before,

To show the sign of "two to one,"
     And hang it o'er your door?

How do you mean your debt to pay?
     Will one discharge the other's?
Or shall you work by subterfuge,
     And say, "Ah, that's my brother's"?[2]

Published in England in January 1831, just as Chang and Eng were leaving the country, Lytton's new work, *The Siamese Twins: A Satirical Tale of the Times with Other Poems*, would become the first book-length portrayal. In the ensuing decades and even centuries, the incredible story of Chang and Eng would spawn countless representations—fictional, biographical, satirical, scholarly, dramatic, operatic, and cinematic. It is a cultural tradition set in motion by Lytton as a representative man of Victorian letters, whose poetic wit filled every page of his light-footed narrative verse.

Running more than 250 pages, *The Siamese Twins* took much liberty with facts and tailored them to fit a Molière-like romantic comedy full of farce and satire. For comic and metrical effects, Lytton changed the twins' names to Chang and Ching, and their father's to Fiam to rhyme with Siam. To counterbalance fictionalization, Lytton drew heavily on the canon of British travel narratives for ethnographic details and stereotypes, such as the flat noses and blackened teeth of the Siamese. The following portrait of Fiam was hardly flattering:

Our Fiam was a handsome fellow,
His nose was flat, his skin was yellow;
Tho' black his locks, with truth you'd swear
His teeth were blacker than his hair.[3]

References to the Finlayson Mission, the Crawfurd account, and other travel journals littered the footnotes in this book of light verse. Lytton recast Robert Hunter as a Mr. Hodges, "the member of a mission, / To

probe the Siam trade's condition." Hodges was so shocked by his first
sight of the conjoined twins that he passed out:

> He lay so flat, he lay so still,
> He seem'd beyond all farther ill.
> They pinch'd his side, they shook his head,
> And then they cried, "The man is dead!"

Regaining consciousness, Hodges, like Hunter, immediately saw a business opportunity. The twins were subsequently brought to England. After
undergoing an examination by the eminent doctor Sir Astley Cooper, as
they did in real life, they were put on display and became a sensation:

> From ten to five o'clock each day,
> There thronged to see them such a bevy,
> Such cabs and chariots blocked the way,
> The crowd was like a new King's levée.

Money flowed into Hodges's pocket. But the youthful twins resented
being treated like animals by their owner and seen as freaks by the audience, as Chang put it to Ching:

> How hard a thing it is to be
> Teased, worried, questioned, pulled about,
> Stared at and quizzed by every lout,
> And give a right to all the town
> To laugh at us for half-a-crown.

In response, Ching suggested a radical change to their predicament:

> Tomorrow, 'gad, we'll make them all dumb
> By cutting this confounded thraldom.
> We'll claim old Hodges's account,
> Keep house upon our share's amount.

It is a bold idea that was never put into practice in the fictional narrative by Lytton, but it strangely foreshadowed what was to come in the real life of the Siamese Twins. At times, fiction makes a claim on reality and conjures it into being.

Chang, the dandy of the two, fell in love with Hodges's daughter Mary, and he also attracted the interest of some society ladies who took a fancy to his exoticism. But his conjoined state presented quite a dilemma for romance. When a Lady Gower invited Chang to a rendezvous, she wondered if "he would not bring / His vulgar brother, Mr. Ching"—an impossible request, of course, but juicy fodder for Lytton's satire.

Absurdities, as in a Sheridan comedy, abounded. The twins got into a fistfight with a fellow at a bar one night and were arrested by a Peeler. The next morning, Ching took all the blame in court and made a passionate plea to exonerate his twin brother, a tactful maneuver actually adopted by Chang and Eng whenever they had a run-in with the law:

But he—my brother—no offence
Committed; you must let *him* hence!
Take me to prison, if you please,
But first this gentleman release.

The bond might save them from the wrath of the law, but it proved to be an insurmountable obstacle to Chang's pursuit of love. In the depths of melancholy and depression, Chang carried a knife into their room. But he did not have the courage to do the unthinkable. Sympathetic to his painful plight, Mary went to Chang's assistance. Like the biblical Eve tempting Adam with the forbidden fruit, she slipped opium into the twins' wine cups. When the twins fell under the influence of the drug, a surgeon entered the room and severed their tie forever.

Their rude awakening the next morning was not their separation, however, but the horrific truth Mary revealed—that she did not love Chang and that she was already engaged to someone else. While Ching would never regain his former self in spirit, let alone in body, Chang paid the ultimate price for unrequited love, falling victim to a seductive plot. Brokenhearted, he disappeared from London, wandered around the world, and was never heard from again. This was, as the satirical narrator summarized the moral of the tale, "what Liberty hath cost."

The handful of scholars who have studied the rise and fall of Lytton's literary career agree that *The Siamese Twins* possesses an autobiographical relevance to the contradictions that plagued this enigmatic Victorian man of letters: Lytton was deeply tied to his mother and to his wife, but he also desperately and repeatedly tried to sever those bonds. As they would do for future generations of writers ranging from Herman Melville and Mark Twain in the nineteenth century to Mark Slouka and Darin Strauss in the twenty-first century, the Siamese boys gave Lytton perfect raw material to work out his own issues or to fathom the mystery of the human bond, physical or metaphysical.

Published around the time of Chang and Eng's departure from England in January 1831, Lytton's book literally chased its eponymous protagonists across the Atlantic. It hit American bookstands in March, just in time for the opening of the twins' exhibition in New York. Newspapers reprinted long excerpts of the book, along with rave reviews. "As a whole," opined one reviewer, *The Siamese Twins* was "an excellent satirical poem." Even though this reviewer for the *Connecticut Mirror* found fault with the "Don Juan abruptness" with which Lytton closed lines and reversed sentences, he agreed with the editor of the *Philadelphia Gazette* in maintaining that "we regard [Lytton's] works, flowing as they have freshly and spontaneously forth, with something akin to the feelings of beholding the sorceries of a magician. The human heart, with all its countless springs of love, avarice, and ambition, is to him, like the leaves of an open book."[4]

Many of these reviews and reprints appeared in the newspapers that closely followed the movements of the Siamese Twins or carried advertisements for their shows. A popular book-length treatment of their story, albeit fictional, by a major author, went a long way toward cementing the twins' position in the Anglo-American imagination. Pretty soon, the fictional plot of Lytton's book became entangled with journalistic reports on the twins, as evidenced by this short article in the *Eastern Argus Semi-Weekly*: "The Siamese Twins have lately, each of them, drawn a prize in a lottery in Philadelphia. These young fellows will, by and by, be enabled to cut a splash in society—be the 'observed of all observers'—and possibly realize some of the scenes written down for them by Bulwer [Lytton] in his late poem. Young, charming and rich! They may make many a fair damsel's heart to palpitate."[5]

No verisimilitude, however, could prepare us for the dramatic turns that the conjoined life of Chang and Eng would take. Reality sometimes eclipses the wildest imagination.

The Lynnfield Battle

The winter of 1831 was brutal, the worst in many years. Big snowstorms devastated the Eastern Seaboard from Georgia to Maine. New York City was repeatedly buried under mountains of snow that heaped up to several feet. Violent northeaster gales hurled snowdrifts in all directions and drove in tides so high that wharves were overtopped and waterfront cellars were flooded. Mail delivery was disrupted. Sleds, sleighs, and horses had to be employed day and night to clean up the snow on the streets.

While the city was busy battling the weather on the night of March 19, an English shoemaker named Edward Smith carried a duplicate set of keys, walked into the City Bank of New York (the present-day Citibank) on Wall Street, and absconded with $245,000 in banknotes and Spanish doubloons. This was the first recorded bank heist in the United States. Smith, a denizen of the Lower East Side, was quickly nabbed, convicted of the crime, and sentenced to five years in Sing Sing.

Blizzards might provide a convenient cover for bank heists, but they were bad for showbiz. As James Hale wrote on March 16, 1831, to Susan Coffin, who had returned home to Newburyport, the receipts for the first two days of the twins' exhibition came to only $55. "I hope to do better every day," Hale wrote, trying to sound upbeat.[1] But his hope was dashed when another storm hit the wider area, greatly diminishing traffic. Hale wrote to Mrs. Coffin again two weeks later: "The weather has been very stormy here . . . the walking is bad—We have not had forty ladies since we opened—they you know are our best customers, if we can get them—Our receipts have averaged but $20 per day—and two nights at the Theatre paid $50 per night amounting in all—15 days to 425 dollars."[2]

A rare ray of sunshine arrived in the midst of the dreary weather and business doldrums. Chang and Eng received news from their mother, Nok. By now they had been away from Siam for almost two years. Even though they enjoyed their new lives in the West, homesickness for the two young men was palpable. The welcome messenger who delivered the news, along with a letter from their mother, was one Mr. Holyoke. As Hale described, "Mr. Holyoke came on Monday and gave Chang Eng news from their mother, also a letter from her which has been translated to them. They are now quite easy."[3] We do not know the contents of the letter, or whether it was written in Siamese or Chinese or English. Anyway, through layers of intermediaries, they could hear their mother's words, like endearing echoes. It reminded them of their audience with the king a few years earlier, when words were whispered back and forth at the court through interpreters. It brought back memories of the hissing sound of raindrops falling on palm leaves, and the lazy lapping of waves on the muddy banks of the Meklong. For a moment, they had a sudden urge to go home. But they were not free, not yet their own men, according to the contract they had signed with Abel Coffin.

Feeling that they had tapped out the New York market and needing to change their locale, the small troupe—Hale, the twins, and a man named Tom Dwyer, who drove the buggy—decided to brave the weather and hit the road. What followed was a series of extended stays and whistle-stop visits in the Northeast, ranging from big cities to tiny hamlets, basically anywhere they could set up a show. A cross-check of Hale's correspondence and newspaper reports gives us a glimpse into their taxing itinerary.

They reprised their visit to Philadelphia for three weeks in April, again using the Masonic Hall as their base. Hale was able to send Mrs. Coffin only $150 in receipts, partly due to the fact that the twins had been under the weather for a while. As Hale told Mrs. Coffin in a letter dated April 23, "Chang Eng have been very ill—a touch of the liver complaint—they are now heartier than ever—they were confined to the bed 4 days & under the Doctor's hands."[4]

Next they went to Baltimore, staying at the historic Fountain Inn, an imposing brick-clad Georgian structure with keystone façades, mahogany interiors, and a paved courtyard for coaches. The inn was said to have been George Washington's favorite hostelry in town, where he had first stayed in May 1775 as a member of the Virginia delegation on his way to the Second Continental Congress in Philadelphia. As the *Baltimore Patriot* reported on April 26,

> The public are respectfully informed that these wonderful boys, having returned from Europe, will be exhibited for a few days only at their rooms, Fountain Inn, No. 7 Light Street. Any comment upon them is deemed unnecessary as their credit has been fully established by the reception they have met with, from the numerous, honorable and renowned gentlemen in England, as also from our own most distinguished countrymen. Hours of admission from 11 to 3, and 7 to 9 P.M. Admittance 50 cents—Children half price.[5]

Also on sale at the exhibition was the promotional pamphlet penned by Hale, *An Historical Account of the Siamese Twins*, along with a full-length lithographic portrait of the twins, which added another twelve and a half cents apiece to the receipts. The show in Baltimore seemed to have gone well, and their stay was extended to Saturday, May 14.

In the weeks from late May to July, the troupe visited Portsmouth, New Haven, Hartford, Salem, Worcester, and a cluster of villages in the area. Apparently the fifty-cent admission charge was rather steep for small-towners, so Hale tried two strategies to attract more visitors. He put an ad in local papers that read, "As it is thought by some that the price of admission (the same as has invariably been charged in large cities) is too high, all gentlemen who visit the Twins, and after having seen them still think as aforesaid, will receive their gratification without money and without price. 'The Union must be maintained.'"[6] And when this discount scheme did not spur enough activity, he put another notice in the papers: "In order that none need be disappointed in witnessing the 'Greatest Curiosity of nature ever known,' the admission will be reduced to 25 cents only."[7]

In that scorching summer of 1831, the twins, traveling in New England, did have some competition—not from another human oddity but from an Ourang Outang, recently imported from Batavia by one Captain Shirley. Also hailed as a "Great Natural Curiosity," the three-year-old female creature was on display in Boston while the twins were canvassing villages outside the city. The way the newspapers publicized the Ourang Outang bore a strong resemblance to the way they had reported on the twins less than two years earlier, as seen in this excerpt from the *Boston Transcript*:

> The brig Harley, Captain Shirley, which arrived here 3d inst. from Batavia, has on board a young female Ourang Outang. She has suffered much on the voyage and is very sick. She is greatly affected by cold, and keeps a blanket constantly wrapped about her. She has been visited by Dr. Smith, the Quarantine Physician, who examined her, felt her pulse and ordered milk to be given to her, which occasioned a temporary revival of her spirits. She is still able to walk, although she totters from weakness. When she stands erect her hands nearly touch the ground. She eats, drinks and spits, like a human being.

The article went on to say that this was the first successful attempt to "introduce one of these remarkable animals alive into this country." An earlier attempt to import an Ourang Outang had resulted in one dead in the harbor upon arrival. Despite the death, all was not lost, for the skeleton was "frequently exhibited by Dr. Smith at his annual Anatomical Lecture."[8]

The Siamese Twins, after all, were not animals, even though in the eyes of the gawkers who paid fifty cents or less to see them in a small parlor of a country inn or a crowded ballroom of a city hotel, they were as exotic and freakish as an Ourang Outang. They needed a break from the backbreaking schedule of exhibitions, away from the maddening crowd. Especially when heat waves hit New England, the showrooms, unaired and stuffy with sweat and scent, had become rather like animal cages, increasingly unbearable. Finally, much to their relief, the twins were allowed a brief hiatus from road travel. At the end of July, they retired to Lynnfield, Massachusetts, for what a local paper reported as "a little relaxation and amusement, boarding at the Hotel, and going out occasionally for the purpose of fishing, shooting, etc."[9]

Peace, however, was the last thing they could find in this otherwise sleepy town of a few hundred souls. And their hunting guns ended up pointing not at wild birds in the sylvan woods but at not-so-civilized humans who regarded the twins—as if anticipating the drama of Hawthorne's *Scarlet Letter*—as less than human. One incident was so dramatic that it merits a lengthy quote from one of the newspaper reports, entitled "Commonwealth vs. Chang and Eng":

> Chang and Eng, the Siamese Twins, were arrested on a Warrant from a Magistrate for a breach of the Peace at Lynnfield, on Monday last, and bound over to be of good behavior and to keep the Peace, in the sum of two hundred dollars.
>
> They have for a few days past been rusticating for recreation and staying at the Lynnfield Hotel, so as to enjoy the sports of fishing on the pond and shooting in the woods. The neighboring inhabitants have had a very eager curiosity to catch a glimpse of their movements while on their excursions, and have sometimes been rather troublesomely obtrusive to the Siamese, whose object was seclusion. Last Saturday afternoon they were in the fields, shooting, each with his fowling piece: a considerable number, 15 or 20, idle persons, followed to observe their motions, and some of the men or boys were probably obtrusive and impertinent. Two persons from Stoneham, Col. Elbridge Gerry, and Mr. Prescott, went toward them in the field, after they had been harassed and irritated considerably by

others—the attendant of the Siamese requested these persons to keep off, and by way of bravado threatened that, if they did not, the Siamese would fire at them. The Colonel opened his waistcoat and dared them or him to fire, but they did not,—the Colonel then indiscreetly accused them or him of telling a lie,—the attendant spoke to the Siamese about the charge of lying,—they exclaimed, "He accuse us of lying!" and one of them struck the Colonel with the butt of his gun,—the Colonel snatched up a heavy stone and threw it at the Siamese, hit him on the head, broke through his leather cap, and made the blood flow,—the Siamese then wheeled and fired by platoon at the Colonel, who was horribly frightened, as most other people would have been, though it turned out afterward that their pieces were charged only with powder. The noise and smoke were just as great as if they had been loaded with ball. The Siamese went immediately into the Hotel and loaded with ball,—the Colonel and Mr. Prescott, learning this, were greatly alarmed, and endeavored to keep out of the way; Mr. Prescott fled to the barn and secreted himself in a haymow. The Colonel went to Danvers and lodged a complaint against the Siamese and their attendant, a young Englishman, for breach of the peace. An officer went to arrest them, but by the interposition of a gentleman, who happened to be at the Hotel, a truce was concluded.

On Monday, however, Prescott made complaint to Mr. Justice Savage of this town, and they were taken before him and bound over.

Concluding the otherwise straight-faced narrative, the anonymous writer could not resist the temptation to toss in a little gem of badinage: "It cannot be said to be any great hardship to the Siamese to be bound over, for from the day of their birth they have been under *bond*."[10]

One of the parties involved in this incident, Colonel Elbridge Gerry, was a relative of Elbridge Thomas Gerry (1744–1814), one of the nation's founding fathers. That elder Gerry, much maligned for his aristocratic haughtiness, had served for two terms as governor of Massachusetts before becoming James Madison's vice president. It was during his contentious governorship that he bestowed upon the great democracy the obnoxious term and practice of "gerrymandering." Unable to live up to the legacy of his illustrious ancestor, Stoneham's Colonel Gerry nonetheless felt the need to defend his family name and personal honor not only during his confrontation with the twins but also afterward. He soon wrote a letter to the local paper to present his side of the story, "to state the facts as they were." According to the colonel, the blame lay squarely on the twins and their attendant, and it was the evil trio who had viciously attacked a man minding his own business and defending his honor. "I thought the conduct of the three highly improper, and that they deserved to be punished—particularly the young Englishman (whom they called William) who attended 'the twins,' as he was the origin and cause of the affray."[11]

Dubbed the "Lynnfield Battle" by the newspapers, this incident, occasioning plenty of jibes and jests, might have brought much-needed comic relief to the readers during a summer lull. For the twins, however, the event was a sobering reminder of their precarious position. A later newspaper report painted a far more sinister picture of what had actually transpired, the fact being that they were being hounded by the nineteenth-century equivalent of paparazzi. According to this writer, who simply signed his article as "Carlo":

In the first place, while the twins were amusing themselves with shooting in the fields, attended by their servant, a lad of about eighteen years of age, (Mr. Hale being absent,) a mob of from twenty to thirty persons gathered about them, following them from place to place, and dodging after them in the woods. They repeatedly requested the people not to follow them, but without effect. They were as zealous as if in pursuit of a wild beast. This hunt lasted all the afternoon. About night-fall, as they were returning to the hotel, their followers began to insult them, calling them "damned niggers," and using, in a most foul and disgraceful manner, opprobrious epithets in relation to their mother, which excited them in a high degree; and before anything was done on their part, their pursuers cried out, "Let's take away their guns and give 'em a thrashing."[12]

It seems that the twins were first pursued like "a wild beast" by a curious mob that, in face of resistance, turned verbally abusive and threatened physical violence. Such a mob scene foreshadowed the anti-Chinese riots that would run rampant in the United States in the postbellum decades. In 1871, twenty-one Chinese were shot, hanged, or burned to death by white mobs in Los Angeles. In 1885 in Rock Springs, Wyoming, a mob of 150 disgruntled white miners, armed with rifles, stormed into the Chinese quarters and killed twenty-eight Chinese and burned the district to the ground. In fact, the word *hoodlum* comes from the anti-Chinese cry of "huddle 'em," a signal for mobs to surround and harass the Chinese, as they did here with the Siamese Twins: "Let's take away their guns and give 'em a thrashing."[13] And to call them "damned niggers" and conflate them with blacks was further indication that the cause of this "affray" in the peaceful New England town was as much curiosity chasing as racism. Once again, the twins were regarded as racial freaks.

According to the mysterious author Carlo, the twins had their final say in the matter, demonstrating their unsurpassable wit by turning their courtroom appearance into a carnival of laughter. To defend themselves in front of the judge, one of the twins addressed Mr. Prescott, the plaintiff: "You swear you fraid o' me; you fraid I kill you, shoot you—at same time you know I have guns—you see I shoot you if I choose—I ask you civilly not to follow me—you wont let me go away—you call me and my mother hard name—and yet you swear you fraid I kill you. Now, suppose I see a man in my country, in Siam—he goes out into woods, and sees a lion asleep—he say 'Oh! I fraid that lion kill me'—what I think of that man if he go up and give that lion a kick and say 'get out you ugly beast?' I wish you'd answer me that." Amusing as it was, the twins' pidgin-flavored rhetorical flourish did not, however, convince the honorable judge, improbably named Savage, who fined them two hundred dollars for the assault and disturbance of the peace.[14]

With their vacation ruined by a mob, the twins had to move on. Enduring horrendous heat in a tiny buggy, they arrived in Newburyport, hometown of the Coffins. Their visit inspired local poet Hannah F. Gould to pen a poem that was published in the town paper, *The Newburyport Advertiser*. Simply titled "To the Siamese Twins," the first stanza runs:

> Mysterious tie by the Hand above,
>   Which nothing below must part!
> Thou visible image of faithful love—
>   Firm union of heart and heart—
> The mind to her utmost bound may run,
>   And summon her light in vain
> To scan the twain that must still be one—
>   The one that will still be twain![15]

Though no Emily Dickinson, who was but an infant in the summer of 1831, Gould did share with the future belle of Amherst a fondness for using a dash at the end of a line and the penchant for puns and metaphysical musings. Like Dickinson, Gould was also a spinster, staying unmarried to provide companionship for her widowed father, a Revolutionary War veteran. In fact, she had just begun writing poetry in her thirties, "first entertaining Newburyport citizens with mock-epitaphs of local celebrities, then contributing pieces to magazines and annuals," as she did here with the poem dedicated to the twins.[16] She would gain quite a reputation as the author of religious, historical, commemorative, and antislavery poems, many of which appeared in *The Liberator*, the abolitionist flagship journal edited by fellow Newburyport resident William Lloyd Garrison.

In some ways, the twins, arriving in Newburyport in late August of 1831, walked into a tempest of national significance without the slightest inkling of the storm clouds ahead.

⇌ 16 ⇌

An Intimate Rebellion

"**A** revolution," Chairman Mao once quipped, "is not a dinner party." But the Great Helmsman did not say that a revolution, or a rebellion with revolutionary consequences, cannot *begin* with a dinner party. And that was exactly how the Nat Turner slave revolt, an apocalyptic event that shook the nation, got started.

On Sunday, August 21, 1831, still smarting from the loss of the Lynn-field Battle, the Siamese Twins were convalescing at their owner's manor in Newburyport. Mrs. Coffin had taken her children, Susan and Abel, to church, as she would do every Sunday. James Hale was traveling in New Hampshire, trying to arrange a show in Portsmouth for the twins.

Seven hundred miles away, in a wooded swamp near Cabin Pond in Southampton, Virginia, a small group of black slaves gathered for a barbecue dinner. Hark had arrived early in the morning, carrying a pig. Henry had brought brandy. Sam, Nelson, Will, and Jack soon joined them. Around three o'clock, when the pig turned golden in the make-shift pit, glistening with grease that would make a carnivore drool, the group's leader, Nat Turner, made his belated appearance. In the ensuing hours, over a feast of barbecue and brandy, Turner and his followers hashed out a plan to "commence the work of death."

A man "moved to action by reading and interpreting the signs of heaven and earth," Nat Turner was what some historians call a semiotic rebel.[1] Born on October 2, 1800, Turner had been the slave of Benjamin Turner of Southampton, Virginia. In the next decades, the ownership of Turner changed hands a few times and eventually came to a carriage-maker named Joseph Travis, who would become the first victim of the 1831 insurrection. As Turner explained in his jail-cell confession, he had, even as a child, always known that he was intended for some great purpose. He claimed that he had been born with a parcel of extra hairs on his head and chest, and he had showed uncommon intelligence for a child, being able to read a book without having learned the alphabet. The fact that he would claim to know certain things that had happened before his birth further confirmed the belief that he was a prophet blessed with divine inspiration and would never be of any service to anyone as a slave. Compelled by such a sense of destiny, he went ahead and acted like a prophet—studiously avoiding society, wrapping himself in mystery, and devoting his time to fasting and prayer. Soon divine messages reached him under many guises: When he was praying at the plough one day, a spirit spoke to him a line from the scriptures: "Seek ye the kingdom of Heaven and all things shall be added unto you." Another time, he had a vision and saw white and black spirits battling in the heavens, while a voice said to him, "Such is your luck, such you are called to see, and let it come rough or smooth, you must surely bear it." Other signs included lights in the sky showing "forms of men in different attitudes," "drops of blood on the corn as though it were dew from heaven," and hieroglyphic characters written in blood on tree leaves.

Like a true prophet, he had been communicating these revelations to his fellow slaves and making converts among them. On May 12, 1828, Turner said he heard a loud noise in the heavens, and the spirit again appeared to him. According to Turner, the spirit told him that "the Serpent was loosened, and Christ had laid down the yoke he had borne for the sins of men, and that I should take it on and fight the Serpent, for the time was fast approaching when the first should be the last and the last should be the first." He interpreted this as a message that he should plan for action. A clear go-ahead signal then came in the form of the great solar eclipse in February 1831. Turner gathered his most trusted followers and drew a plan, according to which they would have begun the "work of death" on July 4. But Turner fell sick, or, as some claimed, he hesitated and delayed the action. Then another divine signal came in the guise of a green-tinted sun on August 13. Turner and his men convened in the woods for a last supper.

After a long night of feasting and drinking, while arming themselves, the rebels struck the first blow before dawn on August 22. They arrived at the house of Turner's master. What happened next, as narrated in Turner's confession and embellished by Thomas Gray, a two-bit lawyer who took the dictation with an eye for profit, read like a horror scene from a crime thriller. It was every bit as gory as Truman Capote's *In Cold Blood*:

> Hark went to the door with an axe, for the purpose of breaking it open, as we knew we were strong enough to murder the family, if they were waked by the noise; but reflecting that it might create an alarm in the neighborhood, we determined to enter the house secretly, and murder them whilst sleeping. Hark got a ladder and set it against the chimney, on which I ascended, and hoisting a window, entered and came down the stairs, unbarred the door, and removed the guns from their places. It was then observed that I must spill the first blood. On which, armed with a hatchet, and accompanied by Will, I entered my master's chamber, it being dark, I could not give a death blow, the hatchet glanced from his head, he sprang from the bed and called his wife, it was his last word, Will laid him dead, with a blow of his axe, and Mrs. Travis shared the same fate, as she lay in bed. The murder of this family, five in number, was the work of a moment, not one of them awoke; there was a little infant sleeping in a cradle, that was forgotten, until we had left the house and gone some distance, when Henry and Will returned and killed it.

Their tactic was to kill all the whites in the houses they struck, no matter their age or gender. "It was my object," Turner said, "to carry terror and devastation wherever we went." In this fashion, they methodically struck house after house, farm after farm, recruiting more rebels and picking up more weapons along the way. By midday, they had hit eleven farms in the area and enlisted about sixty mounted insurgents. Thirsty for blood, revenge, and freedom, they were getting ready to attack the county seat, Jerusalem, when the better-equipped local militia stopped their advance and began to stage a forceful counterattack. Turner's rebel band disintegrated. At daybreak the next morning, the militia had captured or killed all the rebels except for Turner, who had fled and would elude his pursuers for more than two months, his escape as dramatic a period in nineteenth-century American history as any, given the waves of fear that the revolt started. He hid himself in different shallow holes he had dug with a sword, until one day a hunting dog, lured by some meat Turner had kept in his cave, exposed his hideout. A local farmer captured him at gunpoint. It was Sunday, October 30.

Ironically, what had begun with a barbecue dinner also came to an end on a carnivorous note. The slaughtered pig turned out to be a sacrificial symbol of the extreme violence. Turner was put on trial in November and sentenced to die by hanging. The court judgment ended on a bloodthirsty tone, full of hatred and vengeance: "You . . . be hung by the neck until you are dead! dead! dead. . . ." After Turner's execution, some claimed that he was skinned, his flesh fried into grease, his bones ground into powder and baked into ginger cakes.

Turner's was not the only body that suffered mutilation in an insurrection defined by raw brutality. The rebel slaves as well as the militia assaulted their victims with animal ferocity. As a historian acknowledged, "Violence on the part of the slaves is precisely what a slave revolt is all about. A rebellion directed indiscriminately against men, women, and children, and fought largely with swords, axes, and farm implements might be expected to produce horrible scenes of cruelty and devastation." In his confession, Turner repeatedly spoke of the almost perverted satisfaction of viewing "the mangled bodies as they lay," and, almost like a modern-day voyeuristic photojournalist, he described scene after scene of butchery: "Having murdered Mrs. Waller and ten children, we started for Mr. William Williams'—having killed him and two little boys that were there; while engaged in this, Mrs. Williams fled and got some distance from the house, but she was pursued, overtaken, and compelled to get up behind one of the company, who brought her back, and after showing her the mangled body of her lifeless husband, she was told to get down and lay by his side, where she was shot dead." Likewise, Virginia Governor John Floyd's diary captured the degree of brutality perpetrated by the rebels: "Throughout this affair the most appalling accounts have been given of the conduct of the negroes, the most inhuman butcheries the mind can conceive of, men, women, infants, their heads chopped off, their bowels ripped out, ears, noses, hands, and legs cut off, no instance of mercy shown."

What Governor Floyd forgot to mention, however, was that "blacks did not have a monopoly on decapitation and other forms of mutilation. One group of whites had cut off the head of rebel Henry Porter. It ended up in the hands of a militia surgeon who reportedly carried it with him around the county. The cavalry company from Murfreesboro decapitated as many as fifteen suspected rebels and placed the heads on poles for display. One head was posted at the intersection of the Barrow Road and Jerusalem Highway—a crossing which then became known as 'Blackhead Sign Post.'"

Despite the degree of cold-blooded brutality, or maybe because of it, this slave revolt has been dubbed an "intimate rebellion," an event that took place in a tight-knit community where everyone knew each other. In a sense, it was a homicidal drama that unfolded under the same roof shared by the masters and slaves as a family. In fact, "many of the 200 black and white casualties knew the people who killed them." Like a plot from a Greek tragedy, familiarity bred hatred of greater intensity, and intimacy led to killing with more savagery.

Even though the revolt was repressed in a single day and it barely went beyond the county lines of Southampton, the slayings served as a toxin that spewed shock waves all over the country, sending a chill down the spines of Southern slaveholders. In Virginia, there were about half a million slaves, and the total throughout the South was about two million. Fanned by rumor and exaggeration, Southern whites, without any cause or provocation, dreaded the imagery of their slaves running wild and committing barbaric acts of murder, plunder, and rape. Many of them blamed antislavery Northerners for having incited the revolt. Chief among those suspected agitators was William Lloyd Garrison, who had himself penned a fiery editorial in the inaugural issue of *The Liberator*, condemning human bondage. It had also contained a poem that eerily portended the tragedy in Southampton:

Wo if it come with storm, and blood, and fire,
   When midnight darkness veils the earth and sky!
Wo to the innocent babe—the guilty sire—
   Mother and daughter—friends of kindred tie!
   Stranger and citizen alike shall die![2]

When word of Turner's revolt came, Garrison wrote in the journal's September editorial: "What was poetry—imagination—in January, is now a bloody reality." But he took no credit and denied that his words had provoked the horror of revolt; instead, he blamed the slaveholders: "The slaves need no incentives at our hands. They will find them in their stripes—in their emaciated bodies—in their ceaseless toil—in their ignorant minds—in every field, in every valley, on every hill-top and mountain, wherever you and your fathers have fought for liberty—in your speeches, your conversations, your celebrations, your pamphlets, your newspapers. . . . What more do they need?"[3]

Garrison's self-defense did not, however, stop Southerners from going after him. Within weeks of the insurrection, while the Vigilance Association of Columbia, South Carolina, offered a fifteen-hundred-dollar reward for the arrest and conviction of any white person disseminating "seditious" abolitionist literature, Georgia's Senate passed a resolution offering a reward of five thousand dollars for Garrison's arrest and conviction.[4]

This was not the first time Garrison had a run-in with the slavehold-

ing class. In fact, the turning point of his career as a crusading abolitionist was a fight with one of his townsmen. Born in 1805 to a father
who was a retired merchant-marine master, Garrison grew up in Newburyport and began an apprenticeship at the *Newburyport Herald* at the
tender age of thirteen. Growing sympathetic with the antislavery movement, in 1829 he became coeditor of the Quaker newspaper *Genius of
Universal Emancipation* in Baltimore. "When he discovered that a fellow
townsman from Newburyport, Francis Todd, owned the brig *Francis*,
which transported seventy slaves from Baltimore to New Orleans," he
was resolved, as he proclaimed, to "cover in thick infamy all who are
concerned in this nefarious business." In the *Genius*, he excoriated Todd
for his part in the slave trade:

> Exposing the source of their wealth, he labeled them "enemies of
> their own species—highway robbers and murderers." "Unless they
> speedily repent," Garrison warned, they would one day "occupy the
> lowest depths of perdition." For his vituperative comments, Garri-
> son faced criminal and civil charges of libel. Following a brief trial,
> the editor was found guilty and fined fifty dollars and costs. He
> refused to pay, and authorities imprisoned him in the Baltimore
> jail for seven weeks in 1830 until a wealthy New York abolitionist
> paid the fine.[5]

The imprisonment galvanized Garrison, turning him into a full-fledged
crusader for the abolitionist cause.

We don't know whether Garrison ever took issue with another of
his townsmen—namely, Captain Abel Coffin—for his ownership of
the Siamese Twins. Given Garrison's outright condemnation of human
bondage, it would not be surprising if he would have despised Coffin, a
seaman like his own father, for exploiting slave labor by the twins. Nor
do we know how Chang and Eng reacted to the news of a slave rebellion
in a faraway place called Southampton, Virginia. Would they have felt
sympathy with the plight and misery of the slaves? Or would they have

objected to the brutality of the killing? Either way, at this point they would not know how the insurrection was somehow related to their own destiny—not only tangentially through Newburyport and its abolitionist native son Garrison, but also more directly. They would not know about their rendezvous with American history until they arrived in Virginia a few months later.

Old Dominion

At the height of the Nat Turner frenzy in that anguished fall of 1831, Chang and Eng continued to tour in New England, hitting small villages and big cities, working like a pair of mules yoked to a grindstone, churning out cash for their owner day in and day out. Even in Newburyport, the home base of the Coffins, they had enjoyed only one day of rest—on that fated Sunday of the Turner revolt—before a showroom was booked and they were put on display again.

In late October, unfavorable working conditions and his disagreements with Mrs. Coffin compelled James Hale to quit his job as the twins' manager. His replacement was an Irishman, one Charles Harris, who, like Hale, was an accountant by training but listed his profession as a doctor. Like his predecessor, Harris accompanied the twins on tours, sometimes traveling with them and sometimes going ahead to make arrangements and drum up interest.

As winter approached, the mercury plummeted below zero. Frozen roads posed a big challenge for the small troupe endlessly on the move. Corduroy roads—primitive paths built of logs and saplings laid side by side—caused nightmares for travelers in carriages and threatened horses' legs. Quite a few foreign travelers commented on the perils of this unique American construction mode and the overall atrocious state of the nation's roads. Charles Dickens, during his 1842 trip, wrote, "A great portion of the way was over what is called a corduroy road, which is made by throwing trunks of trees into a marsh, and leaving them to settle there. The very slightest of the jolts with which the ponderous carriage fell from log to log, was enough, it seemed, to have dislocated all the bones in the human body."[1] Alexis de Tocqueville, who was then touring the country to study the American prison system and might have crossed paths with the twins in 1831, also deplored riding on stages—he called them "diligences"—driven at a fast trot on roads "as deplorable as those in Lower Brittany." As he told his mother in a letter, "One feels quite rattled after a few miles."[2] Traveling from Philadelphia to Pittsburgh in late November, a route Chang and Eng would follow in a few months, Tocqueville noted how cold the winter was, as "this would indeed turn out to be the most brutal fall and winter for at least fifty years."[3]

On these roads in the dead of winter, riding in a buggy driven by Tom Dwyer and a single horse named Charley, the twins and their troupe brushed with disaster constantly. They had one bad accident on Schooley's Mountain in northern New Jersey, putting the driver in bed for days. The wagon repair cost between four and five dollars. In central Pennsylvania, on their way to Shippensburg, they had another narrow escape. "After leaving Carlisle we got along very merrily & had completed 6 miles of the 21," Charles Harris told Mrs. Coffin in a letter, "when the Axle of the Gig snapped & down came one side flat on the ground." Frightened, Charley the horse set off at full speed, dragging the broken buggy for about seventy yards before the twins, experienced horse-whisperers, managed to calm it down. Getting out of the vehicle and assessing the damage, they found that the right side of Eng's head was swelling. The twins sat by the roadside, trying to figure out what to do next. Fortunately, an empty carriage passed by, and they were able to get into it, "leaving the gig and broken wheel in care of a cottager near to whose house the accident took place."[4]

A prolific letter writer, Harris gave us a detailed account of those difficult days in late December 1831, when everyone else seemed to be celebrating the holidays—Tocqueville and his travel companion, Gustave de Beaumont, after a tough trip in the Northeast, were now relaxing on a Mississippi steamboat, while twenty-two-year-old Charles Darwin had just set sail in the *Beagle* for the Galápagos Islands. The twenty-year-old twins continued to travel and work. Between Christmas and the New Year, Harris wrote, "The weather still continues sadly against us, but nevertheless we have today a Balance of nearly $150 remaining on hand." Planning to send Mrs. Coffin the money, Harris enumerated how they had earned it by a series of whistle-stop shows in small Pennsylvania towns: Easton, $80; Bethlehem, barely enough to pay the bills; Allentown, $20; Reading, $50. They would set out for Lancaster the next day, stopping at Reamstown for the night and traveling at a speed of eighteen miles a day, weather permitting.[5]

The snow drove the twins farther and farther toward the South. In March 1832, the troupe reached Virginia, where nerves remained raw from the shock of Turner's revolt. Here they hit a snag trying to put up a show and found themselves at the center of a public debate—or, in the view of a historian, their visit "opened up a can of worms" in state politics.[6]

In the wake of the violent revolt, brutal suppression, and summary execution of Turner, a fierce debate over the future of slavery broke out in the Virginia General Assembly. On December 14, 1831, William Henry Roane, grandson of the patriarch Patrick Henry, introduced an antislavery petition in the legislature, calling for emancipation. Roane was supported by Thomas Jefferson's grandson, Thomas Jefferson Randolph, and other delegates who wanted to cleanse "the escutcheon of Virginia of the foul stain of Slavery."[7] But they were met with strong resistance from delegates who argued that slavery was a "necessary evil"—necessary because the system provided the state with labor and wealth.

The Virginia debate encapsulated the tensions that gripped the nation after the Turner revolt. The fear of insurrections took hold in the white imagination. Traveling in New Orleans, Johann August Roebling, a German immigrant who would later build the Brooklyn Bridge, heard rumors that "the blacks . . . had made a plan to massacre the whites, and thus attain their freedom by force."[8] Roebling's account was substantiated by another traveler, Sir James Alexander, who noted in his

Transatlantic Sketches that "there was an alarm of a slave insurrection" in New Orleans.[9] Rumors of a rebellion in North Carolina led authorities to arrest every free black in Raleigh. In Fayetteville, Tennessee, it was believed that a group of slaves had plotted to set fire to buildings and "commence a general massacre." Jane Randolph, the wife of Thomas Jefferson Randolph, was so shaken by the horrors in Southampton that she even begged her husband to consider moving west to Ohio. The Turner event, she said, "had aroused all my fears which had nearly become dormant, and indeed have increased them to the most agonizing degree."[10]

When Randolph rose in the Virginia General Assembly and spoke in favor of emancipation, he represented not just the declared principles of equality and justice but also the widespread, deep-seated fear of another black rebellion. But the opposition party, made up mostly of slaveholders from the Tidewater and Piedmont regions, was not willing even to consider the proposal for emancipation. The Select Committee, chaired by William Henry Broadnax, who had led the militia suppressing the Turner revolt, reported that it was "inexpedient for the present legislature to make any legislative enactment for the abolition of slavery." In January, by a vote of sixty-seven to sixty, the emancipation proposal was tabled by the assembly, and the Virginia debate came to an end. "Unable to act against slavery, the legislature acted against what it believed to be the source of insurrectionary spirit," as Louis Masur writes. "Within weeks, a colonization bill to provide for the removal of free blacks moved swiftly through the legislature. A 'police bill' further eroded the rights of free blacks, denying them trial by jury and allowing for their sale and transportation if convicted of a crime. The legislature also revised the black codes, barring slaves and free blacks from preaching or attending religious meetings unaccompanied by whites."[11]

Such was the cauldron of racial tensions into which Chang and Eng walked. Unwittingly, their visit forced the legislature to consider again the question it had just put to bed. By provisions of a tax law passed in 1813, the state imposed a licensing fee of thirty dollars on "every exhibitor of a show" in every county, city, or borough. This meant that much of Virginia would be off limits for the twins—in small villages where they would stay for no more than a night or two, they wouldn't even be able to gross more than $30 a day. On behalf of Chang and Eng, Harris had to make an appeal to Virginia's General Assembly, hoping for an exemption from the prohibitive tax.[12]

At the beginning, things looked promising, for the finance committee reported favorably on the twins' request. But, as Harris recalled later, when the assembly turned to the matter, the discussion took an unexpected turn. One assemblyman got up, stating that they would be quite mistaken if they considered themselves doing anything to favor the Siamese Twins by lifting the tax, because "it would only do good to some fellow in one of the Eastern States who had bought them of their mother." Obviously, the members of the Virginia legislature regarded the twins as slaves, property of their owner. Imposing taxation on the twins' exhibition pertained, therefore, to the financial welfare of their owner, not to Chang and Eng. Based on this assumption, the legislature dismissed the twins' request. Adding insult to injury, a newspaper in Norfolk published an article by a local doctor, stating that the twins "were sold by their Mother to Mr. Hunter and Captain Coffin" in Siam and therefore were indeed slaves. "On hearing this CE's [Chang and Eng's] rage knew no bounds," as Harris described it, "and they made me go immediately to the Young Doctor who drew out the Memorandum and ask him how he came to state such a thing." The doctor replied nonchalantly that he had obtained the information from a paper published by the esteemed Dr. John Warren, who had given the twins their first examination, and that every medical man in this country had a copy of that paper. In fact, Dr. Warren's article did indeed open with the statement, "These boys were purchased of their mother, by Captain Coffin and Mr. Hunter (the owners) in a village of Siam."[13]

Irked by these reports and the legislature's rejection, Chang and Eng realized for the first time the true nature of their precarious position. Even if they had never thought of themselves as slaves, they had been regarded as such by everyone else and treated accordingly. That realization was, as Joseph Orser puts it, "a wakeup call to the twins."[14]

Since their arrival from Siam, Chang and Eng had not been shy in vocalizing their discontent, complaining about unfair treatment, and fighting for what they deserved. Prior to the ill-fated visit to Virginia, they had just tussled with Mrs. Coffin over a raise in their travel allowance. Their arrangement with her had been for them to pay for the maintenance of their horses and conveyances out of a two-dollar expense allowance each week. But frequent accidents on icy roads had greatly increased maintenance costs. They wrote, via Harris, to Mrs. Coffin and asked her to raise the weekly allowance to three dollars, or they would board their horses and carriage and use public stagecoaches to get around. Mrs. Coffin's reply was slow in coming, and when it did, it was intentionally ambiguous: "about the chaise CE can do as they please." Deeply upset, Chang and Eng wrote again, arguing their case. When her reply was again slow in coming, they wrote for the third time, suggesting that Mrs. Coffin had intended to "place them in an awkward place, and that it was like taking a bird, clipping off his wings & then holding it up on one's hand & saying, 'Now you may fly if you wish.'" Their colorful metaphor was pretty persuasive, and Mrs. Coffin yielded to their demand.[15]

A negotiation over a one-dollar raise was apparently no comparison with a fight over their status, trying to free themselves from bondage and exploitation. Nat Turner and his slave rebels had paid dearly for such a struggle. So would millions of others in the coming years during the bloody Civil War. Yet now was the time for Chang and Eng to wage a war, finally, to obtain independence for themselves.

⪧ 18 ⪦

Emancipation

Buffalo, "a little town on the shores of Lake Erie," as Gustave de Beaumont called it, population 8,500, saw its fortune on the rise in 1832.

The Neutral Nation and then the Iroquois Indians had first settled here, followed by the French, who arrived at Buffalo Creek in the 1750s. And then the British took control of the region and built the town on a radial street system. During the War of 1812, the British army, before famously torching Washington, DC, burned Buffalo to the ground and destroyed all but a handful of its 150 buildings, leaving its residents fleeing in the teeth of a snowstorm. The few who stayed paid dearly for their mistakes. One woman, Sarah Lovejoy, was tomahawked while trying to save her dresses from the looting forces. As a local historian writes, "A few days later, residents trickled back to the village, now mostly piles of smoldering black ashes scattered in the white snow. A solitary cat wandering the ruins was the only living thing left in Buffalo. Strewn in the wreckage were the stripped and scalped bodies of their fellow villagers."[1] The survivors buried the frozen bodies of their neighbors and slowly rebuilt the town.

The 1828 opening of the Erie Canal, however, would start a new chapter in Buffalo's history. It would make the city, blessed by its convenient proximity to Lake Erie and Lake Ontario, a transportation turnpike and a gateway to the western frontier. In 1832, when Michigan had not yet joined the Union and Wisconsin was still a trackless forest beyond the pale of civilization, boomtown Buffalo was incorporated as a city. After an election by the Common Council, Dr. Ebenezer Johnson, the wealthiest Buffalonian, was appointed mayor on May 28, the day the famous Siamese Twins rode into town.

Because they arrived in the evening, after a three-day journey through the woods of western New York, Chang and Eng probably missed the celebration and hoopla surrounding the new mayor. The best hotel in town, the Eagle, with a capacity of two hundred, had been fully booked by rich tourists on their way to Niagara Falls, and its ballroom was abuzz with festivities each night. The twins checked in to the Mansion House, a more modest lodging at $2 a night. We do not know whether they had also missed the rare and memorable sight that had once disgusted Tocqueville and Beaumont when the two Frenchmen arrived there a year earlier. The entry in Tocqueville's notebook for July 19, 1831, which happened to be the day when Indians came to town to collect an installment of federal payment for their lands, reads in English translation as follows:

> Arrival at Buffalo. Walk through the town. A crowd of savages in the streets (day of payment) new idea which they suggest. Their ugliness. Their strange look. Their oily, bronzed skin. Their long, black, stiff hair. Their European clothes worn in savage fashion.

Tocqueville was particularly struck by the scene of a drunken Indian who was treated badly by his fellow Indians and his female companion. "Contrast with the moral and civilized population in the midst of which they are found," the astute student of American democracy observed with plain arrogance, the Indians showed "something of the wild beast."[2]

Distinct from Tocqueville's cryptic brevity, his travel companion Beaumont's description in a letter was more detailed and expressed more empathy:

The evening of our arrival at Buffalo, we witnessed a curious spectacle, which moved us to pity. . . . The streets of Buffalo were full
of drunken Indians when we arrived. We stopped near one who was
dead to the world and perfectly motionless. An Indian woman—his
wife, we were told—approached him, vigorously shook his head,
knocked it against the ground, and, when the poor man gave no
sign of life, wailed and laughed like an idiot. Further on we saw
another woman, this one intoxicated, being carried back to her
forest encampment by two or three tribesmen.[3]

Chang and Eng had no time, nor were they in the mood, for lamenting
the sad plight of "drunken Indians" brutalized by European civilization.
While the local tribesmen, drunk or sober, wandered the streets of Buffalo, the brave Sauk and Fox Indian warriors, led by Black Hawk, were
waging a battle across the West from Illinois to Wisconsin, a conflict
that lasted from April to September, giving the young Captain Abraham Lincoln his brief military stint. Meanwhile, the Siamese Twins
were having their own beef with the whites and their personal battle
to fight.

After their alarming experience in Virginia, Chang and Eng were
inspired to plan their own revolt, though one less violent than the Turner
insurrection. They recruited their former manager, James Hale, as a
confidant and intermediary, and, through Hale and Harris, they repeatedly asked for a face-to-face meeting with Captain Coffin, who was
traveling overseas on business. When the captain, originally due back
in January, was held up indefinitely in Batavia, the twins demanded
that Mrs. Coffin meet with them in Buffalo. All this time, they had
not disclosed to the Coffins the real purpose of the requested meeting,
but their owners must have had an inkling of what was brewing inside
the twins' heads. They knew that the twins would turn twenty-one in
May, which meant they would reach adulthood and could legally make
decisions over their own lives. But, having in hand that contract hast-
ily executed on the eve of the twins' departure from Siam, the Coffins

must have felt reassured of their continued ownership and the lucrative gains from the twins' labor. What could two heathen freaks do in a land of God-fearing people, two human monsters who could barely read and write in God's tongue? Well, a rude surprise awaited the Coffins.

When Mrs. Coffin replied in April that she could not meet them in Buffalo, Chang and Eng decided to take the matter into their own hands. After a long trek through the deep valleys of the Allegheny Mountains, they arrived in Pittsburgh, then a city of more than twelve thousand people. There, on May 11, 1832, the twins celebrated their twenty-first birthday by announcing that their relationship with the Coffins would be terminated by the last day of the month. The news shocked Mrs. Coffin. The prospect of losing the two Asian boys who had been raking in thousands to her coffer was devastating. In letter after letter, she accused them of breaking their promise, threatened them with legal actions, and reminded them how much she had cared for them, "liking and loving them." Calling them ingrates, she refused to let them go.

"As social equality spreads there are more and more people who, though neither rich nor powerful enough to have much hold over others, have gained or kept enough wealth and enough understanding to look after their own needs," opined Tocqueville, who was now back in France and had started working on his classic book on American democracy. He went on to describe, with abundant admiration and a touch of envy, the quintessential character of the American people, whose lives he had observed up close for nine months: "Such folk owe no man anything and hardly expect anything from anybody. They form the habit of thinking of themselves in isolation and imagine that their whole destiny is in their own hands."[4] Tocqueville might just as well have referred to the Siamese Twins, two newly minted American adults fighting fiercely to gain independence, to stand alone *together*, and to take their destiny into their own hands.

Undeterred by Mrs. Coffin's refusal and incensed by her accusation, the twins, as if taking a page from American history, made a declaration to unchain themselves once and for all. On May 29, when Buffalonians continued to celebrate the founding of their city and the Indians sang about chasing the buffalos soon to be extinct, Chang and Eng made Harris sit down in their room at Mansion House and pen a long letter to Mrs. Coffin, in care of Captain William Davis. This declaration of independence is so unique and occupies such an important place in their conjoined life that it merits quoting at great length here:

> *Dear Sir,*
>
> *Your letter of the 22nd came to hand last evening & I must thank you for your promptitude in so quickly replying to mine from Pittsburgh. It was of great importance to me to know that my letter had been received & whether or not Mrs. C. could make it convenient to come on here—as without a letter from you I would have been not a little embarrassed as to the course which I had to pursue on Thursday evening—when they mean to close the concern.*
>
> *I have read your letter over to Chang-Eng & they say that as to the "promise" made to Captain Coffin "that they would stay under Mrs. Coffin until the return of Captn. to the U.S."—as to this they say there must be a great mistake somewhere as they must deny this altogether. When they last saw Captn. C.—they distinctly understood from him that he would in all human probability be home in January (1832)— but on this they stated their wish (in case of any accident to him) to have a memorandum under his hand as to the time they were to consider themselves under his control—he immediately stated that of course when they attained the age of 21—they were "Their Own Men"—to use the words of Captn. C on the occasion. Moreover they say January, February, March, April & May have all passed & the chance of seeing Captn. Coffin seems (they say) as far off as ever.*

Repeatedly using the parenthetical phrase *they say*, like stage directions or novelistic asides, this epistle recorded as closely as possible the voice of the twins. Through Harris, the twins flatly rejected the two lines of reasoning by which Mrs. Coffin had tried to persuade them to stay: their promise to remain until Captain Coffin's return and her love for them. "Suppose, they say," the letter continued, "that Captn. Coffin should prefer remaining altogether in Batavia or any other distant region—is it reasonable that they should wait from month to month & year to year until his return? In fact, they say, such an undefinable term as that of 'till Captn. C. returns' is quite absurd after 4 months having passed since the time fixed for his return."

As for Mrs. Coffin's putative motherly affection for them, the twins pulled no punches in venting their bitter anger by recounting numerous instances of her abuse and exploitation:

> As to Mrs. Coffin doing all she could for their comfort & loving them & liking them—they say, they have no doubt that the number of thousand of hard shining dollars which they have enabled her to spend have made her like them—but let Mrs. C. look into her own heart & they feel confident she will discover that the great loving & liking was not for their own sakes—but for the sake of the said Dollars. If there is any doubt in her mind on this subject they say, she has only to retrace in her mind the cruel manner in which they were forced to go into a crowded room when they were more fit to be in an hospital. If they wanted to give a few instances they would remind her of New York (their first visit) & likewise London & Bath—they say to Mrs. C.—let her look over these things in her own mind (they hope she has not forgotten them), & after this let her make up her mind as to her loving & liking them—In fact, they say, the less she says about loving & liking—the better.

They felt especially resentful about their visit to Newburyport, the Coffins' hometown, when they had expected to have a little rest, but her "wish to make money was so great that instead of having any time to themselves a room was procured & visitors admitted just as it had been a few days before at Boston."

In conclusion, they reemphasized "the fatigues & dangers by Sea & Land in Ships & Carriages—by Night & Day," which they had endured to make money for the Coffins. Fully aware of the importance of this letter, they regretted not being able to draft it by themselves, but they were now sophisticated enough to know how to authenticate their words transcribed by someone else: "They have asked to affix their signature to it to stamp it as their deed, their sentiments & their feelings, concerning the transactions. Chang Eng, Siamese Twins."[5]

For the first time, Chang and Eng affixed to a letter their English signatures, conjoined as their body, raw as their feelings, and emphatically self-asserting as the label they had adopted for themselves, "Siamese Twins." Later, P. T. Barnum would try to claim credit for coining the term *Siamese Twins* for Chang and Eng, but we know better than to trust the words of a serial embellisher who would retrofit his autobiography nine times. "Call me Ishmael" . . . so begins Melville's *Moby-Dick.* "Call us Siamese Twins" . . . thus turns the new chapter in the incredible life of Chang and Eng. A double underline—like a bond bridging the space between words, or like an arrow pointing to the right, a road sign—completed the signature field and concluded the Siamese Declaration of Independence. With the ink barely dry, the Siamese Twins had become "their own men."

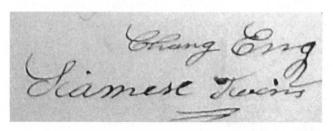

SIGNATURES OF CHANG AND ENG

A Parable

To celebrate their freedom, Chang and Eng went boating at Niagara Falls on June 1, 1832. According to their account book, on that special day they also bought five hundred cigars for $9; Bob, a horse with a decidedly American name, for $72.50; a pocketbook for $1; two suits for $13.50; a trunk for $10; and some other items, both necessary and extravagant. Always economical and never spending beyond their means, the twins also knew how to have a good time and live in style.[1]

Relaxing in a hired boat and cruising down the mile-wide Niagara River, the twins felt the warm northern sunlight and breathed in the sweet summer air. No more harsh words from a master or mistress, no more days of being herded like cattle. There would still be stress and hard work ahead, but at least they were their own masters. As the boat moved closer to the falls, the booming of the cataract became as loud as a buffalo stampede, and the currents became swifter. From afar, they could see a rainbow hanging over the precipice on the Canadian side, festooned by a cloud of spraying mist. On the spur of the moment, they took over the paddles from the boatman and rowed the craft by themselves. Memories of the muddy Meklong came back to them, the bygone days when they chaperoned the quacking ducks down the great river, reeking of weeds and fish after a monsoon storm. Without knowing it, they rowed past Goat Island, where the rapids became dangerously strong. If not for the persistent reminders and then screams from the boatman, they might have taken their chances just to see how perilously close they could get to the edge, where the narrowing river tumbled down a 160-foot-high precipice at a rate of 100 million tons of water per hour.

After landing at Table Rock, they paid the boatman $4 for the rental and twenty-five cents as an extra tip for the scare. They walked away laughing, like two boyish pranksters, arms wrapped around each other's shoulders. Then they descended a steep and slippery wooden staircase that led to a cavern below the cliff and a hundred feet above the water. Looking down into the misty abyss and listening to the thunderous roar, they were thrilled by the sublime scenery and excited by the prospects awaiting them on the road ahead.

They may well have heard that the almost supernatural scene in front of them, overwhelming hundreds of visitors each day, had inspired a popular parable: "A man in a daydream drifts toward the precipice of Niagara Falls unaware of the danger. On the opposite side, someone watches. Just as the man is about to plunge, the observer cries out 'STOP!' The shout awakens the man from his reverie, and at the critical moment he is saved."[2] The charismatic evangelist Charles Finney, who had introduced this parable at his fiery sermons and led a sweeping religious revival called the Second Great Awakening in the early 1830s, had meant to urge wandering sinners, like the daydreamer in the story, to wake up to the voice of God and choose salvation. For the twins, however, Niagara Falls suggested a different allegory. Rather than stop on the edge and return to the safety of the master's arms, they were taking a headlong plunge into the unknown by cutting themselves off from the Coffins. Whether they could land safely or would simply ruin themselves, whether it would be a splash of success or a self-annihilating dive, the answer awaited them at the bottom of the unfathomable abyss.

Having celebrated their freedom, Chang and Eng left the Buffalo area and made their first stop in Rochester, New York. They had kept Charles Harris as their manager, and he would now work for them rather than for the Coffins. They had also bought from Mrs. Coffin the horse Char-

ley, and the carriage in which they had been traveling, at a bargain price
of $103. The kind of business acumen that had once made them suc-
cessful duck farmers in Siam came in handy again as they set out to
manage their own affairs. In fact, before severing ties with the Coffins,
they had secretly prepared themselves for all the challenges of conducting business transactions: improving their English language skills until
they were "able to read and write very creditably" and mastering arithmetic in order to be able to "keep their own accounts and to make their
own calculations."[3] Ready as they were, however, difficulties abounded.

Rochester, the most thoroughly evangelized of American cities in the
1830s, afforded Chang and Eng their first challenge as self-supporting
showmen. Here they had to compete with fervent revivalists—not for
souls, but for paying audiences. The fire of the Great Awakening that
was sweeping across America had an especially powerful effect on this
country town on the banks of the Genesee River. Founded in 1812,
Rochester had been a village of fifteen hundred as recently as 1821.
The opening of the Erie Canal connected the area's vast wheat fields
and ubiquitous mills to the urban centers on the East Coast. By 1830,
the former Rochesterville village had turned into a bustling entrepôt of
ten thousand residents. "But with growth came discord," writes Louis
Masur. "The middle class divided on political and religious issues and
united against the laboring classes on moral questions such as the consumption of alcohol. The story repeated itself in scores of other towns
and cities. With expansion and wealth came dissension and strife. Only
a revival of religion, many believed, could preserve the nation 'from our
vast extent of territory, our numerous and increasing population, from
diversity of local interests, the power of selfishness, and the fury of sectional jealousy and hate.'"[4]

In the fall of 1830, the elders of the Third Church invited Charles
Finney, a rising star in the revival movement, to preach in Rochester.
Born in 1792 and reared in Oneida County, New York—a breeding
ground for nonconformist communities in the nineteenth century—
Finney had begun a career in law when one day, during a walk in the
woods, he experienced an epiphany. The next day, instead of showing

up in court to argue a case, he skipped the appointment and told his client, "I have a retainer from the Lord Jesus Christ to plead his cause." And plead he did, with impressive fervor and enthusiasm. In Rochester, where Finney would do God's work at the pulpit from September 1830 to March 1831, he preached three evenings a week and three times on Sunday, always to overflowing crowds. Like a manager of a circus show, Finney carefully orchestrated all aspects of his sermon to achieve maximum theatrical effects. He would allocate seats near the pulpit for worried sinners, calling those seats "the anxious bench," reserved only for prominent citizens who had spoken with him privately. As Paul E. Johnson points out in his trailblazing study of the revivals in Rochester, "None sat on the anxious bench who was not almost certain to fall. Separated from the regenerate and from hardened sinners, their conversions became grand public spectacles."[5] Finney's final sermon in Rochester was a "Protracted Meeting," which lasted five days, blazing from morning to night, bringing the entire city to a halt.

The direct impact of revivalism on Chang and Eng was its crackdown on leisure activities such as theatergoing, drinking, and circus attendance. Deep down, the Great Awakening was partly a response to the rise of the new working class and the changing habits of life that arrived in tandem with industrialization and capitalism. The revivalists regarded the entertainments of working men as evil and wasteful, beclouding their minds and thus blocking the millennium.[6] In the wake of Finney's evangelical work, a push for temperance began in earnest in Rochester. Foreshadowing the scenes during the Prohibition era in the twentieth century, people rolled barrels of whiskey down to the sidewalk and smashed them in front of cheering Christians and awestruck sinners. While whiskey ran in the gutter or into the canal, two brothers, John and Joseph Christopher, Episcopalian converts, bought the local theater, shut it down, and converted it to a livery stable. The other two brothers, members of the Presbyterian Church, "bought the circus building and turned it into a soap factory."[7]

Against these God-loving brothers who called the shots in town, the Siamese brothers, pagan and freakish, stood only a whisker of a

chance when they arrived in Rochester. They had difficulty even book-
ing a room (a familiar obstacle) to display themselves, let alone luring
paying customers from their daily prayer sessions, busy church events,
and weeklong camp meetings that were in vogue throughout the nation.
Earlier, when traveling in Maryland and still working for the Coffins,
the twins had already tasted the fierce competition from revival activities. As Harris wrote in January 1832, "We opened a room in Green-
castle & only took $15—but the cause of this was evident to me on
learning that there has been (& still continued when we left) a four days
meeting which was protracted to 10 days & as might be expected all the
good folks were literally mad on the subject." Harris concluded the letter on a worrisome note: "I fear religion stood much in our way."[8] And
he was right; religious enthusiasm was raging everywhere in America.
Finney called the movement he had led "the greatest revival of religion
throughout the land that this country had then ever witnessed."[9] Not to
be outdone in hyperbole, Finney's chief rival, Lyman Beecher, declared
the 1831 awakening to be "the greatest work of God, and the greatest
revival of religion, that the world has ever seen."[10] With Rochester as the
epicenter of revival, the entire region of western New York shuddered
and came to be known as the Burnt-Over District, because the blazes
of revivalism roared most intensely there.

Regrettably, the Burnt-Over District was also the stomping ground
of Chang and Eng in the summer of 1832, as they set out to seek their
own destiny. The result, as reflected in cash receipts, was, well, less than
ideal. Except for the little town of Auburn, where the twins got lucky
on the night of July 4, when locals were in an especially festive mood,
they were barely able to cover their expenses at most of the stops. They
even sought other ways of making a profit, including selling cigars on
the side—the five hundred cigars they had bought wholesale in Buffalo
for $9 now went on sale at their exhibitions. But the area was literally
burned out by religious fervor.

Adding to their misfortune, they continued to be dogged by the Coffins, who refused to give them a clean break. Despite repeated requests,
Susan Coffin failed to return some of their personal effects left in her

care in Newburyport. Instead, she sent along her bitter recriminations. Throughout the summer, the twins continued to exchange acrimonious letters with her and fend off her vile accusations. One thorny issue that resurfaced was the matter of their first trip to England in 1829, when Chang and Eng had to travel in steerage while the Coffins had enjoyed the luxuries of first-class cabins on the *Robert Edwards*. At the time, Captain Coffin had blamed the shipmaster for overbooking the cabins, claiming that he had bought the twins first-class tickets. In July, Chang and Eng had an unexpected visit from Captain Samuel Sherburne, who had commanded the *Edwards*. According to Sherburne, Coffin had in fact bought steerage tickets for the twins and listed them as servants. This revelation infuriated the twins, and they shot off an angry missive to Mrs. Coffin, inveighing against the "cold ingratitude of those for whose benefit I have so long & so laboriously toiled & endured hardships."[11] It should be noted that Chang and Eng referred to themselves in writing sometimes by the singular pronoun "I" and sometimes by the plural "we"—a grammatical choice that resembles the speech pattern of two Old Testament brothers. Moses was a stutterer, so Aaron acted as his spokesman. The alternating between singular and plural pronouns and verbs, by both Chang-Eng and Moses-Aaron, would give future scholars of bioethics much fodder for thought.[12]

On October 5, 1832, the long-anticipated showdown finally took place upon Captain Coffin's return to America. After what he dubbed "a wild goose chase," Coffin caught up with the twins in Bath, New York, where the two parties held a long talk. Chang and Eng, as Coffin told his wife in a letter that night, were glad to see him but also seemed "to feel themselves quite free" from him. A ship captain accustomed to giving orders and a master cocksure about ownership, Coffin was shocked by the twins' revolt. Not knowing the degree of their determination, Coffin even had high hopes of whisking them off to France, where they had previously been denied entry.

Counting on the rhetorical prowess that ran in his Puritan blood, Coffin reminded the twins of the contract they had signed, adding that the arrangement with the Siamese government was in fact for seven

years, not five, and that he had intentionally shortened the term of ownership on paper in order to assuage their mother's fears. But Chang and
Eng had learned not to trust Coffin's words, especially after learning
the truth about that voyage on the *Edwards*. They saw through Coffin's ruse and knew instinctively that, as they later told Robert Hunter,
it was a trick calculated to induce them to stay longer with him. They
were adamant about quitting him, telling the former master that they
wanted to settle the score once and for all and be done with it. In his
letter to Susan, Coffin was vague about the terms of the settlement,
stating only that the twins, having become savvy in business dealings,
had referred Coffin to "their man," apparently Harris, to finalize the
separation. "That is the only way I can settle with them," Coffin wrote.
"I shall settle as soon as possible & return home." He felt defeated but
unwilling to admit it: "I am almost beat out with the rough roads." And
he would not cut the twins loose without letting them have a piece
of his mind. A Bible-thumping Puritan, Coffin delivered a sermon on
the spot, à la Charles Finney, chastising the twins for indulging in all
sorts of dissipation—whoring, gambling, and drinking. He urged them
to repent their sins, almost as though God was speaking through him.[13]

These were shocking accusations. The twins were known to be interested in women, just like any other young men. Given their abnormal
condition, they apparently had not had any luck with ordinary females,
so it is not inconceivable that they might have explored sexuality with
prostitutes. They also enjoyed hard liquor, and, based on their later lifestyle, they would indeed try their luck at card tables occasionally, just as
they were interested in chess, checkers, hunting, and fishing. But having
their way of life condemned in such moralistic terms by a Christian who
had exploited and cheated them was more than the twins could bear.
It added fuel to their discontent with those pulpit-pounding preachers
who had kept potential customers from them. Their riposte to Coffin
was succinct and firm: "They had as good right to a woman as he had."

With no other recourse, Coffin settled with the twins and stormed
off the next day. He told others that when the twins refused to repent,
he beat them, giving them "the damnedest thrashing they ever had in

their lives." But James Hale, who knew the twins well and had seen their fistfights with troublemakers, thought that Coffin had made up the story to save his own face. "It cannot have been so," said Hale, because Coffin "is yet alive."

This would be the last time Chang and Eng ever saw the man who had radically changed their destiny, turning them from two Siamese duck fanciers in a remote corner of Earth into world-famous showmen. In less than five years, on August 27, 1837, Captain Coffin, commanding the Boston ship *Gentoo*, would die of consumption on St. Helena Island, the same place where years previously he had sent his wife the good tidings: "Susan, I have two Chinese Boys 17 years old grown together. . . ." Not to put too fine a point on it, but, like adding an extra nail to his coffin, the *New York Spectator* ended his obituary with an acknowledgment of Coffin's major contribution to American cultural history: "The Siamese Twins were brought to this country by Capt. C."[14]

America on the Road

With the Coffins finally no longer able to claim ownership, Chang and Eng did not need to perform tricks, both literally and figuratively, for anyone anymore. Suddenly, they found that what lay between them and their future was only the open road of America—a kind of liberation that was hardly open to freed blacks, who putatively posed a greater threat to America's early nineteenth-century race hierarchy. As the entrepreneur twins would discover, America in the 1830s was a nation on the move; or, as a foreign visitor commented, "There is more travelling in the United States than in any part of the world. . . . Here, the whole population is in motion, whereas, in old countries, there are millions who have never been beyond the sound of the parish bell."[1] Even the slaves, whom this visitor did not mention, were also perpetually on the move, sold to other owners when their masters died or to other areas when the masters deemed it profitable to do so. If mobility then defined the American character, we can already get a glimpse of that trait in the period when Chang and Eng, freakishly exotic and barely human in the eyes of most, visited every nook and cranny of the country. A picturesque sight on the open road, the conjoined Siamese brothers had, we will discover, plenty of company and competition.

Despite the American penchant for motion, the early 1830s remained what Harriet Beecher Stowe called "the ante-railroad times," a period when travel could be excruciatingly slow and challenging. Roads in

America were a confusing quiltwork, controlled even more confusingly by state, county, and local authorities. Since the colonial era, the old Indian trails, after years of exploration by frontiersmen and buckskin marauders like Daniel Boone and Davy Crockett, had turned into tote roads, and then newer paths were cut, followed by highways and toll roads. "In the 1830s," as Jack Larkin describes in his study of everyday life in America between 1790 and 1840, "the best roads in the United States were the major county roads and turnpikes of southern New England, the lower Hudson Valley and southeastern Pennsylvania. . . . Elsewhere the American landscape continued to present impressive obstacles to travel."[2] As we shall see, the twins and their fellow travelers on the American roads would encounter a plethora of challenges—providing insight into the American lifestyle of two centuries ago.

The fall of 1832 was also a time of great political upheaval and change in America. Andrew Jackson fought a bitter reelection battle and ended up beating Henry Clay by 219 to 60 in the Electoral College and by 700,000 to 329,000 in the popular vote. But Old Hickory's landslide victory only served to galvanize his political opponents, the Whigs, who would fight him in major national issues, condemning him as an uncouth lout and a despot. The nation was as ideologically divided as it had ever been since its founding. Reflective of the growing tension was South Carolina's passage of the Nullification bill in October 1832, threatening secession from the Union, a move that threw the political calculus into chaos. On October 8—three days after Chang and Eng freed themselves from Captain Coffin—the US Army, in the wake of the Black Hawk War, took the first step in removing Indians from their homes on the East Coast, thus beginning a six-year campaign that came to be known as the Trail of Tears. "The Indian races are melting in the presence of European civilization like snow beneath the rays of the sun," Tocqueville euphemistically observed in his notebook, suggesting that what we now call "ethnic cleansing" was little more than a literary deliquescence.[3] In fact, the removal of more than forty-five thousand East Coast Indians, of whom thirteen thousand would perish in a forced march on the road, opened up one hundred million acres of land, mainly in the South, including the area where Chang and Eng eventually would settle down. Seeing a golden opportunity for wealth, white settlers quickly poured in—not necessarily to farm but to turn over the land claims to later settlers for profit, a nineteenth-century version of real-estate flipping, an early "land rush." The land-grab craze molded a national character, or malaise, that Tocqueville would once again euphemistically diagnose as "American restlessness." Settlers plunged into the wilderness with as little gear as an ax and the obligatory Bible. In Ohio, a popular staging area for further migration, as well as the stomping ground for the Siamese Twins in the waning months of 1832 and the first half of 1833, one could find, according to a guidebook for settlers, "hundreds of men . . . who have settled for the fourth, fifth, or sixth time on a new spot. To sell out and remove only a few hundred miles makes up a portion of the variety of backwoods life and manners." One fecund woman from Illinois bore twelve children, every one of whom had been born in a different house.[4]

On their peripatetic journeys, these pioneering settlers, hardly people of means, would carry with them only what they could put on a packhorse or an oxcart, if they were lucky enough to be able to afford either. Their material needs created an opportunity for one of the most colorful figures that had ever graced the American open roads in those early years: the Yankee peddler. In fact, most European tourists to this country prior to the Civil War noted two great points of divergence between the crude life in the New World and the more genteel civilization of their own: the seemingly vulgar American habit of spitting and the ubiquitous presence of Yankee peddlers.[5] Claiming a long line of genealogy stretching from early Indian traders to modern-day door-to-door salesmen (whose death knell has once and for all been sounded by Amazon), nineteenth-century peddlers were a familiar sight on the highways, byways, and waterways of America in the 1830s. Carrying a basket or a trunk, or driving a one-horse shay, they hawked an assortment of useful "Yankee notions": pins (from which we get the term *pin money*), needles, hooks, scissors, razors, knives, combs, buttons, spoons, pots, pans, brooms, books, cotton goods, lace, perfume, clocks, chairs, spices, essences, dyes, woodenware, pottery, and so on.

Most of these peddlers hailed from New England, or, to be more specific, Connecticut. Benedict Arnold, the infamous traitor, born in Norwich, Connecticut, spent his youthful years peddling woolen goods up and down the Hudson Valley, through the very same area where he would later operate as a military man and betray George Washington.[6] Perhaps the Connecticut Yankee who had climbed the steepest social ladder was Collis Potter Huntington, best remembered today as the founder of the Southern Pacific and Central Pacific Railroads. Born in Poverty Hollow, Connecticut, west of Hartford, Huntington began his career as a peddler of clocks, watches, silverware, needles, knives, combs, and other Yankee notions that he had packed into two tin boxes two feet long and sixteen inches deep. It was during those early years of hawking and haggling that the future robber baron would hone his skills of profiteering. "These travels gave him an idea of the topography of the land that later helped him in his railroad developments," writes Richardson Wright in *Hawkers and Walkers in Early America*.[7]

These sweet-talking Yankee peddlers, who also went by the term *chapmen*, were the lifeblood of early America, moving the goods around before mass transportation was even conceivable. But their craftiness gave them quite a reputation as well as a unique place in the American cultural imagination. As J. R. Dolan puts it in *The Yankee Peddlers of Early America*, "In the eighteenth century he was considered a rascal, in the nineteenth he was thought to be a cheat: he was sharp, crafty, mean, and always on the lookout for a chance to make a shady deal," while in the early twentieth century he was symbolized by the crooked, ersatz bandleader Harold Hill in *The Music Man*.[8] In the South, long before the atrocity committed by General Sherman and his army of bluecoats, *Damnyankee* had already become one word, without a hyphen, in the Southern lexicon, thanks to these creative peddlers from New England. Timothy Dwight, the stalwart—some might say uptight—president of Yale, had some harsh words reserved for these peddlers, most of whom were about the same age as the Yale students under his charge: "Many of these young men employed in this business, part at an early period with both modesty and principle. Their sobriety is exchanged for cunning, and their decent behavior for coarse impudence. . . . No course of life tends more rapidly or more effectively to eradicate every moral feeling."[9]

In fact, Yankee peddlers were almost synonymous with humbuggery or huckstering. Sam Slick, one of the first humorous figures in American literature (though invented by a Canadian), is a Connecticut clock peddler, and his name says it all about his character, as does his fictional hometown, Slicksville. In Washington Irving's timeless tale about Rip Van Winkle, when the henpecked protagonist wakes up from his twenty-year slumber in the Catskills and returns home, he learns to his relief that his wife died years earlier. His daughter, now a mother with a nursing baby, tells the Dutchman of the peculiar manner of his wife's passing: "She broke a blood-vessel in a fit of passion at a New England peddler."[10] Nathaniel Hawthorne was both annoyed and amused by the peddlers who pestered graduates and guests at the Williams College commencement in 1838:

> The most characteristic part of the scene was where the peddlers, gingerbread-sellers &c were collected, a few hundred yards from the meeting-house. There was a peddler there from New York, who sold his wares by auction; and I could have stood and listened to him all day long. Sometimes he would put up a heterogeny of articles in a lot—as a paper of pins, a lead pencil, and a shaving box—and knock them all down, perhaps, for ninepence. Bunches of lead pencils, steel pens, pound cakes of shaving soap, gilt finger-rings, bracelets, clasps, and other jewelry, cards of pearl buttons, or steel . . . bundles of wooden combs, boxes of loco-focos [matches], suspenders &c, &c &c—in short everything—dipping his hand down into his boxes, with the promise of a wonderful lot, and producing, perhaps, a bottle of opodeldoc [liniment], and joining it with a lead pencil.[11]

Perhaps the only honest, albeit exotic, salesman portrayed in American literature of that period was Herman Melville's Queequeg, the heavily tattooed and tomahawk-wielding cannibal who arises from the South Seas to peddle embalmed human heads in New England. As the innkeeper Peter Coffin tells Ishmael, "He's sold all on 'em but one, and that one he's trying to sell to-night, cause tomorrow's Sunday, and it would not do to be sellin' human heads about the streets when folks is goin' to churches. He wanted to, last Sunday, but I stopped him just as he was goin' out of the door with four heads strung on a string, for all the airth like a string of inions." The Polynesian giant, it turns out, is a generous soul who does not care a farthing for money and has quite a potlatch mentality like the Indians, prompting Ishmael to declare, "Better sleep with a sober cannibal than a drunken Christian."[12]

Exotic and colorful like Queequeg, the Siamese Twins were also, in the loosest but best sense, peddlers. They did not just market their oddity—as Peter Coffin put it, "a great curio"—but they also literally sold merchandise on the side: Cuban cigars, lithographic portraits, and biographical sketches. So it is not surprising that one day, when they tried to quit showbiz and settle down, they would first choose to run a general store as a way to make a living, a career option that seemed inspired by their early years of peddling both as duck farmers in Siam and traveling salesmen on the American roads.

Besides Yankee peddlers, the roster of Chang and Eng's fellow travelers on the open road also included itinerant preachers. As early as the First Great Awakening in the mid-eighteenth century, Puritan ministers like Jonathan Edwards—perhaps not surprisingly, a native of Connecticut—would head out on horseback and give sermons along the circuit. In 1738, George Whitefield would go from Savannah, Georgia, to Boston, drawing crowds as large as thirty thousand, before moving on to Connecticut, New York, and Pennsylvania before heading South again. During the Second Great Awakening, which coincided with America's fast expansion into the wilderness, various churches sent hundreds of traveling preachers to save souls in newly settled areas. Facing practical issues of surviving on the frontier, many of these gospel peddlers also moonlighted, preaching on Sundays and doing productive work on weekdays—carpentry, tailoring, doctoring, and whatnot. Such a dual career sometimes made it hard to distinguish the clergymen from those whose chosen trade required constant itinerancy on the American roads and backwoods trails: blacksmiths, silversmiths, clockmakers, doctors, repairmen, dentists, artists, and more. Another quote from Nathaniel Hawthorne, who also had wandered during 1837 and 1838, might suffice to illustrate how things got done on the road:

> 30th July [1838]. Remarkable character.—A traveling "Surgeon Dentist," who has taken a room here in the North-Adams House, and sticks up his advertising bills on the pillars of the piazza, and all about the town. He is a tall, slim young man, six feet two, dressed in a country-made coat of light blue (taken, as he tells me, in exchange for dental operations) black pantaloons, and clumsy cow-hide boots. Self-conceit—very strongly expressed in his air; and a doctor once told him that he owed his life to that quality; for, by keeping himself so stiffly upright, he opens his chest, and counteracts a consumptive tendency. He is not only a dentist—which trade he follows temporarily—but a licensed preacher of the Baptist persuasion; and is now on his way to the West, to seek a place of settlement in his spiritual vocation.

Habitually curious about human affairs and as insightful about the foibles of humans as any American writer, Hawthorne wrote again in his journal a few days later:

> Scenes and characters—A young country fellow, twenty or thereabouts, pained with a toothache. A doctor, passing on horseback, with his black leather saddlebags behind him, a thin, frosty-haired man. Being asked to operate, he looks at the tooth, lances the gum; and the fellow being content to be operated upon on the spot, he seats himself in a chair on the stoop, with great heroism. The doc-

tor produces a rusty pair of iron forceps; a man holds the patient's head. . . . A turn of the doctor's hand; the patient begins to utter a cry; but the tooth comes out.[13]

One such itinerant dentist was Charles Willson Peale, who had been a traveling portrait painter, coach-maker, silversmith, saddle-maker, taxidermist, and veterinarian before founding the first public museum in Philadelphia in 1786. Given how polymath these traveling professionals were, it is easy to imagine the excitement they caused when they appeared on the village green of an isolated hamlet and opened a pack full of notions, Yankee or not—their often-tarnished reputations notwithstanding.

Nor should we forget the horse-mounted judges who meted out justice and maintained the rule of law. With the settlements of the still-inchoate democracy so far-flung, the American judiciary system, first created in 1789, divided the country into the Eastern, Middle, and Southern Circuits. The justices on these circuit courts had to travel around to hear cases, and most had to spend half a year on "circuit riding." Judge William Cushing of the Eastern Circuit, for instance, would ride around in a four-wheeled phaeton drawn by a pair of horses. According to Richardson Wright, Cushing's was an ingenious equipage, "for the justice enjoyed his comforts and relished the pleasures of the table, and had the carriage built after his own design with storage spaces for books and choice foods. A jet black and faithful negro servant rode behind and gave the requisite touch of dignity to His Honor's peregrinations." The honorable judge would also bring his wife along on the circuit, so that she could read aloud the law books for him. Less pretentious justices without the benefit of phaetons would simply ride their circuits on horseback. Justice Pinckney of Charleston, for example, would start out early each morning and consult with clients and lawyers en route. "As they rode side by side he would listen to their case. If he had to give an opinion, he always made it in writing and cautiously endorsed it as 'given on circuit,' since he had no law books with him to consult." And that was how the colorful term *horseback opinion* came about.[14]

As the country mushroomed, Congress regularly had to expand and reorganize the system of judicial circuits, increasing the number of circuit courts to six in 1801, seven in 1807, and nine in 1837. The swelling roster of circuit judges made them more ubiquitous figures on the road. In the Middle West, they usually traveled by horseback. As one historian put it, "The years when Abraham Lincoln rode the circuit in Illinois form a definite and picturesque phase of his life."[15]

These, in addition to singing masters, clockmakers, tinsmiths, wheelwrights, healers, quacks, dancing teachers, portrait painters, handwriting instructors, silhouette cutters, mesmerizers, and, one day, as we shall see, phrenologists, were some of Chang and Eng's colorful fellow travelers on the American road.

Notwithstanding the fractious political discord and the controversies over the role of a centralized bank, Chang and Eng in the fall and early winter of 1832 continued to tour a broad swath of areas in New York, Pennsylvania, Ohio, and what is now West Virginia. Not yet at the level where they could afford a luxurious phaeton, they traveled in a two-wheeled gig, drawn by a single horse, followed by a wagon. Like all two-wheelers, a gig had a higher accident rate than the more stable four-wheeled varieties, giving credence to the old saying that "half the coachmen were killed out of gigs."[16] As winter descended, the twins, who already had endured frequent accidents on New England's icy roads, tried to stay clear of mountainous regions and moved into the flat terrain of the Ohio Valley.

An examination of the twins' account ledger, kept meticulously in Harris's neat script, reveals a steady, nonstop itinerancy in those waning months of 1832. After bidding a bitter farewell to Captain Coffin in Bath, New York, the twins moved on to the village of Angelica, at the foot of Bald Mountain in New York, on October 5. The next day, they arrived in Ellicottville, followed by Jamestown on the eighth, Mayville on the tenth, and Westfield, close to Lake Erie, on the twelfth. From there, they nipped the northern tip of Pennsylvania, making a stop in North East, before arriving on October 16 in Ashtabula, Ohio. Venturing south the next day, they reached Warren, Ohio, dubbed "the Capital of the Western Reserve" (and also the hometown of Earl Derr Biggers, the future creator of Charlie Chan). From there, they made a stop at Poland and, according to records, paid a bill of $4.50 to stay for two nights at Mr. Bidwell's. They also spent $1.25 for washing and $2.37 for fixing the wagon. Sadly, we have no way of knowing whether the blacksmith who mended the wagon was someone hired by William McKinley Sr., father of the future president, whose family ran foundries and shops in Poland and nearby towns.

And so the journey continued.

October 24, Lisbon.

October 26, Mr. Fitch's at Canfield.

On October 29, Chang and Eng arrived in Youngstown, in northeastern Ohio, and then Salem the next day. While in Canfield, they had left behind a watch and had to pay two dollars to recover it a few days later. The month ended in Wellsville, a hamlet by the Ohio River where, in 1774, a group of Virginia frontiersmen had brutally killed several Mingo Indians at Yellow Creek, triggering the outbreak of Lord Dunmore's War. On the last day of the month, as usual, the twins paid Charles Harris his monthly $50 salary and the driver, Thomas Crocker, $10.

Traveling southward, the twins arrived in Steubenville, Ohio, on November 3 and paid $5 in town tax. A few days later, on their way from Washington, Pennsylvania, to Pittsburgh, they apparently were ripped off, for the November 9 entry read: "Tax to the Wise Men of Canonsburgh $5." An equally colorful entry from the previous day read: "To the one eyed nigger at Irons's $0.50." It must have been for the black servant at Mr. Irons's in Washington, where they had spent the night of November 8. They usually paid hotel servants between twenty-five cents and a dollar as tips, depending on how long they had stayed.

Somewhere along the way, their horse Charley took ill. A vet was called, resulting in two related entries in the ledger: "Horse Doctor for Charley $1.50" and "Hire of a horse from Pittsburgh to Burgettstown $4." Other expenses that regularly show up in the ledger include tolls, postage, candles (spermaceti or tallow), horseshoeing, washing, whips, combs, gloves, horse feeds, cigars (for their own consumption, while those bought at

wholesale would be retailed at exhibits), guns, and haircuts. From Bur-
gettstown, Pennsylvania, they made stops in the following places before
the end of December: in present-day West Virginia, Wellsburgh, Wheel-
ing; in Ohio, St. Clairsville, Barnsville, Washington, Cambridge, Zanes-
ville, Gratiot, Brownsville, Newark, Granville, and Utica.

Just before Christmas, from December 22 to 24, as young urchins
prayed to St. Nicholas, the twins stayed in Mount Vernon, Ohio. They
paid $8 in town tax, 75 cents for advertising, $21 for lodging at Plum-
mer's, and 50 cents for tips to the servants at the inn. Also, the ledger
has an entry, "Dec. 24, Expenses at Kenyon College, Gambier, $1.50,"
indicating that they visited the college that had been founded eight
years earlier to train much-needed clergy. We don't know what those
expenses were for. It could be something they didn't want to describe,
because they were usually very meticulous and exact. They moved on
to Sunbury on Christmas Day, after fixing their gig and wagon. On
December 27, they arrived in Worthington and spent the last days of
1832 at Colonel Kilbourne's Inn outside of Columbus, Ohio.

Chang and Eng celebrated the New Year 1833 with a small shopping
spree: six silk pocket kerchiefs, $6.50; cigars, 18 cents; a pair of scissors,
30 cents; two pairs of suspenders, $1.75; a pair of Monroe shoes for
Eng, $3; and a pair of overshoes for Chang, $3.12. On January 5, they
spent $4 on a book and presented it to Kenyon College, where they
had apparently made some friends during their visit. Today, this two-
volume set of Thomas Moore's *Letters and Journals of Lord Byron*, one of
Chang and Eng's favorite books and a popular item on the bookshelves
of nineteenth-century households, remains in the Special Collections of
Kenyon College's library.[17]

The other expense items for those days included horseshoeing, 45
cents; repair for the gig, $2.25; horse doctor, $1.25; cutting hair, 50 cents;
tipping a boy, 10 cents; postage, 10 cents; and opodeldoc, 40 cents. It
seemed that they were getting ready to open the first show of 1833 and
to spend another year on the road, as the ledger indicates: "Advertising
and Printing at Columbus, O. $9" and "Through brace for wagon and
other repairs $12.87."

Despite the acrimony that came to dominate American politics during that era, the Siamese Twins remained strongly in the public consciousness. In fact, during the 1832 presidential campaign, "the Siamese Twins" was an expression dropped freely by Americans as a metaphor for the freakish or anything deemed inseparable. An anonymous "Citizen of Alabama" wrote to the *United States' Telegraph* to express his utter abhorrence at the nomination of Martin Van Buren to succeed John Calhoun as the vice-presidential candidate. That nomination speech, so opined the Southern gentleman, "may fairly be viewed as a *mental lusus*! It leaves the Siamese Twins far behind."[18] In a marathon speech on the general pension bill in April, Congressman Warren R. Davis of South Carolina insisted that the chain of measures in the proposed legislation was "connected as indissolubly as the Siamese Twins."[19] Even though they had been traveling in backwoods areas rather than in the more metropolitan centers in the Northeast, the twins were very much on the mind of Americans.

In fact, their newsworthy quality was so taken for granted that in March 1833, the *Boston Investigator* printed three news items back to back: The South Carolina Convention had met to repeal the Nullification bill; the Siamese Twins had raided the South, moving from Ohio into Kentucky, with Tennessee in their sight; and "the amount of money deposited in the several Savings Banks in the State of New York is upwards of $3,000,000."[20] The first and third items were in fact major issues. The repeal of the Nullification bill by the South Carolina Convention defused an explosive situation. As David S. Reynolds puts it in his commanding study of the Jacksonian Age, "Resolving the nullification crisis was one of the great achievements of Jackson's presidency. He established the principle that America was not a compact of loosely bound *states* but an enduring union of *people*." It was a principle that Abraham Lincoln would adopt when the eleven Southern states, led again by the Palmetto State, separated from the Union in 1860–61.[21] The third item in the *Boston Investigator* pertains to Jackson's attempt to break up or at least weaken the influence of the Bank of the United States (BUS), forerunner of the Federal Reserve. Jackson never liked the BUS, regarding it "as a fountainhead of the evils" that derived from aristocratic privileges and centralized government. For him, "the bank, which had twenty-nine branches and controlled a third of the nation's bank deposits, stole money from average Americans and handed it over to wealthy stockholders." But his political enemies, Henry Clay and the Republicans, argued that the bank was a stabilizer of the economy, necessary for economic health. The 1832 election, therefore, became largely a referendum on the BUS, as Jackson had vetoed the bill for the bank's recharter and tried to kill the "hydra-headed monster of corruption," while his opponents cried foul and condemned him as the despotic "King Andrew the First."[22] Sandwiched between two explosive news items, the mention of the Siamese Twins' itinerary indicates how much Chang and Eng grabbed the American imagination, and their ubiquity in the press of that era enables us two centuries later to have such a thorough portrait.

Attention proliferated whether in the North or the South. On March 31, 1833, for example, an advertisement appeared in a New Orleans newspaper stating that the Siamese Twins would arrive the next day aboard the steamboat *Tippecanoe* from Memphis. It advised the curious not to miss the opportunity of seeing the famous twins in their characteristic dress as they proceeded from the boat to their lodging on Canal Street. Thousands of people thronged to the show at the hour of the rendezvous, only to find that it was an April Fools' Day prank.[23]

By July, several newspapers, quoting the *Warren News Letter*, reported that Chang and Eng had been tried in Trumbull County, Ohio, "for an assault and battery committed on an old and respectable citizen. The defendants pled guilty and were each fined five dollars and cost."[24] This incident, which took place in late June when the twins returned to the Trumbull–Warren–Youngstown area, was recorded in their ledger as "June 27th, Knock down to Old Hunter at Poland, $13.84." As we know, this was not the first time that the twins had run into troubles with the law. Given their chair-hurling temperament and often fearless courage to stand up to any physical challenge, this would not be the last time, either.

Soon after the trouble in Trumbull County, Chang and Eng arrived in Cleveland, then a city of more than five thousand, where they stayed from July 3 to 5. The receipts from the three days of exhibits were a mixed bag: $26.50 for the opening day, $90 for the second, and $44.25 for the last.[25] The sudden spike of interest on July 4 might have had to do with the holiday, but more likely it was attributable to a visit by a surprise guest, Black Hawk, the legendary Sauk warrior. After his failed attempt in 1832 to retake Indian lands from white settlers in a war named after him, Black Hawk had been captured and jailed in St. Louis, Missouri. In April, on the order of President Jackson, Black Hawk was brought to the East by steamboat, carriage, and railroad, and paraded around cities like a war trophy, to demonstrate the power of the United States. Everywhere Black Hawk went, large crowds awaited him, to get a peek at a real Indian, something that most white Easterners had seen only in pictures or plays. He had become a curiosity much like the Siamese Twins. In Washington, Black Hawk was met by President Jackson at the White House, about which the Indian warrior said in his autobiography, published later that year, "His wigwam is well furnished with everything good and pretty, and is very strongly built." Jackson, an Indian fighter who had once adopted an orphaned Creek boy, acted like a stern father determined to punish his prodigal son and teach him a lesson. He sent Black Hawk to be imprisoned at Fort Monroe in Norfolk, Virginia.

After a few weeks in jail, where Black Hawk posed for portraits so often than he could not find the time to make his calumet (ceremonial pipe), he was released and taken to meet the president again, in Baltimore. Addressing Black Hawk and the accompanying Indians as "my children," Jackson, the notorious Indian fighter, excoriated them for waging the war and warned them against any future mischief. According to newspaper reports, Black Hawk promised Jackson not to fight again, although Black Hawk's version of the exchange, as he would later recount it in his autobiography, carried a slightly different flavor. In any case, Jackson was pleased with Black Hawk's response, and he entertained Black Hawk by taking him to Baltimore's Front Street Theatre, where the Sauk warrior in his traditional garb drew more curiosity and fascination than did the play of the night—in the same manner as the exotic Siamese Twins had once charmed theatergoers in London.[26]

His captivity finally over, Black Hawk was sent back to a reservation west of the Mississippi, but not before he had to do another circus tour in cities along the way. In eastern cities like New York and Philadelphia, Black Hawk, his son, and other tribal members created quite a spectacle. "We were called upon by many of the people, who treated us well, particularly the squaws," Black Hawk recalled. But as they moved farther west and closer to battle sites and areas of conflict, the reception turned hostile. In some places, crowds burned and hanged his effigy, reflecting the hysteria still common among settlers closer to the untrammeled areas.

Cleveland, sitting on the verge of the frontier, was a relatively friendly zone for Black Hawk. Learning that the famous Siamese Twins were also in town, he could not resist the temptation to see the wonder of nature for himself. So, on July 4, Black Hawk and his entourage walked through streets decorated by American flags, their own buntings so extravagant that some curious bystanders mistook them for an Independence Day pageant. The colorful group arrived at the showroom inside Mr. Scovill's hotel, a frame building on Superior Street that the owner, a carpenter by trade, had erected by himself in 1825.[27] Black Hawk, a short man with a prominent nose and dark, beady eyes, addressed the twins through an interpreter for more than five minutes. According to the *Cleveland Advertiser*, the great Indian warrior told Chang and Eng that he and his friends had heard of the twins, and had been very anxious to see them, and that they were pleased to have their wish granted. "The Great Spirit had made them as they were, and would protect them and be their guide and protector, should they go again across the Great Waters," the newspaper reported. "The Great Spirit will call both to him at once."

At the end of the visit, the twins asked the doorkeeper to return the admissions that the Indian entourage had paid to get in. If we remember earlier in New York, Chang and Eng, known for their wry sense of humor, had once refunded half the admission fee to a man with one eye because "he could see only half of what the rest of the audience saw." In this case, they told Black Hawk through the interpreter, "Your money's no good here, chief," eliciting a bittersweet chuckle from the veteran warrior. Chang and Eng also gave the special guest a copy of their lithographic portrait as a gift. Black Hawk was pleased and told the twins that "he would show his Red brethren the portrait which they had presented to him, and would tell them what he and his friends had seen." The entire visit lasted about fifteen minutes.[28]

The spectacle of a powwow on so-called Independence Day between the conjoined twins in their Asian costume and a legendary Indian warrior in his native regalia reverberates down to us with crowning irony, but it must have been a feast for the eyes for the people in Cleveland. In the emerging entertainment business of America, the exhibition of Indians, real or fake, would become standard. In the coming years, whenever Chang and Eng got tired of the road and chose the convenience of displaying themselves at Peale's Museum in New York, Albany, or Baltimore, they would inevitably be joined by exhibitions of Indians, Polynesians, Africans, and members of other exotic tribes who were part of the museum's "collection." But what made the meeting in Cleveland unique was the fact that we don't know who was the gazer and who was the object of the gaze. A case of mutual curiosity, if you will. The Siamese Twins and Black Hawk certainly shared the fate of being looked upon without relinquishing their ability to look at others. Case in point: a week later, on July 11, returning from Painesville to Cleveland, Chang and Eng logged an expenditure of fifty cents in their ledger: "Going to see Lady Jane 'Ourang Outang.'" Their onetime competition in Boston, the Ourang-Outang, with a new anthropomorphic epithet, had apparently followed them to Cleveland. There is no written record to help us fathom the depth of emotion that Chang and Eng must have felt when they joined the crowds and viewed the caged creature. Nor do we know how they felt when they had visited the Cincinnati Museum on February 11 that same year and saw monsters, cannibals, and Indians in wax—they also paid fifty cents for that museum visit, according to their ledger. Did they feel a sense of both wonder and revulsion, the same way the other gawkers felt when looking at them? Or were they gradually becoming like their former white captors, viewing the world through the Caucasian power structure so that they would not see themselves as oppressed underdogs, transferring that burden to those less fortunate? While we can only imagine those scenes, the paradoxical drama of the gazed becoming the gazer, the enslaved becoming the enslaver, will continue to unfold in the incredible life of Chang and Eng.

Despite their best efforts, the Ohio Valley did not prove to be fertile grazing ground for the twins. Ticket receipts could barely keep up with the high costs of travel and other expenses. For the entire month of July 1833, when they toured the Cleveland–Detroit region, they grossed $428.50 but paid $417.32¼ in expenses, leaving them with a paltry net of $11.17¾. August was worse, grossing them the minuscule amount of $136.75. After deducting $310.37 in expenses, they were $173.62 in the red. September was not much better, when they moved between Ohio and Kentucky and netted only a small profit of $126.26. "They appear eager for money," declared a newspaper article published in Elyria, Ohio, where they visited on July 15. However, as the article goes on to say, they were happy. "They are now 22 years old, drive their own equipage, and direct their own movements. . . . They enjoy good health, and a fair flow of spirits, and appear perfectly content and happy. They often remark, that they never saw any single person as happy as themselves."

The writer was very impressed by the deadpan wit that the twins showed during their one-day appearance in Elyria, where they grossed $57.25 in admission fees, second highest in the month of July. "A gentleman in the evening asked them if they ever conversed together when alone? Chang, exchanging a look with Eng, replied, 'Me never alone, Sir.' To the enquiry, why do you not converse together? Eng significantly answered, 'Me no news, Sir.'" And in response to the gentleman's observation that Chang seemed to pocket all the cash, Eng replied with a laugh, "Me rob him tonight. Me good pickpocket."[29]

Despite financial setbacks, the Siamese Twins remained full of humor and verve, happy being their own men but eager to leave the not-so-lucrative Ohio Valley and seek new frontiers of adventure.

≽ 21 ≼

The Deep South

*The Congo is not more different from Massachusetts or Kansas
or California. So I have chosen to write of Alabama not as a state
which is part of a nation, but as a strange country.*
—Carl Carmer, *Stars Fell on Alabama* (1934)

"Whenever I'm asked why Southern writers particularly have a penchant for writing about freaks," remarked Flannery O'Connor, "I say it is because we are still able to recognize one." A great novelist from Georgia, author of gothic stories about escaped criminals exterminating families or Bible salesmen prowling for girls with wooden legs, O'Connor insisted: "To be able to recognize a freak, you have to have some conception of the whole man." She went on to explain that in the Christ-haunted South, "the general conception of man . . . is still theological," a creature "formed in the image and likeness of God." Man, in other words, is a shadow, a ghost, or possibly a freak. Thus conceived "as a figure for our essential displacement," O'Connor concluded, the freak attains the depth and prevalence in Southern culture and literature.[1] Whether or not O'Connor was right in her diagnosis of the Southern fascination with the freakish and abnormal—she did admit that "almost anything you say about Southern belief can be denied in the next breath with equal propriety"[2]—there is no denying that Chang and Eng stumbled upon a gold mine when they ventured into the Southern states in the fall of 1833.

After a brief tour in Kentucky, the young men opened in Nashville, Tennessee, on October 10 and grossed more than $500 during their nine days there. For the month of October, when they moved (as Elvis Presley would do about a century later) between Tennessee and Alabama, their receipts jumped to $1,104.50. If numbers tell a story, their

income ledger suggests that the Deep South was smitten with the men
from Siam: In November, they grossed $985.75, and in December, as
Christmas approached, $1,447.

The road to the South, however, was not a smooth one. It was—as
the twins would come to realize and take to heart—a different country. In this chapter's epigraph, what Carl Carmer said about Alabama
may sound a bit hyperbolic, but as W. J. Cash reminds us, it is a hyperbole "applicable in one measure or another to the entire section" of the
South.[3] Crossing from Tennessee into Alabama, Chang and Eng quickly
learned a lesson about law and punishment and strange ways of life in
the heart of Dixie, where even freed blacks, if they still existed there,
were forbidden to travel. On October 26, roving in Huntsville, Alabama,
the twins were snagged by local authorities for not having obtained a
license. They had to pay a fine and costs of $26.60, and then in Athens,
the next town, they got into trouble again.

A cotton village founded in 1818, Athens, like countless townships
that sprouted in early nineteenth-century America, had an optimistic
name but boasted only a few hundred souls. Yet, it had the unique distinction of being the hometown of William Wyatt Bibb, elected the first
governor of the State of Alabama when it joined the Union in 1819.
In less than a year, however, Bibb died in a fall from his horse, and his
brother Thomas succeeded him in office. The lesson that Chang and
Eng learned in Athens was not about fraternal bonding or how to keep
things in the family, but Southern pride and a penchant for violence.

On the night of their exhibit, October 28, almost the whole town
turned out and crowded the parlor of the only hostel in town, operated
by one Mr. Bass. Ruddy-faced farmers in their overalls drawled melo-
diously, chewed on tobacco, and spat with abandon. Women in their
puffy, flowery dresses brought their crying babies. Restless kids fidgeted
on stools and picked their noses out of habit. Sitting amid the colorful
audience was a local doctor named Bolus, who, trying to distinguish
himself from the crowd, proposed to examine the "connection" of the
twins. The idea pleased the onlookers, who wanted to get their money's
worth by looking at God's miracle up close. But the twins were appalled.

After years of being prodded, poked, and examined by numerous eminent physicians in big cities both in the United States and abroad, they were reluctant to make themselves available to a country doctor. Also, they were now their own men and had to please no master, who surely would have ordered them to strip and gratify the paying crowd. So the twins politely declined the doctor's request.

Ruffled by the two freakish Chinamen's challenge to his authority, Dr. Bolus announced that the twins were imposters, a declaration that caught fire in the room. The insult immediately opened up an old wound for the twins: In Liverpool, during their trip to England, they were attacked by an arrogant Briton who called them frauds after they had refused to undress themselves before the ladies in the room. At that time, as tender youths inexperienced in the world, they rushed toward the man from behind the table, Chang pulling out his purse and giving the man a shilling, asking him to leave. The Briton punched him in the nose instead.

And now, in what purported to be the entertainment center of a Southern village, they again faced the same baseless accusation. Their tempers flaring, they walked up to the doctor, and one of them knocked him down—from the perspective of their opponent and the bystanders, it was hard for anyone to figure out which of the twins had delivered the blow. Regardless, pandemonium ensued. Rushing to the defense of their village doctor, the crowd assailed the twins with a kettle of hot water, chairs, drinks, or whatever came in handy. Chang and Eng "narrowly escaped with their lives," wrote the Alabama *Athenian*. Since they delivered the first blow, the twins were arrested and taken before a magistrate. After an investigation, they "were bound to appear at the next Circuit Court in a bond for three hundred and fifty dollars. They gave the requisite security and were discharged."[4] The news about the incident reached as far as England, where the *Times* lampooned it as a "battle-royal in Athens," stressing the happy fact that the twins were not hurt but "bound over" for the flagellation of a country doctor.[5]

In the twins' income ledger, the entry for October 28 in Athens was marked with a cryptic "~."

A few days later, in Florence, Alabama, they appeared before the circuit judge, Sidney C. Posey. Hailing from Pendleton, South Carolina, Judge Posey also carried the license of a Methodist minister and was attended on his trips by a black slave, a wedding gift from his father-in-law, a wealthy plantation owner in Columbia, Tennessee.[6] During the hearing, Judge Posey, a Southerner who thoroughly understood a man's right to defend his honor in face of a false accusation, took it upon himself to verify the mysterious band, and, after being satisfied with the examination, dismissed the charges against the twins and required only that their manager, Charles Harris, publish a statement of explanation in the local paper so as to appease the agitated Athens citizenry. That judicious ruling led to an entry for November 1 in the twins' expense ledger: "Judge Posey for inserting C.H.'s statement of the Athens affray in Florence 'Gazette' $2."

Ironically, the Athenian fracas seemed to have boosted the twins' popularity in Alabama, for folks down South seemed to like nothing better than a good fight. For the three days Chang and Eng appeared in Florence, the receipts totaled more than $200. Their biggest haul was in Tuscaloosa, then the state capital, in western Alabama. Staying at a local tavern called Mr. Ewing's, Chang and Eng spent two days in this city by the Black Warrior River, paid a steep $27 for corporation tax, but grossed $308 in receipts. The hundred or so students of the newly founded University of Alabama were treated to a rare view of these wonders from afar, not realizing how these Siamese men, outlandish and freakish as they were, would slowly and resolutely inch themselves into a Southern world in ways no one could ever imagine. "For ways that are dark / And for tricks that are vain / The heathen Chinee is peculiar," as F. Bret Harte would suggest in his wildly popular satirical poem, "The Heathen Chinee" (1870).[7] But it was still four decades before that familiar nineteenth-century refrain made its way into the American lexicon.

The Siamese Twins, however, were hardly the only exotics in the Bible belt. In the woods south of Tuscaloosa, an area of backcountry that would become famous in the twentieth century thanks to the work of James Agee and Walker Evans, there was a town named Demopolis, where Chang and Eng would stop for one night. In the words of Carl Carmer, Demopolis was where "the Deep South's most romantic story had its beginning."[8] Just like the Siamese Twins, whose story began on the other side of the globe, the genesis of Demopolis also had to do with events that unfolded in a distant land.

On Bastille Day in 1817, a band of about 150 French exiles, led by General Charles Lefebvre Desnouettes and Colonel Nicolas Raoul, heroes of Napoleonic campaigns across Europe, arrived at what then was known as the White Bluff. They had been banished from their native land by King Louis XVIII following the downfall of Napoleon Bonaparte. Lured by the dream of a new beginning, they decided to settle in the wilderness of Alabama and grow olives and grapes to sustain themselves like common people. They first called their settlement "Aigleville" (French for "Eagleville"), in memory of their dethroned emperor, whose royal insignia included a figure of an eagle, but they later changed the name to "Demopolis" (meaning "city of the people"), in keeping with their desire to live among ordinary folks.

Women in silky, brocaded gowns and men in tricolored military uniforms, these aristocrats, who had never done a day's manual labor in their lives, set out courageously to clear woods, plow fields, raise cattle, milk cows, and cook meals over coals. In the evenings, after the sun had long set behind the white bluff by the river, they would light fires, play guitars, read books, drink rich wines from the Old World, and dance in the moonlight.

But the Gallic tale with a romantic beginning soon came to a tragic ending. The crops of olives and grapes failed year after year because these "farmers manqué" knew nothing about the soil or the frost that would soon ravage the Mediterranean trees and vines. Moreover, fever and diseases also significantly reduced the population of the colony. While the wealthiest among them could afford to live on imported goods (their own meager products were never adequate to sustain the group), the less fortunate had to lead lives severe beyond their imaginations. Colonel Raoul became a ferryman in a nearby creek, while his wife, formerly the Marchioness of Sinabaldi, flipped flapjacks for ferry passengers in a lonely cabin on the bank. When amnesty was finally granted by Louis Philippe a few years later, those who could afford it would either return to France or move on to other American cities. Their history remained star-crossed, for in 1822, on his way back to Europe, General Desnouettes drowned when his ship, the *Albion*, struck a reef off the Irish coast.

By the time Chang and Eng arrived in Demopolis, on February 26, 1834, the former French settlement had already lost most of its Gallic luster. Only a few of the olive trees that had survived frostbite were scattered around town, bearing fruit each year to the delight of the more hardy avian population. Anything else left of this strange episode of Alabama history seemed to be buried in place names scattered in the area, words with etymologies rooted in Napoleonic imperial dreams: Marengo, Linden, Arcola, and Moscow. The twins made stops at these Alabama towns and counties on their way back from a two-month tour in Mississippi and Louisiana, which included a stint in America's capital of carnival, New Orleans. Near Demopolis, they paid Colonel Raoul a dollar to be ferried across the creek and stayed at a hostel run by one Mr. Drummond. In a town of only a few hundred souls, their one-day show grossed $61. At the ticket price of twenty-five cents per person, not including the sale of lithographic portraits, biographical sketches, and cigars, it amounted to more than two hundred visitors. That's nothing less than a riot in the woods.

Perhaps the French authority had been right four years earlier, when they denied entry to the Siamese Twins for fear of maternal impressions. Judging by their phenomenal popularity among the French expatriates, it seems that the twins would not only wield a sort of necromantic power over pregnant women but also appeal to displaced souls, or anyone troubled by a sense of alienation from one's self. Whether it's Dr. Jekyll and Mr. Hyde or the picture of Dorian Gray, the freak, to quote

Flannery O'Connor again, is "a figure for our essential displacement," an estrangement from ourselves, from God.

As the twins traveled in the backwoods, bayous, and swamps of the antebellum Deep South, a fad simultaneously began sweeping through the United States, a new so-called science of mind, one lacking empty theological speculations and futile metaphysical doubts. It was nothing less than a supposed intellectual fever that would grip almost everyone in nineteenth-century America, including Chang and Eng.

Head Bumps

*A phrenologist and a mesmerizer came—and went again and left
the village duller and drearier than ever.*

—Mark Twain, *The Adventures of Tom Sawyer*

"The Siamese Twins," declared Orson and Lorenzo Fowler
in 1837, "furnish another striking example of the truth of
phrenological science."[1] By then, late into the decade when
Martin Van Buren was president, phrenology—which some regarded as
harmless quackery practiced upon the gullible, while others saw it as
a scientific discovery of the relationships between a person's character
and the shape of the skull—had reached the apex of its popularity in
the United States.

Whether chicanery or science, phrenology was first developed in Aus-
tria by German physician Franz Joseph Gall, who proposed that mental
phenomena have natural causes that can be determined. Gall believed
that the human mind is not unitary but is composed of independent
and ascertainable faculties that are catalogued under at least thirty-
seven rubrics, including Combativeness, Veneration, Benevolence,
Adhesiveness, Amativeness, Language, Murder, and so on. These faculties, or aspects of a person's character, are localized in different organs
or regions of the brain. "The development of these thirty-seven organs
affects the size and contour of the cranium, so that a well-developed
region of the head indicates a correspondingly well-developed faculty
(propensity) for that region. Consequently, it was thought possible that
a man could make a fairly accurate character analysis by studying the
shape of a subject's head in conjunction with his temperament."[2]

Gall's phrenological theory was introduced to the Anglo-American world by his collaborator and disciple Johann Gaspar Spurzheim. In Edinburgh, where the prestigious medical establishment regarded the new "science of mind" with skepticism, Spurzheim's lectures and publications in the 1810s found an important convert in a brilliant young barrister, George Combe. Revolting against his own Calvinist roots, Combe eagerly seized upon the optimistic new science that promised a way out of the pessimism, the doom and gloom caused by the Protestant beliefs in predestination and the total depravity of man. In his book *The Constitution of Man* (1828), perhaps the best known and most inspirational of all phrenological publications, Combe asked, "Why should man have existed so long, and made so small an advance in the road to happiness?" He suggested: "The grand sources of human suffering at present arise from bodily disease and mental distress . . . and these will be traced to infringement, through ignorance or otherwise, of physical, organic, moral, or intellectual laws, which when expounded, appear in themselves calculated to promote the happiness of the race." Now phrenology made it clear that "mental talents and dispositions are determined by the size and constitution of the brain," not by what Calvinists would call God's "unconditional election." Morality, therefore, became a science with the aid of phrenology.[3] In this way, phrenology offered a hopeful interpretation, one that banished the threat of dark recesses with an assurance that everything could be brought to light, to the surface.[4]

In 1829, the same year that the Siamese Twins had arrived in Boston, Combe's book was enjoying a vogue in America, a nation that had witnessed the decline of Calvinism and the rise of the common man. Even a skeptic like Ralph Waldo Emerson, otherwise averse to what he called a "shallow Americanism which hopes to get rich by credit, to get knowledge by raps on midnight table, to learn the economy of the mind by phrenology," had to admit that *The Constitution of Man* was "the best Sermon I have read for some time."[5] Whether or not Emerson would concede, there was an affinity between his transcendentalist idea of self-reliance and phrenology's pragmatic motto "Self-made or never made." Or, for that matter, the Jacksonian bugle call of the "manifest destiny" was an optimistic rhetoric just as phrenology was a hopeful hermeneutic.

Many of the pioneers of American medicine were also devotees of phrenology. John Warren, the Brahmin Harvard doctor who first examined Chang and Eng, had studied Gall's works as early as 1808 and had attended Spurzheim's Paris lectures in 1821. Warren incorporated phrenology into his Harvard lectures, and, beginning in 1820, he made it the subject of an annual address to the Massachusetts Medical Society.[6] Similarly, Dr. Philip Physick, another titan of medicine who also happened to have examined the twins, actually spearheaded the formation of the Central Phrenological Society in Philadelphia in March 1822.

When Spurzheim visited the United States in 1832—a trip comparable to Sigmund Freud's historic tour nearly a century later that would bring the gospel of psychoanalysis to America—the German phrenologist sparked a popular enthusiasm transcending the medical and scientific communities. Everywhere he went, he was mobbed; everywhere he spoke, the venue was packed. His landing in New York on August 7 was duly noted by Philip Hone in his diary: "Spurzheim, the celebrated phrenologist, a disciple of Dr. Gall, arrived here on Tuesday in the *Rhone* from Havre."[7] Spurzheim's appearance at Yale College's commencement made "the professors [fall] in love with him," with one of them remarking that "no stranger ever visited the United States who . . . possessed the power at once so fully to absorb and gratify the public mind." At his final stop in Boston, where he gave a series of eighteen public lectures on phrenology, Spurzheim was wined and dined by John Warren in the latter's capacity as the former dean of Harvard Medical School. Unfortunately, however, the strenuous schedule caused Spurzheim's health to fail, and he died in Boston on November 10, just days after Andrew Jackson's reelection. Dr. Warren, ever the impresario of medical theater, did the popularizer of phrenology the ultimate honor by performing a public autopsy on Spurzheim, preceded by a lecture at Harvard (even autopsies by that time had on occasion become public spectacles!). One might even say that Warren literally dined Spurzheim alive and dissected him dead. After a funeral attended by thousands, the man who brought phrenology to Anglo-America became the second person to be buried in Cambridge's newly opened Mount Auburn Cemetery—the nation's first rural cemetery—while his phrenologically superior brain, weighing a massive fifty-seven ounces, was kept at the Boston Athenaeum for posterity.

After Spurzheim's death, the task of championing the cause of phrenology fell to Combe and two newcomers, the Fowler brothers. While Combe remained the brain of phrenology (pun intended), it was the Fowlers who turned the new science into a practical profession and a feverish fad in America. The elder brother, Orson Fowler, who liked to ride the railroad because he believed it energized him with electricity, began his career in phrenology when he was still studying for the ministry at Amherst College. He teamed up with his classmate, Henry Ward Beecher, son of a Calvinist minister and brother of Harriet Beecher Stowe, in lecturing on the new science and giving character readings in nearby western Massachusetts towns. Upon graduation, while Beecher became a minister as planned (although he continued to use the pulpit to harangue his congregation about the virtues of phrenology), Fowler decided to answer his newfound calling. He initiated his younger brother, Lorenzo, into the cause, and the two started a lucrative phrenological tour in the Northeast, lecturing on the new science and examining heads for fees. The success of the Fowler brothers soon drew followers and emulators. "Others of the same stamp, foot-loose young men, some educated but others not, took off on the lecture trail," observes John D. Davies in *Phrenology, Fad and Science* (1955). "During the 1830's and 40's there was probably not a village in the nation that did not entertain at least one visit from an itinerant practical phrenologist."[8] Thus, on the busy open roads of America appeared a new figure—peripatetic as a Yankee peddler, entertaining as the Siamese Twins and other showmen. In Orson Fowler's own words, their modus operandi went like this: "Let me plant a course of lectures in a little village, containing but a single tavern, two stores, and a blacksmith's shop, and a dozen houses, and they flock in from their mountains and their valleys for ten miles in all directions, and fill up any meeting-house that can be found."⁹ The nation's long-lasting craze for phrenology was aptly portrayed in this chapter's Mark Twain epigraph, from *The Adventures of Tom Sawyer*, where the teenage protagonist lamented the unbearable boredom of village life after a spellbinding visit by a phrenologist and a mesmerizer, who often were the same person in disguises, as Melville shrewdly observed in *The Confidence-Man*.

To Combe and other brainier advocates, these practical phrenologists, who would apply calipers to measure head bumps and interpret characters for fees, had degraded the science and reduced it to the level of palmistry and fortune-telling, a mere charlatan's trickery performed at county fairs and in village squares. Some enterprising phrenologists would even stage exhibitions of giants, dwarfs, and other freaks as added attractions, or run a gambling scheme on the side for extra profit. As the con man Duke of Bridgewater admitted in *The Adventures of Huckleberry Finn*, he was a printer by trade but would also "do a little in patent medicines; theatre-actor—tragedy, you know; take a turn in mesmerism and phrenology when there's a chance; teach singing geography school for a change; sling a lecture, sometimes." In other words, he would do "anything that comes handy."¹⁰ But, thanks to the tireless efforts of the Fowler brothers, phrenology became a reputable science and art in nineteenth-century America, with a broad base and popular appeal. Phrenological theory thus was applied to fields as various as education, health, medicine, literature, religion, and career counseling. Celebrities who counted themselves as aficionados came from all walks of life, ranging from presidents to generals, writers, doctors, and tycoons.

It is now a story known to all students of literature that one day in July 1849, Walt Whitman walked into the Phrenological Cabinet on Nassau Street in New York and asked to have his head examined by Lorenzo Fowler. This visit was a turning point in Whitman's career, because his talent as a poet as well as his superior character as a man was confirmed by the phrenological findings:

You were blessed by nature with a good constitution and power to live to a good old age. . . . You have a large sized brain giving you much mentality as a whole. You are well calculated to enjoy social life—Few men have all the social feelings as strong as you have. . . . You choose to fight with tongue and pen rather than with your fist. . . . Your courage is probably more moral than physical. . . . You are a great reader and have a good memory of facts and events much better than their time. . . . You have a good command of language especially if excited.

Numerically, Whitman received top-notch scores on most of his faculties: 6 for Amativeness, Philoprogenitiveness, Adhesiveness, Inhabitiveness, Combativeness, Alimentiveness, Cautiousness, Conscientiousness, Individuality, Form, Size, Weight, Locality, Eventuality, Comparison, and Human Nature; 6 to 7 for Self-Esteem, Firmness, Benevolence, and Sublimity.[11] Whitman liked his phrenological chart so much that he would first publish it in the *Brooklyn Daily Times* and then bind it into the first three editions of *Leaves of Grass*, a collection of experimental poems full of phrenological references, such as

Who are you indeed who would talk or sing to America?
Have you studied out the land, its idioms and men?
Have you learn'd the physiology, phrenology, politics,
     geography, pride, freedom, friendship of the land?

Whitman included the phrenologist among those he called "the lawgivers of poets":

The sailor and traveler underlie the maker of poems, the Answerer,
The builder, geometer, chemist, anatomist, phrenologist, artist,
     all these underlie the maker of poems, the Answerer.

Among the phrenological categories, Adhesiveness, the organ of friendship and social attraction, was of particular interest to Whitman, a sexually active gay man living in the prohibitive milieu of Victorian America. As he wrote in the poem "So Long":

I announce adhesiveness, I say it shall be limitless, unloosen'd,
I say you shall yet find the friend you were looking for.[12]

Whitman's encounter with the Fowlers was not limited to a single head examination. Perhaps the Fowlers truly believed in their phrenological readings and saw real potential in the vivacious young man from Brooklyn. When other booksellers were reluctant to stock the obscure poet's first book, in part due to its erotic excess, Fowler's Phrenological Cabinet continued to keep it on the shelf and promote it for years. Undoubtedly, Whitman's career as a poet was deeply entangled with phrenology and its American champions.[13]

Two other giants of American letters, Melville and Poe, were also steeped in phrenological thinking. Melville devoted several earnest chapters to the hot-button topic in *Moby-Dick*, declaring in chapter 79, "The Prairie": "To scan the lines of his face, or feel the bumps on the head of this Leviathan; this is a thing which no Physiognomist or Phrenologist has as yet undertaken." Having chastised Gall and Spurzheim for failing "to throw out some hints touching the phrenological characteristics of other beings than man," Melville went on to draw an unusual phrenological chart of the sperm whale, from forehead to nose, from skull to hump, concluding that, phrenologically speaking, "the great monster is indomitable."[14]

Ever enthusiastic to probe the darkest recesses of the human heart, Poe wrote a rave review of a book on phrenology in 1836, claiming, "Phrenology is no longer to be laughed at. . . . It has assumed the majesty of a science."[15] In his own work, Poe also sprinkled phrenological gems generously, sparing no ink in describing the head shapes of the characters and discussing their corresponding faculties in such stories as "The Fall of the House of Usher" and "The Murders in the Rue Morgue." Poe's own phrenological portrait, published by the Fowlers in their journal, stated: "His phrenological developments, combined with the fiery intensity of his temperament, serve to explain many of the eccentricities of this remarkable man."[16]

Almost like a nineteenth-century Facebook database, a long gallery of phrenological portraits and readings was published and preserved by the Fowler brothers and their associates—profiles of famous as well as infamous Americans: John Adams, Thomas Jefferson, Andrew Jackson, Abraham Lincoln, Ralph Waldo Emerson, Horace Greeley, Nathaniel Hawthorne, John Brown, Frederick Douglass, Susan B. Anthony, Helen Keller, Louis Agassiz, Thomas Edison, John Jacob Astor, Cornelius Vanderbilt, and Andrew Carnegie, as well as John Wilkes Booth, Lizzie Borden, and Leon Czolgosz.

Also on this long list appear the names of Chang and Eng, whose ontological ambiguity had baffled the world. But the Fowler brothers, as it turned out, were not the first to examine the head bumps of the Siamese brothers. After spending the winter of 1833 in the Deep South, Chang and Eng slowly moved northward like migrating birds as the weather warmed up. From Alabama, they traveled to Georgia in March 1834, followed by Tennessee, South Carolina, North Carolina, and then Virginia, where they toured for two months in July and August. In September, they were booked, rather like a traveling Western show, by Rubens Peale, son of Charles Willson Peale, for display at his museums in New York, Albany, Philadelphia, and Baltimore for a period of twelve days in total, an arrangement that would become routine in the coming years. Fiercely independent, the twins were always proud of the fact that they never consigned themselves to be a permanent fixture at any museum or a part of any circus troupe. Their stints at the Peale museums gave them some needed respite from travel while providing a stable income. But they still kept their eyes on the road, and in the fall and winter of 1834, they continued to travel up and down the coastal states of Maryland, Virginia, and North Carolina, enjoying varying degrees of success.

At some point, their old manager James Hale, with whom they had stayed in constant contact for advice on show business and financial matters, suggested that they visit Cuba—an idea that sounded quite appealing to them. Thus, in March of 1835, Chang and Eng took off for the island country for a month. Upon their return from Cuba in late April, the twins again had an engagement at the Peale Museum in New York, this time for more than a month. After resting their tired feet, Chang and Eng spent the summer months of 1835 peregrinating in northern New York and Canada, shuttling back and forth across the border several times.

In June, when they traveled along the Erie Canal, they received a phrenological reading in the town of Schenectady, New York, an area that was not just the "Burnt-Over District" in the wake of the Great Awakening, but also on the route of the Fowler brothers' phrenology tour. According to a newspaper report, "The Editor of the Schenectady Reflector has taken the phrenological portrait of Chang and Eng, the Siamese Twins. He professes to be an adept in the science, and therefore well qualified to judge of character."[17] The "Editor of the Schenectady Reflector"—in fact, the *Schenectady Democrat and Reflector*—was Giles Fonda Yates, a Schenectady native who had graduated in 1816 from nearby Union College with Phi Beta Kappa honors. Working as a lawyer and editor of the leading local paper, Yates became a phrenology enthusiast at some point and would give head exams to townsfolk or travelers.[18]

On a quiet Sunday, June 14, the famous Siamese Twins rolled into town in a hired coach from Albany, where they had exhibited at Peale's Museum for two weeks. It was an unseasonably hot day for traveling, and the twins and their entourage had had to stop along the way to rest, spending twenty-eight cents on lemonade at a country store to quench their thirst.

Sitting in his empty office, Yates heard about the arrival of the twins. He felt a bit miffed because they had decided to advertise in his rival's paper, the *Schenectady Cabinet*. What he cared about was not the loss of fifty cents in advertising money, but precious publicity. After the twins had settled in at the City Hotel, run by Mr. Matthews, Yates paid them a visit, carrying a set of calipers in his pocket. A silver-tongued lawyer, Yates managed to convince the twins to allow a phrenological reading, despite the strong Siamese aversion to letting others touch their heads for fear of bad luck. As he later reported, Yates gave the twins "a very good set of bumps," complimenting them for their Mirthfulness, Benevolence, and Adhesiveness. One key finding of the examination was that the twins' "cerebral development indicates different powers of intellect." Based on that, Yates denied "the alleged identity of thought and feelings in the Twins." He cited as supporting evidence the 1831 Lynnfield Battle, when Chang was said to have been the "refractory" of the two who reacted more violently to the insult by the mob.[19]

Yates's amateurish reading and his assertion that the twins thought and felt differently would be disputed by the Fowler brothers, who would give them two official phrenological examinations. The first one took place in the fall of 1836. On that October day in New York City, when the leaves turned golden and the air filled with light and sparkle, Orson Fowler and his assistant, Samuel Kirkham, met up with the twins at the Washington Hotel on Broadway. Since their last examination by an obscure amateur, the twins had come to understand better the fad that had enthralled the nation. It seemed that everyone was eager to have a head-bump check—just as, in a few decades, Americans of every stripe would sit for their photographic portraits. In some ways, Fowler was less interested in the heads of the twins than trying to prove a point—that is, as he put it at the very beginning of the resulting report, the twins would "furnish another striking example of the truth of phrenological science." Against the enemies and skeptics of his cause, Fowler felt he could use the findings to prove the scientific nature of phrenology, for the conjoined bodies of Chang and Eng presented a unique opportunity. The Fowler brothers, who cowrote the report even though Lorenzo was absent from the exam, presented their case this way:

It is well known that their traits of character, including their feelings, passions, abilities, dispositions, modes of thinking, of acting, and so forth, are so much alike as frequently to start the pretense, and induce the belief, that they possess but *one mind*, or, at least, that, in consequence of the wonderful, *physical connexion* of their bodies, there exists between them a similar union of mind, or such a one as to cause both minds to think, feel, and act simultaneously and *alike*. Although this is a mere pretense, yet the foundation of it remained to be developed and explained by phrenology.

Unlike Yates, who amateurishly used his findings to dispel the common belief, the Fowlers started out with the unverified common assumption and ended up proving it with phrenological evidence: The twins were "found to be most wonderfully and strikingly *alike*, not only in size and general outline, but even in the minute development of nearly *all the phrenological organs*." Their heads, in other words, were near alike as two pins.[20] Strictly speaking, this report, published in 1837, was not a phrenological reading, for it contains no measurements, character analysis, or career predictions. The Fowlers were mostly interested in making their case against the charges of their opponents.

Eighteen years later, in 1854, when their cause had won the hearts and minds of most Americans—by then it was almost taken for granted that an applicant for a position as a train conductor or a jailer should present his phrenology chart as proof of his qualification—the Fowlers would perform another exam on the twins. This time, the report would be more detailed and, consequently, more revealing about the nature of phrenology as a racial discourse.

Like most phrenological readings, this one begins with the shape of the twins' heads, which were described as "very peculiar," for "nothing like it is ever found in the Caucasian head." Sounding a note of condescension toward both women and racial minorities, the report went on to say, "We have never before seen, even in our women, as high, long, and full a moral lobe, along with as narrow a head at the ears, as those of these twins." Again and again, the Fowler brothers ascribed phrenological results to racial differences and Siamese national character: "Their Benevolence is of the very largest order," whereas "Veneration is much larger than we almost ever find it in our own race," corresponding undoubtedly with "their nation's extreme devotion to their religion." Their Adhesiveness is also larger than any found in Caucasian men, and so is Parental Love or Inhabitiveness. "Judging from this," the phrenologists opined, "they must be a most affectionate and domestic people." Other national characteristics included small Hope and Conscientiousness, deficient Spirituality, moderate Mirth and Ideality, but very large Imitation. In conclusion, "Their organism, movement and texture, betoken a far less active, intense state of the nervous and cerebral systems, than is generally found in our own race. That is, their organic quality by no means comes up to the general average of the Caucasian variety."[21]

In this phrenological reading, conducted when the Civil War was looming on the horizon, we can detect a more virulent form of racism dominating popular thought. Phrenology, as we now know, was a precursor to some of the eugenic theories and racial discourses that would come to characterize America in the late nineteenth and early twentieth centuries. It was, as Nathaniel Mackey puts it, "a white way of knowing," a notion of racial determinism that assumed "human surfaces offer incontestable evidence of the qualities, capacities and traits not only of individuals but of groups."[22]

Unsurprisingly, the Fowler brothers' report was quite in keeping with some of the racially biased descriptions of the Siamese published by Western travelers during the same period. For instance, George Finlayson, the British surgeon on the Crawfurd Mission in 1821–22, applying principles of physiognomy and phrenology, made the following observations in his memoir: "The face of the Siamese is remarkably large, the forehead very broad, prominent on each side, and covered with the hairy scalp in greater proportion than I have observed in any other people." Based on these descriptions, Finlayson concluded that the Siamese, reflective of a larger Asian population supposedly more suited to perform menial labor, "would appear to be admirably calculated to execute and to undergo the more toilsome and laborious, but mechanical, operations which are the usual lot of the laboring classes of mankind. They have the frame, without the energy of London porters. The greater number of them are indeed more distinguished for mechanical skill, and patience under laborious occupations, than for brightness of imagination or mental capacity."[23]

In 1836, the same year when Orson Fowler was inspecting the heads of Chang and Eng in New York, William Ruschenberger, surgeon on the American mission, was applying calipers to the skulls of the Siamese in their native land. Here are some highlights from Dr. Ruschenberger's phrenological examination:

The forehead is narrow at the superior part, the face between the cheek bones broad, and the chin is, again narrow, so that the whole contour is rather lozenge-shaped than oval. The eyes are remarkable for the upper lid being extended below the under, at the corner next to the nose, but it is not elongated like that organ in the Chinese or Tartar races. The eyes are dark or black, and the white is dirty or of a yellowish tint. The nostrils are broad, but the nose is not flattened, like that of the African. The mouth is not well formed, the lips projecting slightly.

Ruschenberger, who would later practice in Philadelphia and become involved in the autopsy of Chang and Eng, went on to detail exact measurements of "four purely Siamese heads." Based on these phrenological numbers, the doctor, his conclusions portending more racially charged stereotypes of Asians in the next century, reached verdicts that resembled those of the Fowlers and Finlayson in racial views: "The Siamese, like all Asiatics of low latitudes, are disposed to indolence, and to the indulgence of the animal propensities. . . . They are mean, rapacious, and cruel; and never betray any of that high-toned generosity of feeling which wins our admiration or demands our respect. . . . The only commendable quality of the Siamese character, so far as I could learn, is their filial respect. . . . Like all ignorant and uneducated people, they are superstitious."[24]

As if it was not enough for Ruschenberger to degrade the character of the Siamese as a group, he went even further to tarnish the reputation of Siam's most famous representatives, robbing Chang and Eng of the only virtue he had generously granted the Siamese—filial piety. In his *Narrative of a Voyage Round the World*, Ruschenberger told this story:

We sat on the floor smoking and sipping tea for an hour or two with Piadadè, whom we found to be a mild good-hearted old man. The famous Siamese Twins were a theme of conversation. . . . "Where are the twins?" was asked of every one who visited the shore. Piadadè shook his head: "Their poor mother cry plenty about those boys. They say, they make plenty money—no send never any to their poor mother." In fact, they have in Siam the character of being dissipated and unfilial.[25]

When his two-volume travelogue was published in 1838, Ruschenberger's mention of the Siamese Twins caught the eye of a few newspaper editors, who reprinted the above snippet or paraphrased it, to the consternation of Chang and Eng.[26]

Despite these racially charged phrenological readings, ethnographic stereotypes, and character smears, the Siamese Twins were determined to pursue their happiness and liberty just as all white Americans, native or foreign-born, did, only with more grit and gusto. Even the most imaginative phrenologist, perhaps one gifted with a Whitmanesque vision, could not have prophesied a shocking new development in their singular American story.

Part Four

LOOK HOMEWARD, ANGEL

(1839–1861)

CHANG AND ENG'S HOUSE, TRAPHILL

☆ 23 ☆

Wilkesboro

O n a blissfully tranquil June morning in 1839, when the dogwood rioted in bloom and the honeysuckle drooped in heavy masses, a rickety buggy whisked into the dusty street of Wilkesboro, North Carolina.

A sleepy "holler" nestled in the foothills of the Blue Ridge Mountains, Wilkesboro lay on a lush, fertile land rimmed by the Yadkin River, whose headwaters in the mountains were nicknamed "the Tigris and the Euphrates of the Carolinas." Native Americans called the Yadkin the Sapona River, after the Saponi tribe.[1] Approaching Wilkesboro from the west, the Yadkin did a head fake and then snaked around the village, surging over the rocky bed. The roaring river was so limpid that when a Tory captain during the Revolutionary War tried to elude capture by hiding under water, he was easily spotted by his pursuers. The village center, built on the south side of the river, was a loose cluster of dull frame buildings, including a nondescript courthouse that had been built in the 1820s, a couple of churches, a jail, and a doctor's office. What truly distinguished this village center from countless others was a stately oak standing on a corner of the courthouse lawn. Known locally as the "Tory Oak," it had served during the American Revolution as a gibbet for five Tories hanged by Colonel Benjamin Cleveland, one of the founding fathers of Wilkesboro.

As if sensing the palpable presence of the historic tree, which had remained stalwart through the currents of time, the single-horse buggy stopped under the giant oak's sprawling shade. A small, tattered door opened, and out came, nimbly, the famous Siamese Twins. Patting the dust off each other's shoulders and recovering a bit from the rocky ride over mountain roads, the conjoined duo scanned the courthouse square with their squinting eyes. "Freaks!" yelled a snotty-nosed kid, stopping a few scattered pedestrians dead in their tracks. Everyone stared. The twins stared back, as they had done thousands of times, in cities as glamorous as London, Paris, and New York, and in seedy towns whose names they had long forgotten. Would this village by the Yadkin River become yet another insignificant smudge in their business ledger, with cash receipts and miscellaneous expenses squared off and balanced out?

Wilkes County was named, as was the town of Wilkesboro, in honor of John Wilkes, an English statesman and champion of American rights at the time of the Revolution. John Wilkes Booth, the future assassin of Lincoln, was related to the English political leader through his paternal grandmother.[2] Equal parts piedmont and mountain, the county in the heart of the Yadkin basin had been inhabited by Siouan-speaking tribes prior to the arrival of Europeans. Then colonial settlers of primarily Scots-Irish, German, and English extraction migrated here from Virginia and Pennsylvania via the Great Wagon Road and the Carolina Road. The most famous of these migrants was Christopher Gist, believed to be the first white man to settle in the area. Friendly with the Cherokees, Gist became a legendary Indian scout and surveyor— credited, perhaps apocryphally, with twice saving the life of Colonel George Washington. One of Gist's sons married an Indian girl, who gave birth to Sequoyah, the legendary inventor of the Cherokee alphabet.

As if Wilkes and Gist were not sufficient, Daniel Boone, the coonskin-hatted trailblazer of the American frontier, had a strong connection to Wilkes County. Brought by his parents to the Yadkin Valley as a kid from Pennsylvania, Boone had spent his formative years in the county, using it as a launch pad for his hunting expeditions to Kentucky, where he would eventually earn his reputation.

In addition to the highest-profile locals, many of the residents in this area were veterans of the American Revolution and the subsequent wars with the British and the Indians. Respectable gentlemen with names prefixed by titles of colonel, major, and captain, these decorated war heroes were joined by doctors, ministers, and planters to form the county's upper echelon, who lived on better, more fertile lands, while the less fortunate scattered around the woodland hills of the area, subsiding in huts, log cabins, and even in mountain caves. Geographically sliced off from the outside world, these mountaineers were fiercely independent, relying on what the land produced for sustenance: corn, tobacco, wheat, rye, oats, apples, peaches, grapes, and so on. In addition, some mountaineers eked out a living by what was known as "yarbin' it," the local colloquialism for gathering and selling roots, barks, and herbs.[3]

Not even the most renowned soothsayer could have guessed that this Arcadian locale would become, as I describe in the epilogue, the setting for one of the most popular sitcoms (or, rather, rubecoms) in twentieth-century America, *The Andy Griffith Show*. In the nineteenth century, a landing on the moon would have been even more imaginable than the arrival of television. To this day, we do not know what exactly had brought Chang and Eng to this sleepy holler, an even more rustic version of what would become the mythical Mayberry. During their decade-long tour, the twins had traversed the Rip Van Winkle State many times, but they had always traveled along the Eastern Seaboard or through the middle Piedmont Plateau, never to the remote upper airs of the mountainous western part of the state. The only time they almost came this way was in October 1834, when traveling from Virginia into North Carolina. They had planned to go from Danville, Virginia, to Wilkesboro, and they even had the handbills printed already, advertising that, "For One Day only, the United Brothers, Chang and Eng, will receive Visitors at the TENT," but for some unknown reason that trip never materialized. (Perhaps their horse took ill, as a bill from a veterinarian seems to suggest.)

Biographers, in fact, have speculated about the reason the Siamese Twins went to Wilkesboro. Shepherd M. Dugger, a Tar Heeler who claimed to have met the twins in person, maintained in his book, *Romance of the Siamese Twins* (1936), that it was a Wilkesboro doctor by the name of James Calloway who had invited the twins to come visit. Dugger believed that Dr. Calloway, a great-nephew of Daniel Boone and a graduate of the University of Pennsylvania, saw the twins' show in New York in the spring of 1839 and struck up a friendly conversation with them. Learning of Chang and Eng's fondness for outdoor sports, Calloway told the twins that Wilkes County, where he had set up a medical practice, "was replete with clear streams teeming with fine fishes; that the hills and mountains abounded in deer and wild-turkeys, with smaller game, as squirrels and pheasant galore." Calloway warmly invited the twins to come visit. This was an explanation perpetuated by Irving Wallace and Amy Wallace in their biography. But recently, Joseph Orser, in his superb study of the twins, dismissed Dugger's view, citing evidence that Calloway could not have met the twins in New York in the spring of 1839 because they were touring in the South during those months—as indeed they were.[4]

Regardless, Chang and Eng clearly had planned for this trip and paid Dr. Calloway a friendly visit after their arrival. Earlier, when they were still touring in Georgia, Charles Harris had left the caravan and gone to New York on May 8. He would stay there for two weeks, apparently to make arrangements for his and the twins' retirement from a life on the road. On June 7, when the twins got closer to Wilkesboro, Harris returned from New York to join them. After a long stagecoach ride, Harris arrived in Wilkesboro on June 20. According to the expense ledger, Harris paid "one stage fare extra for luggage," indicating that he had brought an unusually large amount of provisions. Ledger entries under the heading "Payments by C Harris when at New York" give us a clue: "a Box to hold clothes for CE," "6 Cakes of Windsor Soap," "a Nail Brush," "getting Shirts from Jersey City," "2 Horse Collars," "2 Pole Straps," "2 Breast Straps," "a Pair of Driving Gloves for Chang," and so on. It seemed that they were making plans for a long or even permanent stay.

This remote area had much to offer as a retirement place for Chang and Eng, who by now were road-weary and tired of the prying eyes of the public. The forests, creeks, and rivers were also ideal for hunting and fishing, a fact borne out again by their ledger. In early June, en route from Salisbury to Wilkesboro, the twins incurred costs on many items related to outdoors sportsmanship: "Copper Caps for gun $0.75," "Shot $0.50," "Lead for bullets $0.70," "Two Hats $2.50," "Copper Caps $2.00," "Gun Smith $0.38," and "Fishing Hooks & Lines $0.30." Riding along the same route about a decade earlier, Elisha Mitchell, a geologist from the University of North Carolina at Chapel Hill, had contemplated the suitableness of this area for a reclusive life. In July 1828, Mitchell wrote in one of his diary letters to his wife: "Here, according to some men calling themselves philosophers, in retirement shut out from intercourse with the world by the sides of these streams and hemmed in by these mountains—man may, if he will, be happy."[5] In another letter a few days later, Mitchell compared the local scenery to Pennsylvania's bucolic Wyoming Valley before the onslaught of industrialization, and he considered it to be "the place for a person to retire to, who has been ill-treated by the world and is disgusted with it." He recommended it as a retreat to a lawyer friend, painting a scene of rustic living in the woods, "telling him how finely he could shoot bears for his wife to eat and get fine skins to warm her—the orchard would also furnish fine whisky for her as well as the field the best of wheat and he could present the whole to her as the product of his own labor and a testimonial of his love."[6] Chang and Eng's imagination did not extend yet to domestic bliss, but they certainly yearned for seclusion.

They were now twenty-eight years old—healthy, energetic, and experienced in the ways of the world. After a decade of hard work and frugal living, they impressively had amassed more than $10,000 in savings. There was one item in their ledger that recurred almost every month: a $3 payment for "Premium on Draft to NY," presumably for the cost of sending their hard-earned dollars to a New York savings bank. The press, prone to exaggeration, had speculated that they were worth between $40,000 and $60,000. The New Orleans *Times-Picayune* even claimed that by the end of 1838, the twins had "made upwards of $100,000 clear by exhibiting themselves in this country."[7] Still, the $10,000 they had stashed away was a handsome sum and could go a long way in a remote and economically moribund area like western North Carolina.

Things were clearly winding down, as revealed by their relaxing schedule en route to Wilkesboro. They did, however, have one show in Salisbury on June 1 and then another in Statesville on June 3, netting $28.36 and $35.50, respectively.

For the rest of the time, almost as if returning to their country roots, they hunted, fished, or simply drove around to take in the mountains. The closer they got to their destination, the more they seemed to enjoy the area. Though it was a different kind of lushness from their native Siamese tropical green, with no palm fronds sounding off the quick beat of a monsoon rain, they felt weirdly at home immersing themselves in the running streams, soft hills, sparkling air, and blue mountains as ancient as time. They had never felt so happy since leaving Siam, free like the early days when they were kids cruising down the muddy Meklong in their dinghy, herding a team of quacking ducks.

On the night of June 10, they repaired to an old Dutchman's hostel a few miles outside of Wilkesboro. The next morning, after fixing the halter of the buggy, they trundled into the village under the curious eyes of the townsfolk, who, having been tipped off by an advance notice, were expecting the famous twins. Stopping under the oak tree in the village square, they walked up to a boardinghouse run by Abner Carmichael, the county sheriff and father-in-law of Dr. Calloway.

After freshening up, they began to receive visitors, which took on all the hoopla of a papal visit, because the small front room of Carmichael's boardinghouse was suddenly choked with every vestige of local humanity. Peter Marsh, the advance runner sent by the twins to Wilkesboro a few days earlier, had done a stellar job of advertising with handbills and posters, and word spread among mountain folk faster than a patch of kudzu. By the day's end, the twins had grossed the opulent sum of $47.25. At a stiff price of twenty-five cents per head, it meant that there had been a gaggle of two hundred visitors.

Having satisfied the curiosity of the good folks of Wilkesboro, the twins spent the next two weeks exploring the area. They each got a haircut, eschewing the Chinese queues they had maintained for mercenary purposes since the days in Meklong. They bought two hats to

shade them from the warm June sun and two pairs of summer trou-
sers. Equipped with hunting rifles and fishing gear, they roamed the
mountains, woods, and creeks, almost like two Siamese Daniel Boones.
Cherries were in season, and they bought baskets of them from "an old
negro woman," as recorded in their ledger. The return of Charles Harris
from New York on June 20 brought a temporary break from these happy
outings in the woods, as they rummaged through the luggage for items
they would need for setting up a homestead. All five of them—Chang
and Eng, Harris, Marsh, and the driver, George Prendergast—would
stay, on and off, for two months at Carmichael's boardinghouse, using
it as a base for their local adventures.

As they wound down life on the road, the twins did a few more shows
in neighboring counties: Jonesville on June 24, Williamsburg on June
25, grossing meager amounts of $18.50 and $13.75, respectively. Then
they traveled to Ashe County, on the border between North Carolina
and Virginia, for one last hurrah. The entourage left Wilkesboro two
days before the Fourth of July and rode along the foothills of the Blue
Ridge. They stayed for one night at Mrs. Colvard's, a hostel at the foot
of the Blue Ridge where Elisha Mitchell had also stayed in July 1828.
Mitchell wrote in his diary letter: "At Mrs. Colvards the fare was rather
hard; no tea or coffee but excellent potatoes."[8]

The next morning, as the twins continued to ride through the ragged
ranges, more than a thousand miles to the south the American-built
schooner *La Amistad* had quietly departed Havana, Cuba, where the
twins had once toured. On this day, fifty-three Mende slaves, led by
Sengbe Pieh, revolted against the Spanish crew and attempted to steer
the ship back to Africa. The subsequent capture and trial of the rebel
slaves would spark a firestorm in the United States. In the heat of the
public debate over what to do with the captives if they were to gain
freedom, the freakish figure of the conjoined twins came to the mind
of some opinion makers, who suggested that "they will not be allowed
by a Christian public, to be led about for show, like the Siamese Twins,
where the benign rays of Christianity can never reach them."[9]

Ashe County, the location of the twins' last performance, was a mountainous plateau more than three thousand feet in mean elevation, named after the state's governor, Samuel Ashe. "There are more cattle than people in the county, and more sheep than cattle," was a local saying used to describe the area. Jefferson, the county seat, was surrounded by mountains: To the west, cutting off the afternoon sun, was Paddy, named for a man hanged at its base. Phoenix Mountain was to the north. To the south lay "Nigger Mountain," named for a cave at its summit, five thousand feet above sea level, which often was used as a hideout by fugitive slaves. The other explanation for the name, however, "points to the mountain's black granite outcrop," a feature identified by Dr. Mitchell during his field trip in 1827 but reflecting the preponderance of racism even built into the geography.[10]

The sparsely populated area around Jefferson had a long history of conflict and strife. Settled by veterans of the Revolutionary War, the town was one of the first in America to be named after the nation's founding father, Thomas Jefferson. Many of the county's residents were living embodiments of frontier trials and patriotic sacrifice, real-life stories that would make James Fenimore Cooper's *Leatherstocking Tales* or Mary Rowlandson's captivity narrative sound like preposterous Yankee concoctions. One woman by the name of Lydia Waters, though not as literary as Mary Rowlandson, had an experience just as horrific as what was depicted in that classic captivity narrative: "In 1800 unidentified Indians captured eleven-year-old Lydia and her younger brother as the family approached their new home on the South Fork," as Martin Crawford tells us in his in-depth historical study of Ashe County. "Spared her brother's scalping and death on account of her 'beautiful golden hair,' Lydia was enslaved and for two years suffered brutal hardships at the hands of her captors. These included having her hair torn out and being branded on the neck with hot spears and irons. After an exchange of prisoners, Lydia was released and returned to her family, but they did not initially recognize her because she was so disfigured by the branding and her hair had turned pure white." And now Lydia Waters Brown, a widow in her fifties, was presiding over a large family household on the North Fork.[11]

The story of Captain Martin Gambill was also a local yarn that had regional and national resonance: In 1780, Captain Gambill, a thirty-year-old Virginia-born pioneer, rode a hundred miles to warn the American commander of the impending British approach, thus playing a pivotal role in a battle that proved a turning point in the war. Disabled in the left arm at the Battle of Kings Mountain, this southern Paul Revere settled with his family in the area, serving as the county's first tax collector and first sheriff.[12] When the Siamese Twins arrived in 1839, Captain Gambill had passed away, but his widow, Nancy, and their sons Martin and Jesse, still resided in the area. In the coming years, the twins would frequently carry on commercial transactions with the Gambills, buying fodder, brandy, and livestock from them.

Now, however, after half a day of hard riding on mountain roads, the twins and their party finally arrived in Jefferson, locale of their last performance. On Main Street, lined by rows of blackheart cherry, the twins pulled up at the boardinghouse run by Colonel George Bower, Ashe County's wealthiest man and leading politician. Settlers in the central part of the county in the wake of the Revolutionary War, the Bowers were true founders—in 1800, the family had provided, at the nominal price of $100, the fifty-acre land upon which Jefferson, as the county seat, was to be located. In his prime, Bower could boast of more than a thousand acres of improved land, thirty-four slaves, and a fortune estimated to be over $122,000.[13] In 1861, while pursuing a fugitive slave, Bower drowned in the Yadkin near Wilkesboro. The *North Carolina Standard* eulogized him as "a striking example of the honest, straightforward old time public men of the state who are rapidly passing away."[14] The twins would stay at this old-timer's boardinghouse for two nights and incur $10 in expenses, in addition to thirteen cents paid to the hostel's black servant for shining their boots, a behavior anticipating their complicity with a binary white–black hierarchy in which they clearly identified with the white.

Befittingly, given the area's illustrious patriotic past, it was in Jefferson on July Fourth that Chang and Eng gave their career-ending performance—while fireworks and guns popped off everywhere in this young nation. Far away in New York, where President Martin Van Buren was visiting, the whole city, as someone told Edgar Allan Poe in a letter, was "in perfect confusion." Poe's confidant continued to inform him: "The President's visit and the celebration of the Fourth of July have turned people's brains. I have never heard such an incessant popping and squibbing in my life before. The whole place appears under arms."[15] Western North Carolina was not noted for raucous celebrations of the Fourth of July, with the possible exception of Salem, where the Moravians would pray for peace and sing "The Psalm of Joy," accompanied by a trombone. That annual performance had first started in 1783 and was in fact the nation's earliest official Independence Day celebration.[16]

In Jefferson, the twins discovered that a horse show was the local custom on the Fourth. The program included a horse race down the Main Street, a display of jumping horses, and pony rides for kids. On this day in 1839, the appearance of the twins in Ashe County seemed to instantiate a new national existence for the town. After the horse show was over, trophies awarded and ribbons taped, the locals packed the courthouse for a peek at the famous Siamese Twins. Sensing that this might be the grand finale of their decade-long road show, Chang and Eng put in extra effort entertaining and indulging these mountain folks, who had no idea that the twins were planning to settle down among them. For too long, the twins had been carnival clowns. On this carnivalesque holiday, no one really understood what Chang and Eng were secretly celebrating, perhaps with a stifled chuckle, while grossing $38.60 in receipts.

≈ 24 ≈

Traphill

Traphill—a rustic name derived from rail-pen traps that an early settler had built on the hills to ensnare wild turkeys—sat quietly in a verdant valley between the Blue Ridge and Stone Mountain, twenty miles northeast of Wilkesboro. Close to the Roaring River, Traphill was so isolated that later it would become the locale of frequent robberies and murders by bushwhackers and deserters during the Civil War. And if we move the needle of time even a bit farther toward the future, Traphill would become a center for mass production and exportation of moonshine in the Prohibition era. In the hills, hollows, caves, and "cutthroat ridges"—so named because they were inaccessible to intruders without the use of lethal force—flourished countless moonshine stills hidden well beyond the reach of law. Even as late as the 1960s, as depicted on *The Andy Griffith Show*, the area was still a haven for bootleggers.

It was here that Chang and Eng, outlaws in a very different sense, would build their first homestead, buying a plot of land and signing a deed:

> October 17, 1839. From Caleb Martin to the Siamese Twins, Chang & Eng. 100 acres plus 50 acres, for $300. Along Little Sandy Creek.[1]

Closing the deal, the seller, an honest, red-faced planter, was flummoxed when both of his hands were shaken simultaneously over a transaction.

To make the occasion even more surreal, at least for the mountaineer, the twins, as legend has it, paid for the purchase with a bag of tingling silver coins.[2]

The land purchase was the first step the twins took to plant their roots in the Southern soil, after a summer of peregrination, search, and happenstance. Having performed their last show in Jefferson on July Fourth, the twins spent the next three months roaming the hills and hollows, looking for game, fish, scenery, and a place they could call home. Once again, their expense record captured a vivid picture of their movements. For the months of July and August, expense items that constantly showed up in their ledger included lead, buckshot, bullets, gunpowder, copper caps, and bills for boarding outside Wilkesboro. They had traveled so much during these hot months that horseshoe-ing became a recurrent entry, as did laundry and bootblacking: "July 18. Charles the negro for cleaning boots $1.50." On July 20, they paid sixty cents for a tin bucket in Traphill, possibly for holding fish they had caught in the nearby river. That fishing and hunting trip might have led to their eventual move to Traphill. According to Joseph Orser, their initial connection to this neck of the woods was Robert J. Baugus, a slaveholding farmer, who also ran a boardinghouse.[3] When the twins and their entourage—in addition to Charles Harris, two other men, Peter Marsh and George Prendergast, continued to be on the payroll until the end of August—stayed at Baugus's, affections grew between Harris and one of the Baugus girls, Fanny. The budding romance soon blossomed into earnest courtship. Over the years, thanks to the gener-ous salary the twins had paid him, Harris had built up a sizable nest egg, which would make him a good catch for any young woman in Wil-kes County. In October, Harris and Fanny became engaged to marry, and Harris decided to settle permanently in the area where his in-laws had an extensive network of family ties. In this way, Harris, an Irish-man and a stranger who ordinarily would have been viewed with suspi-cion by the mountaineers, was accepted into the community. In turn, this opened the door for Harris's closest associates, Chang and Eng.

October became a month for celebration, and the twins and Harris seemed to be having their own Oktoberfest, a ritual for which North Carolina would become famous. In addition to the twins' buying land and Harris's getting hitched, the three foreigners also took another major step toward acclimating themselves in America: applying for citizenship. On October 12, 1839, Chang and Eng filed a petition to the Superior Court of North Carolina to become naturalized United States citizens. Their sworn statement—in essence, a micro-autobiography submitted on October 1—read:

Chang and Eng (commonly known as the Siamese Twins) represent to this Honorable Court that they are natives of the kingdom of Siam, in Asia; that they arrived in Boston, Massachusetts, United States, on the 16th day of August, 1829. In October of that year they went to England and returned to the United States in March, 1831, and resided therein without leaving there until the fall of 1835, when they went to lower Canada, soon after they went to the continent of Europe and were absent about 12 months. After their return in 1836, they went to the province of lower Canada where they remained until October 1836, when they returned to the United States and have continued therein without leaving there ever since; and since the 1st day of June 1839, have continued within the State of North Carolina; they further represent that during their continuance within the United States they have behaved as men of good moral character; that they are attached to the principles of the Constitution of the United States and are well disposed to the good order and happiness of the same—and they here before this Honorable Court declare their intention to become citizens of the United States and to renounce his [sic] allegiance to the King of Siam and of every other state, King or Prince and Potentate, and they respectfully pray that this Honorable Court may receive their declaration, made before this Court with the view of becoming naturalized citizens of the United States and

that a record thereof be made and such order or judgment in the
premises as is by law required.

CHANG

ENG

Sworn to before me, Oct. 1,
1839. J. Gwyn, Jr. C.S.C.[4]

It was puzzling that the twins were able to acquire citizenship when
federal laws at the time forbade this. The 1790 Naturalization Act limited the privileges of naturalized citizenship to "free white persons," a
legislation that, incredibly, would not be repealed until 1952. Even the
two laws enacted later—the Fifteenth Amendment of 1870 granting
citizenship to African Americans and the Snyder Act of 1924 recognizing indigenous people as citizens—would not have applied to Chang
and Eng. But in the years before the rise of anti-Asian or anti-Chinese
sentiments, loopholes did exist to allow a small number of "Orientals"
to become citizens. According to John Tchen, at least one Chinese-born
male had been naturalized by the time the twins took their oath, a seaman who had come to America in the same year as did the twins, anglicized his name to John Houston, and married an Irish woman in New
York. In subsequent years, a handful of Chinese were also naturalized
in the state of New York.[5]

One reason why some Chinese were able to fly under the radar might
have had to do with the fact that before the 1849 gold rush, the number
of Chinese in the United States was minuscule. Sightings of individual
Chinese were reported in Pennsylvania as early as 1785, and the few
documented examples of migration were mostly caused by returning
missionaries who had brought Chinese men and women back with them
to work either as servants or interpreters. For instance, in 1842, Reverend William J. Boone, founder of the American Episcopal Mission in
China—or, one might say, a trailblazer like his distant relative, Daniel Boone—brought back Sin Say, a language teacher, and Wong Kong
Chai, a young man who helped to care for Boone's children.[6] These
long-queued Chinese were rare sights in America—as rare as the Sia-

mese Twins in North Carolina. In fact, the US Census Bureau did not have a category for Chinese until 1870, when the color/race question was expanded to include "C" for Chinese, which in turn stood for all East Asians. Before that, the Chinese were considered white for census purposes. In the early nineteenth century, the near-invisibility of the Chinese as a racial group ironically had worked in their favor at times, as in the case of the naturalization of the Siamese Twins.

In circumventing legal restrictions, the twins might also have received help through the local network. Orser points out that the county's superior court clerk, James Gwyn, who notarized and processed the twins' petition, knew them well because he had also stayed at Abner Carmichael's boardinghouse whenever court was in session. Friendships struck up among fellow boarders at a country inn might not always have been as strong as the bond between Ishmael and Queequeg, but familiarity grown out of greetings at the breakfast table, postprandial fireside chats, and bed sharing (called "bunking" at the time) when necessary would foment a relationship good enough to get things done at the county courthouse. As Orser puts it:

> Until the 1870s, county officials determined a person's fitness for citizenship. Local standards, not national laws, influenced the process. The twins were applying in a county that had very few immigrants and no other Asians, in a region whose color line was drawn decisively between white and black, in a court where they had been neighbors with the man administering the oaths. The twins were able to take advantage of the community's standards and its social network to gain citizenship.[7]

The drama of what sociologists have called *Gemeinschaft* (community) versus *Gesellschaft* (society)—the dichotomy between communal, personal dealings and systemic, impersonal interfaces—seemed to be played out in full view by the twins' experience. Even more than a century later, in the early 1990s, when I, as a struggling foreign student in Alabama, wanted to open a Chinese restaurant in Tuscaloosa and went to the city hall to apply for a business license, the amiable clerks there, looking at me as though I were fresh off the boat, never bothered to inquire about my immigration status, which could have jeopardized my chances of getting a license. Federal law be darned, these local folks were just happy to see a new business in town, another place where they could order egg rolls and General Tso's chicken, followed by the obligatory reading of fortune cookies.

In the case of the twins, they might also have benefited from the fact that they were world-class "celebrities," which would open many doors for them in a small place like Traphill.

Having acquired land and citizenship, these two new Americans set out to get themselves settled. The first order of business was to have a house built. Next to the bubbling creek and overlooking the single-rock Stone Mountain, the wooden house eventually was "two stories high, with a spacious veranda on three sides of the ground floor." It sported an extra-wide staircase to make it easier for the twins to ascend side by side to the second floor. There were two smaller buildings next to the house, one used as a kitchen, which contained "the largest fireplace in the area," and the other as "a dwelling for slaves, a storehouse, and a stable for horses." One other special feature about the house was that most of the rooms were designed with oversize windows, because the twins "wanted a view from every part of the house, as well as plenty of daylight inside."[8] The windows in the back, in particular, presented a spectacular view of Stone Mountain, the largest monadnock in North America, a twenty-five-square-mile pluton with a dome shape and a surface resembling a lunar landscape. The mountain air was, in the words of the geologist Dr. Mitchell, "salubrious and healthy." In the coming years, tourists seeking to restore health would, as their doctors recommend, come to this area for clean air and mineral waters.[9]

While their house was being built, Chang and Eng, almost as though they were newlyweds, slowly began to accumulate such household items as dishes, knives and forks, linen for sheets, funnels, pitchers, door locks, candlestands, and so on. When the house was ready for them to move in, they dispatched Harris to New York for a shopping spree. Their house might not have been as gorgeous as those big mansions along the Yadkin River, but, given a certain acquisitive proclivity, they knew how to live, and in style. The luxurious items Harris brought back from the big city, recorded in their ledger as "Articles purchased for the private use of CE by Harris at New York in June 1840," included rugs, silverware, ivory knives and forks, ivory carvers, brass candlesticks, tea trays, glasses, tumblers, tablecloths, silk handkerchiefs, wool shirts, soap, tea, coffee, brandy, sauce, spice, and more. They spent a total of $467.62½ on these eighty or so items.

Even though their $10,000 savings would make them two of the richest men in Wilkes County, Chang and Eng, parsimonious by nature, did not want to live the idle life of country squires. Some newspapers reported that they had "purchased a farm" in North Carolina and had "gone farming."[10] In reality, they had at first tried their hands at commerce. These former duck fanciers set up a general store in Traphill and started trading merchandise. Most of the store inventory, an assortment of groceries, hardware, crockery, and other "notions," came from local sources. They bought beef, pork, corn, brandy, potatoes, coffee, turkey, bacon, eggs, cloth, and household articles from farmers and suppliers in the area, and they sold or bartered these at a profit. For instance, according to their account book, for a bushel of wheat they paid 75 cents and sold at 96 cents, netting a 28 percent profit. Or, they paid 37½ cents for a bushel of corn and sold at 49 cents on average, netting a 30 percent profit. They also bought beef, coffee, and cows from James Gwyn, their inside man at the county court; pigs from Nancy Gambill, widow of the famous patriot; brandy and cutting knives from her son, Martin Gambill; and honey from farmer Hardin Spicer. When a local planter died and his effects went on sale, the twins grabbed the opportunity and bought a gallimaufry of household things that they could retail at their store: stone jars, mugs, scythe blade, shear plough, hinges, and cast fire-iron. Their customers were also local; often the names that showed up in their expense book as sellers would reappear on their sale slips as buyers of other merchandise.[11] This was a close-knit community where almost everything was produced and consumed locally, giving these mountaineers the strength of rugged individualism but also limiting the prospect of economic growth due to a lack of commerce with the outside world.

While running the general store, the twins continued to improve their homestead and their land, behaving more like gentry than greenhorns. They had no problem hiring maids to do household work, borrowing slaves from neighbors to do odd jobs, and employing masons and carpenters for home improvements. The names of some local women— such as Charlotte Pratt, Sally Walker, Rodha Rose, Polly Rose, Hetty Poplin, and Mary Tallby—regularly appeared on the ledger as recipients of wages. In November 1839, the twins borrowed slaves from David Yates and Abner Carmichael, and the next February they twice hired a slave named Lunn and paid his owner, Captain John Johnson, for the temporary employment. The male counterparts of some of those hired maids also showed up in the ledger: In 1840, Jesse Poplin was paid forty-five cents for splitting rails on February 27, and then $4 for the more demanding work of cleaning up the swamp on their land on August 8. Edward Rose was paid seventy-five cents for making two pairs of shoes and fifty cents for repairing boots on March 13. After a stormy spring in 1841, the house needed more work. In June, John Holloway of Traphill was hired for five days to build a chimney, fix the hearth, and put rock pillars under the house; he was assisted by another local man, John Sparks, a regular visitor at the general store. Records do not indicate how the local craftsmen felt about working for the twins, but money surely overcame any prejudice, while the slaves simply had no choice. Whether the slaves particularly resented being treated like chattel by these "freaks" who were only off the boat by a dozen years is another question that will remain buried in history, but the fact that local community members trusted Chang and Eng enough to rent out their slaves is telling, and it reveals both how the twins came to see their own new status in the Southern hierarchy and how they quickly came to be accepted as part of the oppressor class.

In this insulated rural community, far from the madding crowd, Chang and Eng, as a reporter from nearby Salisbury put it, "appeared in their unconstrained condition much more amiable and interesting than when encountering the gaze of the wondering crowd." They were, in fact, "as happy as lords," which they, as soon-to-be slaveholders, had become.[12]

A letter the twins wrote to their "discoverer," Robert Hunter, described in their own words the kind of leisurely life these two country lords were living:

> We live way off in the back wood at the foot of the mountains called the Blue Ridge—in a very healthy country within 25 miles of the State of Virginia and fifty miles from the State of Tennessee. We have wood and water in great abundance and our neighbors *are all on an equality* [italics added], and none are very rich—people live comfortably, but each man tills his own soil. . . . We enjoy ourselves pretty well, but have not as yet got married. But we are making love pretty fast, and if we get a couple of nice wives we will be sure to let you know about it.[13]

The letter is revealing in several ways, especially since it does not regard the slaves as "people" and certainly not people benefiting from any sort of "equality" bestowed on the white—and, in this case, Chinese—population with regard to social caste or wealth. Finally, the last sentence may sound like a joke, a typical Siamese Twins' tongue-in-cheek self-mockery. But as the world would soon find out, they were, to use the local parlance, serious as a stone.

A Universal Truth

It is a truth universally acknowledged," Jane Austen declared in her classic opening of *Pride and Prejudice* (1813), "that a single man in possession of a good fortune, must be in want of a wife."[1] What the astute observer of the cloistered life of British landed gentry at the end of the eighteenth century could not have imagined was the possible complication involving the status of "a single man." What if the single man were physically tied to another, as in the case of the Siamese Twins? Would the universal truth still be universal?

It would be decidedly unfair for us to disparage Austen for her lack of imagination or foresight. In 1843, when the news surfaced about the double wedding of Chang and Eng to two white sisters in a remote corner of North Carolina, most Americans were surprised, shocked, stunned, disgusted, or simply incredulous. MARRIAGE EXTRAORDINARY, screamed the headline in the *Carolina Watchman*. "Ought not the wives of the Siamese Twins to be indicted for marrying a quadruped?" asked the *Louisville* (Kentucky) *Journal*. William Lloyd Garrison's *The Liberator*, touting abolitionist and highly religious agendas, condemned the union as "bestial." The *Greensborough* (North Carolina) *Patriot* resorted to a bare-bones notice of the fact and a disdainful aside, "Comment is useless."[2] Nonetheless, everyone was asking, "How did it happen?" To answer that question, we need not only heed the wisdom of Austen's seemingly universal truth but also examine Chang and Eng's real-life situation against the larger canvas of American culture as it entered the straitlaced, chastity-belted Victorian Age.

Since their arrival in North Carolina in June 1839, Chang and Eng, having been accepted as honorary whites in the Southern hierarchy of races, were two reasonably happy "lords" busy running their general store, raising corn and hogs, and traveling constantly to Wilkesboro and the surrounding area for business or pleasure. About eight miles northwest of the county seat was Mulberry Creek, a valley that grew out of a natural pass through the Blue Ridge, cut by a steep and twisting road that presented broad vistas. Traveling in this direction, the twins often stopped by the residence of David Yates, a rich planter with six children, seven slaves, and an estate that grew to a thousand acres. In his biography of the twins, Judge Jesse Graves described the Yates domicile as a large house standing upon a high hill, painted in white, surrounded by orchards and slave cabins, which gave the place "an aristocratic aspect."[3] Alston Yates, David's oldest son, was a frequent customer at the twins' store, having purchased such items as linens, ladles, axes, locks, hinges, coats, shirts, pantaloons, dried fruits, tables, tubs, buckets, and even a book on constellations. Occasionally, the twins would "borrow" a slave from David Yates to work on their land. Since state laws did not allow slaves to hire themselves out for extra work, the twins would have to pay Yates the wages. Their relationship became even closer when, in November 1840, the oldest Yates daughter, Letha, married Samuel Baugus, brother of Charles Harris's wife, Fanny. In this remote mountainous region, blood is certainly thicker than water. "So in their frequent visits to and from town," as Graves put it, "Chang and Eng fell into the habit of stopping at Esq. Yates for dinner, or in the evening to stay all night and chat with the old gentleman and the old lady."[4]

As the friendship grew, the twins turned their not-inconsiderable attention to the two younger Yates daughters, Sarah and Adelaide, who had reached the prime age of (as was said then) maidenhood at eighteen and seventeen, respectively. Not regarded as classic beauties, the two girls, nurtured by the mountain climate, were vivacious, imaginative, and, in nineteenth-century parlance, exuberant like wildflowers. Simpler in personality and plumper in body than her younger sister, Sarah had "rich, auburn hair, fine teeth, and hazel eyes." Adelaide was a tall, slender brunette with "a free and open countenance."[5]

The twins had first met these girls at the wedding of either Charles Harris and Fanny Baugus or Samuel Baugus and Letha Yates. Either way, the attraction was immediate. Their initial lively tête-à-tête was described by Shepherd Dugger:

> Eng said [to the girls], "My brother wants to marry; and if any young lady here will have him, we will have a wedding today."
>
> "It is he who wants to marry," said Chang, "and he is putting it off on me just to raise a conversation with you about love. He'd marry at the drop of a hat, and drop it himself, if he could get the ugliest girl in town to say 'yes.'"
>
> "The reason I don't marry," said Eng, "is because I'm fast to him."
>
> "The reason I don't marry," said Chang, "is because I'm fast to him. Isn't it a pity that neither of two brothers can marry, because he is fast to the other?"
>
> "Indeed it is," said Sarah, "is there no chance for you to be separated?"
>
> "The doctors say not," said Eng, "and each of us decided that we would rather look on pretty girls, with a lean and hungry love-look, and continue to want a wife than to be in our graves."
>
> "What a pity," said Adelaide, "that you who love ladies so dearly can't marry, and that two young ladies can't have such lovely husbands as you would have been."
>
> "Good-bye," said the girls. "Good-bye," said Chang.
>
> Eng said, "Good-bye, my brother will be back to see you some day."
>
> "If I come back," said Chang, "I will leave him behind, because he always monopolizes the conversation of the girl I love best."
>
> Eng said, "To show that I want to be fair, I will let him take

choice of you girls now, and if we get back, the other shall be no less a choice to me."

Chang chose Adelaide, and they parted joking as the young ladies left.[6]

Even though Dugger claimed to have known the twins and interviewed their descendants for details about their lives, the above conversation might have been imaginary, judging by the numerous factual errors Dugger made in his book. But it certainly captures the dynamics between the twins, the kind of Click-and-Clack Tappet Brothers humor ("Don't drive like my brother"), a comic routine Chang and Eng had practiced to perfection in their decade-long performance.

A more reliable account of how the romance began is supplied by Judge Graves, who had befriended the twins for many years. Graves claimed that the twins had first met the Yates girls at Charles Harris's wedding, when guests came from miles away to enjoy the banquet and celebration in Traphill. The next morning, when everyone was leaving, "Chang observed that a rather handsome young fellow dashed up by the side of Miss Adelaide as she cantered off on the prancing bay; and Eng saw that a rather good looking young Methodist preacher, named Colson, rode more soberly along by the side of Miss Sally [i.e., Sarah]. If any emotion of interest stirred the breast of any of the parties at that time it is one of the unrevealed secrets."[7]

It was at this point that the twins began to make what one might describe as more frequent "rutting trips" to the Yates house in Mulberry Creek. As they became more familiar with the Yateses, Graves wrote, "they often devoted much of their time to the young ladies, whom they entertained most agreeably with accounts of their adventures and the amusing scenes they had witnessed—interspersed with very soft, sweet notes on their flutes—melody very greatly admired by the girls who had never heard such instruments before."[8] Like Odysseus returning from his epic journey, these two seasoned globetrotters, who had honed their interpersonal skills in front of millions of faceless strangers, undoubtedly

were fascinating interlocutors to the two young women who probably
had never ventured beyond the county line. The twins' charm, aided by
their worldwide fame and substantial wealth, proved almost irresistible.

Their obstacles, however, were also nearly insurmountable.

Laws prohibiting marriage and sex between whites and people of
color had been in existence since colonial times. In 1691, Virginia
passed the first anti-miscegenation law in the colonies, followed by
Maryland in 1692 and then by Pennsylvania, Massachusetts, and others in the years to come. In North Carolina, a 1741 statute fined any
white man or woman who married "an Indian, negro, mustee [octoroon]
or mulatto man or woman, or any person of mixed race to the third
generation." A second 1741 statute forbade any cleric or justice of the
peace from performing any such marriage. In 1839, just when Chang
and Eng arrived in North Carolina, the state assembly, as if anticipating troubles brewing in its northwestern mountains, "took a step to
strengthen normative marriage by prohibiting marriage between free
persons of color and white persons and by declaring any such marriage
already entered into to be null and void."[9] The issue of miscegenation
also drew national attention that year when the Massachusetts General
Assembly waged a debate over repealing the ban on interracial marriage. The repeal, opposed by the abolitionists, who advocated freedom
for blacks but feared racial mixing, failed in the former Bay Colony. It
was not until 1967 that the ban on marriage between people of different races was, finally and definitively, ruled unconstitutional by the US
Supreme Court in the landmark case *Loving v. Virginia*. At the time of
the ruling, sixteen states still had miscegenation laws on their books.

Legal clarity notwithstanding, reality was murkier. The mere fact that
in 1839 the North Carolina state assembly needed to pass a new bill to
reinforce the existing prohibition was a clear indication that interracial
liaisons must have taken place in spite of the laws. In her book on interracial sex in the nineteenth-century South, Martha Hodes points out
that white anxiety about sex between white women and men of color,
especially blacks, is not a timeless phenomenon in the United States
and that the most virulent racist ideology about black male sexuality

emerged in the decades that followed the Civil War. In the antebellum era, "white Southerners could respond to sexual liaisons between white women and black men with a measure of toleration; only with black freedom did such liaisons begin to provoke a near-inevitable alarm." In North Carolina in the 1830s, as Hodes's research uncovers, "marriage between free people of color and whites was more explicitly prohibited, yet such alliances did not cease." In a western county, a black man and a white woman had lived together and cohabited as man and wife for a decade before the court voided their union in 1842. In eastern North Carolina, a black man and a white woman had no trouble getting a marriage license from a county clerk in 1840, and the census taker that year recorded the household as consisting of one white female and one free man of color.[10]

This is not to paint a rosy picture of North Carolina in the 1840s, but only to reveal the gray area where interracial unions were allowed to take place despite state laws and communal sanctions against them. In her study, Hodes draws an important distinction between tolerance and toleration: "Tolerance implies a liberal spirit toward those of a different mind; toleration by contrast suggests a measure of forbearance for that which is not approved." The latter, not the former, describes white attitudes toward sexual liaisons between men of color and white women in the antebellum South. Yet, as Hodes reminds us, "the phenomenon of toleration, no matter how carefully defined, cannot convey the complexity of responses: white neighbors judged harshly, gossiped viciously, and could completely ostracize the transgressing white woman."[11] These were the racial dynamics and communal forces at work when Chang and Eng courted the Yates sisters with their globetrotting tales and tintinnabulating flute notes.

Just as the twins obtained citizenship by benefiting from the invisibility of Chinese as a racial category, they might also have been able to circumvent marriage laws by jumping through the same loophole. In US Census Bureau documents, Chang and Eng, like many Chinese at the time, were—given the white–black hierarchy—considered "honorary" whites. Even in 1870, when "C" had been created as a catchall category for Chinese and all Asians on the US census, Chang and Eng were still recorded as being white by the census takers. But what is recorded on paper can have very little bearing on how people really feel about race. Chang and Eng were Asian in the eyes of Wilkes County residents, no matter what the census taker decided to put on the form. So we are back to square one, to the question: Would the white sisters marry these Asian men? In the words of Judge Graves, the initial difficulty the twins encountered in their courtship came not from the fact that these prospective husbands were attached at the liver, but from the "ineradicable prejudice against their race and nationality."[12] Even if the girls were tempted by the twins' advances, their father was appalled by the prospect of marrying his two daughters to two swarthy Chinese who, to make matters worse, were freaks.

Over the years, newspapers had now and then published idle speculation and made a farce out of rumors about Chang and Eng's romantic intrigues. The very first of such reports came when they arrived in England in 1829. As previously quoted, the twins were portrayed as being innocently flirtatious with the hotel chambermaid in London. From that period, there was also the story about a British society woman named Sophie, who was enamored of one of the twins but had to give up her amorous designs because of the fear of bigamy. In November 1834, a rumor surfaced again, according to the *Mobile* [Alabama] *Register* and the *Baltimore Patriot*, that "the Siamese Twins have had a falling out with each other, and that a duel would have ensued sometime since, but the parties could not agree upon the distance. The quarrel originated from the interference of Chang, in a love intrigue of his twin brother Eng." But other newspapers soon disputed the claim and tried to set the record straight, as did the *Pittsfield* [Massachusetts] *Sun*: "The Siamese Twins are at Columbia, S.C. The report that they had quarreled about a love affair turns out to be 'a weak invention of the enemy.'" Or, as the *New Hampshire Sentinel* put it, "Chang and Eng are still good friends, though some malicious people did report that Chang had a love affair on hand which he wished to conceal from Eng." In December 1836, the *Portsmouth* [New Hampshire] *Journal* reported: "One of the Siamese Twins is said to have fallen in love with a young lady at Wilmington, Del. She likes Chang well enough, but objects to marrying both." A few months later, in February 1837, the *New Hampshire Sentinel*, quoting other sources, claimed that the twins "flatly deny the story, which some mischievous persons have put in circulation, respecting their having fallen in love with the same young lady, and fought a duel at ten paces. Eng says he wishes to marry, but he cannot, without the consent of his brother, who is inclined to a life of a single blessedness." The latest, and most farcical, update on this front came out in the New Orleans *Times-Picayune* on June 6, 1838, claiming that one of the twins would marry "Miss Afong Moy, the little Chinese lady," a popular exhibition at New York's Peale Museum, where she had often shared the stage with the twins since her debut in 1834. "The happy bridegroom," the newspaper added, "had invited his brother to stand up with him and act as groomsman."[13]

Many of these reports were nothing but tabloid pabulum concocted by editors to sell papers at the expense of the twins' perceived monstrosity. But it is true that the twins, despite their abnormality, had always pursued an interest in women, as any heterosexual men would. Based on what the twins later recalled for interviewers, the mythical Sophia from the London days might have been real. Nor did their dalliance with the British chambermaid sound too far-fetched. Completely different from visitors who came and went in public, maids or daughters of innkeepers were the only members of the opposite sex the twins could meet for an extended period in a more intimate setting. Their ledger reveals expenses on gifts apparently for these women. For instance, on August 5, 1833, they spent $1.50 on a ring as a present, romantic or not, for one Caroline Scovill, daughter of the hotel owner in Cleveland, Philo Scovill. Though she was not the romantic interest for the twins, Fanny Harris (née Baugus), if we recall, was the charming daughter of the boardinghouse keeper in Traphill.

And then there was Catherine Bunker, daughter of a New York businessman, with whom Chang had allegedly fallen in love. According to some biographers, Chang had such a lingering crush on her that when

the twins later had to adopt an official surname, they chose "Bunker."
Moreover, when Chang drew up his first will, he even named Catherine,
by then married to someone else, as his major heir.[14] Also, in early 1832,
about the time they turned twenty-one, Chang and Eng had tried to use
their former manager, James Hale, as an intermediary in their wooing
of a young lady in the Northeast. They sent her at least two letters via
Hale, who mocked them as "my old stick-in-the-mud rapscallions" and
tried to boost their morale when she failed to reply: "Don't be uneasy
my dear fellows for I expect the former letter must have miscarried—
and no doubt the last will be shortly answered."[15]

None of these romantic capers, real or fictional, had been taken seri-
ously by the press or the twins' associates. They only helped to pique
interest in the freak show, inviting the public to visualize the conjoined
twins in a fool's errand of wooing a single damsel. As long as they played
the part of fools, the twins could be celebrated and ridiculed as carnival clowns, and expressions of their carnal desire, genuine or contrived,
only further spiced up the comedy. But now, at the foot of the Blue
Ridge, the carnival play was about to become a reality—to the horror of
the peering and cheering crowd.

Earnest as they were, the twins were no fools regarding the mountainous hurdle facing them in the matter of matrimony. The five-inch
ligament that connected them would stop any maiden dead in her
tracks. A bedroom dialogue between the twins after their meeting with
the Yates girls, a sort of chest-baring in the dark, is dramatized by Shepherd Dugger in his biography:

> Chang said to Eng, "We will keep in touch with those girls, for they
> think more of us than we are thought of by all else in America."
>
> "Maybe you are mistaken," said Eng. "It was only a show
> acquaintance, and they did not want to render things unpleasant
> by bluffing our familiarity."
>
> "It was more than that," said Chang. "I felt the thrill of their
> sympathy deep down in my soul. Maybe they will marry us."
>
> "Marrying with us is a forlorn hope," said Eng. "No modest girl

is apt to marry, where the pleasures of her bridal bed would be exposed, as ours would have to be."

Chang, always more the go-getter of the pair, would not accept Eng's defeatism. And he saw a reason to remain hopeful.

> "Brother, you see it wrong," said Chang. "It is the refined (and those only) who can excuse whatever is necessary to become a mother. We are not responsible for our physical condition, and we should not have to die childless on that account. We will see again, the dear girls who talked so good to us today, and, through their love we may have children to carry our blood and image in the world, when we and their mothers have gone to the Glory Land."
>
> "Brother," said Eng, "I never saw you so great a philosopher as you are now. Those girls inspired you, and when you go back to see them, don't fail to take me, and I will do my best in helping you win Adelaide, who sent that thrill to the bottom of your craw. I know you have sand enough in your gizzard to digest it."[16]

Chang probably would not have minded such a gentle ribbing from his twin, but still, they needed to do something to turn things around.

In Austen's *Pride and Prejudice*, there is a crucial turn of events, a dramatic change of heart when the heroine, Elizabeth Bennet, visits Pemberley, the sprawling estate of Mr. Darcy, whose marriage proposal she earlier rejected. In Darcy's absence, Elizabeth tours the estate and is charmed by the grandeur and beauty of the place. She also hears convincing testimonials from Darcy's servants about the kindness and generosity of the master:

> It was a large, handsome stone building, standing well on rising ground, and backed by a ridge of high woody hills;—and in front, a stream of some natural importance was swelled into greater, but without any artificial appearance. Its banks were neither formal, nor falsely adorned. Elizabeth was delighted. She had never seen a

place for which nature had done more, or where natural beauty had
been so little counteracted by an awkward taste.[17]

As the Chinese saying goes, "When you love a house, you will also love
the crow that lands on its roof [ai wu ji wu]." Elizabeth begins to wonder
whether she has misjudged Darcy and whether she has made a mistake
by turning down his proposal. At that moment, she imagines herself
being the mistress of Pemberley, which "might be something!"

The house Chang and Eng had built in Traphill was certainly not as
grand as Pemberley, but the twins' courtship of the Yates sisters proceeded apace, almost as though it had taken a page from the classic
British novel. It was said that Adelaide was more receptive to Chang's
advances than Sarah was to Eng's, which created a dilemma for all four.
Both Adelaide and Chang knew, of course, that their relationship would
not stand a chance if Sarah did not come along, or Eng was, in a manner of speaking, to be left alone. The calculus was such that if one sister
were to marry one of the twins and yet to bed both of them, it would
certainly be considered polygamy; if the two sisters were to marry the
twins, at least the numbers would be right—even if the situation would
still seem mind-boggling to all concerned or curious. Winning over
Sarah, then, became a must for the marriage plot to work. Eng turned
to Adelaide for help, and Adelaide, having her own interest at stake,
willingly became Eng's confidant and messenger. When necessary, she
would add a few words of approval of Eng and some sisterly advice to
Sarah. Eng's advances and Adelaide's whispers softened Sarah's heart,
but still, as Graves put it, "she gave but slight encouragement" to Eng.[18]

Against Sarah's "pride and prejudice," the twins came up with an
idea to impress the recalcitrant young woman: "quiltin'," as it was called
in this part of the world. One of the traditional means of sociability
for women, a quilting party brought together the community, mostly
women, for chat, gossip, courtship, and other forms of interaction while
sewing a quilt, which provided a symbolic coherence. With their special purpose in mind, Chang and Eng were determined to make this
the fanciest quiltin' anyone had ever seen. As Graves described in his

biography, "Preparations on an adequate scale were duly made. Pigs and lambs and 'the fatted calf' were slain to make ready for the feast."[19] Then, on the appointed day, farm wives and daughters from nearby, including Adelaide and Sarah, dressed in their best gowns, cambric collars, and lace caps, arrived at the twins' house for an evening of merriment and a feast on a Homeric scale. They took their places in the big sitting room, much bigger than their ordinary farmhouse living rooms, and arranged themselves around the four sides of a quilting frame. While the women began to stitch and chat, the twins circled around them, entertaining, wisecracking, and paying special attention to the two Yates sisters— treating them like princesses and making them the envy of all the others. As the delicate fingers flew through stitches and words of banter bounced around, most of the women there had no clue that they were participating in the Niobe-like weaving of the biggest local "scandal." They would be shocked to learn that the freakish "Sime twins," as they called them, were not just flirting innocently with the Yates girls. As Graves continues in his account of the fated night and after, "The quilting was soon done, and the supper over, the young folks betook themselves to the various amusements in which they enjoyed until a late hour. The next day Miss Sally did not leave for home until she had heard the earnest vows of her lover, nor did he cease to plead, with that persuasive eloquence sincere passion lends, until success was attained."[20] Sarah apparently was impressed by what she saw at the twins' home at Traphill. Though not a grand mansion, the house was, in the words of Graves, "uncommonly elegant," equipped with silverware, brass candlesticks, ivory-handled knives, tablecloths, and so on, all bought in New York—which could have been Paris, as far as the local women were concerned. The rooms were airy and spacious, neatly furnished with tables and benches of solid wood and chairs made of hickory and bottomed with polished splits of white oak. In the corner of the parlor were "several clay pipes with long cane stems while nearby hung the calico poke filled with smoking tobacco, native grown, but of the choicest flavor."[21] Overall, everything showed the good taste of the house's masters. Like Elizabeth Bennet imagining her future as mistress of Pemberley, Sarah had begun to see the bright side of being wedded to the twins, or one of them. Such a bright side may be summarized succinctly in the words of Adelaide, as she is portrayed in Burton Cohen's play *The Wedding of the Siamese Twins* (1989), "They've traveled. They're interestin'. They've got money. They want us real good."[22]

Having finally won the hearts of both sisters, Chang and Eng would now need to clear the hurdle of the parents. David Yates was adamant in his opposition, and so was his wife, Nancy, even though her own physical condition should have made her more malleable in her feelings toward these two Asian "freaks." According to contemporary testimonies, Nancy was morbidly obese. "This lady was about five feet seven inches in height and nearly nine feet in circumference," describes Graves.

> Her accurate weight was never ascertained for the reason that there were in that neighborhood no adequate means of weighing her. Several contrivances were resorted to ascertain her weight, but the nearest approach to success was by using two pairs of steel yards drawing together four hundred and fifty pounds which being firmly secured a sort of swinging platform was attached thereto. When this good woman stepped upon the platform both beams flew up; but the gentleman engaged in the enterprise estimated that her weight could not have been less than five hundred pounds. She was unquestionably the largest woman in the state, perhaps in America. Long after the time we have been speaking of, she died of obesity. When her coffin was taken from the undertakers it could not be gotten into the house until an opening was made for it.[23]

In fact, Nancy was sometimes visited as an object of curiosity just like the Siamese Twins. Shared physical abnormality could have turned Nancy into the twins' sympathizer. But it did not, although growing up with a mother who was "abnormal" might have made the girls more receptive to the twins in the first place. Having encountered curiosity, if not stares, from the local people as a result of their mother's enormity, the sisters, one can suspect, might have already been inured to associating the disabled with Hester Prynne–like outcasts of the community. As portrayed in *The Wedding of the Siamese Twins*, the sisters' attitudes toward the twins as freaks were indeed influenced by their own mother's abnormality:

> ADELAIDE. Why? They're farmers just like Poppa.
>
> SALLY. And real peculiar lookin' ones, too.
>
> ADELAIDE. Anymore peculiar lookin' than Momma?
>
> SALLY. *(Shocked.)* You're talkin' about our Momma who has loved you to pieces ever since you showed your nasty mouth on this good green land.
>
> ADELAIDE. My mouth ain't nasty. I'm speakin' the truth. Momma don't look like anyone else we ever saw. Do you love her any less because of it?[24]

Although it is fictional, Cohen's Broadway play contains more than a kernel of truth.

Parental opposition, however, did not stop the girls from wanting to unite with these two united brothers. Defying their parents' order, they rendezvoused, though stealthily, with the twins. They sought the help of the pastor of the Baptist Church, Colby Sparks, who agreed to intervene and spoke to the parents, but to no avail. In desperation, the girls and their Siamese sweethearts resorted to the time-honored tactic of elopement to fulfill their conjugal dream. They came up with a plot:

> For a time the matter was to be apparently dropped until the ensuing county court week when Esquire Yates, who was one of the county justices, would go to Wilkesboro to assist in holding the court, then the parties at an appointed hour should meet at a "Covenant Meeting House" which stands on the hill near the South Fork of Roaring River, and there, their old friend Colby Sparks, the Baptist Pastor, was to be in waiting ready to perform the ceremony, easy to be done before there could be any danger from pursuit. They understood pretty well there could then be no pursuit, for

the irate father could not know of their flight in some time, and the mother who weighed five hundred pounds could not follow over such roads as lay between the Yates homestead and Covenant Meeting House.[25]

In the end, it turned out that they did not have to resort to such a desperate measure. The parents relented before the planned elopement. We are not entirely sure what had caused the parents to change their minds—perhaps they were well aware of the stubbornness of their daughters; perhaps the mother's disability eventually made the Yateses feel more receptive to the twins' abnormal condition; perhaps the twins' wealth made the match easier for the parents to stomach, knowing that their daughters would be well provided for; or perhaps it was a combination of these factors. In any case, the wedding was set for April of 1843.

When the sleepy community awoke to the shocking news, the good folks did not take it well. When they saw the conjoined twins riding with the Yates girls in an open carriage, their resentment, already at a high point because of fears of liaisons between whites and blacks, reached a boiling point. A few men, according to Kay Hunter, smashed windows at the Yates house. Some neighbors "threatened to burn his crops if he did not promise to control his daughters."[26] Having world-famous freaks live among them was one thing, but seeing them united with two of their young women in an "unholy alliance" was quite another. The community outrage might not have been as violent as those dramatic scenes in *The Hunchback of Notre Dame*, when the enraged crowd attacked the clown and the beauty, but it was enough to make all concerned pause.

The longtime associates of the twins were also aghast. Charles Harris, who had now settled comfortably in Traphill after marrying a local girl and siring an heir, was appalled by the twins' desire for the same thing. As someone who had traveled the world with the twins and taken care of their various interests and needs for a decade, Harris seemed unable to accept the possibility that the conjoined twins could live a life as normal as his. He tried to talk the twins out of what he regarded as their foolishness, but to no avail. Disappointed, Harris communicated with James Hale, whose reaction was even more indignant and nasty. "Give me all the particulars of the marriage," Hale replied to Harris. "I am *very* anxious to know how they got into such a stupid scrape. If they only wanted *skin*, I think they might have managed to get it for *less* than for life."[27] As I described earlier, Hale had showed a willingness, genuine or feigned, to facilitate the twins' romantic pursuits—or, to put it in his crude words, to satisfy their carnal desire for "skin." But, just like Harris, Hale found it absurd that the twins would try to marry and live a "normal" life. Fallout then ensued between the twins and Harris. They had no choice but to distance themselves from their former manager and old friend.

Neither the outcry of community members nor the opposition from friends and associates could derail the twins from executing their conjugal plan. It had been more than two years since they had settled in Traphill, and they had built a strong enough social network to sustain a temporary outburst of cries and grumblings. Also, David Yates, though not a pillar of the community, was after all a wealthy planter and county justice—in other words, a force to be reckoned with. As soon as he gave his blessing to the marriage, the cow, so to speak, was out of the barn.

Accordingly, on April 13, 1843, a very fine early spring day, the most unusual double wedding took place at David Yates's house in Mulberry Creek, officiated by Reverend Colby Sparks. Considering the extraordinary nature of the union, the twins and the Yates family took care to follow the law to the letter—never mind the part that forbade miscegenation—and posted a bond of $1,000 for each marriage. North Carolina required postings of such bonds to ensure that there was no legal obstacle to the proposed marriage. Volunteering as the bondsman for the Yates party was Sarah and Adelaide's elder brother, Jesse. The bond for Eng and Sarah reads:

> Know all men by these presents that we Eng one of the Siamese Twins and Jesse Yates are held and firmly bound unto the state of North Carolina in the sum of one thousand Dollars, current money, to be paid to the said state of North Carolina for payment

whereof, well and truly to be made and done we bind ourselves our Heirs executors and administrators jointly and severally, firmly by these presents sealed with our seal and dated this 13th day of April A.D. 1843.

The condition of the above obligation is such, that the above bounden Eng one of the Siamese Twins has made application for a license for marriage to be celebrated between him and Sarah Yates of the County aforesaid now in case it should not hereafter appear that there is any lawful cause or impediment to obstruct said marriage, then the above obligation is to be void otherwise to remain in full force and virtue.

Eng

Jesse Yates.

Chang's bond was identical except for the names of the bride and groom. Most extraordinarily, even on these bonds, Chang and Eng still had no last name. They were each known as "one of the Siamese Twins," and each signed only his given name. However, on the marriage licenses issued by a county clerk a few days earlier, the last name "Bunker" mysteriously appeared. The crucial part of the licenses reads, "You are hereby licensed and authorized, to solemnize the rites of matrimony between Eng Bunker and Sarah Yates, and join them together as man and wife." It seemed that the twins had no problem using their unique brand, "the Siamese Twins," for official purposes, legal or financial. But the absence of a surname would not do for the women they were about to marry. They needed to choose something for the misses.[28]

As for how they landed on the name of Bunker, there have been a few theories and stories. As noted earlier, Judge Graves believed that the twins had chosen the name in honor of Catherine Bunker, the woman for whom Chang had still carried a torch. Bunker was also the name of the New York company with which the twins had maintained a lasting business and banking relationship, an enterprise run by Frederick, William, and Barthuel Bunker—Catherine's father and uncles.

Another explanation of the name's provenance sounds more comical: When the twins went to the Naturalization Office to sign citizenship papers, the clerk asked for their names, and "Chang and Eng" was the answer they gave. The dismayed clerk told them that unless they could provide a Christian name or a surname, they would not be able to complete the application process. While the twins stood in confusion, a gentleman named Fred Bunker came to their rescue by suggesting that he would consider it an honor if the twins would adopt his family name, which the twins happily obliged.[29] This story, though intriguing, is apocryphal. The twins had acquired citizenship in 1839, and if they had adopted the Bunker name at that time, there had been no sign of it. None of the documents to date, including court summonses, business records, and personal correspondence, contained a trace of the Bunker name until its sudden appearance on the marriage licenses. In fact, records at the superior court in Wilkes County show that it was not until 1844, a year after their marriage, that the twins petitioned the court to legally adopt the Bunker name. Also, in the county archive, the marriage bonds are now accompanied by a slip of paper that states, "TOOK NAME OF BUNKER, FOR SURNAME." It seems that the twins did indeed adopt the surname around the time of their marriage but did not legalize it until a year later.[30]

Another explanation of the name might be far less plausible than poetic: Bunker sounds like a corrupt form of Bangkok, a city that still tugged at the heartstrings of the twins.

Whatever the real reason, the twins had now settled on a name by which they would be known—and one that their brides would assume. In the quiet living room of the Yates house, shielded from the peering eyes of the public but still within earshot of neighborly guffaws and grumblings, the famous Siamese Twins were wedded to the two sisters: first Eng and Sarah, and then Chang and Adelaide. It was probably moot to speculate who the best man was for Eng and who for Chang. The marriage vow that contains the phrase "until death do you part" would certainly carry extra meaning for that occasion.

After the ceremony, the small gathering of family and friends were treated to "a most elegant supper," followed by the Virginia reel, a group dance popular in this mountainous region. After the festivities were over, Chang and Eng took their brides home to Traphill, where an extra-wide bed—widest perhaps in all of North Carolina or even North America—awaited the four of them.[31]

≈ 26 ≈

Foursome

*When a conjoined twin has sex with a third person, is the sex—by virtue of the
conjoinment—incestuous? Homosexual? Group sex? Well, it definitely is sex.
You can tell, because everyone wants to talk about it.*
—Alice Dreger, "The Sex Lives of Conjoined Twins" (2012)

Against the drab backdrop of the corseted Victorian Age,
what happened in the quiet upstairs bedroom at the Siamese
Twins' house in Traphill, North Carolina—or how the conjoined Asian men consummated their double union to the two white
sisters in a Brobdingnagian bed, made of pinewood, devoid of fancy
drapery, facing a large window that overlooked the single-rock Stone
Mountain—sounded like a racial burlesque utterly out of place. That
sexual congress, condemned openly in the penny press and maligned
secretly behind closed doors by neighbors, flew in the face of the norm
of a historical era known for the erotic reserve and moral earnestness
of the middle class, for the endless social campaigns for propriety, modesty, and conformity.

As in those early Puritan colonies, or in Confucian China or any
human congregation that tries to live by some rigid fundamental principles, sex for Victorian America, in the words of John S. Haller and
Robin M. Haller, "represented a pandering to the lower instincts, a less-
ening of family structure, and a serious weakening of society's order
and stability." The dissemination of carnal knowledge, the so-called twilight talk, concealed in hygiene manuals, etiquette books, and religious
pamphlets, was calculated, according to the Hallers, "to impress their
readers with sentiments of virtue and chastity, and offered the notion
that physical love somehow interfered with the realization of society's
greater objectives. Discussions of sex predisposed the Victorians to an

assortment of inferences in which sexual urges were somehow at vari-
ance with the search for morality and the proper definition of virtue."
Combining an undertone of Old Testament vengeance with strands of
modern science and pseudoscience, which included Thomsonianism,
Swedenborgianism, homeopathy, phrenology, and animal magnetism,
the purity literature of Victorian America "portrayed sex as the most
primitive human tendency . . . the aberrations of which were invariably
detected and punished through disease and mental anguish."

One of the leading crusaders against sexual promiscuity around the
time the Siamese Twins got married was Dr. Sylvester Graham, who
prescribed in his widely circulated writings certain rules regarding the
frequency of intercourse for married couples. Graham observed that
American men were suffering from impotence, skin and lung disease,
headaches, nervousness, and other maladies, and he blamed all of it on
sexual excess in the conjugal bed. Believing that an ounce of semen
equaled nearly forty ounces of blood, Graham recommended that, to
avoid disease and premature death, healthy and robust husbands should
limit their sexual indulgences to twelve times each year. In addition, he
prescribed dietary changes for men to include such foods as unbolted
wheat, rye meal, hominy, and his trademarked Graham flour.

Another health crusader was John Harvey Kellogg, cofounder of the
Kellogg cereal company, whose promotion of health foods went hand
in hand with his advocacy for abstinence. Kellogg advised parents to
prevent "silly letter-writing" between boys and girls in their early school
years and campaigned for "eternal vigilance," enjoining parents to guard
the chastity of daughters in all their relations. Orson Fowler, the phrenology promoter, also joined in the crusade, stressing "the importance
of phrenology in choosing marriage partners, which would enable men
and women to seek those of similar thought and feeling through a
searching analysis of the brain's 'soul-chambers,'" rather than relying on
the ever-deceptive corporeal attraction and sex appeal.[1] In addition, the
tremendously popular behavior manual, *Mrs. Beeton's Book of Household
Management*, combining cooking recipes with domestic protocols, also
helped to codify Victorian sexual norms.

Despite these social campaigns that earned the Victorian period a sterling reputation, reality was far more complex beneath the veneer of moral earnestness. As Peter Gay reminds us in his monumental study of Victorian sexuality, "The bourgeois experience was far richer than its expression, rich as it was; and it included a substantial measure of sensuality for both sexes, and of candor—in sheltered surroundings. It would be a gross misreading of this experience to think that nineteenth-century bourgeois did not know, or did not practice, or did not enjoy, what they did not discuss." Tapping into a vast historical archive, Gay shows that the Victorians were publicly prudish but secretly prurient.[2]

In nineteenth-century America, there was also a plethora of religious groups and utopian communities that openly explored nonconventional sexuality and challenged the traditional paradigm of monogamous marriage. The rise of Mormonism and its practice of polygamy was one obvious example. Also, in the wake of religious revivalism and under the influence of utopian ideologies imported from Europe, there arose in America sects, cults, and spiritualist settlements that experimented with different models of government, marriage, labor, and wealth: New Harmony, Yellow Springs, Nashoba, Brook Farm, Hopedale, Skaneateles, Sylvania Association, and the Oneida Community. Take the last group, for example: It was a religion-based socialist commune, founded in Oneida, New York, by John Humphrey Noyes in 1848 and dedicated to living as one family and to sharing all property, work, and love. In addition to communal sharing of all property and possessions, the Oneida members also believed strongly in a system of free love known as "complex marriage," which allowed a member to have sex with any other member who consented. Regarding childbearing as a communal responsibility, the Oneidans paired women over the age of forty with adolescent boys, and older men with young women. As their guru Noyes put it, "the main idea was the enlargement of home—the extension of family union beyond the little man-and-wife circle to large corporations."[3] To avoid pregnancy, Noyes advocated "male continence," which became a voguish form of contraception in the late nineteenth century. "Noyes divided the sexual act into three stages: the presence of the male organ in the vagina, the series of reciprocal motions, and last, the ejaculation of semen. Since the only uncontrollable portion of the sexual act was the final orgasm, he claimed that with sufficient mental control, the male could voluntarily govern the first two stages, prolonging the motions of sex so that mutual satisfaction could be obtained without orgasm."[4] While some doctors looked enviously on the ability of the Oneida communitarians to prolong carnal pleasures, and others suspected that the only result of Noyes's sexual experimentation was the substitution of "wet dreams" for natural ejaculation, moralists, not surprisingly, condemned the Oneidans. In 1843, the year of Chang and Eng's double wedding, some of these utopian experiments, such as New Harmony and Brook Farm, which would inspire the Oneidans, reached their peaks. Comparing the frenzy of utopianism to the fire of the Great Awakening, Noyes wrote, "The Millennium seemed as near in 1831, as [Charles] Fourier's Age of Harmony seemed in 1843."[5]

Adhering to no ideology other than the pursuit of personal freedom and happiness—however one defines or questions what "personal" means here—the Siamese Twins and their wives built a unique commune, a conjugal structure that was both within and outside the contours of traditional marriage. Having for so long lived a very public existence, the twins could not shelter their bedroom acts from the insidious speculations of tabloid peddlers and curious neighbors. There was never any direct how-they-did-it revelation, nor any unbuttoned discussion in contemporary print media, but the fact that two conjoined Asian men went to bed with two white women was enough to provoke outrage and condemnation. As we saw earlier, while the local *Carolina Watchman* merely referred to the union as a "marriage extraordinary," and concluded the report with a comical jab, "May the connection be as happy as it will be close," other newspapers were not so merciful in their attacks on the presumably unnatural, ungodly union. One paper suggested an indictment against the Yates sisters for marrying a "quadruped." Another newspaper editor opined, "Were it not for the evidence daily afforded of what unnatural things men and women will do, we should pronounce the account incredible. What sort of women can they be who have entered into such a marriage? What sort of father to consent? What sort of clergyman to perform the unnatural ceremony?" As Orser points out, the fiercest denunciation came from Northern abolitionist papers, which blamed sinful slavery for such an unsavory union. These papers printed the wedding notice in the column titled "Southern Scenes," a section devoted to sensationalized stories of "murder, matricide, duels, drunken assaults, robberies, judicial corruption, and insanity" coming out of the slaveholding South. The papers treated the wedding as yet another proof of how the institution of slavery had corrupted the Southern soul. As Garrison editorialized in the *Liberator*, "None but a priest whose mind had become besotted by the impurities of slavery could 'solemnize' so bestial a union as this; and none but a community sunk below the very Sodomites in lasciviousness, from the same cause, would tolerate it."[6] What Flannery O'Connor said about Southern grotesque seems apropos again: "Anything that comes out of the South is going to be called grotesque by the Northern reader, unless it is grotesque, in which case it is going to be called realistic."[7]

While the world looked on with horror and contempt, the twins and their wives went on to live their lives as married couples. Lacking information about those most intimate moments, biographers, novelists, and medical professionals have all tried to figure out the nature of the conjoined twins' sex life. How did they do it? In the words of Alice Dreger, "People really want to know: what do conjoined twins feel when they have sex? If one is sexually stimulated, does the other feel it? If one has an orgasm, does the other enjoy the same, however unwittingly?" Was there competition, however playful, over male prowess? Was there peer pressure, encouragement, advice, or coaching? What about the wives? Did they feel embarrassed or excited about having sex in the presence of another man, a brother-in-law, who was literally lying next to her in bed? Would one sister feel jealous, suspicious, or resentful when the other was in bed with her man? Or—and here is the question many must have been dying to ask and yet afraid to do so for the sake of politeness—did the twins ever swap wives? Medical experts have stated that, "based on what we know about the significant variability of one conjoined twin to feel a body part (e.g., an arm) that putatively 'belongs' to the other twin, it's hard to guess how any conjoinment will turn out in practice. Nerves, muscles, hormones, and psychology all probably factor in to who feels what." Ultimately, as Dreger puts it succinctly, it all depends on what you mean by "having sex."[8]

Among the biographers of Chang and Eng, Irving Wallace and Amy Wallace were perhaps the first to unbutton the taboo topic in a fair-minded way, without any hint of voyeurism. In their book *The Two* (1978), the father–daughter best-seller team speculated on how the twins might have carried out the bedroom act, when no sex manual, marriage tract, or etiquette book—all of which were widely distributed in Victorian America—could teach them how to go about it:

> Physically, the twins could not maneuver very far apart. They were bound tightly when lying down, too close for either to achieve any real degree of independent performance or privacy. In sexual inter-course, only the obvious missionary position—with the man on top—could have worked well. Yet it could not have worked too well. The anatomical restriction was always there. If Eng mounted Sallie [Sarah], then Chang could not be far behind—indeed, he would be dangling seven or eight inches to one side. Moreover, it meant Chang had to be curled against Sallie, partially covering her body throughout. The same condition would have occurred when Chang made love to Adelaide. Eng would have been drawn against or partially across Adelaide.
>
> Another likely position of copulation that may have been employed was that of the woman mounting the man. Whether the straitlaced prudery of the period would have allowed such lovemak-ing by Sallie and Adelaide will probably never be known. . . . As to the possibility of both couples making love simultaneously, it was quite possible with both women on top, but quite improbable with both men on top, because their mates beneath would have had to

be lying one partially across the side of the other's body, evoking images of an incredible orgy of flesh.[9]

In his best-selling novel *Chang and Eng* (2001), Darin Strauss also tries to flesh out the details of the bedroom act, creating a plausibly complicated drama of sexual attraction among the four players. In a key section of the story, narrated in Eng's voice, Strauss imagines the consummation of the double marriage in bold, descriptive language:

> My brother's wife glanced at me, then her eyes darted away. She seemed to be talking to both of us through the anxious disappearance and reappearance of her smile. . . . I shut my eyes tight. The sensation of her leg touching mine was faint and natural. . . . And then my brother and his wife began to have relations. Chang stirred me yet again as he climbed on top of his wife and me. He was touching her breasts at the nipples as if he feared he'd never get the chance again. My arm was wrapped around my brother's shoulder, and to make this positioning possible, our band extended farther than it should go. The inopportune logistics meant I had no choice but to curl against Adelaide, to cover her body partially—at the curve of her hip—and move along her leg as my brother rocked back and forth. . . . When she and my brother were finished, it took Chang a moment to separate himself from his wife. He was panting like a mackerel plucked into the air. And then Adelaide, smiling, was covering Chang's mouth with her tiny hand, resting her head on his breast, and staring back at me.[10]

In our treatment of this delicate matter, there is a risk of sensationalizing what might not have been so sensational a scene. The picture of two men in bed with one woman, for which the French have an elegant epithet, or of two men with two women, easily provokes, as the Wallaces term it, images of orgy. But the reality might not have been as shocking as we would imagine. The closest evidence we have ever gotten in this regard came from Dr. William Pancoast, the physician in charge of the

twins' autopsy in 1874. The eminent Philadelphia surgeon, after cutting open the twins' corpses and examining every part of the anatomy,
including the genitalia, also asked the widows the most sensitive question about their sex life and got an answer in return, as he wrote in the
autopsy report:

> The twins . . . had become so accustomed to their curious relation
> as to act and live under certain regulations of their own as one
> individual. We were told in North Carolina that they had agreed
> that each should in turn control the action of the other. Thus Eng
> would for one week be complete master . . . and Chang would sub-
> mit his will and desires completely to those of Eng, and vice versa.
> Though it seems most immoral and shocking that the two should
> occupy the same marital couch with the wife of one, yet so thor-
> ough was this understanding of alternate mastery, that, as I was
> told by one of the widows, there had never been any improper rela-
> tions between the wives and the brothers.[11]

What evolved in this strategy of "alternate mastery" was for one party to
completely yield to the will of the other, a sort of self-imposed "blanking
out," a mental withdrawal. As incredulous as it might sound, at least one
other pair of Siamese Twins, the Hilton Sisters, would attest to the feasibility of the psychological trick. Violet and Daisy Hilton, born in England in 1908 and joined at the hips, followed in the footsteps of Chang
and Eng and became world-famous entertainers. Brought to the United
States in their teens, they grew up to be vivacious young women, outgo-
ing with men and attracting many suitors. Unlike Chang and Eng, however, the Hilton Sisters had trouble tying the knot when one of them fell
in love with a man. Violet and her fiancé were denied a marriage license
in twenty-one states on grounds of morality. In their self-defense, the
Hilton Sisters explained how they managed their romantic involvements
in order to avoid any hint of *ménage à trois*: They had "acquired the ability to blank out the other" in those key moments. When one sister had a

date, the other would quit paying attention, sometimes by reading and sometimes by taking a nap.[12]

In *The Tragedy of Pudd'nhead Wilson; and the Comedy, Those Extraordinary Twins*, Mark Twain worked the element of "alternate mastery" into a novel based on real-life Italian twins, the Tocci Brothers. His sobriquet indicating a preoccupation with two-ness, Twain had first seen an exhibition picture of Giovanni and Giacomo Tocci and had never been able to forget the striking image of "this freak of nature," which he described as "a combination consisting of two heads and four arms joined to a single body and a single pair of legs."[13] In *Pudd'nhead Wilson*, a work that unites two novels as one, like Siamese Twins, Luigi, one of the Italian twins, speaks to his brother Angelo: "My friend, when I am in command of our body, I choose my apparel according to my own convenience, as I have remarked more than several times already. When you are in command, I beg you will do as you please." Angelo replies, "When I am in command I treat you as a guest; I try to make you feel at home; when you are in command you treat me as an intruder."[14]

How successfully Chang and Eng practiced "alternate mastery," we will never know for sure. Their wives, as quoted above, did say that there was never any improper behavior in their shared bedroom. But *impropriety* is a loaded word, charged with biases, hypocrisy, and whatnot. Mormons were attacked for their practice of polygamy; Oneida communitarians would justify their sexual promiscuity in the name of a lofty idea, as would free-love advocacy groups of assorted stripes and colors. A *ménage à trois* among three singletons, depending on where one stands, would be considered variously as debauched, deviant, or delightful, while the sex act between two people in the unavoidable presence of the third person, as in the case of the Siamese Twins, would be considered freakish and bestial. Somewhere Sigmund Freud, the father of modern sexuality studies, admitted, "In matters of sexuality we are, all of us, the healthy as much as the sick, hypocrites nowadays."[15]

When asked in an interview about his illustrious ancestors' bedroom acts that had led to his creation and that of his clan, Milton Haynes, the great-grandson of Chang, interviewed by Josh Gibson for the documentary film *The Siamese Connection*, gave what I believe to be the best answer, which should put the matter to bed: "How did they do it? As simple as you did." Or, as Karen Tei Yamashita puts it in her fictional rendering of the Chang and Eng story, "Whatever speculations you may have about that incredible night and nights to come pale when one reflects on the reality and mathematic possibilities of position, sexuality, culture, race, politics, genetics, DNA. Bodies entangled upon bodies, the great union of Asian America with all women, with all America— mind, body, and spirit—the great gift. Amen."[16]

Mount Airy, or Monticello

She was a slave, and salable as such.
—Mark Twain, *The Tragedy of Pudd'nhead Wilson*

llow me to fast forward 160 years in our story and describe an event of which the seed, like everything else, was sown in the past. In July 2003, about a hundred descendants of the Siamese Twins congregated in Mount Airy, North Carolina, for their Bunker reunion. A tradition that began years ago, the annual gathering is always held on the last weekend of July, at the White Plains Baptist Church, which the twins had helped build with their bare hands on a hill adjacent to the farmland that still belongs to the family. By some estimates, there are about fifteen hundred Bunker descendants today, spread throughout the world, although most of them have stayed close to their ancestral haunt in North Carolina.

Like most family reunions, the festivities consist of a potluck buffet, speeches, and updates on the clan news. One year, they even watched a show about their illustrious ancestors, the Burton Cohen play, *The Wedding of the Siamese Twins*, which had premiered on Broadway in March 1988. A field trip to the twins' original homestead, now retooled as Mayberry Campground to attract from all over the world diehard fans of Sheriff Andy and Deputy Fife (more on that later), is also on the program. Journalists from the local media, following a tradition that began with the twins' arrival in this area in 1839, are usually in attendance. Sometimes, researchers and historians are also present as honored guests. The Bunkers are a convivial, welcoming bunch.

At the family jamboree in 2003, however, something unexpected happened. An African American named Brenda Ethridge stepped up to the microphone. She introduced herself as a descendant of Aunt Grace, the first slave owned by Chang and Eng. Ethridge had learned of her connection to the famous twins through stories passed down in her own family but had never been able to verify the details. Nor did she know much about her distant ancestor, who is buried in the same cemetery as Chang and Eng, along with generations of their offspring. According to Cynthia Wu, a Chinese-American historian who was present at this reunion, the sudden appearance of an African American in their midst hit a nerve. While Ethridge was a welcome presence for most on that occasion, a flurry of exchanges ensued among several concerned Bunkers, museum curators, and DNA experts. Only six years had elapsed since the official confirmation that Thomas Jefferson had fathered children with his slave Sally Hemings, and that subject was still hanging in the air. Across the state line, it seemed, the ghost of Monticello lingered in Mount Airy.[1]

To understand how we arrive at this juncture, or how the conjoined brothers could have spawned thousands of offspring, and why a black woman would challenge the veracity of their genealogy, we need to return to the mountain wedding in 1843, to the quiet house that today still stands in Traphill, where the Bunker clan, as a quintessentially American, multiracial family, was just getting started.

At the time of the twins' wedding, some local folks wagered over how long the marriage could last and whether such a "freakish union" would produce any offspring. In their mind, bestiality was godforsaken, unnatural, and surely doomed to infertility. They also wondered how long the Yates sisters could stand the ignominy of having to bed two swarthy Asian freaks. James Hale predicted that unless the twins were separated, the marriage would not stand a chance. "Depend upon it," he wrote to Charles Harris, "the result will be, a desire to attempt a surgical operation upon themselves."[2]

Those skeptics might have been surprised to know that the twins had indeed considered surgically untying themselves so that they could lead "normal" lives with their respective wives. It was their wives, however, who vehemently opposed such a move. According to some biographers, the twins, prior to their wedding, had consulted with physicians in Philadelphia and were ready to go under the knife. Aghast at the news, Sarah and Adelaide begged the men not to follow through with the dangerous procedure and reassured the men that they would be happy to marry them "as they were."

The skeptics must have been even more surprised when they heard, ten months after the wedding, that each couple had produced a "fine, fat, bouncing daughter." On February 10, 1844, Sarah and Eng became proud parents of a baby girl named Katherine; only six days later, Adelaide and Chang welcomed into the world a baby girl named Josephine. If there was any lingering doubt about the procreative aspect of the unions, there would be even more evidence to put the matter to rest: In their lifetime, the two couples would produce twenty-one children in total, with Eng and Sarah claiming eleven and Chang and Adelaide, ten. Out of these twelve daughters and nine sons, two would die at young ages from accidents, while two were deaf and mute. There were no twins, let alone conjoined twins or babies with any other discernible deformity.

Twenty-one children for two couples may seem extraordinary and could possibly feed into some of the prevailing stereotypes that portrayed primitive "Orientals" engaging in bestial sex and breeding like animals. Thomas de Quincey, if we remember, called the Asian continent the "workshop of men." Herman Melville, hardly conventional in his choice of bedfellows, imagined in *Moby-Dick* that those ghostly aboriginals "of earth's primal generations" in insulated Asia "engaged in mundane amours."[3] In reality, however, it was not unusual for a couple living in the Appalachians during this era to have a score of children. Visiting the area in 1828, Dr. Elisha Mitchell, the geologist who had earlier given us the on-the-ground account of the lay of the land in Wilkes and neighboring counties, was struck by the "swarms" of children he encountered everywhere—a phenomenon confirmed by studies of demographics and birth rates. As Martin Crawford points out, "Families with ten or more offspring were common in this period." One couple from northwestern North Carolina produced eighteen children in the decades straddling the Civil War, while another couple had seventeen. One woman, Jane Richardson, "was reported in 1855 as possessing no less than 174 living children, grandchildren, and great-grandchildren."[4]

A year after the birth of their first children, the twins and their wives celebrated the arrival of two more additions to brood, born again only about a week apart: a baby girl named Julia for Eng and Sarah on March 31, 1845, and the first boy, named Christopher, for Chang and Adelaide on April 8. As the family grew, the house in Traphill became too small for them. In the spring of that year, Chang and Eng purchased a farm in nearby Surry County for $3,750. Straddling bubbling Stewart's Creek outside the village of Mount Airy, this 650-acre farmland would become their Xanadu—or, more pertinent and closer to home, their Monticello.

On this new land, Chang and Eng—two brothers formerly sold into indentured servitude and treated no better than slaves—began farming by using black slaves. Here our story takes a significant turn, entering what Primo Levi called "the gray zone" of humanity, a treacherously murky area where the persecuted becomes the persecutor, the victim turns victimizer.

The first slave Chang and Eng owned, as mentioned earlier, was Aunt Grace, the ancestor of Brenda Ethridge, who attended the 2003 Bunker reunion. Legally known as Grace Gates, and born a slave in Alabama around 1790, Aunt Grace was sold to North Carolina at a young age and became the property of David Yates. Chang and Eng received her as a "wedding gift," the same way that the nameless black servant standing behind Alabama circuit judge Sidney Posey, presiding over the assault case against the twins years earlier, had been a wedding present from the young judge's in-laws. Known for her exceptionally large feet, Grace would assume the slave–nanny role and exert a large influence in the twins' family, nursing all of the Bunker children as well as her own.

Soon after their relocation to Surry County, the twins began to purchase more slaves and even engage in slave trading. What is unquestionably clear is that the twins by this time had adopted the mindset, in all its permutations, of the oppressor class, the whites who owned slaves. In

GRACE ("AUNT GRACE") GATES, FIRST SLAVE
OWNED BY CHANG AND ENG BUNKER

September 1845, they bought from Mount Airy planter Thomas F. Prather two black girls, aged seven and five, for $450, and from another neighbor a three-year-old boy for $175. Within just a few years, they had eighteen slaves. Out of these eighteen, according to the 1850 census, more than half were younger than eight years old. As Judge Graves admitted candidly, "Some few of their slaves were valuable to them for their present ability to labor; but much the greater number of them were an absolute burden but very valuable on account of the marketable price and prospective usefulness."[5] According to the twins' descendant Melvin Miles, Chang and Eng would buy slaves younger than eight, keep them, and work them until they were in their early twenties, when they would be sold or traded for younger ones to carry on the work. With very few exceptions, they would not keep a male slave older than twenty-five, because "the twins thought that by then the male slaves were of the

BILL OF SALE FOR TWO SLAVES SOLD TO
CHANG AND ENG BUNKER

mindset of trying to escape or rebel against their owners."[6] Perhaps the twins remembered the horror of the Nat Turner revolt in 1831. Female slaves, by contrast, would be kept for as long as needed, because they were less likely to run away or to rebel, and they would bring additional value when they had babies—the so-called increase. Aunt Grace, for instance, gave birth to nine children, three of whom—Jacob, Jack, and James—survived and became the property of her masters.[7] In fact, Grace's three sons all assumed the Bunker name, according to the 1870 census.

Living in squalid cabins, the slaves were divided into "house slaves" and "field slaves." The former, including Aunt Grace, worked mostly around the houses, helping to cook, clean, sew, nurse babies, and do other domestic chores. The field slaves would rise before dawn and work in the field till sunset. How the twins treated their slaves was a contentious topic both during their lifetimes and after their deaths. There were accounts that portrayed them as humane and kind, while others described them as "severe taskmasters." According to Judge Graves, whenever the twins took long trips, they would always bring gifts for each member of the family, "not even forgetting the colored servants down to the youngest."[8] In the field, they also patiently taught the slaves some of the new farming techniques they had learned from agricultural magazines. The twins were allegedly among the first farmers in North Carolina to produce "bright leaf" tobacco, and they taught the slaves how to use their newly acquired press to make "plug" chewing tobacco. Possum-hunting being one of their favorite sports, the twins would frequently take some of the slaves out with them on early mornings for expeditions, which were recreational to them but not necessarily to the slaves.

These descriptions of the so-called harmonious relationship between masters and slaves, suggesting that the twins "did not drive their slaves but supervised them," were complicated by allegations to the contrary.[9] The first of these negative reports appeared in a newspaper article published in the *Greensborough Patriot* in 1852. The author of the article, who signed himself merely "D.," did a profile of the twins, describing them as

shrewd and industrious businessmen with belligerent and fiery dispositions. He claimed that the twins had once split "a board into splinters
over the head of a man who had insulted them" and were "fined fifteen
dollars and costs. . . . Woe to the unfortunate wight who dares to insult
them." This prelude led to a more devastating revelation: "When they
chop or fight, they do so double-handed; and in driving a horse or chastising their negroes, both of them use the lash without mercy. A gentleman who purchased a black man a short time ago from them, informed
the writer that he was 'the worst whipped negro he ever saw.'"[10]

Such an unflattering depiction of them as cruel masters drew an
immediate response from the twins, who were acutely aware of the
importance of public image. They shot off a long letter to the newspaper, defending their own character and integrity and objecting vehemently to the article's claims:

> The portion of said piece relating to the inhuman manner in which
> we had chastised a negro man which we afterwards sold, is a sheer
> fabrication and infamous falsehood. We have never sold to any man
> a negro as described, except to Mr. Thos. F. Prather, who denies
> the truth of said accusation, or of ever having told any person that
> which the author of said communication says he heard. We are well
> aware that to some who have not seen us, we are to some extent an
> object of curiosity, but that we were to be objects of such vile and
> infamous misrepresentation, we could not before believe.

Along with the letter, the twins attached an endorsement by thirteen
local citizens and neighbors attesting to the truthfulness of their statement, signatories who included Thomas Prather, from whom the twins
had made their first purchase of young slaves and to whom they had
now sold an older one.[11]

Then there were other stories about often-poisoned relations between
the twins and their slaves. One, reported years later, tells of a black slave
who one day appeared at the front door of the twins' house and wanted
to see them on business. While the Southern custom dictated that a

"colored" man would have to use the back door of a white man's home, this black man might have thought the rule would not apply to two tawny Asians with slanting eyes. "When the Twins saw the negro standing in the front door," as the story goes, "they instantly made for him with a malignant air and the negro lost no time in taking himself away. After that he knew his place."[12]

Another story, reported in the *Mount Airy News*, is about a slave who had "developed into a desperado and was considered dangerous":

> He usually was a pest, for the hand of every man was against him. There was no law to protect such slaves and it was considered the proper thing to do to kill him on sight. This bad negro, the property of Chang, was reported one night to be in the negro cabins of a slave owner near Mount Airy. The citizen went with his gun to investigate and the negro ran from the cabin and as he ran the citizen fired his gun intending to shoot him in the legs. But as luck would have it he aimed too high and killed the negro.
>
> There was no law to punish him for his deed; but he saw a big bill facing him in the way of pay for the value of the dead slave. At once he went to the home of the Twins hoping to make the best settlement possible. Imagine his surprise when the Twins refused to accept a cent and expressed their satisfaction that the negro was out of the way.[13]

In the antebellum South, such tragic events were certainly not rare occurrences. Nor would such conduct by a slave master raise any eyebrows. The twins themselves were said to be fond of bragging about how they had bet on slaves at card games, treating them as disposable property, no better than livestock:

> One time, when they were traveling in Virginia with a neighbor, they were urged by some gamblers to join in a game of cards. They did not engage in gambling games, and so they refused. However, they agreed to back the neighbor, who was "handy with cards." The

neighbor won royally, and the gamblers, in their desperation, bet "a negro." The twins won him, and then sold him back to the unlucky gamblers for $600.[14]

Stories like the above, both the positive and the disparaging portrayals of people treated as subhuman, starring two Asian freaks consorting with two white women and lording over a squad of black slaves, certainly had much traction in the antebellum South. They became perfect fodder for scandal-starved newspapers and readymade material for Southern Gothic, with its endless obsession with sexual peccadilloes, racial violence, deranged cravings, and morbid humor. The following profile, filed in early 1850 by a curiosity-seeking journalist and featured in a publication aptly entitled *The Southerner*, would require very little touchup for it to fit into a plantation pastoral with decidedly racist undertones:

> When we got off the stage at Mt. Airy we were told by the townspeople that the Twins were moody, sulky people and often refused to see anyone who called on them.
>
> After a few glasses of ale and a meal at the Blue Ridge Inn in Mt. Airy we felt more in place in calling on the Twins. It was an extremely warm day and the driver gave the horses plenty of time, in addition to taking the long way around. After having arrived we drove up into a shade of a large cottonwood tree. Everything seemed quiet except a colored boy doing some metal work in a shop nearby. There was a large male peafowl strutting across the yard. Then the twins appeared in the doorway dressed in rough cotton. Each had a quid of tobacco in his mouth, each was barefooted. They stood in the doorway a minute or so, then waved good naturedly. They approached our carriage and asked how they could serve us. . . .
>
> They led us into the living room which contained a bed and other necessities. We found them to be extremely interested in farming as well as moderate conversationalists, often speaking in unbroken English. One would talk awhile then the other would

take over and talk for a few minutes. A colored boy was instructed
to bring in some fresh cider, which we really enjoyed.[15]

What might otherwise pass as a run-of-the-mill antebellum encounter,
in which landed Southern gentry were being served by domestic slaves
while hosting visitors, was complicated by the fact that the masters
in question were, simultaneously, Asian and freakish. The journalistic
preamble about the twins being moody and sulky, the gothic setting
of an exotic bird milling around and a "colored boy" doing handiwork
nearby, and finally the dramatic entry of the real exotic bird, the conjoined twins, in the doorway, clad in coarse cotton, chewing tobacco,
like some ominous creature, barefoot no less—as if reprising a scene
from *1001 Arabian Nights*, the most popular contraband book in colonial America—busting out of a cage, all combined to suggest something
bestial, crude, scandalous.

Nineteenth-century Americans were not new to the scandal or outrage of nonwhite men luxuriating in the privilege of the slaveholding
class. Prior to the arrival of the Europeans, many Native American
tribes had owned slaves, though none exploited slave labor on a large
scale. With the introduction of African slavery, Indian nations also participated in the practice. At the time of Chang and Eng's settlement
in North Carolina, the Cherokee Nation possessed a few thousand
black slaves. The wealthy family of the Cherokee chief, James Vann,
owned more than a hundred in 1835.[16] What magnified the scandal
of Chang and Eng as slave masters was their perceived monstrosity
and miscegenation.

It would be hard to overestimate the enormous impact these percep-
tions had on the populace, both the wealthy and the poor, who lived in
the vicinity of the twins' homestead and in the surrounding areas. The
rich white unquestionably begrudged having to share class and status
with two Asians; just consider the reaction of the twins' closest associates when Chang and Eng expressed their wishes to live the normal
lives of country squires. The poor white was especially resentful and
envious, his place on the social ladder suddenly at risk. Local rumor

mills churned out endlessly salacious stories about the foursome that was going on by Stewart's Creek, on farmland owned by two "colored" men with slanting eyes, masters to a bunch of Negroes. The résumé of a local boy, who would later become a leading voice in explosive national issues such as abolitionism and the anti-Chinese campaign, might give us a rare glimpse into how the unusual lifestyle of the twins as slaveholding landed gentry had affected the American heart and soul.

Born the same year as Chang and Eng's arrival in America, Hinton Rowan Helper (1829–1909) was the son of a struggling North Carolina farmer who owned a small plot of land and a family of four slaves in Mocksville, about sixty miles south of Mount Airy. When Helper was less than a year old, his father died from mumps, leaving his widow and seven children near poverty. Living under his mother's care until he was a teenager, Helper graduated from Mocksville Academy in 1848 and went to California in 1851 to seek his fortune. He was utterly disappointed, because he had difficulty finding a job in a region flooded with non-Caucasian immigrants such as Mexicans and Chinese. Disillusioned with his California experience, he turned to writing to vent his resentment and to prescribe a cure for what he thought had afflicted the nation. Drawing upon his three years of drifting in the Wild West, Helper's first book, *The Land of Gold* (1855), exposed the California dream as a hoax perpetrated by greedy financiers and inept politicians. He was particularly alarmed by the state's estimated forty thousand Chinese, whose presence offended his strong Anglo-Saxon prejudice. In a sensational chapter titled "California Celestials," he waged an all-out war against the Chinese, mocking their appearances, dismissing their habits, and condemning their immorality. "I cannot perceive," he wrote, "what more right or business these semi-barbarians have in California than flocks of blackbirds have in a wheatfield." But no worries, he reasoned, because fate was against the Chinese. "No inferior race of men can exist in these United States without becoming subordinate to the will of the Anglo-Saxons," as it had been with the Negroes in the South, whose enslavement stood as the central issue in his subsequent book, *The Impending*

Crisis of the South (1857).[17] Combining statistical charts and provocative prose, the new book attacked the evils of slavery and its devastating effects upon the people to whom the book was officially dedicated, "The Nonslaveholding Whites of the South." Enjoying popularity exceeded by no antebellum publication other than *Uncle Tom's Cabin*, this abolitionist tome argued that slavery ruined the South by preventing economic development and industrialization, and that it hurt the Southern whites of moderate means, who were oppressed by a small aristocracy of wealthy slaveholders.

Although there was no direct evidence linking Helper's animus toward both the Chinese and the slaveholding aristocracy to his in-person experience with the Siamese Twins, it is not inconceivable that, as Robert G. Lee suggests, "the young Hinton Helper, in addition to sharing the salacious but almost universal fascination with the imagined sexual practice of the twins and their wives, resented the fact that the Siamese twins were land owners of substance and slaveholders to boot, while Helper's own family found itself in reduced financial circumstances on its small farm as the result of his father's early death."[18] When the twins gave one of their last performances in the summer of 1839 in Statesville, ten-year-old Helper was but a few miles away. Spending his formative years in Mocksville, Helper, if he did not live within a stone's throw of Chang and Eng's domicile, certainly came of age within the earshot of all those ribald rumors that rippled through the hills and hollows of western North Carolina.

There are at least two central motifs in Helper's writings that can assist us in detecting the invisible but discernible presence of the Siamese Twins in his racial imagination. First, he was obsessed with the Chinese in California "as a deterrent to the immigration of respectable white women and thus a barrier to 'normal' family development."[19] To Helper, nothing would be more abnormal as a family unit, both racially and structurally, than the abominable union of the Asian twins and their white wives. Second, Helper's belittling descriptions of Chinese people made them seem like freaks, evoking the eerie monstrosity of the conjoined twins:

[John Chinaman's] feet enclosed in rude wooden shoes, his legs bare, his breeches loosely flapping against his knees, his skirtless, long-sleeved, big-bodied pea-jacket, hanging in large folds around his waist, his broad-brimmed chapeau rocking carelessly on his head, and his cue [sic] suspended and gently sweeping about his back! I can compare him to nothing so appropriately as to a tadpole walking upon stilts.[20]

What offended Helper's Anglo-Saxon sensibility was not just the freakish, exotic appearance of the Chinese but also the strange phenomenon that the Chinese all looked alike to him. "All their garments look as if they were made after the same pattern out of the same material and from the same piece of cloth. In short, one Chinaman looks almost exactly like another, but very unlike anybody else."[21] We know for sure that in mid-nineteenth-century America, no two Chinese men looked more alike than Chang and Eng, who in fact always wore clothes "made after the same pattern out of the same material and from the same piece of cloth." As Helper wandered around the city square or walked down Telegraph Hill in San Francisco, where the Chinese thronged the "cow-pens" and "human stables," as he put it, his mind might have easily been tricked by the memories of the Siamese Twins, who had undoubtedly haunted his childhood.[22]

In the early 1850s, when Helper returned from the California nightmare to his humble homestead in North Carolina to nurse his injured sensibility while writing his first two books, the gentrified life of Chang and Eng in the next county was just getting more complicated. Since 1844, each twin and his wife had increased their brood at a steady pace of one child a year. The crowded house led to more tension. The two sisters squabbled, spurring the twins to set up two households within a mile of each other on their farm outside Mount Airy. Since they could not go separate ways as ordinary men would, they alternated three days at each home and each conjugal bed—a rigid routine they would follow religiously till their last breath. While the fear of miscegenation between black and white had remained the driving force behind Helper's abolitionist rhetoric, the union between Asian and white, let alone the abnormal kind, would only intensify racial anxiety. In fact, white supremacists like Helper rallied under the banner of abolitionism not with the purpose of saving blacks from the injustice of slavery but with the goal of protecting the purity of the white race from the menace of miscegenation. In this regard, Chang and Eng might have disturbed the racial paradise as imagined by the ilk of Helper not only through their marriage to two white women but also through their possible relations with their slave women.

Now—back to the Bunker reunion in 2003. It was a grand occasion of celebration, a gathering of people who were products of a union unthinkable to most. The Bunker descendants certainly proved how wrongheaded Helper and other nineteenth-century racial apologists were, or how unfounded their crackpot racial theories were. Contrary to the fear of racial contamination and degradation, the Bunker progeny were all respectable citizens. Many of them were highly educated, smart, savvy; some were army generals, presidents of major corporations, and elected government officials. In the midst of this multiracial harmony, however, the appearance of a black woman with a claim on the proud Bunker genealogy wreaked no small havoc. Subsequent steps taken by some of the Bunker descendants indicated how sensitive the matter was, or how unbearably haunting family history can be.

Even before the 2003 reunion, some Bunker descendants, perhaps motivated by the Jefferson/Hemings controversy, had made inquiries in May of 2002 to the staff at the College of Physicians of Philadelphia, where the autopsy of Chang and Eng had been conducted in 1874 and where the fused liver of the twins is still preserved. These descendants had asked about "the possibility of testing hair trapped in the plaster of Chang and Eng's body cast to confirm anecdotes about hereditary lineages that issued from their slaves." Although there was no extant record or newspaper report on such a matter during or after the twins' lifetime, these descendants had grown up with family stories about how Patrick Bunker, Eng's son, "used to play with his half-sisters and half-brothers who were enslaved." Now that a descendant of a Bunker slave woman had surfaced, the issue took on added urgency and interest. Gretchen Worden, the curator of the Mütter Museum, who received the inquiry from the Bunker descendants, contacted a forensic scientist at George Washington University about the possibility of "obtaining DNA from either Chang and Eng's hair or liver." The expert replied and affirmed the feasibility of conducting such a test if nuclear DNA was available in the hair root, "if any part of it came away from the follicle when it was pulled away by the plaster."[23]

There was, however, no follow-up to this flurry of inquiries. There is no definitive conclusion. Unlike the Jefferson/Hemings situation, in which DNA results brought clarity to a past that many of Jefferson's white descendants had denied for centuries, most Bunker family secrets remain shrouded in the fog of time. However, even without scientific corroboration, family lore still endures, such as the following about the twins:

They attended the local shooting matches, where a turkey or beef was the reward for the best marksman, and Chang and Eng acquired reputations as crackshots with rifles or pistols. It was the object of much curious speculation on the neighbor's part how two men tied together could be so adept, often more adept than a single man.

The farmers in Surry County were frequently plagued by wolves, who wreaked havoc among their livestock. There existed one particularly notorious wolf, christened "Bob-Tail," because he had lost part of his tail in a trap. This wolf did not merely limit his dinings to sheep and cattle, but was believed to have eaten a negro baby who wandered into the woods. Bob-Tail made trouble for three years, and no one was able to trap him, until one night when Chang and Eng were awoken by noises coming from among their livestock. They ran out, taking with them a gun and a slave carrying a lantern. It was Bob-Tail, and the wolf breathed his last at the twins' hands. This coup gave Chang and Eng considerable prestige in the community, especially as no more negro babies were ever known to be stolen or eaten.[24]

This family vignette, passed down orally through generations, seems to be about the twins' remarkable marksmanship and heroic deed of ridding the community of a dangerous pest. But a more discerning and curious reader, mindful of the genealogical intricacy of a slave-owning household in the antebellum South like that of the twins, might rightly ask, "Negro babies? Whose Negro babies?"

The Age of Humbugs

There's a sucker born every minute.

—attributed to P. T. Barnum

It little profits that an idle king,
By this still hearth, among these barren crags,
Matched with an aged wife, I mete and dole
Unequal laws unto a savage race,
That hoard, and sleep, and feed, and know not me.

In "Ulysses," Alfred, Lord Tennyson, imagined that the eponymous hero, having returned from his epic journey and reunited with his wife, Penelope, and son, Telemachus, grows weary of the humdrum life of domesticity. Speaking in dramatic monologue, the former voyager yearns for the road again: "I cannot rest from travel; I will drink / Life to the lees."

Mount Airy was decidedly no Ithaca, and the Siamese Twins were certainly not mythical characters—although they had been regarded as living proof of a miracle from God. But they did share with the Homeric hero the discontent with lassitude and the urge for action. Avid readers who stocked their bookshelves with the works of Shakespeare, Pope, Byron, and other eminent British authors, Chang and Eng could easily have read "Ulysses," a popular poem published in 1842 by the most popular poet of the Victorian Era. The twins would certainly recognize that raw yearning for the road.

In the spring of 1849, opportunity knocked at their door, offering the twins a reprieve from the rustic life of landed gentry. An old friend,

Edmund Doty, whom they had met during their decade-long odyssey, approached them with a proposal. Now that they had married and had kids, Doty wanted to exhibit two of their brood as well as their conjoined bodies, to show the world that however abnormal they might look, their conjugal ties to two white women were able to produce normal children. Making the twins a handsome offer of $8,000 a year, all expenses paid, Doty rekindled the twins' wanderlust and financial appetite.[1]

In April, as gold dreamers from all over the world flocked to California for a chance to "strike it rich," Chang and Eng journeyed with their five-year-old daughters, Katherine and Josephine, to New York to dig for their own gold. It had been ten years since their withdrawal from the public eye and their settlement in the Rip Van Winkle State. Just as the henpecked Dutchman in Washington Irving's classic tale who slumbers through the Revolutionary War in the misty Catskills and wakes up to a world beyond recognition, Chang and Eng also found that the country, which they now proudly called their own, had profoundly changed during their somnambulant decade in the mountains. Show business, in particular, had entered a golden age of chicanery, at the center of which now stood the Prince of Humbugs, P. T. Barnum.

Even before Barnum burst onto the scene, America had already seen many elaborate hoaxes or sensational scams. Under Jacksonian democracy, which was now entering its third decade, the rise of the common man meant that everyone had an opinion or was entitled to have one. When the popular will becomes paramount in a nation's political life, the manipulation of public opinion also becomes a necessary art and evil, thus giving rise to a new army of confidence men, crooks, tricksters, charlatans, swindlers, fakers, frauds, cheats, hustlers, bilkers, sharks, racketeers, mountebanks, and humbugs, who pervade every trade and every walk of life. One of the most elaborate hoaxes was pulled off in New York in the summer of 1824, when two men, a retired carpenter by the name of Lozier and a butcher who went by the affectionate epithet of Uncle John, announced that they had been hired to saw off Manhattan Island and turn it around. The duo emerged from City Hall, where they supposedly had held a meeting with Mayor Stephen Allen, and claimed that Manhattan Island was beginning to sag because of the weight of new business buildings on its southern end. Flaunting a huge ledger containing the names of out-of-work laborers who had applied for the task, the two con artists managed to engage scores of carpenters and contractors to furnish lumber to build barracks for the workmen. They also hired butchers for the purposes of preparing cattle, hogs, and fowl to feed the workmen. And, of course, they drew up plans for hundred-foot saws and other mechanical appliances, which blacksmiths and mechanics feverishly set to work designing. Five hundred to a thousand people turned up on a July day at the designated street corner. But, as if anticipating the turn-of-the-twentieth-century exploits of Meredith Willson's *The Music Man*, Lozier and Uncle John never showed up or were heard from again.[2]

Another scam took the nation by storm in August 1835, when a series of six articles appeared in the New York *Sun*, that era's version of the *National Enquirer*, announcing the discovery of lunar life with the aid of a seven-ton telescope invented by Sir John Herschel. The articles claimed that scientists had observed fourteen species of animal life on the moon, including unicorns, two-legged beavers, and brown quadrupeds resembling bison. These fantastical animals were seen to roam a lunar landscape of massive craters, pyramid-shaped mountains of amethyst crystals, rushing rivers, and lush vegetation consisting of about thirty-eight species of trees. The most astonishing discovery of all was winged humanoids walking on the moon. "They averaged four feet in height, were covered, except on the face, with short and glossy copper-colored hair. . . . The face, which was of a yellowish flesh-color, was a slight improvement upon that of the large orang-outang." These stories were so sensational that they fooled not only the gullible readers of the penny press but also a committee of Yale University scientists, who traveled to New York for further investigation. A women's club in Springfield, Massachusetts, eagerly raised funds for sending missionaries to the moon.[3]

One may wonder whether those devout Christian ladies in Springfield had ever considered how in the name of sweet Jesus their missionaries would travel to the moon. Interestingly, someone else had already taken care of the need for space travel. Just two months earlier, Edgar Allan Poe, always game for a spoof, had published in the *Southern Literary Messenger* a story titled "The Unparalleled Adventure of One Hans Pfaall," which details a journey to the moon via a revolutionary new balloon and a device that compresses the vacuum of space into breathable air. In fact, Poe had planned to write sequels to the "scoop" and to continue to keep readers on tenterhooks of curiosity, but the Great Moon Hoax stole the thunder from him. However, nine years later, Poe got to pull another fast one on the credulous when he sold a sensational story to the *Sun*, the same tabloid that had upstaged him with the Great Moon Hoax. On April 13, 1844, the newspaper carried the headline,

ASTONISHING INTELLIGENCE BY PRIVATE EXPRESS FROM
CHARLESTON VIA NORFOLK! THE ATLANTIC OCEAN
CROSSED IN THREE DAYS!! ARRIVAL AT SULLIVAN'S ISLAND
OF A STERLING BALLOON INVENTED BY
MR. MONK MASON!!

The news of eight people in a balloon crossing the Atlantic in three days spread like a prairie fire, and both the earlier and the later editions of the newspaper were sold out. "I never witnessed more intense excitement to get possession of a newspaper," Poe gloated privately. The newspaper boys jacked up the prices so high that even Poe himself could not get hold of a copy all that day.[4]

Most of these hoaxes were committed for the purpose of selling papers. While making good copy, they also earned the perpetrators notoriety and money. Poe, for instance, in addition to earning much-needed cash to eke out a precarious living, was also credited with having inspired such later science-fiction writers as Jules Verne and H. G. Wells. But no one in nineteenth-century America was more successful in making a fortune out of tomfoolery, or did so with more swagger

P. T. BARNUM AND GENERAL TOM THUMB

and braggadocio, than P. T. Barnum, the nation's first great purveyor
of mass entertainment, a brash Connecticut Yankee who believed with
evangelical fervor that "the American people like to be humbugged."

Phineas Taylor Barnum, born in Bethel, Connecticut, on July 5, 1810, was a tireless polisher of his own résumé later in life. Barnum certainly wished that he had not dillydallied in his mother's womb a day too long so that he could have basked in the patriotic glory of having entered into the world to the jovial fanfare of July Fourth. Or, in the words of one biographer who knows all too well his subject's unusual hunger for attention, "Probably his tardiness was for the best; competition between P. T. Barnum and the national holiday would have been too much—for the national holiday."[5] Named after his maternal grandfather, Phineas Taylor, Barnum certainly would live up to the romantic significance of "Phineas," a biblical name meaning "brazen mouth." Even though Bethel, a town known for manufacturing combs and hats, was "a tight little prison of Puritanism" ruled by the iron fist of the blue laws, out of this religious crucible would come a man whose lifetime mission was, as he put it himself, "to cater to that insatiate want of human nature—the love of amusement."[6]

Appropriately, the future Prince of Humbugs learned his first lesson in humbuggery from his namesake, Grandfather Taylor, who enjoyed a reputation as a village wit and wag. At his birth, Barnum not only was christened with the name of his grandfather, but the latter, an inveterate prankster, also gifted the baby with a plot of land he called "Ivy Island." As Barnum retold it in his autobiography—a narrative feat retrofitted nine times and said by many to be the most widely read book, after the Bible, in the second half of the nineteenth century—"My grandfather always spoke of me . . . to the neighbors and to strangers as the richest child in town, since I owned the whole of 'Ivy Island,' one of the most valuable farms in the State."[7] Always feeling his oats as a rich landowner, young Barnum could not wait to see his prized dominion. After repeated begging, he was finally allowed to take a peek. To his utter dismay, his so-called inheritance was "a tract of swampy, snake-infested land." At that moment, everyone hooted, and young Barnum learned the truth that he had been the laughingstock of the family and neighborhood for years. More important, he learned his first lesson in chicanery, the art of pulling off a practical joke at another's expense.

Barnum bragged in his autobiography that his "organ of 'acquisitive-

ness' was manifest at an early age," acquisitiveness being a phrenological faculty responsible for one's compulsion to acquire and hoard. He
did not know that when Franz Joseph Gall, the father of phrenology,
had first identified this organ in many of the prisoners he was studying,
he had called it in German *Diebssinn*, the "organ of thieving." Whether
criminally pilfering or just Yankee shrewd, the acquisitive young Barnum was "always ready for a trade," peddling molasses candy, ginger-
bread, cookies, and cherry rum. Like Poor Richard, Benjamin Franklin's
industrious alter ego, young Barnum generally found himself "a dollar
or two richer at the end of a holiday" than he had been at the beginning.[8] Averse to manual labor, he was not a great help on the farm, so
his father opened a country store and made twelve-year-old Barnum
the clerk.

While Melville had called the whaling ship his "Harvard and Yale
College," Barnum could have made the same claim about the country
store for what it could teach him. As he later recalled:

> There is a great deal to be learned in a country store, and princi-
> pally this—that sharp trades, tricks, dishonesty and deception are
> by no means confined to the city. More than once, in cutting open
> bundles of rags, brought to be exchanged for goods, and warranted
> to be all linen and cotton, I have discovered in the interior worth-
> less woolen trash and sometimes stones, gravel or ashes. Some-
> times, too, when measuring loads of oats, corn or rye, declared to
> contain a specified number of bushels, say sixty, I have found them
> four or five bushels short.[9]

Deception was so common in this business that the grocer would make
it into the hall of fame for humbugs when many years later Barnum
wrote a book called *The Humbugs of the World*.

From a country store, Barnum quickly graduated to the lottery business, another common scheme for scamming the gullible. One time, to
move a large quantity of worthless glass bottles and worn tinware from
his store, Barnum "conceived the idea of a lottery in which the high-

est prize should be twenty-five dollars. . . . It is unnecessary to state that the minor prizes consisted mainly of glass and tin ware," Barnum gloated in his memoir. "The tickets sold like wildfire, and the worn tin and glass bottles were speedily turned into cash."[10] From this cocoon of country-store trickery would emerge the most fabulous showman of the age, and what occasioned the metamorphosis was a chance encounter with Joice Heth's freak show.

Wizened like a mummy and blind like a bat, Joice Heth, the toothless black woman, was believed to be 161 years old in 1835. Paralyzed either from age or disease, Heth was nonetheless pert and sociable at exhibitions, garrulous about her protégé, "dear little George," for she claimed to have been the nurse of the nation's founding father, George Washington. Like love at first sight, when Barnum saw her display in Philadelphia, he sensed an opportunity and bought her from her owner for a thousand dollars. Whether or not Barnum actually believed in Heth's authenticity was beside the point. What Barnum found in her was the greater truth, something that would become the cornerstone of his success as a showman.

"Everything depended upon getting people to think, and talk, and become curious and excited over and about the 'rare spectacle,'" Barnum shrewdly put it. "Accordingly, posters, transparencies, advertisements, newspaper paragraphs—all calculated to extort attention—were employed, regardless of expense."[11] Thanks to publicity, the exhibition rooms where Barnum showcased Heth—in New York, Boston, Philadelphia, Albany, and other large and small cities—were continually thronged by the gullible and skeptical alike, because both wanted to see the rarity in person in order to add some weight to their own opinions. When Heth died the next year and her autopsy revealed that she could not have been older than eighty, the scandal of a hoax provoked even more interest than when she was alive. And more money flowed into Barnum's pocket, making him recognize "the perfect good nature with which the American public submit to a clever humbug," and the fact that untruths succeed better than truths.

Having found his true vocation, Barnum spent the next few years on the road, working with different partners, showcasing oddities and talents, and running circuses. But he hated the life of a traveling entertainer and yearned for something more stable and glamorous. His big moment came on January 1, 1842, when he opened the American Museum in New York, an institution with which his name would forever be associated, a ladder by which he rose to fortune and fame. Like the Disneyland of today, almost no American living in the mid-nineteenth century had not heard of or dreamed about visiting Barnum's museum. Open every day from sunrise to sundown, the museum assaulted the senses of visitors with a superfluity of permanent collectibles and transient novelties, including

> . . . educated dogs, industrious fleas, automatons, jugglers, ventriloquists, living statuary, tableaux, gipsies, Albinoes, fat boys, giants, dwarfs, rope-dancers, live "Yankees," pantomime, instrumental music, singing and dancing in great variety, dioramas, panoramas, models of Niagara, Dublin, Paris, and Jerusalem; Hannington's dioramas of the Creation, the Deluge, Fairy Grotto, Storm at Sea; the first English Punch and Judy in this country, Italian Fantoccini, mechanical figures, fancy glass-blowing, knitting machines and other triumphs in the mechanical arts; dissolving views, American Indians, who enacted their warlike and religious ceremonies on the stage.[12]

The secret of Barnum's success was the art of advertising, not merely by means of printer's ink but by turning every possible circumstance to his advantage. "It was my monomania," he said, "to make the Museum the town wonder and town talk." An indefatigable carnival barker, Barnum was never short of ingenious ideas for ensnaring crowds and making them pay. "When people expect to get 'something for nothing,'" he remarked with candor, "they are sure to be cheated, and generally deserve to be." At one point, Barnum realized that his museum was getting too crowded because the visitors, once inside, had been milling around for too long. Some of them even brought their dinners, with the evident intention of literally "making a day of it," while hundreds were waiting outside to pay up and get in. To speed up the flow of the crowd and the money into his coffers, Barnum creatively erected a big sign over the door leading to the back stairs that read in large letters: TO THE EGRESS. Mistaking the arcane word for a rare species of animal they had not seen, the dallying throng began to pour down the back stairs, only to realize too late that they were back on the street. Their loss was Barnum's gain, because he was now able to "accommodate those who had long been waiting with their money at the Broadway entrance."[13]

"Advertising is like learning," Barnum said, "a little is a dangerous thing. . . . When an advertisement first appears, a man does not see it; the second time he notices; the third time he reads it; the fourth he thinks about it; the fifth he speaks to his wife about it; and the sixth or seventh he is ready to purchase." In a unique scheme to advertise his museum, Barnum once put an elephant to work plowing on his farm in Bridgeport right next to the train tracks. To maximize the effect, he dressed an elephant keeper in an Oriental costume and gave him a time-table of the railway, "with special instructions to be busily engaged in his work whenever passenger trains from either way were passing through." Pretty soon, the whole world was talking about how the proprietor of the celebrated American Museum had introduced elephant farming.[14]

For his unscrupulous ways of grabbing public attention, Barnum never felt any remorse. Instead, he believed that he had his finger on the pulse of the nation. "I fell in with the world's way," he said. "If my 'puffing' was more persistent, my advertising more authentic, my posters more glaring, my pictures more exaggerated, my flags more patriotic and my transparencies more brilliant than they would have been under the management of my neighbors, it was not because I had less scruple than they, but more energy, far more ingenuity, and a better foundation for such promise."[15]

In the spring of 1849, when Chang and Eng arrived in New York and tried to restart their career as showmen, they faced a daunting competitor in the American Museum, which had dominated showbiz since its inception. That year, General Tom Thumb, a twenty-five-inch midget, the crown jewel of Barnum's exhibition, was all the rage. Barnum had discovered his pygmy prodigy a few years earlier in Bridgeport, Connecticut. After signing a contract with the parents, Barnum changed the name of his prized acquisition from the plain-as-shoe Charles S. Stratton to the fanciful General Tom Thumb and turned him into an even bigger cash cow than the Siamese Twins had once been for the Coffins. As Philip Hone duly recorded in his diary, Tom Thumb was the lion of the city at the time:

> I went last evening with my daughter Margaret to the American Museum to see the greatest *little* mortal who has ever been exhibited; a handsome well-formed boy, eleven years of age, who is twenty-five inches in height and weighs fifteen pounds . . . lively, agreeable, sprightly, and talkative, with no deficiency of intellect. . . . His hand is about the size of a half dollar and his foot three inches in length, and in walking alongside of him, the top of his head did not reach above my knee. When I entered the room he came up to me, offered his hand, and said, "How d'ye do, Mr. Hone?"[16]

Compared with this smooth-talking, cigar-puffing dwarf, even the famous Siamese Twins might have seemed a little passé, especially when they did not have an ingenious and indefatigable carnival barker like Barnum backing them. Their own promoter, Doty, was apparently no Barnum; no one could be. The other disadvantage for the twins lay in the fact that, as Barnum had learned from his own experience, in the pyramidal hierarchy of showbiz, "ranging from the mammoth wholesale establishment down to the corner stand," a traveling, single-installation display was really at the bottom of the ladder. Thanks to Barnum and his ilk, Americans had by this time become more accustomed to glittery extravaganzas in museum galleries than scruffy freak shows in drawing rooms and on street corners.

Even Doty's clever scheme of displaying the twins' children, as well as recycling the old promotional line that the twins were considering (again) surgical separation, did not do much to boost ticket sales. But the twins' return to the world stage did get some attention from the press. As the *New York Tribune* announced on April 23:

> After ten or twelve years of retired life on their farm in N. Carolina, the celebrated Siamese Twins, Chang and Eng, are about to start another tour of exhibition. They will commence in this City in a few weeks, and after visiting the principal cities of the North and East, will proceed to Europe. One object of their travel, we learn, is to obtain the opinion of eminent surgeons as to the possibility of their separation. They will be accompanied by several of their children, who will also be included in the exhibition.[17]

Against the formidable competition from Barnum's menagerie of freaks and curios, the Siamese Twins opened their show in New York in late April of 1849 without much fanfare. The exhibition lasted but six weeks, during which time they also made a quick trip to Washington, where, as the *New Hampshire Patriot* noted on May 17, they "receiv[ed] calls at the modest price of a quarter of a dollar admission." The ambitious Northeast tour did not happen, nor did the planned trip to Europe pan out, nor did the financial arrangement with Doty. In July, when the twins and their daughters returned to North Carolina, they had "nothing to show for their trouble but an IOU from Doty." Their disappointing homecoming garnered only a scant mention in the *Pittsfield Sun*: "The Siamese Twins have gone back to their homes and their wives." In the Age of Humbugs, authenticity was destined to be outgunned by sales puffery, an indignation that would become routine in the coming era of billboards, neon signs, and "Mad Men."[18]

The show, however, had to go on. A few years later, Chang and Eng accepted an offer from a Mr. Howes to do another tour, again with their children. This time, they did tour the Northeast, traveling along the Atlantic Seaboard all the way up to Nova Scotia and then back to central and upstate New York before moving northward again as far as Quebec. Touring with them this time were Chang's son Christopher and Eng's daughter Katherine. From April 1853 to March 1854, the quartet made 130 stops and covered about forty-seven hundred miles.

All this time, Barnum had kept a hovering eye on the twins, a rare specimen that had so far eluded his capture. Over the years, as Barnum added more novelties—his dwarfs shrinking and giants expanding—to his collection, the Siamese Twins had remained missing from his menagerie, or refused to be *Barnumized*, a term Barnum proudly used to describe the process by which he would discover, acquire, prep, and control oddities, human or not.[19] Perhaps they were too independent, or perhaps they were weary of the ill repute of the Prince of Humbugs; Chang and Eng had repeatedly spurned Barnum's overtures. But the pitiful tour in 1849 and the lackluster one in 1853–54 made the twins wonder whether they should indeed give the crass Yankee a second look. In the autumn of 1860, only weeks before the election of Abraham Lincoln as president, they agreed to be put on display at Barnum's museum for a fee of $100 a week.

Compared to the weekly $300 fee they used to get from Peale's Museum, which had by now been forced out of business and taken over by Barnum, $100 was an insulting amount, especially considering that they were now accompanied by two of their children. But for Barnum, this was already proverbial highway robbery compared to the wages he had been paying the living curios of his establishment. This arrangement between the twins and Barnum was really a marriage of convenience, one full of distrust and misgivings at the outset. According to Patrick Bunker, Eng's son who was displayed at the American Museum along with his father and uncle, the twins found Barnum to be tight-fisted and exploitative. "They never liked Barnum," Patrick said. "He was too much of a Yankee, and wanted too much for his share of the money."[20] The ill feeling was mutual: Barnum resented the fact that, unlike the other oddities under his wing, the twins were too independent and they drove a hard bargain. Despite these niggles, having the Siamese Twins inside his museum gave Barnum plenty of bragging rights. Contrary to all the facts and evidence, Barnum would later claim that he had discovered the united brothers and also coined the term *Siamese Twins*, a fib that still holds sway in some quarters of popular culture.

During the monthlong engagement at Barnum's museum, the twins and two of their children, twelve-year-old Montgomery and ten-year-old Patrick, were displayed next to an albino family and an exhibition called "What Is It?" The former consisted of a European couple and their son, all albinos with pink eyes, discovered on a human spelunking mission in Holland by Barnum and then recast as "Negroes from Madagascar." The latter was "a deformed, intelligent Negro named William Jackson," whom Barnum had renamed "Zip, the Monkey Man" and promoted as the missing link between man and the ape.[21] Having experienced the leisurely life of slaveholding Southern gentry, the twins must have found it hard to swallow the humiliation of being put on display along with "Barnum's freaks," or being regarded as one of them. Standing next to the deceptively labeled albino family and the Monkey Man, they were especially appalled by Barnum's sales puffery. They felt that Barnum was probably the most freakish of all the men they had met, a natural wonder in his own right, a new incarnation of the ubiquitous Yankee Peddler they had encountered during their decade-long life on the road. It was a sentiment shared by none other than Albert Edward, Prince of Wales, who visited the museum about a week after the twins had opened there. Arriving on a day when Barnum was out of town, and having inspected thousands of oddities at the American Museum, the future King Edward VII of England asked, "I suppose I have seen all the curiosities; but where is Mr. Barnum?" With a touch of British humor, His Royal Highness was suggesting that he had missed "the most interesting feature of the establishment," the owner himself.[22]

To allude to Barnum as a curiosity, making him one of the freaks and wonders he had corralled and caged at his own museum, is to acknowledge the unique character of a humbug and his special place in American history and culture. A humbug, flimflam man, shingle man, confidence man, or, to some, just Yankee, is a trickster. As Melville recognized long ago, a trickster is not necessarily the Devil, although he could traf-

fic in devilish ways. "Trickster is amoral, not immoral," declares Lewis
Hyde in his book on the trickster as a covert but quintessential American hero, an interpretation resonating with many thinkers and writers.[23]
Anthropologists who study the myriad manifestations of the trickster
in diverse cultures—Native American coyote, Polynesian Maui, West
African Eshu, Hindu Krishna, Chinese Monkey King, Greek Hermes,
and others—have all recognized the figure as one of the most archaic of
mythical generators. In the words of Paul Radin, "Trickster is at one and
the same time creator and destroyer, giver and negator, he who dupes
others and who is always duped himself. . . . He knows neither good
nor evil yet he is responsible for both. He possesses no values, moral or
social . . . yet through his actions all values come into being."[24]

    In the American context, some have argued that the confidence man
as a trickster—a colorful figure ubiquitous in literature and film—is
"one of America's unacknowledged founding fathers." In *The Confidence
Game in American Literature* (1975), Warwick Wadlington goes so far as to
suggest that "Americans have always been, in one sense or another, confidence men," because Americans are "peddlers of assurance." America
was founded on the loftiest metaphor of its being the land of promise,
the New Jerusalem. The soaring language from statesmen and orators
ranging from Benjamin Franklin to Ralph Waldo Emerson vivified the
myth of self-reliance and economic optimism, a matrix of robust confidence.[25] In the Jacksonian Age, democracy also became a game of confidence, in the double sense of the word: political representatives gain
the trust of the common men and pull a con on them. The most successful politicians, Jackson being the best example, are those who show an
extraordinary capacity for identifying the needs of others and play them
for suckers, as a shrewd confidence man would. The founding myth
of promise, the ideology of rugged individualism, and the politics of
democratic representation all joined forces to make America a breeding
ground for confidence. From Yankee peddlers to sly politicians, smart
investors, and even imaginative writers, every American was involved,
as Melville put it, in the creative act of "godly gamesomeness."

In nineteenth-century America, no one did it better than P. T. Barnum in turning confidence into entertainment; no one was a better trickster than the Prince of Humbugs. For that reason, both the Prince of Wales and the Siamese Twins were correct in recognizing the curator of the freak show as the most freakish figure at the aptly named American Museum.

Minstrel Freaks

After a rather humiliating stint at Barnum's American Museum in New York, Chang and Eng struck out again on their own. Considering themselves gentry, they no longer wanted to be dime-museum freaks or sideshow riffraff. So in November 1860, when the nation was roiling as a result of the presidential election, the twins took two of their children, Montgomery and Patrick, and boarded a ship for California.

Judging by their latest two attempts, Chang and Eng astutely concluded that the East Coast market had been tapped out and that the fast-growing West, to which people continued to flock, might present better opportunities. Since the discovery of gold twelve years earlier, California had boomed. San Francisco, initially a loose cluster of adobe haciendas, had mushroomed into a city overnight; or, as Will Rogers quipped, it "was never a town." But getting to the fabled Gold Mountain before the completion of the transcontinental railroad in 1869 or the Panama Canal in 1914 required a lengthy journey. From New York, the twins and their sons sailed for eight days down to Panama City, and then took a train across the Isthmus of Panama to catch the steamship *Uncle Sam* on the other side.

Aboard the 1,800-ton Pacific Mail steamer, the Bunker quartet sailed for the new Eldorado. During the sixteen-day journey, they saw, as teenage Montgomery wrote in a family letter, plenty of whales and flying fish, and enjoyed a diet of fresh green corn, beans, and peas. When the ship stopped at Acapulco, Mexico, for coal, the ubiquitous palm trees and the verdant tropical vistas caused a stir in the twins' hearts, a sudden pang of homesickness—not for North Carolina but for Siam, which lay far beyond the horizon of the blue Pacific, the "heart-beating center of the world," as Melville put it. Among the passengers was a Reverend J. A. Benton, native of Sacramento, who had left California for China a

CHANG AND ENG BUNKER AND THEIR CHILDREN

year and a half earlier on a mission to demonstrate that, "if one will but keep going in the same direction he will get home again at last." Speaking at length with the globetrotting reverend, the twins were hungry for any tiny morsel of tidings about the native land they had left almost a lifetime earlier.[1]

Arriving in San Francisco, Chang and Eng were surprised to find that their reputation had preceded them. Not only were they household names, but their success as showmen had also spawned imitation and mockery in the hands of a new breed of performers, who represented an emerging American art: the minstrel show. In fact, when they were still in New York, they had already witnessed the increasing popularity of blackface minstrelsy. During the month of their exhibition at the American Museum, at least half a dozen minstrel bands were performing every night at popular local joints, including Niblo's Saloon, Mechanics Hall, and the New Bowery Theatre.

Minstrelsy had begun in the early 1800s with white men in blackface portraying Negro characters and performing putative Negro songs and dances. By the mid-nineteenth century, it had expanded its repertoire, or racial cast, to include Chinese, Irish, Japanese, Native American, and other ethnic minority characters. Originating in East Coast cities, minstrelsy had also spread geographically, especially to California. According to Robert C. Toll, "When a large number of people trekked across the continent in search of California gold . . . minstrelsy quickly established itself there. First presented in 1849 by local amateur groups scattered throughout the goldfields, minstrelsy by 1855 claimed five professional troupes in San Francisco alone."[2] A sure sign that San Francisco had become a hub for minstrelsy, one of the most famous troupes at the time, the Christie Minstrels, led by E. P. Christie and others, "changed their name to Christie's San Francisco Minstrels to add to their luster when traveling around the country."[3]

What made California a particularly fertile ground for minstrelsy was not only the prevalence of rowdy, gun-toting, pleasure-seeking crowds but also the huge influx of immigrants who made for a more racially mixed population. The Chinese, especially, had a strong presence in California, a fact repugnant to many and one that, as we saw, had irked the ilk of Hinton Helper, Chang and Eng's fellow Tar Heeler-turned-Sinophobe. Chinese immigration to the United States had been sporadic before the mid-nineteenth century, but the discovery of gold at John Sutter's mill suddenly spiked the number of Chinese arriving in North America: 325 in 1849, 450 more in 1850, 2,716 in 1851, and 20,026 in 1852. By 1860, there were about 37,000 Chinese in the United States, most in California. At first, Chinese were welcomed in the state that had just joined the Union in 1850. Their arrivals were routinely reported in the newspapers as increases to a "worthy integer of population." But as the competition in the goldfields became more intense, the tide soon turned against the Chinese, and the affectionate feelings soured. When Emerson said in 1854, "The disgust of California has not been able to drive or kick the Chinaman back to his home," the New England sage seemed well informed about the happenings in the Wild West and the rise of anti-Chinese sentiments, which would soon lead to mob violence and the passage of discriminatory laws. A sure sign of change in the air: The word *Chinaman*, previously a neutral, catchall term for Asian men, had already picked up a negative tone when Emerson used it.[4]

Rising hostility toward the Chinese led to demeaning portrayals in minstrel shows. The stock character of John Chinaman—in yellowface, sporting a long queue and a pair of loose pantaloons, speaking in a caricatured dialect—often appeared on the minstrel stage, as depicted in the following song, "Big Long John":

Big Long John was a Chinaman,
and he lived in the land of the free . . .
He wore a long tail from the top of his head
Which hung way down to his heels . . .
He went to San Francisco for Chinee gal to see,
Feeling tired, he laid down to rest,
Beneath the shade of huckleberry tree.

Or, as in another minstrel song, "Hong Kong," in which John Chinaman speaks of his doomed love for his "lillee gal":

> Me stopee long me lillee gal nicee
> Wellee happee Chinaman, me no care,
> Me smokee, smokee, lillie gal talkee,
> Chinaman and lillee gal wellee jollee pair.[5]

As a predecessor to Ah Sin, the other stock character created and popularized by F. Bret Harte in his satirical poem "The Heathen Chinee," John Chinaman was the Asian counterpart to such blackface figures as Jim Crow and Zip Coon. During his disappointing adventure in the West, Hinton Helper must have been so impressed by these minstrel songs that he would later adopt "John Chinaman" as the generic name for all the "Celestials" maligned in his books.

Arguably the most famous "Chinamen" in the nineteenth century, the Siamese Twins naturally were featured in minstrel shows that parodied the Chinese. Their nonstop tour across the country from 1829 to 1839, followed by sensational stories of their married lives in the South, had turned them into cultural icons as familiar as Charlie Chan and Fu Manchu were in the twentieth century. In *Orientals: Asian Americans in Popular Culture*, a study of the representation of Asians in American culture, Robert G. Lee astutely identifies two motifs of change embodied by the Siamese Twins: "The forty-year career of Chang and Eng suggests both the shift in the signification of the Chinese from object of curiosity to symbol of racial crisis and the shift in the popular sites of that signification from museum to minstrel show."[6] In other words, if a freak show, as I have suggested earlier, often staged racial freaks, the rise of minstrelsy in the 1840s and the surge of anti-Chinese sentiments in the 1850s had opened up a new arena for the staging of racial others. Freak show was transitioning to minstrel show, or at least the two were joining forces to channel the boiling racial tensions in antebellum America. It was a historical change experienced, and indeed embodied, by Chang and Eng.

On December 10, 1860, when the twins opened their exhibition at

Platt's New Music Hall in San Francisco, many in the audience had already seen or would soon see minstrel renditions of the freak show. Chief among those minstrel appropriations were the skits performed by Charley Fox and Frank B. Converse, both pioneers of blackface minstrelsy. Fox was known for the popular songbooks he edited, and Converse was regarded as the "Father of Banjo." As seen in a songster cover, the Fox–Converse team performed banjo duets by impersonating the Siamese Twins, tossing their pigtails and kicking around the stage with pointed wooden shoes. Chang and Eng's unique physicality, something that the twins themselves had exploited successfully in their onstage repartee, also made it convenient for Fox and Converse to appropriate the twins as characters for skits such as "Conundrums," which featured chin-wags between two speakers:

When is a bedstead not a bedstead?
When it's a little buggy.
Why is a railroad-car like a bed-bug?
Because it runs on sleepers.
Why is a poor man like a baker?
Because he needs de dough.
Who was the oldest woman?
Aunt-Iniquity.[7]

Arriving in the West after the Civil War broke out, hence too late to see Chang and Eng's California shows in person, Mark Twain nonetheless had an obsession with the Siamese Twins that was part of his lifelong infatuation with what he called the "genuine nigger show." Twain, or little Sam, first saw minstrel shows when he was growing up in Hannibal, Missouri. He was struck by the "loud and extravagant burlesque."[8] Like Jakie Rabinowitz, the boy who fell in love with "negro numbers" (jazz songs) against his Orthodox Jewish father's strictures in the iconic film *The Jazz Singer* (1927), Twain became enamored with minstrelsy despite his mother's warnings. After he arrived in the West, he regularly attended performances of the San Francisco Minstrels, whose core members included Billy Birch, Dave Wambold, and Charley Backus. In his *Autobiography*, Twain devoted an entire chapter to minstrelsy, detailing his childhood fascination with it, his later acquaintance and friendship with blackface artists, and his lament over the passing of the golden age of minstrelsy, declaring that, "if I could have the nigger show back again in its pristine purity and perfection I should have but little further use for opera."[9] As for Twain's literary work, there has been ample scholarship shedding light on the fact that Twain, very much like Melville and other major American writers of that era, was indebted to blackface minstrelsy both aesthetically and ideologically. Critics have noted how, for instance, in both *Adventures of Huckleberry Finn* and *Tom Sawyer Abroad*, Twain appropriated the three-part structure of a minstrel show as a controlling framework for narrative; or how he lifted many of his most radical elements from minstrelsy when he absorbed its costuming, vernacular, and stock figures; or how he learned beneficially from minstrelsy "its insistence on a self that was complexly constituted from a mixed gender, class, and racial sourcepool."[10] Ralph Ellison's astute remark that Nigger Jim in *Huckleberry Finn* rarely emerges from behind the minstrel mask also speaks to blackface's profound influence on Twain's literary imagination.[11]

Scholars have also noticed that Twain carried his avowed love for blackface minstrelsy into his obsession with the Siamese Twins. Around 1868, he wrote the burlesque sketch "Personal Habits of the Siamese Twins," which traffics more in exaggeration than fact. The beginning of the story resembles closely the standard opening of a minstrel routine called a "stump speech," which always starts with a personal pitch to gain the audience's confidence: "I do not wish to write of the personal *habits* of these strange creatures solely, but also of certain curious details of various kinds concerning them, which, belonging only to their private life, have never crept into print. Knowing the twins intimately, I feel that I am peculiarly well qualified for the task I have taken upon myself." After plenty of absurdities, the piece ends with an obviously facetious factoid: "Having forgotten to mention it sooner, I will remark in conclusion that the ages of the Siamese Twins are respectively fifty-one and fifty-three years."[12] And then there was the book known as *The Tragedy of Pudd'nhead Wilson*, to which is attached, like Siamese Twins, a sequel called *The Comedy, Those Extraordinary Twins*. Twain himself admits candidly to the defect of his creation: "two stories in one, a farce and a tragedy." Even though *Pudd'nhead Wilson* is allegedly based on a different set of Siamese Twins, Twain worked some of Chang and Eng's life stories into the novel, full of burlesque and other features of black-face minstrelsy: disguises, cross-dressing, racial mixing, and pastiche.[13]

The epitome of Twain's appropriation of the Siamese Twins as min-strel figures, however, was his stage performance. A successful public speaker who made almost as much money from lectures as from book royalties, Twain often tapped the repertoire of minstrelsy in his delivery of speeches, casually reeling off anecdotes, scrapping rhetorical flour-ishes, and shooting for foolery and the tall tale. The famous tagline for his lectures, "The Trouble Begins at Eight," was actually a standard byline in minstrel-show advertisements.[14] On February 28, 1889, when storyteller James Riley and humorist Edgar "Bill" Nye gave a program of readings at Tremont Temple in Boston, their manager induced Twain on short notice to introduce the duo. His unexpected appearance on the stage "provoked a great waving of handkerchiefs and a tumult of applause and cheering, the organist doing his bit by sounding off fortissimo." Not missing a beat, Twain stepped into the spotlight and introduced Riley and Nye as Chang and Eng. His opening salvo ripped a page from his own earlier sketch of the famous twins, establishing his own credibility as the speaker while making the audience chuckle and roar: "I saw them first, a great many years ago, when Barnum had them, and they were just fresh from Siam. The ligature was their best bond then, but literature became their best hold later, when one of them committed an indiscretion, and they had to cut the old bond to accommodate the sheriff."[15]

As if turning others into the Siamese Twins were not enough, Twain would eventually act in character himself. On December 31, 1906, more than twenty years after the deaths of Chang and Eng, Twain put on a Siamese Twins performance with the aid of a young man at a New Year's Eve dinner party on New York's Fifth Avenue. Both dressed in white and tied together by a pink sash, which stood for the connecting band, the pair had their arms around each other. Harking back to teetotaler Eng in "Personal Habits" and upright Angelo in *Pudd'nhead Wilson*, Twain's character pleaded the temperance cause while his twin brother kept nipping from a flask:

> We come from afar. We come from very far; very far, indeed—as far as New Jersey. We are the Siamese Twins. . . . We are so much to each other, my brother and I, that what I eat nourishes him and what he drinks—ahem!—nourishes me. . . . I am sorry to say that he is a confirmed consumer of liquor—liquor, that awful, awful curse—while I, from principle, and also from the fact that I don't like the taste, never touch a drop.

As he continued to stump for reform and his twin continued to nip, the alcohol apparently influenced both. The two began to stagger around the stage, the speech slowly becoming a slurring jumble:

> Wonder'l 'form we are 'gaged in. Glorious work—we doin' glorious work—glori-o-u-s work. Best work ever done, my brother and work of reform, reform work, glorious work. I don' feel jus' right.

According to a report on the front page of the *New York Times* the next day, Twain's skit brought down the house so noisily that he could not continue the "lecture."[16] As the telharmonium, an electrical device invented by Thaddeus Cahill that year, transmitted the music of "Auld Lang Syne" from Broadway, the dinner guests and the host bade farewell to another year gone by, a year when Twain famously and openly lamented that the minstrel show had "degenerated into a variety show" and that he missed the good old days of the "real negro show," days when he was roaming the Wild West, when the tam and bones of Birch, Wambold, and Backus caused uproarious laughter that shook Frisco harder than the big quake that year, and when the real Siamese Twins and their dog-gone "authentic" imitations drew in crowds as thick as flies.

Twain might have been carried away by nostalgia, but it is certainly true that whether appearing as yellowface characters in a minstrel skit or acting in person in a freak show, the Siamese Twins were a big attraction in the West, even in a period when the political crisis leading to the Civil War dominated the news. As the *Daily Alta California* reported on December 15, 1860, "The interest in these wonders of nature continues unabated." Or, a week later, when they moved north along the Sacramento River to hit the gold-mine towns newly populated by modern-day Argonauts, the *Sacramento Daily Union*—which would one day give Twain a head start as a writer—reviewed Chang and Eng's show on December 22: "The Siamese Twins held their levée at the Forrest Theater yesterday afternoon and evening, and were visited by a large number of citizens. They are introduced to the audience by their agent, who gives a brief sketch of their history, etc.; after which, they mingle with their visitors, conversing freely and pleasantly, in good English."[17]

There were also reports that the twins advertised among the Chinese, using Chinese-language flyers to attract the "Celestials" to their exhibition tent.[18] We don't know how successful those efforts were, for the Chinese had been driven out of the minefields by white prospectors. A lethal combination of unfair tax laws targeting the Chinese and anti-Chinese violence had made mining an unfeasible choice of profession for these Chinese immigrants, thus giving birth to a saying that would echo throughout the nineteenth century, "no Chinaman's chance." In fact, Twain had gone to California because he had lost his job as a journalist in Nevada after he had expressed sympathy for abused "Chinamen." Standing no chance in mining, Chinese men, who had never done domestic chores like washing clothes and cooking in their native China (those jobs were for women), opened laundromats and fast-food joints in order to earn a living. As laundrymen toiling away with steam and starch, or as cooks stir-frying endless orders of chop suey, they would have been unlikely attendees at the Siamese Twins' shows.

Whether or not the twins were able to meet up with local Chinese, they had kept in contact with their families back home in North Carolina and continued to concern themselves with seemingly mundane

details of husbandry on their farms. In a rare extant letter penned by
the twins themselves, Eng wrote:

> *Dear wife and children we wanted to know very much how are you
> coming on. we have not hear from you for 6 weeks. we got two letters
> from you since we left. i hope you has done hauld the corn from Mr.
> Whitlock before now Tell Mary to take care of catle & pigs—i wanted
> to know very much how mill coming on—most likely we will be back in
> march—maybe not till may or june—you must tell Mary to have every
> thing carige on wright— leave a truk in n york with Mr. Hale he send
> it home by way of Marmadow tell Mr. Gilmer if we have any thing to
> hauld from their to have our truk bring it on too—nothing in them but
> shoese & coat for Mary—We has not seen much gold yet but hope to
> get some befor long—i must bring this close—Hope this will fine you all
> well & happy take good care of the five—write soon to this Place your
> has ever E.[19]*

Pretty soon they would have more than cattle and pigs to worry about.
At the end of 1860 and the beginning of 1861, after the election of Abraham Lincoln, daily headlines in the newspapers portended a national
crisis on the horizon. In fact, on the days after the historic election and
before the twins had left New York for the West Coast, Chang and Eng
had already seen their own names linked in the news to the crisis. While
minstrel artists had exploited the twins' image for entertainment, the
raging national debate over the fate of the union had also used the conjoined twins as a most salient and powerful metaphor. As seen in this
political burlesque printed in the *New York Tribune*,

> The "Union" in Danger—Chang threatens to secede—There is a
> report in circulation that a dreadful quarrel took place between
> the Siamese twins, at the American Museum, on the 7th inst. It
> seems that Chang, who is a North Carolinian and a secession-
> ist, had insisted upon painting the ligament black which binds
> them together. To this Eng objected, preferring the natural color;

whereupon Chang resolved to "sever the union" with Eng, which he declared to be "no longer worth preserving." Eng, who is of a calmer temperament, finally persuaded him to wait a little—until the 4th day of March next. Dr. Lincoln, a pupil of the celebrated Jackson, was called in, who gave his opinion that the operation would be dangerous for both parties, and said the union must and shall be preserved. A system of non-intercourse will probably be adopted—each party preserving to himself the privilege of biting his own nose off.[20]

Alluding to Lincoln's inauguration on March 4 and his famous speech about the imperative of preserving the union, the newspaper satire made full use of the symbolic valence of the Siamese Twins in American lexicon and cultural lore. In the coming days, as the North and the South veered closer to a calamitous clash, newspapers invoked the conjoined twins again and again as an allegory for the union, as the *Baltimore American* did in the following verbal skit, likening secession to a supposed separation of Chang and Eng:

If one of the Siamese brothers, disgusted with his life-long contact with the other, rudely tears himself away, snapping asunder a bond that God and nature intended to be perpetual, he inflicts upon himself the same precise injury that he inflicts upon his fellow. Each spouting artery, each quivering muscle, each wounded nerve that he tears in the lacerated side of his discarded companion, has an exact counterpart in his own equally lacerated side. He commits fratricide and suicide at once.[21]

With a storm brewing, the twins could no longer linger in the West looking for gold. On February 11, 1861, they boarded the steamer *Golden Age* and started their homecoming journey. Always steadfast in their own bond, Chang and Eng had no idea how strong the state of the national union was, or how the catastrophe would wreak havoc in their conjoined life while also tearing the country apart.

⋟ Part Five ⋞

THE CIVIL WAR
AND BEYOND

(1860–1874)

UNION AND CONFEDERATE DEAD, GETTYSBURG BATTLEFIELD,
PENNSYLVANIA, JULY 1863

Seeing the Elephant

I n the wee hours of April 12, 1861, when shots were fired at Fort Sumter outside Charleston, South Carolina, the Siamese Twins were sleeping in bed in Mount Airy, likely next to one of their wives. Recuperating from their recent California trip, they were at that moment about three hundred miles from this flashpoint of history.

Their subsequent wartime experience, however, was not so peripheral. Indeed, no one in the country could escape the impact of the fraternal bloodbath that would cost 620,000 lives, the rough equivalent of six million in proportion to today's population. To quote again from the *Baltimore American*, the newly waged war was like the Siamese Twins being violently ripped apart, "fratricide and suicide" all at once.

Just days after the Confederate attack, President Lincoln called for volunteers to form an army to restore the Union. He also ordered a blockade of the Southern ports. In response, the Confederate Congress declared war on May 6. North Carolina, where the sentiment for secession was far from unanimous, joined the Confederacy on May 20 and became, in fact, the last state to secede. Both Union and Confederate sides were confident about victory, anticipating a conflict of only transitory duration. In fact, the first Union soldiers were recruited for just three months, whereas North Carolina's first troops were signed up for only six months. In Surry County, Chang and Eng's home area, citizens congregated at the courthouse in Dobson to volunteer for fighting the Yankees. One militiaman, boasting of the skills of his pals in hunting and riding, claimed that "Southerners could whip the Yankees with cornstalks." Another local boy, joining the new cavalry company and marching through the main street, bragged about bringing back "Abe Lincoln's ears." Reminded of his boast after the war, the militiaman, who miraculously was still alive, laid the blame squarely on the darn Yankees: "But they wouldn't fight with cornstalks." As for the local farm boy who wanted to clip Honest Abe's ears, his body was shipped back home, having given what Lincoln would solemnly call the "last full measure of devotion," albeit to "The Lost Cause."[1]

It was to the same Lost Cause that Chang and Eng would devote their resources, loyalty, and manpower. As slaveholding landed gentry, they sided steadfastly with the Confederacy. Since acquiring citizenship, they had taken a lively interest in national politics and local elections. They were described as "zealous followers of Henry Clay and the Whig party," although they felt threatened by the members of the anti-Catholic and xenophobic wing of the party who would later reinvent themselves as the Know-Nothings.[2] When journeying in the Northern states prior to the war, the twins often had had trouble controlling their indignation against the Fugitive Slave Law, passed in 1850 and enforced by the federal government. When the final conflict came, as Judge Graves put it, "in all questions of a sectional character the feelings and sentiments of Chang and Eng were all strongly with the South, with whose people and institutions they had become so thoroughly identified."[3]

Living in a remote area of the country, however, the twins were not directly affected by the bloodshed during the first two years. North Carolina proved to be a minor arena for military conflicts, having witnessed only seventy-three skirmishes and eleven battles during the Civil War. One year into the war, the twins, according to county records, were still financially stable and comfortable, with Eng possessing 300 acres of land and nineteen slaves, and Chang owning 425 acres and eleven slaves. By 1863, tax records showed that Eng was still worth $17,850 and Chang was worth $16,130. And during these war years, Chang and Adelaide gave birth to two more children, Jesse Lafayette in April 1861 and Margaret Elizabeth in October 1863. Never far behind, Eng and

Sarah also had two children, Georgianna Columbia in May 1863 and Robert Edward in April 1865. The last one was born just days after the war ended and named after the Confederate hero General Robert E. Lee, whom the twins greatly admired.[4]

While Chang and Eng continued to enjoy financial prosperity and domestic bliss, they could not avoid the impact of the war on the community. To finance the unexpectedly protracted conflict, the state levied an increasingly heavy tax on the citizens. The Conscription Act, passed by the Confederacy on April 16, 1862, also threatened the peace of mind in every household. North Carolina contributed a total of 111,000 troops, 19,000 of them draftees, to the Confederate Army. For western North Carolina, a region known for its economic self-sufficiency, with scant need for external goods and services, the loss of manpower was disastrous for its way of life. As a result of volunteer enlistment and a compulsory draft, the community was in dire need of artisanal workers, "men whose skills as blacksmiths, millers, carpenters, tanners, and shoemakers could be dispensed with or readily imported." In nearby Ashe County, citizens of the Horse Creek district had to petition the governor to release Morgan Testerman, a local craftsman, from conscription. "Arguing that the Confederacy would be better served by employing Testerman as a carpenter than as a soldier," the petitioners detailed the tasks for which Testerman's specialized skills were required, including "the manufacture of spinning wheels, chairs, tables, bedsteads, farming tools, and in particular the construction of a new gristmill, of which, they contended, the Horse Creek neighborhood was urgently in need."[5] The Union blockade created other hardships, particularly when salt became unavailable. An essential dietary condiment, salt was also needed for the preservation of pork, beef, and vegetables. By the end of 1862, the staple was selling for $30 a bushel in the local market. To make matters worse, the mountain region was hit by near-drought conditions in the summer of 1862, leading to a scarcity of corn and other necessary staples. As winter set in, famine suddenly loomed as a real possibility. Compounding the misery, fugitives, draft dodgers, and deserters of all stripes and convictions found a haven in the remote mountain ranges lying between North Carolina and Tennessee. The "bushwhackers" constantly rampaged through the area, robbing, looting, and even murdering defenseless citizens.

The psychological effects would be even harder to handle. The scale of carnage was shocking—the Civil War is often regarded as the first warfare of the modern era, pitting mechanized weaponry against human flesh. The reports from the battlefields were gruesome and chilling. In a two-day battle at Shiloh, Tennessee, in April 1862, a total of twenty-four thousand soldiers died, surpassing the combined American casualties in the Revolutionary War, the War of 1812, and the Mexican War. Ambrose Bierce, who fought at Shiloh on the Union side, described the battlefield as a smoking jungle covered in pools of blood, with trees reduced to blasted stumps, and "knapsacks, canteens, haversacks distended with soaken and swollen biscuits, gaping to disgorge, blankets beaten into soil by the rain, rifles with bent barrels or splintered stocks, waist-belts, hats and the omnipresent sardine-box." A seemingly endless wasteland of dead horses presented a horrific tableau, the stench of rotten flesh making the scene that much more horrendous. But most appalling of all was the human suffering. Bierce went on: "Men? There were men enough; all dead apparently, except one, who lay near where I had halted my platoon to await the slower movement of the line—a Federal sergeant, variously hurt, who had been a fine giant in his time. He lay face upward, taking in his breath in convulsive, rattling snorts, and blowing it out in sputters of froth which crawled creamily down his cheeks, piling itself alongside his neck and ears. A bullet had clipped a groove in his skull, above the temple; from this the brain protruded in bosses, dropping off in flakes and strings. I had not previously known one could get on, even in this unsatisfactory fashion, with so little brain." One of Sergeant-Major Bierce's men, not usually known for his courage, asked whether he should put his bayonet through this "fine giant," the dying fellow soldier. Bierce was "shocked by the cold-blooded proposal."[6] It is this kind of reprehensible cruelty of war and unspeakable human misery that has led one historian, Drew Gilpin Faust, to call America during the Civil War a "republic of suffering."[7] Out of the 111,000 Tar

Heelers who went to war and "saw the elephant," 40,275—or more than one-third—would not return. It proved to be the greatest loss of lives suffered by any Confederate state. Apparently it was far from a barn-yard fight with cornstalks, as some Southerners had expected.

While "seeing the elephant" was a popular phrase signifying a battle-tested experience, the soldiers fighting the War Between the States would have seen real pachyderms stomping the battlefields if President Lincoln had accepted a generous offer from the king of Siam, a bizarre interlude in the goriest chapter of American history. Before the war, King Mongkut—better known to Americans as the Asian monarch who hired the British governess Anna Leonowens to educate his harem of concubines and kids—had addressed two letters to President James Buchanan, along with gifts that included a sword, a photograph of His Majesty and one of his favorite princesses, and two long tusks from Siamese elephants. In the letters, the king expressed wishes to send over a stock of elephants to be raised in America and deployed as means of transportation in war or peace, as they had been used in Siam for centuries.

Arriving too late for the intended addressee, His Majesty's gifts and missives fell into the hands of the bachelor president's successor, Abraham Lincoln. On February 3, 1862, three days after issuing General War Order No. 1, calling for all United States naval and land forces to begin a general advance by George Washington's birthday, Lincoln replied to King Mongkut and declined the generous offer. With a hint of condescension, the president touted the superiority of steam power over animal strength: "I appreciate most highly Your Majesty's tender of good offices in forwarding to this Government a stock from which a supply of elephants might be raised on our own soil. This Government would not hesitate to avail itself of so generous an offer if the object were one which could be made practically useful in the present condition of the United States. Our political jurisdiction, however, does not reach a latitude so low as to favor the multiplication of the elephant, and steam on land, as well as on water, has been our best and most efficient agent of transportation in internal commerce."

This friendly exchange has elicited some fanciful what-ifs from Civil War buffs: What if the Union or the Confederate Army had used battalions of war elephants? Could there have been herds of angry pachyderms at Pickett's Charge or emerging from the forest lines at Shiloh? In ancient Siamese warfare, elephants were indeed mighty weapons for frontal assaults and for cleaning up battlefields by stomping the life out of the luckless and wounded.[8]

While Lincoln employed his presidential jurisdiction to prevent the military use of Siamese elephants, thus consigning them to circus rings and menageries, he could not stop a sprinkling of Siamese-descended men from entering the war. On April 1, 1863, a week before he turned eighteen, Christopher Wren Bunker, Chang's first son, enlisted in the Confederate Army to fight for a cause that his father and uncle cherished. On that spring morning, Christopher said teary farewells to his family and rode across the state line into Wythe, Virginia, where he joined the 37th Battalion of the Virginia Cavalry as a private.[9] Unlike Union cavalrymen, who were usually provided with a government-owned horse, Confederate officers and mounted troopers were required to bring their own animals, for which they were partially reimbursed. Always fond of horses, Chang and Eng had quite a collection of steeds from which Christopher could choose. The Bunkers would also have to pay for the upkeep of the horse, costs that would rise to a few hundred dollars in Confederate money by the end of the war.[10] They also gave Christopher a rifle with the initials "CWB" inscribed on the stock.

Christopher would not be the last Bunker to join the war, nor was he by any means the only Asian soldier involved in the conflict. The Civil War has always been remembered as a struggle between the Union Blue and the Confederate Gray, a fratricide committed by white brothers and aided by black soldiers on opposite sides of the Mason-Dixon line. But, as recent research reveals, there were at least several hundred soldiers of Asian descent who participated in the bloodbath. The real number perhaps was higher, but anglicized names have made it hard for historians to identify and track them down in the records. In fact, the Civil War was not the first time we saw Asian participation in the nation's military affairs. During the War of 1812, several Filipinos had fought in the Battle of New Orleans against the British, a dramatic episode that turned Major General Andrew Jackson into a folk hero and paved his way to the presidency.

There were, however, fewer than forty thousand Asian men and women living in the United States during the Civil War, a small number in a nation that by the 1860 census had a population of 31,433,321. This figure included more than thirty-seven thousand Chinese living in California and fewer than a thousand living east of the Mississippi. Judging by this ratio, as Ruthanne Lum McCunn points out in her pioneering research, "The number of Asian men who volunteered to serve in the [Civil War], proportionately speaking, is remarkably high."[11] Most of the Asian volunteers served in the navies—prior to the war, many had already been working on ships as stewards, cabin boys, cooks, and sailors. Among those whose identities have been verified, many had adventuresome life stories that could have been fine fodder for historical fiction.

Take, for example, Thomas Sylvanus, whose Chinese name was Ah Yee Way. Born in Hong Kong, he was rescued from an orphanage by an American missionary and brought to Philadelphia for schooling at the age of eight or nine. The 1860 census showed his age as fifteen; for the question of race, the census taker "made something akin to an exclamation mark." Still a minor, he enlisted in Company D, 81st Pennsylvania Volunteer Infantry, on August 31, 1861. Repeatedly battle-tested at Fair Oaks, Allen's Farm, Savage's Station, Charles City Crossroads, and Malvern Hill, he went partially blind and was discharged on December 10, 1862. Living in Philadelphia, he heard that the city was threatened by a possible Confederate victory at Gettysburg. He immediately reenlisted, joining the 51st Pennsylvania Volunteer Infantry on the third day of the famous battle that ended with a victory for the Union, albeit a Pyrrhic one, given the tremendous cost in loss of lives. Desperate to replace fallen troops, Congress enacted conscription and drafted men between the ages of twenty and forty-five. Anyone whose name was drawn by lottery could be exempted by paying a commutation fee of $300 or finding a substitute. Sylvanus ended up enlisting again as a substitute for an umbrella merchant in New York on September 11, 1863. Despite his parlous vision, Sylvanus fought valiantly and was promoted to corporal after four months in Company D, 42nd New York Volunteer Infantry. Injured in the leg, he was taken prisoner at Cold Harbor, along with seventeen hundred other Union soldiers. After the war, this twenty-year-old Chinese veteran—vision impaired, leg injured, and health damaged—was denied a pension. Adding insult to injury, when he reapplied for a pension in 1877, the doctor appointed by the Bureau of Pensions attributed his bad vision partially to inflammation caused by manual labor and partially to "the peculiar look characteristic of his race." Even though he was eventually granted a far smaller pension than he deserved, his common-law Irish wife, Mathilde, could not get the widow's pension to which she was entitled after his death at the age of forty-six in 1891. She ended up having to send two of their children to an orphanage, thus bringing a tragic end to the Sylvanus story, which itself had begun in an orphanage in Hong Kong.[12]

Like Thomas Sylvanus, Siam-born George Dupont also was underage when he enlisted. While working at a foundry in Jersey City, Dupont was enticed by the $75 enlistment bonus. On August 12, 1862, though only fifteen, he was accepted into a White unit, Company B, 13th New Jersey Volunteers, even though he had a dark complexion. The recruitment officers, eager to meet the quota imposed by the federal government, entered Dupont's age as eighteen and doctored the "CONSENT IN CASE OF MINOR" form by crossing out his purported guardian's name. Together with his regiment, Dupont fought in the Battle of Antietam, the bloodiest one-day conflict in American history, and then at Chancellorsville and Gettysburg. Taking part in General Sherman's merciless campaign in Atlanta, Dupont was injured at Kolb's Farm on June 22 and hospitalized until the war's end. In 1869, like his fellow countrymen Chang and Eng, Dupont vacated his oath to the king of Siam and became a naturalized American citizen.[13]

And then there was John Williams, a five-foot-tall, brown-eyed, black-haired Japanese samurai, who served as a substitute for a Brooklyn man. A soldier in the legendary 1st New York Cavalry, comprising mostly immigrants of German, Irish, and English extraction, the pixie Japanese enlistee fought hard for three years in various battles, ranging from the Peninsula Campaign to the Shenandoah Valley Campaign. As we saw earlier, the racial category for Asians at this time was still unsettled in the United States, so some of these Asian soldiers were able to enlist in the White units and received the monthly pay of $13, while others had to join the Colored regiments and received the lesser pay of $10. Either way, they caused bewilderment and confusion on both sides of the fighting line. When John Tomney, a Chinese soldier in the Union Army, was captured, a Confederate general wondered whether he was "a mulatto, Indian, or what?"[14]

The same question could have been put to Christopher Bunker by any of the military men who saw his mixed physical features. They might have been even more curious if he had told them about his origin. At eighteen, Christopher was "a handsome blend of Chinese and European": five-foot-eight, slender, black-haired, with a neatly-trimmed moustache, a strong nose, a broad forehead, brown eyes, and a tinted skin color. It would have been hard to figure out his race from his appearance. But no one could question his pride as a Southerner and his devotion to the Confederate cause. His most noteworthy war experience was his participation in the raid of Chambersburg, Pennsylvania. In July 1864, in retaliation for the damage done by General David Hunter's federal troops in the Shenandoah Valley, Brigadier General John McCausland led twenty-four hundred Confederate cavalrymen as they moved toward Chambersburg. Along the way, they swept aside Union cavalry and captured many of them, as Christopher described in a family letter about similar encounters earlier:

About two weeks ago we all went out on a scout and was gone about five days we travelled three nights and days before we made a halt. The second night got me it rained all night as hard as it could pour and we had to travel over the rockiest and the muddiest road that I ever saw and the next morning we ran up on the Yankee pickets and captured them and went on to a little town called Rogersville and there we saw a

little fun catching Yankees, we captured about 150 Yankees and started
back about twelve o'clock and travelled all night that night and in the
whole scout we did not take our saddles off of our horses but once or
twice and did not feed but once or twice a day and when we got back to
camp every horse in the battalion had scratches so bad that they could
hardly travel.[15]

On the morning of July 30, the Confederate brigade reached Chambersburg. McCausland issued a proclamation to the townspeople, demanding $100,000 in gold or $500,000 in greenbacks within three hours or the city would be put to the torch and its leading citizens arrested. "When its inhabitants failed to raise the money, McCausland destroyed it, and while the city burned, drunken soldiers plundered freely, even tearing brooches, rings, and earrings off women in the streets."[16] Chambersburg was the only town in the North destroyed by Confederate forces.

Fleeing from pursuing Union troops, McCausland got as far as Moorefield, West Virginia. Mistakenly thinking that he was in the clear, he ordered his men to set up camp in a level field that was militarily indefensible. A special unit of Union troops known as the Jessie Scouts disguised themselves in Confederate gray and pretended to be a relief column. In a surprise predawn attack, they routed the Confederates. In the mayhem, Christopher was shot out of his saddle, becoming one of the more than four hundred Confederates wounded or killed in that battle.

Earlier, prior to the raid on Chambersburg, Christopher had told his family in the same letter we saw earlier, "My horse corked himself and became very lame and I had to leave him with a gentleman who lives five miles this side of Lexington . . . and if I should get killed or captured on this raid you can send and get him." After his capture, Christopher's blood-spattered horse was brought back to Mount Airy. Seeing the riderless steed, Chang and Adelaide felt certain their first son had died.

Fortunately, however, Christopher was only wounded. He was taken to Camp Chase near Columbus, Ohio. One of the largest military pris-

ons, Camp Chase was infamous for its lax policy of allowing Confederate inmates to be accompanied by their former household slaves. But by
the time Christopher arrived, the prison had discontinued such hospitality. On October 12, more than two months after his capture, Christopher was finally able to write home:

> Dear Father, Mother, Brothers and Sisters: It is with pleasure I take the
> present opportunity to drop you a few lines to let you know how I am
> getting along. I was captured the 7th of last August and brought to this
> place. I have no news of interest to write to you as there are none allowed
> to come in prison. You must write to me as soon as you get this and let
> me know how you are getting along. I would like to hear from you all
> as it has been a long time since I heard from you. But I hope it will not
> be very long before I hear from you and see you too although I see no
> chance for an exchange. I have not seen many well days since I came to
> this place. I have had the smallpox and now got the diareea [sic] but I
> hope that I will be well in the course of a week. . . . We are drawing very
> light rashions [sic] here just enough to keep breath and body together.[17]

Nothing could have brought more relief and elation to the Bunker household than this plainly worded epistle. From this point on, "packages
from home supplemented his meager rations. His father, Chang, also
sent him money so he could buy items—such as cigars, underclothes,
pocketknives, and smoked beef—from the prison store."[18] Christopher
remained a POW until a parole exchange of prisoners was agreed upon
between the Federal Government and the Confederate States in March
1865. On April 17, he arrived home, a hero to the family.

Family lore holds that Christopher's cousin and Eng's oldest son, Stephen Decatur Bunker, also enlisted in the 37th Battalion of the Virginia
Cavalry after he turned eighteen in July 1864. This would mean that the
two Bunker cousins had fought side by side for almost a month before
Christopher's capture. But no record has been found to confirm Stephen's enlistment in the unit; in fact, there was no trace of Stephen at all
in the Compiled Service Record, except that a D. C. Bunker was listed

in the Confederate Cavalry. As one historian puts it, "It is possible that the clerk got the name confused or maybe misunderstood the accent of the part Chinese cavalryman."[19] To strengthen the family's claim, a North Carolina pension record does exist for Stephen. According to the later testimony of his sons, Stephen eluded capture at Moorefield but was wounded a month later, on September 3, 1864, near Winchester, Virginia, when Sheridan's fifty thousand Union troops clashed with the Confederate Army led by Lieutenant General Jubal Early, forcing the latter to retreat. In April 1865, as the Union victory was all but set in stone after Appomattox, Stephen was wounded again and taken prisoner. A Northern doctor plucked from his shoulder a .44 caliber bullet, a bloody souvenir that would become a family heirloom for generations.

While two of their adult sons "saw the elephant" with their naked eyes and proved their gallantry with their battle wounds, Chang and Eng themselves were said to have been almost drafted—ironically, not by the Confederate Army but by the Union. In the last days of the war, as the armies of Sherman and Grant were delivering the death blows to the South, a division of six thousand Union troops, led by General George Stoneman, moved into North Carolina across the mountain ranges from Tennessee. A former West Point roommate of Thomas J. "Stonewall" Jackson and the future governor of California (1883–1887), Stoneman up to this point had held a mixed record in the war. He had earlier launched a failed raid in Georgia, during which he was embarrassingly captured by home guards. And then later he led a successful raid against the saltworks in Virginia, winning back some lost glory and respect from his peers. The move into North Carolina in 1865 would be Stoneman's last raid. His original instructions were to "penetrate South Carolina well down toward Columbia, destroying the railroad and military resources of the country . . . to return to East Tennessee by way of Salisbury, North Carolina [and] release some of . . . [the Federal] prisoners of war in the rebel hands."[20] But fast-developing events, especially Sherman's swift capture and punitive burning of Columbia on February 17, changed the course of Stoneman's movements, unexpectedly bringing the Union blue to the door of the Siamese Twins.

Stoneman's Raid, as it is known in history, a two-month campaign tearing up rebel havens in western North Carolina and southwest Virginia, commenced on a rainy day in late March. As one of the soldiers in the 15th Pennsylvania Volunteer Cavalry wrote in his diary, "We started from Knoxville in an ordinary rainstorm, which increased in intensity during the day, and at night had developed into a furious hailstorm. We are in the lightest marching order, and our shelter tents are a poor protection at such a time."[21] The dirt roads cutting across the gaps in the Blue Ridge Mountains were in poor condition, now made worse by the storm. For each company, only two pack mules were allowed— one for carrying ammunition, the other for absolute necessities, such as food and cooking utensils. No baggage was allowed except overcoats.[22] On March 28, the advance guard of this force, a detachment of the 12th Kentucky Cavalry under Major Myles Keogh, entered Boone, the county seat of Watauga, taking the citizens by surprise. "We arrived here this a.m.," read Stoneman's official mention of his first hit in the state, "captured the place, killing nine, capturing sixty-two home guards and 40 horses."[23] After burning down the Boone jail and destroying all of the county records, Stoneman divided his forces and led a brigade himself eastward, through Deep Gap to Wilkesboro, where Chang and Eng had first settled. Along the Yadkin River, Stoneman's forces left behind a bloody trail of dead home guards, looted houses, burned factories, and stolen horses and mules.

On Sunday, April 2, Stoneman's cavalry forded the Yadkin and turned north toward Virginia. At nightfall, more than four thousand blue-uniformed men on horseback rode into Mount Airy, which the troopers described as "very ordinary." They picked up, or, "liberated," the mail at the post office and read the letters for amusement. They also hit the homes of prominent citizens, such as Gilmer, Hollingsworth, Prather, and Graves, pilfering additional horses. Cavalryman Frank Frankenberry, tired of camping but too chivalrous to foist himself upon the locals, took a room at the Blue Ridge Hotel. At midnight, word of a seventeen-wagon Confederate train passing through sent some of the troopers scurrying out of town to capture it. When they did, "ani-

mals were turned over to the quartermaster's department and the wag-
ons were burned." According to Thomas Perry in *Civil War Stories from
Mount Airy and Surry County*, the only injury that Stoneman's cavalrymen suffered in Mount Airy was at the hands of the Bunkers: Knowing of the presence of the famous Siamese Twins, Stoneman ordered
his men to leave the family alone. But one foolish Yankee trooper, out
of curiosity, ignored the order and visited one of the Bunker homes,
where he grabbed a Bunker daughter. He "received the only wound the
cavalry got that day when he received a slap across the face from the
same daughter."[24]

It was also said that when Stoneman decided to draft some of the
locals, the name of Eng Bunker was drawn from the lottery wheel. When
Stoneman saw the conjoined twins, he had to let Eng go, because he
could not take both. While most biographers have dismissed this story
as apocryphal, some are willing to accord family lore a special place in
history, including Irving Wallace and Amy Wallace, who seem to cher-
ish this too-good-to-be-true yarn.[25]

Either way, the impact of Stoneman's Raid on the area was palpable
for years to come. A local schoolgirl, Bettie Dobson, wrote in a letter
to her sister, "I expected they would destroy every thang and burn the
houses."[26] When that did not happen and Stoneman's cavalry moved on
to Hillsville, Virginia, western North Carolinians, thinking that the raid
was over, breathed a sigh of relief.[27] But the relief was short-lived, or simply an illusion. Not only did Stoneman's forces, after wreaking havoc in
Virginia, make a U-turn and return to North Carolina for more killing,
looting, burning, and other wartime atrocities, for which the infamous
raid on Salisbury is the best example. But also, the real consequences of
the war would be felt only after the military conflict was over.

Reconstruction

*The Civil War and Reconstruction represent in their primary aspect
an attempt on the part of the Yankee to achieve by force what he had failed
to achieve by political means . . . to make over the South in the prevailing
American image and to sweep it into the main current of the nation.*
—W. J. Cash, *The Mind of the South* (1941)

The South after the war presented a bleak picture of destruction
and destitution. The embers were slowly cooling off in Atlanta
and Columbia, where the stench of unburied dead animals
pervaded the air for months. Weeds overran barren fields at burned-
out plantations. Railroads lay trackless, like bruised gums missing their
teeth. The psychological damage went even deeper. The defeat would
leave a permanent wound in the Southern consciousness, fostering a
deep-seated defiance and enmity toward the Yankees, perpetuating a
distrust of Yankee peddlers and sundry charlatans who had been hawking their notions to folks in the South. One of the twins' fellow North
Carolinians, an innkeeper who had lost his sons and whose house was
burned by the Union Army, said it all, "They've left me one inestimate
privilege—to hate 'em. I git up at half-past four in the morning, and sit
up till twelve at night, to hate 'em."[1]

Chang and Eng, however, could hardly afford to sit around all day
just to hurl imprecations at the Yankees, whether in Siamese or Southern patois. They had large families to support, and their financial situation suddenly was dire. The war had decimated their major asset—the
thirty-two slaves they had owned, worth $26,550 according to 1864
county tax records. Some of their former slaves, after a short-lived
euphoria in the wake of Emancipation, returned to work for the twins,
but they were now wage earners, thus increasing the overhead expenses

CHANG AND ENG BUNKER FAMILIES, 1870

for the farms. By 1870, the census taker noted at least five ex-slaves still living under the Bunker roofs: Peter Razy, listed as "farm laborer"; Aunt Grace, "maidservant"; and her three sons, Jacob, Jack, and James, all listed as "servants." In the family photograph taken the same year, we can see at least two black faces. The one in the front row first right is most likely Aunt Grace, holding one of the Bunker kids. The middle-aged man in the back row, first left, looks African American.

The war had also wiped out their other financial investments. Shrewd as they were, the twins did not anticipate the fall of the Confederacy and the attendant collapse of its currency. At the beginning of the war, they had enjoyed a steady income from loans made in Confederate money. They had thought they were making a killing when Confederate money went on a fire sale. According to the New York *Sun*, the twins "had a good deal of money loaned out on the best securities in the early part of the war when Confederate money went down to about 15c a bushel. Their debtors hastened to liquidate their obligations and redeem their securities with the worthless stuff which they could not refuse." After the war, the twins were stuck with loads of Confederate notes that were valuable only as souvenirs. In fact, the same article in the *Sun* ended with a sales pitch, more or less as a jab at the twins' plight: "Any person wishing to purchase a huge quantity of Confederate notes at very low rates will do well to address Chang-Eng Bunker, Esq., Mount Airy, Surry County, North Carolina."[2] This notice drew the attention of at least one New York collector, J. C. Shields, who immediately was enticed to write a letter to the twins, expressing interest in a deal: "Sirs, I noticed an advertisement on the 10th inst in the Sun that you had a lot of confederate money for sale. If you have please send me a state-ment of how you sell it as I would like to purchase some. I have a great many curiosities and I would like to add some of each denomination of confederate money to my curiosities." The collector added a P.S.: "If satisfactory my friends will purchase a lot."[3]

We don't know whether Chang and Eng ever replied to Mr. Shields. Even if they did, his purchase would not have been enough to help them begin recouping their losses. Let the numbers speak for themselves: During the war, the twins' combined worth hovered around $34,000. After the war, in 1866, the Mount Airy tax assessor estimated Chang and Eng's total worth to be about $9,300, of which $7,000 was in the value of land and the other $2,300 in actual currency and miscellaneous possessions. While they might not have been as desperate as the eighty-five thousand widows and two hundred thousand fatherless children left behind by the deaths of 260,000 Confederate soldiers, they were, for the first time in more than three decades, strapped for cash.

While worthless currency sold as collectibles would not improve their finances in any appreciable way, there remained one curio that might still be construed as a valuable asset: their conjoined body. Hence, now in their mid-fifties, they had no choice but to hit the road again as itin-erant showmen.

In those bleak postwar years, the twins partnered with an assortment of managers and promoters who had checkered histories—the war's devastation had brought out the charlatanism in almost everyone. Or, as the Chinese would say, "The circumstance creates a character." The first manager was one Simon Bolivar Zimmerman, a Baltimore native

and formerly wealthy railroad investor who had settled in North Carolina and then lost everything in the war. He was so debt-ridden and
ashamed of his own parlous state that he would hide in a hotel room
when the twins toured in Baltimore. Working together with Zimmerman was his brother-in-law, Henry Armand London, an eighteen-year-
old war veteran who "had been selected at Appomattox as the courier to
carry General Lee's last order of the war, an order stating that Lee was
surrendering and that all troops must cease fire."[4] When the shows run
by these two inexperienced brothers-in-law did poorly, the twins sought
a new manager and found an entrepreneurial New Yorker named Judge
H. P. Ingalls. We don't know whether Judge Ingalls's title was professional or a self-aggrandizing label, invented in much the same way that
the two confidence men in *The Adventures of Huckleberry Finn* conveniently assumed the titles of king and duke on a raft drifting down the
Mississippi. In any case, the putative judge was a far more capable manager than his predecessors. With an eye for publicity, Ingalls arranged
for a photo session at the studio of Mathew Brady in New York. Having
captured for posterity such luminaries as Abraham Lincoln, Robert E.
Lee, Ulysses Grant, and Walt Whitman, as well as countless soldiers,
living and dead, Brady was the most renowned photographer of the
Civil War era. On this occasion, sometime in the spring of 1866, Chang
and Eng brought their wives and two of their children, Patrick and
Albert, to New York to sit for a Brady photograph.

Realizing that the Siamese Twins were a hotter commodity than he
could handle himself, Ingalls then set them up with the ultimate impresario, P. T. Barnum. By the time Ingalls approached the circus avatar in
1868, Barnum had suffered a patch of bad luck. On December 17, 1857,
a fire had destroyed Iranistan, an Oriental-themed mansion Barnum
had built in Bridgeport, Connecticut, inspired by George IV's Oriental
Pavilion and Kublai Khan's Xanadu. Part Byzantine, part Moorish, part
Turkish, Iranistan was one of those exotic celebrity "dream homes" that
ever so occasionally, through their outlandishness, have become part
of the historical American identity. Iranistan was a precursor to such
overblown monstrosities as Orson Fowler's octagonal mansion, William

CHANG AND ENG BUNKER AND THEIR WIVES AND CHILDREN

Randolph Hearst's eponymous castle, Hugh Hefner's Playboy Mansion, Michael Jackson's Neverland, and Donald Trump's Mar-a-Lago, itself a corrupted reinvention of heiress Marjorie Merriweather Post's 128-room mansion.

The destruction of Iranistan was merely the opening salvo in a chain of fires. On July 13, 1865, in the aftermath of the Civil War, Barnum's American Museum went up in flames, leveling the five-story marble structure as well as nine nearby buildings. Many animals perished in the inferno, including two whales that were boiled alive in their tanks, a fate also suffered by the "Man-Eater" alligator. Those critters that managed to get out—pythons, anacondas, birds, and human freaks—created pandemonium in Lower Manhattan. The rumor that a lion was running loose on Broadway caused a minor stampede, and the police had to be called to calm the crowd. The total loss caused by this Noah's Ark inferno was estimated at a million dollars.[5] Never easily defeated, however, Barnum opened a new museum in 1866, also on Broadway, only blocks away from the original location. But barely two years later, on March 3, 1868, the new museum burned to the ground, again ruining Barnum financially.

A paragon of American optimism, Barnum looked for ways to begin anew. He became a partner in the around-the-world venture of two of his former employees, Lavinia and Tom Thumb, two midgets now happily married. When Ingalls called to discuss the Siamese Twins, Barnum felt that, as much as he loathed working with the tough-as-nail twins, there was money to be made. The feeling of reluctance was mutual; if the twins had disliked Barnum before, the Civil War had only made them distrust the Yankee braggart even less. Just like their previous partnership, the union of Barnum and the twins was solely a marriage of convenience. According to Judge Graves, the health of Eng's oldest daughter, Kate, "a young lady of brilliant and well cultivated mind," was growing more delicate, following a pattern in which Eng's second daughter, Julia, had died at the age of twenty-two in 1865. Deeply concerned about Kate's condition, the twins had considered taking her to England to consult with doctors.[6] Using Ingalls as the intermediary, the twins struck a deal with Barnum to arrange a British tour. At Barnum's insistence, Anna Swan, a Nova Scotian "giantess" of seven foot five and a half inches tall, who previously had been "Barnumized" at his museum, would join the twins and their daughters on the tour.

As chilly winds whipped off the Hudson River, the twins boarded the steamer *Iowa*, with both Kate and Chang's daughter Nannie in tow, and departed New York on December 5, 1868, for Great Britain. Prior to the departure, twenty-one-year-old Nannie described the scene at the dock in her diary: "When we crossed the ferry at Jersey City many people flocked around us crying here are the 'Siamese Twins and their wives.'"[7] Apparently the starstruck mob, willing to believe almost anything, mistook the two young women for the twins' wives.

It was a rough and bitter season for transatlantic travel. Both girls, on their first trip abroad, got seasick. Kate was worried about her health, fearing that "possibly she might never return to their home." Nannie, not inured to the wear-and-tear of a circus tour, "felt a great repugnance to going before the public," which they would have to do when they arrived in Britain. The twins, however, having spent a lifetime of travel under far more primitive conditions, not only got their sea legs but also tried to enjoy the ocean voyage by playing chess, smoking cigars, and chatting amiably with other passengers.

After going ashore fourteen days later in Liverpool, itself a port city tarnished by its dependence on the slave trade, they immediately proceeded to Edinburgh, where Mr. Cassidy, an agent commissioned by Barnum, was waiting. Nannie left a wide-eyed description of the Scotland she saw for the first time: "We looked around on the hills of Scotland with wonder and admiration. The solitary peaks rising out of a vast plain without any chain of hills or mountains as is the case in America. Scotland is a beautiful country indeed, quite romantic in appearance." But the sense of wonder quickly dissipated when the Bunker quartet debuted in Edinburgh on December 21. Here is Nannie's diary entry for that dreadful day: "Was a very disagreeable rainy day. For the first time in my life I was compelled to go before the public. I felt quite embarrassed when the hour came. It was not as I had imagined. We had very few visitors in the forenoon but the number increased quite rapidly during the afternoon & evening receptions."

A few days later, she again confided her frustrations, some of them racial in nature: "All day we were housed up receiving visitors, a thing exceedingly irksome to me when I think of the many beautiful things of antiquity I could see if I could go out. I never felt so indignant in all my life as I did this afternoon. One man I will not say gentleman—asked me if my grandmother or grandfather was a negro. I was so angry I could scarcely speak but was compelled to say nothing." Another visitor, a lady "far advanced in age & somewhat childish in manner," lectured her on the subject of religion and on the welfare of her soul's salvation, completely oblivious to the fact that Nannie had been raised by a mother and an aunt who were devout Christians. The old lady must have thought that the girl was a chip off her father–uncle's pagan block and therefore needed salvation.

Having been the object of curiosity all their lives, the twins knew well how to deal with the slings and arrows of the visitors. But for Nannie and Kate, bred in the foothills of the Appalachians, it was hard to handle the embarrassment of exhibiting themselves in public. This was, however, of no concern to the impresario who had arranged these shows from across the Atlantic. Barnum, irked by the fact that he could not claim credit for having discovered the twins, made only one passing reference to them in the nine versions of his autobiography: "I sent them to Great Britain where, in all the principal places, and for about a year, their levées were continually crowded." And he would not miss any opportunity to attribute the success to his own advertising skills and gimmicks, as he added: "In all probability the great success attending this enterprise was much enhanced, if not actually caused, by extensive announcements in advance, that the main purpose of Chang–Eng's visit to Europe was to consult the most eminent medical and surgical talent with regard to the safety of separating the twins."[8]

Whatever Barnum claimed, the real purpose for the twins' Scottish sojourn was to consult the doctors about Kate's condition. Therefore, outside the busy exhibition schedule, they took her to see the physicians at the prestigious medical school of the University of Edinburgh. The diagnosis was grim: consumption, a disease that before the discovery of penicillin was the equivalent of a death sentence. The doctors stated that her condition was "so far advanced that in all human probability their skill would be unavailing and that the only aid which they could hope to render would be simply mitigate the suffering of the invalid."[9]

The news shattered the twins, especially Eng, who already had lost a daughter to the malady. They had counted themselves lucky to see their sons return from the war, but they could not seem to win the battle against disease. It reminded them of those agonizing days in Siam when, as two green youths, they had seen cholera, the "Curse of Asia," claim their father, and there was nothing they could do.

"Papa and uncle are quite bad off with colds and coughs," Nannie wrote in her diary. The doctors knew that the Bunkers were no ordinary patients; they were medical specimens. One of the Edinburgh physicians came to call on them almost immediately after their arrival, and his interest had less to do with the general welfare of Kate and the twins than with his own academic pursuits. Like the many doctors before him, Sir James Simpson, a professor of medicine at the University of Edinburgh, had a stellar résumé and an impeccable reputation. The first physician to use ether in obstetrics, Simpson had also invented a forceps named after him. The result of Simpson's meeting with the twins and the subsequent examination was a paper, titled "A Lecture on the Siamese Twins and Other Viable United Twins," published in the *British Medical Journal* in 1869. However, Simpson's report revealed no radical departure from the voluminous medical and quasi-medical literature on Chang and Eng that had predated his examination. Four decades after the twins' arrival in the West, doctors had in essence run out of things to say about these rare specimens. Simpson tried to use the most advanced electrical lighting technology to probe into the mysterious band connecting the twins, but to no avail. Failing to reveal anything new, the renowned physician ended up describing instead the exotic appearance of the Siamese Twins after their years of acclimation in America: "Dressed, as they are, in the ordinary American fashion, with the hair cut short, and talking English, as they do, with the American accent, they retain little or nothing of the appearance of Eastern subjects; except their black hair and their features."[10]

Just like some of the gawkers who no longer found the twins shocking to their senses, the medical doctors also seemed to have exhausted their curious speculations about the conjoined twins alive. To gain more medical knowledge about them would require going deeper into their bodies. The doctors and the gawkers alike waited for the twins to perform their final act.

The Last Radiance
of the Setting Sun

Death is the black camel that kneels unbid at every gate.
—Charlie Chan

Friday night, January 16, 1874, was bitter cold. The field was frozen, pines crusted with snow, junipers lacquered with ice. The mountain air, moving heavily like an invisible glacier, cut the skin like a sharp blade. The Cherokee called the month of January *Unolvtana,* "windblown." There was no moon in the sky; it was the penultimate day of the lunar month.

Eng's house stood quietly on the icy farm, looking from afar like a desolate bird's nest abandoned on a barren tree. In the parlor, the conjoined brothers sat on a double chair in front of the fireplace. Chang was coughing, complaining of cold. All day he had been in a foul mood, sullen, sulky, and snappy. Eng tried his best to humor his peevish brother, but his patience began to wear thin. The room was too hot for him. Tossing another log into the fire, Eng might have cursed under his breath. Nothing could escape his brother, whether a wordless mumble or even a fleeting fancy. There was such telepathy between the twins. Chang snapped, struggling to get up. Eng angrily pulled him down by the sheer weight of his own body and the resilience of their connective band. He reminded Chang whose house this was—it was Eng's; and by the rule of the agreement to which they had steadfastly adhered all these years, his brother would have to defer to Eng's wish in everything. Chang whimpered like an injured dog.[1]

Many writers have tried to imagine this unusual scene, when one twin is sick while the other remains well. William Linn Keese, a witty

ENG'S HOUSE, WHERE THE TWINS DIED

poet of mediocre repute, would write about it in a poem published in 1902:

Suppose, for a moment, Chang were ill,
And felt like remaining perfectly still,
And Eng felt splendidly, *au contraire,*
And of all things wanted to take the air—
How would they fix it! Why Eng, of course,
Must stick to his brother's side, perforce,
And hear him fret and murmur and groan,
And see pills and powders down him thrown—
Be dragged off finally, willy-nilly,
To bed at an hour absurdly silly,
And lie there, trying to sleep in vain,
With thoughts that were certainly most profane.[2]

Comedy aside, there were rumors of sibling squabbling, which allegedly had turned violent at times. Chang's addiction to the bottle not only had ruined his health but also made him more irritable, becoming a nuisance to his brother and turning their connecting band into a virtual thorn in Eng's side. Kay Hunter, in *Duet for a Lifetime*, mentions one occasion when the two got into an argument, with an inebriated Chang throwing a featherbed on the fire.[3] Irving Wallace and Amy Wallace also describe one particularly bitter quarrel between the brothers, "during which one of them, probably Chang, pulled a knife and shouted, 'I'm going to cut your gut out!'" Eng dragged his brother to Dr. Hollingsworth, their family physician, and begged him to separate them at once.[4] Though fictional, Mark Twain's humorous sketch, "Personal Habits of the Siamese Twins," published in 1869, five years before Chang and Eng's demise, might also contain a nugget of truth in its description of the brotherly brawl: "Upon one occasion the brothers fell out about something, and Chang knocked Eng down, and then tripped and fell on him, whereupon both clinched and began to beat and gouge each other without mercy. The bystanders interfered and tried to separate them, but they could not do it, and so allowed them to fight it out. In the end both were disabled, and were carried to the hospital on one and the same shutter."[5] In fact, the twins had indeed gotten into a fistfight in 1845 and were hauled into court for disturbing the peace. The presiding judge, Jesse Graves, whose unpublished biography of the twins I have drawn upon, gave us the final word on the outcome of this earlier fracas: "Mr. Lee Reeves, then county attorney, sent a bill for an affray against them which was returned a true bill. They appeared at the next term of the court and submitted to be fined; and as they had become entirely reconciled and were as friendly with each other as they had once been the court imposed only a nominal fee."[6]

Curiously, the extant version of Judge Graves's manuscript, kept at the State Archives of North Carolina, ends abruptly, indicating that pages may be missing, pages that might shed more light on the relationship between the twins during their final days. Instead, we find a postscript in a woman's handwriting that reads:

Eng's treatment of his brother was very kind and forebearing [*sic*] during all the long period of his sickness, showing great tenderness and affection for him and endeavoring by every means in his power to alleviate his suffering. His kindness was received with the warmest appreciation by Chang, whose disposition was very different from the morose, ill nature so falsely ascribed to him.[7]

This postscript, apparently intended to dispel rumors about bad blood between the seemingly companionable twins, raises more questions than answers.

Whatever the truth, the twilight years of the world-famous Siamese Twins presented a bleak picture, almost as gloomy as that of the South, mired in the protracted and painful Reconstruction. After receiving a grim prognosis from the British doctors, Kate, Eng's firstborn, never recovered her health. She died in 1871 at twenty-seven, plunging the conjoined Bunker households into the depths of mourning. As the Chinese would say, "Misfortune never travels alone." Nannie, Kate's confidant and travel companion in Great Britain, contracted the same disease and soon, like her cousin, fell victim to tuberculosis. (Ironically, Nannie would outlive the twins only by a month.) Two other Bunker children, Louisa and Jesse, being deaf and mute from birth, had been sent to the Institute for the Deaf and Dumb and the Blind in Raleigh, far from home. Pushing sixty, the twins themselves had become hard of hearing—Chang in both ears and Eng in his left, the one closer to Chang, as if he would not need it to hear what his twin brother had to say while keeping his right ear tuned to the world, listening on behalf of both. What the world was saying, however, perturbed them.

As they slowly lost their appeal as curiosities, the twins seemed to become more desperate. Throughout their performing career, they had always taken pride in the fact that they were never part of a circus. But in 1870, they were booked for a three-week stint at a German circus in Berlin. For that trip, they took along Eng's twenty-one-year-old son James and Chang's twelve-year-old son Albert. Their appearance at the Circus Renz on Friedrichstrasse, in the momentous year of German unification and on the eve of the Franco-Prussian War, was a traumatizing ordeal for them, akin perhaps to France's impending ignominious defeat by Germany. Every night for three weeks, after a high-wire act, clowns, and bareback riders, the brassy circus band's fanfare brought out the Siamese Twins as the highlight of the night. As a sympathetic observer later recalled, "Two aging men trotted out on the podium, cavorted and bowed, and instead of being greeted with applause they were met with laughter. . . . The two seam-faced, sixty-year-old men, stiffly, awkwardly moving about, seemed ridiculous in this carnival atmosphere. . . . It was pathetic that they had to perform in this undignified manner and in this place. What might have been charming and amusing when they were younger now appeared infinitely sad." In the words of another writer, "They had lost their vigour, and were two elderly men, with the result that their performance had become merely freakish and tasteless. Behind their pleasant, but now wrinkled smiles, and their stiffer bows lay fear in their eyes, and a hatred of those who came to stare and deride." Even though they could not hear well, the guffawing faces of the audience, like stony gargoyles, turned the whole scene into a mime, one in which the whole world ridiculed them silently and mercilessly.[8]

As soon as their Berlin engagement was over, they wanted to move on to tsarist Russia and then France, to strike out again on their own, as they had used to do when they were young. But on July 19, 1870, France declared war on Germany, putting an end to the twins' European dream and, unbeknownst to them, to their career as performers.

As described in the prologue of this book, the twins and their sons boarded the *Palmyra* on July 30 in Liverpool and started their homeward journey. On the steamer, they played a game of chess with Edward James Roye, an American expatriate and son of a fugitive slave, newly elected president of Liberia. The game ended abruptly when Chang suffered a stroke and became paralyzed on the left side of his body. Years of hard drinking had finally caught up with him. Even though Eng, a teetotaler but an addict of late-night poker, was still healthy, the two became bedridden for the remainder of the voyage.

After the twins arrived back home, and while they convalesced, bad news reached them concerning President Roye in Liberia. The railroad funds he had tried to raise in America never materialized. The usurious loan the London bankers had forced upon his country went bad and subsequently doomed his presidency. In October 1871, one year after his chess game with the twins, Roye's political enemies staged a coup d'état, and he was killed by an angry mob that dragged his naked body through the streets of Monrovia. Upon Roye's death, mayhem and violence continued for sixty days in the capital city—named after James Monroe, one of the architects of the American dream of liberty for blacks.[9]

During those turbulent months, the twins would enjoy sitting on the porch on fine days, in their double elm chair, under the shadow of the Blue Ridge. Often they would read, rather than lollygag or whittle, as their fellow Southerners were wont to do. They were avid readers; ever since they had set foot in the Western Hemisphere and learned to read and write, they were always eager to acquire new words and embrace books, reading anything they could get their hands on—newspapers, farmer's almanacs, encyclopedias, and, best of all, literature. On long winter nights by the fireplace or cool summer afternoons on the porch, they would each pick something to read, or share a book by reading aloud to each other. They had read Alexander Pope at least ten times because Eng was partial to this semi-invalid English master for his writing about the conjoined Hungarian Sisters who shared a single pair of legs. If that Missouri boy Samuel Clemens had published *Pudd'nhead Wilson* a bit earlier, they would have loved the story about those extraordinary Italian twins, who also walked around with only one pair of legs, and they certainly did not mind his caricature of them in that humorous sketch; it was all for good fun.

Now that Chang was not well, Eng would read everything for him.

In the local papers, they came across disturbing news about the rioting mobs in faraway Liberia and reports about the death of President Roye. They were no strangers to mobs, whether a crowd of gawkers packing an exhibition hall or an angry throng taunting them with accusations of "fraud." Several times they had even got into fistfights, tables turned over, chairs flying. But Roye's death grieved and infuriated the twins. As much as they had disagreed with him over the evils of slavery—a topic cautiously broached and then quickly dropped during their conversation aboard the *Palmyra*—they liked Roye, because he was, like them, a self-made man. They recalled Roye's words, as the former Negro barber-turned-president of a free nation told them his life story. Roye explained why he had left America: "I have steadily had mind fixed upon a foreign land since early youth, a land of African government; for there I believed our elevation would take place."[10] Those were the words of a man pursuing his dream, seeking freedom and liberty in spite of who he was. But what is freedom, and what is liberty, after which Liberia was named?

Inside their house, lying on the mantel above the fireplace, next to Pope, Shakespeare, Lord Byron, and John Fleetwood's *Life of Christ*, was a tattered copy of George Crabb's *Dictionary of General Knowledge*. It was the first book they had ever owned, given to them as a gift during their first visit to London in 1830, when they were still learning their ABCs. In that dictionary, where they had seen for the first time half-nude pictures of women, all goddesses of Greek and Roman mythologies, the word *liberty* was defined as "a privilege by which men enjoy some favour or benefit beyond the ordinary subject."[11] That definition puzzled them. Their experience with the real meaning of the word had been a bag full of ironies. And irony hardly has any place in a dictionary. They had been sold into slavery by their loving mother, later managed to free themselves and became their own men, and then they bought and owned slaves. In fact, when Roye asked offhandedly, while moving a piece on the chessboard, whether they had ever whipped their slaves, the genial chat ended abruptly. The penny press had reported that the twins were hard on their slaves, prone to using the lash without mercy. Some even claimed, falsely or truthfully, that they had once rewarded a bounty hunter for having shot and killed one of their runaway slaves, and that they bet and traded Negroes during card games. They would not deign to comment on whether or not those rumors contained a kernel of truth. The populace, attracted to a Manichaean tendency that shunned half-tints, liked to reduce the river of human variations to diametric opposites: good vs. evil, master vs. slave, victimizer vs. victim. Those people could not stand, or understand, the gray zone of humanity, a treacherous terrain of ambiguity where an exchange of roles between oppressor and victim constantly occurred.[12] P. T. Barnum, that Connecticut Yankee, a character the twins otherwise loathed with their guts, rightly called those people "suckers." The truth, as Chang and Eng insisted proudly, was something between them and their Maker.

On this winter night of January 16, 1874, the twins again thought of President Roye, their shipboard acquaintance. They had tried not to read too much into that encounter on the *Palmyra*, but it was, in fact, the beginning of their decline, because after Chang became ill during their chess game, he had never fully recovered.

Earlier on Monday, January 12, Chang had suffered from a bout of bronchitis, coughing and wheezing. The doctor was called in, and Chang was better the next day and the day after that. Come Thursday, it was time to move to Eng's house, according to their three-day rotation schedule. Considering Chang's condition and the doctor's advice to stay indoors and keep warm, Eng suggested that perhaps they should break the rule for once and stay put. Chang, however, was adamant about leaving, refusing to let illness or weather stop him from taking the one-mile ride. Besides, he insisted, they were in his house; therefore, he could decide what they should or should not do. Eng had no choice but to get ready for the move.

They rode in an open carriage, as they always did. Chang donned extra clothes and wrapped himself in a horse blanket. Eng drove the horse over the rough and frozen road, Chang clinging on to him like the baby brother he was. Bouncing and huddling together on this coldest day of winter, as frost covered everything, white as the ashes they remembered from their father's funeral, they suddenly felt closer than ever before. Momentarily, they forgot about the cold, wishing they could go on forever, as they had used to do on the open road of this country they were happy to call home.

Upon arriving at Eng's house, Chang started coughing again. The lack of alcohol at his brother's house, a deliberate choice, made it even harder for him to cope with the worsening of his condition. He turned nasty, indigent, and snappy. Eng built a fire in the parlor and sat with his brother in front of the fireplace for a long time, until Chang felt a bit better and was sleepy enough to go to bed.

The next morning, Friday, Chang seemed fine when he woke up. Apparently it was, as the Chinese say, *hui guang fan zhao* (the last radiance of the setting sun). The ray of hope quickly dimmed after the twins got up. Having been away from his home for three days, Eng needed to take care of some routine business, but dragging a cachectic and disgruntled Chang around the house was like trying to swim with a dead weight tied around his neck. Chang only became worse. According to a report later provided by the *Philadelphia Medical Times*, Chang complained by nightfall of a severe pain in the chest, and "so much distress that he thought he should have died." Eng coaxed him into turning in early, but only for a short while. Chang, however, could not fall asleep, his breathing becoming increasingly stertorous. Tossing and turning, he constantly had to sit up in bed, claiming that "it would kill him to lie down." Because of their conjoinment, Eng, of course, had to do everything in tandem. If Chang wanted to turn over in bed, Eng would have to roll over the top of his brother and move to the other side, and vice versa. And if Chang had to sit up, so would Eng. Because of Chang's restlessness, Eng, too, was now exhausted.[13]

At some point, the twins got up and went out to the porch to have a drink of water. On a moonless night, it was pitch dark. Yet beyond the light of the gasoline lantern, they could sense the dark presence of the Blue Ridge in the distance. The stillness of the night was unsettling. Even the wind had died.

Refreshed by the cold water and frozen air, they returned to bed. Soon Chang roused Eng again and said he was too cold. He wanted to go to the parlor and start a fire. Eng refused at first, saying that it would be warmer to stay in bed than to sit by the fire at such an ungodly hour. But Chang persisted, and Eng, always the more thoughtful of the two, obliged, even though this was his house and he could decide on everything. They hobbled to the parlor, like those Italian twins conjoined by a single pair of legs. Eng started a fire and again sat with his brother in the double chair. Even though the fire toasted Eng like a loaf of bread, Chang still shivered and whimpered, a leaf clinging to a limb.

Thankfully, perhaps out of sheer exhaustion, Chang finally dozed off, and Eng managed to drag both of them back to bed.

In the wee hours of January 17, the family heard a scream that might have come from the twins' bedroom. Or was it just someone's nightmare? The house fell quiet again. No one stirred until dawn cracked open a chink in the eggshell of the dark, frozen world. One of Eng's sons got up and went to check on his father and his uncle. Holding up a lamp, the boy saw the ashen face of Chang and said to his father, "Uncle Chang is dead."

"Then I'm going too," Eng whispered faintly.

The next hour or so found the family running about, trying to figure out what to do—or at least how to save Eng. Someone was sent to get Dr. Joseph Hollingsworth, who had previously made known his plan to separate the twins surgically if one of them died. But the doctor lived three miles away, and he also happened to be out of town. His brother, William Hollingsworth, a doctor as well, stepped in and rushed to Eng's house, carrying a case of surgical tools.

Before the doctor's arrival, Eng languished in agony. Now that his twin brother was dead, though still attached to him, Eng felt deserted, and, we can imagine, terrified. He did not know what to do, or how he was supposed to act. Throughout their conjoined lives, they had acted in metronomic harmony, leaning on each other to navigate the world. Suddenly Eng's shadow was no more, just a stone, more like a pebble, if you will, no longer skipping across the pond, but sinking into the murky beyond.

Eng, for only a few hours, became one.

Perhaps that Missouri boy Samuel Clemens did know a thing or two about conjoined twins. In his curtain speech at the performance of a theatrical rendition of *Pudd'nhead Wilson* in April 1895, the maestro of American letters bowed to the applauding audience from his box and admitted publicly to the Achilles' heel in his work, a fatal weakness haunting the novel as soon as he decided to separate the twins: "To save the righteous brother I had to pull the consolidated twins apart and make two separate and distinct twins of them. Well, as soon as I did that, they lost all their energy and took no further interest in life. They were wholly futile and useless in the book, they became mere shadows, and so they remain."[14]

That was how Eng felt now, a mere shadow. A shadow of the dark, solid mass lying next to him—something he still recognized but now a wraith to whom he still looked to find himself. But then that image was gone, and this life, as Shakespeare wrote in the volume that Eng had read for Chang only recently, became "but a walking shadow."

Lingering in pain, fear, confusion, and, above all, loneliness, Eng told Sarah that he was very "bad off." The *Philadelphia Medical Times* reported, as did countless newspapers throughout the world, that Eng, in his final moments, asked his wife and children to rub his legs and arms, and pull and stretch them forcibly. About an hour later, he sank into a stupor—which continued until he died. Before lapsing into oblivion, according to some, Eng spoke his last words: "May the Lord have mercy upon my soul."[15]

Indeed, that last mile had proved to be fatal.

Afterlife

*We must observe that all nations, barbarous as well as civilized, though separately
founded because remote from each other in time and space, must keep these three human
customs: all have some religion, all contract solemn marriages, all bury their dead.*
—Giambattista Vico, *The New Science* (1725)

W hile the burial of the dead may be, as Vico believed, one
of humanity's defining customs, a practice that supposedly
separates *Homo sapiens* from the other species on earth,
how we bury the dead, or how we handle the bodies before and after
burial, varies significantly across the spectrum of culture and time.
This is no place to dive into a lengthy ethnographic survey of diverse
burial practices, ranging from the Siamese cremation by throwing a
body onto a burning pyre—something Chang and Eng had witnessed
at their father's funeral—to the Tibetan "sky burial" by exposing a body
on a rocky cliff and allowing vultures to peck clean the flesh before collecting the bones for preservation. The families of Chang and Eng only
wanted a simple Christian burial: a plain wooden coffin—extra wide
perhaps—a sedate churchyard, a robed minister holding a Bible, and
a circle of mourners. But modern science—with its persistent desire to
pry, and with the almost prurient interest that had dogged the twins
in their lifetime and intensified after their deaths—rendered the family's wishes about as valuable as a Confederate greenback. Even as
corpses, the famous Siamese Twins had to perform one more time in
the public eye.

In *Stiff: The Curious Lives of Human Cadavers* (2003), Mary Roach
provides a fascinating account of how dead bodies have continued to
live public lives:

For two thousand years, cadavers—some willingly, some unwittingly— have been involved in science's boldest strides and weirdest under- takings. Cadavers were around to help test France's first guillotine, the "humane" alternative to hanging. They were there at the labs of Lenin's embalmers, helping test the latest techniques. They've been there (on paper) at Congressional hearings, helping make the case for mandatory seat belts. They've ridden the Space Shut- tle . . . helped a graduate student in Tennessee debunk spontane- ous human combustion, been crucified in a Parisian laboratory to test the authenticity of the Shroud of Turin.[1]

Likewise, the bodies of Chang and Eng enjoyed or suffered—depending on your point of view—a dramatic resurrection, so to speak, in the afterlife.

The news of the twins' death spread quickly, traveling by word of mouth and wire from this remote hamlet to the entire thirty-seven states, then to Great Britain and beyond. The *New York Herald* ran a front-page story, emblazoned with the headline: THE DEAD SIA- MESE TWINS. A LIGATURE THAT JOINED THEM IN LIFE AND DEATH. Their obituaries, some lengthy and others succinct, filled the pages of newspapers big and small all over the country.

While the world was abuzz with the news, the twins' families, prin- cipally Adelaide and Sarah, faced a difficult decision. As much as they wanted a normal burial, that seemed out of the question. As their fam- ily doctors warned them, rapacious grave robbers would spirit away the bodies within days if the twins were simply buried in the ground. Nannie conveyed such a fear vividly in her letter to Christopher, who was traveling in California at the time and was being urged to return home promptly: "Dr. Joe [Hollingsworth] says their bodies would not remain in the grave three nights if they were put there, that [even] the best friends we have can be bought." A reward for the bodies had been secretly put out, and Nannie worried that "some paid demon would drag them from their resting place in less than three nights. And once gone we could not help ourselves, that they would make Merchandise of the bodies in spite of all we can do, or could do."[2]

Neither the doctors' cautions nor the family's fears were unfounded. In the nineteenth century, body-snatching was a time-honored, though hardly honorable, profession. To be a "resurrectionist," as a body snatcher was euphemistically called, one only needed a shovel, a sack, and a good nose or tip for the location of a freshly buried body. What made body snatching particularly lucrative at the time was the increasing influence of medical science and the subsequent demand for human cadavers for anatomical study. Although dissecting corpses for anatomical knowledge had begun as early as 300 BC, under the auspices of Ptolemy I of Egypt, the religious belief or superstitious notion that a body had to be in one piece in order to enter the gates of heaven had created a perennial shortage of cadavers for doctors and medical students. For centuries, only the corpses of executed murderers were legally available for dissection in Britain. The simultaneous spike in demand for human cadavers in medical science and the decrease in execution cases in the nineteenth century, however, created a perfect storm. As Roach describes in her book, in attempting to cope with the shortage, "Some anatomy instructors mined the timeless affinity of university students for late-night pranks by encouraging their enrollees to raid graveyards and provide bodies for the class. . . . By 1828, the demands of London's anatomy schools were such that ten full-time body snatchers and two hundred or so part-timers were kept busy throughout the dissecting 'season.'"[3] Such a high demand for cadavers had even inspired William Burke and William Hare, a lodger and a manager of a boardinghouse in Edinburgh, as we saw earlier, to create their own supply of corpses by murder. It was the trial of these two serial killers and the hanging of Burke that had made the headlines in New York when Chang and Eng first visited there in the fall of 1829.

After years of lobbying by prominent surgeons, and in response to a public outcry over human body trafficking, the British Parliament in 1832 finally passed the Anatomy Act, allowing licensed doctors, anatomy teachers, and medical students to dissect donated corpses, not just bodies of executed murderers. Among the proponents of this act was Sir Astley Cooper, the first British surgeon who had laid his hands on the

Siamese Twins in 1829. An outspoken defender of human dissection, Cooper once said, "He must mangle the living if he has not operated on the dead." According to Roach, Cooper would show no compunction about cutting up strangers' family members or slicing into his own former patients. In fact, he would keep in touch with those he had operated on and, when hearing of their passing, he would commission their resurrection, "so that he might have a look at how his handiwork had held up."[4] Sharing Cooper's almost morbid obsession with cadavers was Harvard professor and physician John Collins Warren, the other surgeon who had also played a key role in the public life of the Siamese Twins. In his journals, Warren referred to dissecting a body as "a primary occupation and a pleasure . . . my daily meat and drink." He admitted that "the idea of nicely injecting a delicate piece of anatomy, of macerating it to a snow-like whiteness, and of enclosing it in an elegant glass vessel of perfectly transparent liquid, had more charms for me than games or plays or parties." When some of his students got into legal trouble for breaking into Boston cemeteries at night and stealing corpses, Warren came to their defense with no reservation or apology: "Such instances as the above may appear improper to those who do not appreciate the importance of the objects. But the surgeon and the teacher have a high moral duty to perform to their patients and to the community; and, in the eye of reason and religion, they will be less culpable for preserving articles so very important and useful, than if, through fear or neglect, they allowed them to be wasted in the bottom of a grave."[5]

Although the new generation of surgeons did not wield the same degree of power as did Cooper and Warren, they certainly shared the passion and hunger for cadavers, especially a unique specimen like Chang and Eng. And these were the men with whom Adelaide and Sarah would have to deal. The alternative would be other kinds of men, the impresarios of showbiz, carpetbaggers of the worst sort, who had also expressed interest in the bodies. Some had already contacted the widows to make offers for the twins' bodies. "Name your price," barked one letter from three Brooklyn entrepreneurs to the grieving widows.[6]

Adelaide and Sarah had to figure out what to do—whether to allow

the northern doctors to cut open their dead husbands, or to let showmen parade their husbands' bodies like stuffed animals, brined in form-
aldehyde in a macabre diorama, all over the world, or, worst of all, to
wait for the grave robbers to spirit them away to the doctors or showmen for the same purposes. They decided to preserve the bodies first,
because they were also waiting for the four adult Bunker sons to return
home and help them make a decision about their fathers' afterlife. After
the twins died on a Saturday, the families ordered a tin box made by a
local smith. On Sunday, January 18, as the *Charlotte Observer* reported,
"a large number of persons, from every direction of the country, visited the residence to see them for the last time."[7] After members of the
public had paid their respects, the bodies were placed inside a walnut
casket, very securely fastened. The coffin was then encased in a large
tin box, soldered, and sealed airtight. Then the latter was put in a large
wooden crate, packed in charcoal and secured, once again, tightly. A
shallow grave was dug in the cellar of Eng's house, and the bodies were
temporarily interred there.[8] The Siamese Twins' temporary resting place
was rather like a Chinese box, waiting for the doctors or anyone else to
unpack the mystery.

   With the twins safely interred, at least for the moment, Adelaide and
Sarah dispatched Joseph Hollingsworth to New England to find out
what noted medical authorities had in mind or had to offer. As a doctor,
Hollingsworth knew how much his colleagues in the North would relish
the chance, like foxhounds licking their chops, to apply their scalpels to
the bodies of a most famous set of twins. Even his own brother, William,
who had attended the twins on the morning of their death, had wanted
to conduct a postmortem but was barred by the widows. While Hollingsworth traveled northward, a missive was going in the other direction,
a telegram on behalf of Dr. William H. Pancoast of Jefferson Medical College in Philadelphia to the Bunker widows, making inquiries
into the status of the twins' bodies and expressing wishes to conduct a
postmortem examination. Learning about the telegram, Hollingsworth
detoured to Philadelphia immediately and met up with the members
of the College of Physicians to discuss the matter. Some newspapers

reported that Hollingsworth, negotiating on behalf of the Bunkers, had asked for a price between $8,000 and $10,000 for the bodies, and that, due to the large sum, several medical institutions in Boston, New York, and Philadelphia would have to work together to raise the funds. Some later accounts, however, dismissed these as unfounded rumors.

At any rate, after the meetings in Philadelphia, a commission was formed, consisting of Doctors John Neill, Joseph Leidy, William Ruschenberger, and others. (Ruschenberger was the surgeon on the 1836 American mission to Siam who had given an expert phrenological reading of Siamese heads.) The commission entrusted three doctors—Pancoast, Harrison Allen, and Thomas Andrews—to travel to North Carolina to conduct the autopsy.

On the evening of Saturday, January 31, two weeks after the deaths, the trio of Philadelphia doctors arrived in Mount Airy. They were met by the widows, who granted them permission to exhume and examine the entombed bodies, under one condition: No incisions could be made that would impair the external surface of the connecting band. Dismayed, these three highly respected men—but medical carpetbaggers nonetheless—tried to reason with the widows, stressing that the band was medicine's Holy Grail. Pancoast maintained, as he would in an article later, that "It was held to be a duty to science and humanity, that the family of the deceased should permit an autopsy. The twins had availed themselves most freely of the services of our profession in both hemispheres, and it was considered by many but as a proper and necessary return, that at their death this *quaestio vexata* (the possibility of a successful section of the band) should be settled by an examination of its anatomical structure."[9] Under pressure, the widows yielded to these Northern medicine men, agreeing that limited incisions would be allowed on the posterior surface of the band, but in no way to deface it in front, nor to pull it asunder.

Finally, reaching an accord with the bereaved women, the doctors proceeded to exhume the bodies. As the *Philadelphia Medical Times* reported:

After unsoldering the tin box, the coffin was carried to the second floor of the house, to a large chamber. The lid was unscrewed, and the object of the search of the Commission was exposed to view. It was certainly an anxious moment. Fifteen days had elapsed since death, and no preservative had been employed. It was an agreeable surprise, therefore, that no odor of decomposition escaped into the room, and that the features gave no evidence of impending decay. On the contrary, the face of Eng was that of one sleeping; and the only unfavorable appearance in Chang was a slight lividity of the lips and a purplish discoloration about the ears. The widows at this point entered the room, and, amid the respectful silence of all present, took a last look at the remains.[10]

Pancoast and his colleagues proceeded to strip the bodies of all clothing and propped them up to a standing position. Then the doctors took photographs of the naked bodies, zeroing in on the connecting band. Next they made incisions into the corpses to start the embalming procedure, for they wanted to do the autopsy in a professional setting in Philadelphia rather than in rural North Carolina. After injecting antiseptic fluid into the twins, the doctors, behaving like Charon's henchmen, sewed up the bodies and packed them back into the casket and the tin box. The package was then driven down to Salem, North Carolina, and shipped by train to Philadelphia. Curiously, the shipment also included one of the two double chairs used by the twins, prompting some newspapers to speculate that the twins would go on a roadshow in the afterlife, as they had done in life: "Once again the Siamese Twins will appear in the world, not as living, breathing souls—a strange freak of nature—but as dull and stark corpses."[11]

While the notion of a roadshow-turned-freak exhibition was mere idle chatter, the twins did unwittingly go before the public eye. On February 10, the official autopsy was conducted at the Mütter Museum, affiliated with the College of Physicians. Or, as the *Philadelphia Medical Times* (granted exclusive media access to the procedure) put it in its editorial: The twins "were exposed for study." Under the watchful eyes of his colleagues, Pancoast opened up the twins' bodies again, hoping to uncover the mystery once and for all:

> The dreaded scalpel was first used on the connecting band between the two brothers. The abdominal cavities were entered for the purpose of examining the viscera. This investigation was attended with most gratifying results, and the physicians were rewarded in their efforts in finding that the lungs, heart, pancreas, liver, spleen and alimentary canal were excellently developed in each, and that all the parts above-named resembled those of ordinary mortals.[12]

A second autopsy followed a week later, and doctors made some important discoveries:

> The two livers which were supposed to be joined only by blood vessels, were really one body, the parenchymatous tissue being continuous between them, so that when they were removed from the bodies and placed on a table they formed one mass. The so-called tract of portal continuity is therefore the liver tissue. It will be remembered that Chang was said to be possessed of one more pouch than Eng. When the liver was removed, however, an upper hepatic pouch was found also proceeding from Eng, so that the band contained four pouches of peritoneum, besides liver-tissue. These disclosures show that any attempt during life to separate the twins would in all probability have proved fatal.

In other words, Chang and Eng were destined, for life as it turned out, to be bound together. The boundary between them, as Raleigh's *Daily News* put it, was "clear as mud."[13]

In addition to these discoveries about the band, other peculiar details became public, such as the fact that each twin had pubic hair that was gray on the left and black on the right, and that Eng's bladder had become overdistended and his right testicle retracted, suggesting that fright contributed to the poor man's death. Having sated their curiosity about what they continued to consider a "monster," the doctors finally sent the bodies back to North Carolina in March, sans the liver, lungs, and entrails. When Christopher and Stephen Bunker met the train and received the bodies in Salem, they were shocked to see "only the shells" of their fathers. Outraged, the two battle-wounded Confederate veterans shot off a terse letter to the conniving Yankee doctors:

Sir

Enclosed you will find the receipt for bringing the bodies of Papa and Uncle from Salem to our home. You will please send the Money by post-office order.

My Mother and Aunt was very sorry that we did not bring the lungs and entrails of our Fathers with the bodies home. And as we did not bring them, you can keep them until further orders from the families.

Respectfully

CW and SD Bunker[14]

Today, visitors to the Mütter Museum in Philadelphia are still treated to a mind-boggling display of medical, anatomical, and pathological specimens, millions of oddities that include a section of the brain of President Garfield's assassin, a piece of tissue removed from the thorax of assassin John Wilkes Booth, and bullets removed from bodies of Civil War soldiers. Standing at the center of this dioramalike shrine of curiosity is the conjoined liver of Chang and Eng, soaking in a tub of formalin. The doctors had taken it out of their bodies during the autopsy and kept it for posterity in the name of science and knowledge. We don't know what became of the lungs and entrails. It seems morbidly fitting then that the twins, who were repeatedly exhibited throughout almost half of the nineteenth century, are now perpetually instantiated through the preservation of their liver—exhibited, as if for eternity, still in the twenty-first century.

Mayberry, USA

On the last day of summer in 2015, after giving a lecture in Knoxville, Tennessee, I rented a car and drove across the state line, over the Great Smokies and the Blue Ridge, to visit the picturesque town of Mount Airy, North Carolina, better known nowadays as Mayberry, USA.

In *The Andy Griffith Show* (or *TAGS*, as it has become known), Mayberry is portrayed as a sleepy town filled with oddball characters and quaint customs. With a population of eighteen hundred souls (exactly the same as Winesburg, Ohio, in Sherwood Anderson's eponymous short-story cycle), Mayberry, though curiously lacking racial minorities in its depiction by CBS during the tumultuous decade of 1960s, remains a quintessential American small town. It is an Arcadia where life's troubles—whether a family feud, a farmer looking for a wife, a pickle-contest debacle, property foreclosure, or baby delivery—can all be solved in twenty-five minutes with the help of amiable Sheriff Andy Taylor and his bungling deputy, Barney Fife. In the words of the garrulous barber Floyd, Mayberry is "a nice, clean community, tucked away in a peaceful valley, where all our children have good teeth."

In reality, Mount Airy, nestled in the foothills of western North Carolina, population 10,388 by the 2010 census, is not only the actual birthplace of Andy Griffith, the star on America's most popular rubecom, bearing his name. It is also, unknown to most, the adopted hometown of Chang and Eng, the original Siamese Twins (as readers of *Inseparable* already know).

It was a good day for driving. The September sun, after a brief bounce off the ragged ridges in the east, had finally disappeared behind rainclouds. A soft drizzle followed, moistening the highway till it became smooth and curvy like a bamboo strip, or perhaps spaghetti. The dogwood—which appeared in literature as early as Chaucer's *Canterbury Tales* as a whipple-tree—dotted hills as ancient as the Bible. Red and flying squirrels flashed their fluffy tails here and there in the woods, which had deepened in color. Winding through gaps between mountains, my rented Jeep Grand Cherokee navigated terrains where real Cherokee had once thrived, as had General George Stoneman's six-thousand-strong cavalry during his famous raid into North Carolina in the waning days of the Civil War.

The news on the radio that day was about the arrival of Pope Francis in the United States. Switching between news and Appalachian bluegrass, I reflected on the long journey that had brought me to Mayberry. The lecture I had given a day earlier at the University of Tennessee was about Charlie Chan, a chubby, aphorism-spouting Chinese detective from Honolulu. Unlike Chan, who had hooked me from the get-go, Sheriff Andy Taylor was a more recently acquired taste. I had sporadically watched some reruns of *Matlock* on TV, and, as a mystery aficionado, I had enjoyed Griffith's new incarnation as a silver-haired lawyer with hayseed wisdom and a steel-trap mind, drawling his vowels and outsmarting suspects, in a manner not so different from Charlie Chan, with his broken English and overpolite demeanor. *TAGS*, however, was no love at first sight. A bachelor sheriff mollycoddled by an aging aunt, or a blabbermouth deputy with a mild case of malapropism and a perpetual habit of misfiring a gun like a Keystone cop, was not really my cup of tea. Only after I began to research western North Carolina did my interest in Mayberry and its piquant citizens blossom. Slowly but surely, the "Magic of Mayberry" grew on me. I began to get the hang of the cornball sheriff constantly ribbing his horny deputy, and to appre-

ciate the hick burg that runs its jail like a motor lodge for a henpecked
town drunk or uses it as a nursery for babies.

After three hours of driving, I cleared Tennessee, rounded the
southern tip of Virginia, and came down from a high plateau overlooking the lush hills and sleepy hollows of the western edge of the Tar
Heel State. On this last day of summer, under gray skies, the broad valley far below was a dense mass of green wilderness, tinted by patches
of autumnal gold and crimson. The tranquility and timelessness of
the vista reminded me of the Chinese *shi wai tao yuan*, the Land of
Peach Blossoms, a mythical paradise of eternal peace and happiness.
When the Moravians first arrived in this area in the 1750s, they simply
called it "The Hollow." I could see why the Siamese Twins would, in
1839, choose "The Hollow" as a place to settle down after a decade of
globetrotting. They considered this area a "garden spot of the world,"
and they had indeed traveled a very long distance to get here. Their
story from Meklong to Mayberry, as I have described in *Inseparable*, is
patently astonishing. Or, as Sheriff Andy says, "If you wrote this into a
play, nobody'd believe it."

Coming down from the high plateau, I was soon on flat land. Sand-
wiched between fields of big-leaf tobacco, of which the twins had been
early pioneering growers, Interstate 74 was not really the crowded
Highway 6 portrayed in *TAGS*, where the speed limit was kept under
thirty-five miles an hour. I had read somewhere that I-74 cut through
the farm that had once belonged to the Siamese Twins. As soon as I
turned off the highway, I came across twin bridges spanning a creek
and saw a sign marked ENG AND CHANG BUNKER MEMORIAL BRIDGE. I
knew immediately I was in the twins' land. But as I drove farther into
town, the ubiquity of "Mayberry"—"Mayberry Auto Sales," "Mayberry
Insurance," "Mayberry Antique Mall," and so on—began to assault my
sense of history and reality. These sensory attacks, however, were only
the beginning, rather like the initial excitement one feels when pulling
in to a parking lot at Disney World.

Unsure of the parking protocol in town, I pulled in to a small lot next to the public library and parked the Jeep there. The Mount Airy Public Library, an award-winning architectural gem, actually occupies the spot where the Jesse Franklin Graves house once stood. Judge Graves, an old friend of Chang and Eng, had written the first complete, though unpublished, biography of the Siamese Twins, which became a goldmine for later writers.

Across the street from the library was the police department, no longer the ancient brick-front courthouse featured in *TAGS*, but a modern, stand-alone concrete building with big glass doors and windows. I knew there would be no amiable Sheriff Andy sitting there behind his desk, clacking away on a typewriter with two fingers, talking on the phone to reassure Mrs. Vickers that the loud bangs she had heard were not Yankee cannons but blasts from highway construction. Nor would there be an overzealous Deputy Fife marching out the door, whipping out a pad from his hip to write me a citation for jaywalking or illegal parking. Since it was not a weekend, there would be no inebriated Otis snoring away on a cozy cot in Cell No. 2. For those imaginary scenes, I would need to walk down the street to visit the local shrine, The Andy Griffith Museum.

Built on the street where little Andy had gone to school, the museum features hundreds of items from the life and career of Mount Airy's favorite son in movies, television, and music. It also collects memorabilia donated by cast members from *TAGS*, including a special section devoted to current Mount Airy resident Betty Lynn, better known as Thelma Lou, Barney's steady. When Lynn retired from acting in 2006, the Missouri native decided to settle in the town that had made her famous. Interestingly, the Surry Arts Council, which oversees the museum, is headed by Tanya Jones, a descendant of Chang Bunker.

In front of the museum, standing under the green canopy of a Bradford pear tree, was a bronze statue of Andy and Opie carrying fishing poles, as they always do in the opening sequence of *TAGS*. I could almost hear the sprightly tune Andy whistles, as he walks Opie down to Myers Lake, possibly playing hooky for a day. After passing the statue, I came to a neatly designed sunken garden, full of manicured viburnum,

STATUE OF ANDY AND OPIE TAYLOR,
MOUNT AIRY, NORTH CAROLINA

holly, arborvitae, English laurel, and autumn cherry. A walking path led
me to the entrance to the museum, whose lobby had a cutout of Goober
Pyle, the gas jockey at Wally's filling station, standing next to two Acme
gasoline pumps marked "Ethyl" and "Regular." I paid the $6 admission
fee—not to Goober, but to a lovely lady sitting behind a window. She
kindly reminded me that when I finished the tour, I could go out and
walk down to the back garden to visit the special Siamese Twins exhibition. "It's free," she emphasized. Imagine her surprise when I made a
beeline for the door and went straight to the twins' exhibition!

At the bottom of the garden, I pushed open a heavy, faceless door that looked like a back entrance to a theater stage. Perhaps the Siamese Twins, in the eyes of many, were merely a sideshow to *TAGS*, which competes with the likes of *Father Knows Best* and *Leave It to Beaver* as classic depictions of 1950s and 1960s American "normalcy" in a period of affluence, suburban sprawls, and middle-class lassitude. Most episodes of *TAGS* end with "things back to normal," as Andy puts it, with a sigh of relief. In one episode, when a carnival comes to town and some of the local women are shocked by an exotic dance show, Sheriff Andy asks the manager to "tone it down a little," essentially shutting down the "gootchie-hootchie dance." In contrast, the story of Chang and Eng, with their physical abnormalities, double matrimony, miscegenation, and slaveholding, was anything but normal. They were regarded as carnival freaks in their day—like Victor Hugo's Quasimodo, "an almost." To open the door to the twins' show in the basement of the Andy Griffith Museum is in some sense to reveal the "underbelly" of America, to see how the normal is built on top of the abnormal, in a manner that Leslie Fiedler, as I mention in the preface, dubs the "tyranny of the normal."

The basement room had no other visitors when I entered. Dimly lit, the walls were covered with posters, photos, paintings, newspaper clippings, and framed documents related to the twins. Next to the entrance, an antique trunk was displayed inside a glass cabinet like a Keatsian urn, that "foster child of silence and slow time." Made by the venerable New York firm of Crouch & Fitzgerald, the old trunk was missing a leather strap, and above the keyhole was the date of manufacture: "May 12, 1868." Judging by the time stamp, the trunk must have been used by the twins during their trips to Europe after the Civil War.

In a corner of the room, next to the trunk, were disassembled bedframes, displayed on the wall. They were extra wide—understandable, considering the number of people the conjugal bed needed to accommodate—and made of solid pine. The twins were said to have been excellent carpenters and might have made this bed themselves. In fact, they were jacks-of-all-trades, skilled in breaking horses, trapping wild animals, target shooting, and stoneworking. Three years earlier, during my last visit to this area, I had seen some of the household utensils, such as a rolling pin, that the twins had made, and a church that the twins had helped build, an architectural gem.

On that earlier trip, in the spring of 2012, I had driven more than three thousand miles from Santa Barbara, California. En route, I stopped to see friends and family and arrived in North Carolina just when the dogwood was in full bloom. Like Ronnie Howard's Opie doing research for his essay on the Battle of Mayberry, I had first spent a week at the State Archives in downtown Raleigh, mining information from the records and documents in the collection. Then I moved on to Chapel Hill to examine the papers archived at the University of North Carolina. After two weeks of research—laying my hands on old letters, faded photographs, tax records, land deeds, court papers, and the twins' meticulously kept ledgers—I made a field trip to the state's western mountains to see the old stomping ground of Chang and Eng.

My first stop that day was Wilkesboro, where the twins had first settled. On a quiet Sunday morning, with all stores shut for the day or, for that matter, permanently, the one-street downtown proudly showed off its centerpiece—a rusted cannon pointing toward a small war memorial that stood like a totem pole on the town square. Except for a Tyson Foods processing facility down the road, Wilkesboro seemed to be reposing in time. I circled around the war memorial, reading the names of the fallen heroes. One name that caught my attention was "Roby P. Yates," killed in World War II, possibly a descendant of the Yates family, the clan of the twins' wives.

I soon hit the road again, following a winding rural route northward, and arrived in Mount Airy about half an hour later. In my ignorance, not having been raised in America, I had not yet made a connection between the Siamese Twins and Mayberry on that trip, so I did not look out for traces of Sheriff Taylor or Deputy Fife. Nor, when I pulled in to a gas station, was I surprised that no friendly Gomer or Goober came out to help me fill up. My destination that day was the cemetery where

CHANG AND ENG BUNKER'S GRAVE, WHITE PLAINS, NORTH CAROLINA

Chang and Eng were buried. I quickly found the spot, a churchyard
on a small mound by a quiet country road, facing the ramparts of the
Blue Ridge to the north. I had seen the photos of the twins' grave many
times, but I was surprised by the sheer number of other Bunkers buried
here. It was essentially their family graveyard.

Most impressive of all was the wood-framed church, painted white,
with a remarkable beauty of symmetry like a perfect mathematical
equation. While I was walking around and admiring the building, a
woman emerged from a side door. "Are you looking for the Siamese
Twins' grave?" she asked. She then handed me a pamphlet that intro-
duces the history of the White Plains Baptist Church. According to the
four-page pamphlet, the twins' wives—daughters of a Baptist pastor—
were avid congregants, whereas the twins were born Buddhist. But
what they lacked in evangelical background, they made up in material
support—not only did they donate the land for the church, they also
helped to build it. Glancing at my California license plate, the woman

WHITE PLAINS BAPTIST CHURCH, NORTH CAROLIINA

realized that I had come a long way to visit the place, so she chatted with me, as if to reward my effort. She told me of an incident that occurred when the twins were building the church, after the wood frame had been raised. One day when they were working on the roof, one of the twins accidentally hit the thumb of the other with a hammer. Tempers flared and an argument broke out, leading to a fistfight. They ended up tumbling down the roof together. The woman chuckled as she wrapped up the anecdote and handed me a smaller church brochure titled "The

Only Doorway." Having attended Sunday sermons in Alabama, I did indeed know where the doorway was supposed to be: Jesus Christ.

The sound of music from a TV monitor on the wall broke my reverie. A documentary film had just started, showing two child actors reenacting the conjoined twins' early life in old Siam. Judging by the images, it must have been *The Siamese Connection*, the film by Josh Gibson. I had watched its excellent documentary during my previous adventure in North Carolina, sitting in the library at UNC and wearing a headset.

I went around the basement room, looking at items displayed on the walls. I had already seen most of them during my research, but there were some surprising finds: copies of the twins' wills, a rare nineteenth-century photograph of Mount Airy's muddy main street, and pictures of some of the Bunker descendants in rural settings. A black curtain shielded one corner of the room. Out of curiosity, I delicately pulled aside the curtain and found a stack of binders on a table. Inside the binders were newspaper clippings about Bunker descendants, arranged chronologically, with dates scribbled in longhand. What particularly caught my attention were clippings from the *Tallahassee Democrat*, all articles about Alex Sink, the 2010 Democratic gubernatorial candidate in Florida. Great-granddaughter of Chang, Sink had grown up in Mount Airy, at the twins' homestead. A savvy businesswoman like her forefathers, Sink started out in the banking business in North Carolina before heading down to the Sunshine State and being elected Florida's chief financial officer. When she ran for governor in 2010, I had watched her debate against Rick Scott on CNN and greatly admired her aplomb and acumen. In interviews, she had often reminisced about growing up in America's quintessential small town. Because of her mixed look, townspeople who saw her on the streets would say, "You must be one of the Bunkers." Maybe it was her appearance, or maybe it was the quixotic hanging-chad politics of Florida, but she lost the election by a hair-thin margin to a scandal-ridden Republican opponent.

After lingering for a while, I left the twins' show and went upstairs for the Andy Tour. Unlike the deserted basement, the museum hall was packed with visitors. It turned out that I had arrived on the eve of Mayberry Days, an annual celebration lasting three to five days and featuring the return of actors, reenactment of characters and scenes, pickle contests, bluegrass music, and even Aunt Bee's bake sale. It all culminates in a parade down Main Street. Unfortunately, the new school year was about to start at my home university, so I needed to return to California the next day, thus having to miss the festival.

A shrine to the favorite son of Mount Airy, the museum holds the largest collection of Andy Griffith memorabilia in the country, ranging from baby Andy's well-worn rocking chair to the comically large keys to jail cells used in *TAGS*, as well as the familiar sheriff's shirt Andy wore on the show. The walls were plastered with movie bills, TV posters, and publicity photos. In contrast to the basement room where I had been able to poke around a little and take pictures freely, this place was almost sacred. There were signs everywhere warning against touching, photographing, or video recording. In the words of the museum's founder, the late Emmett Forrest, who used to play "kick the can" with Andy on the street, this museum is an attempt at "fixin' Andy in time."

In a twisted way, however, *TAGS* may rightly be called a misfit in time. Most revealing is the virtual absence of African Americans in Mayberry, a glaring omission typical of 1950s and 1960s American television. In fact, critics of *TAGS* and other sixties sitcoms have pointed out the near-invisibility of any racial minority in the shows. As Gustavo Pérez Firmat astutely points out in *A Cuban in Mayberry*, "During its original run, Mayberry barely registered a tremor of the social and political upheavals that were sweeping the country. Never mind that in February 1960, a few months before *TAGS* premiered, African American college students staged a sit-in at a segregated lunch counter in Greensboro, a stone's throw away from the fictional location of Mayberry, an event that set off similar protests in other segregated facilities in North Carolina."[1] In the entire run of 249 episodes, with only one exception, *TAGS* never featured a speaking role by a black actor. The only blacks were anonymous faces of a few extras in exterior crowd scenes, a remarkable incongruence with the reality that African Americans accounted for about a quarter of North Carolina's population in the 1960s. Even though for Mount Airy that number was much lower— under 5 percent, according to the 1960 census—the absence of black Mayberrians was so hard to justify that it prompted the NAACP to complain to CBS in 1966 that the show had "never showed a black face." The seventh season of TAGS was in part a response, however belated and woefully inadequate, to those complaints. In the twenty-sixth episode of the season, "Opie's Piano Lessons," the character Flip Conroy, a former NFL star returning to his hometown to work in his father's business and to coach the school football team, was played by a black actor, Rockne Tarkington.

Before the first appearance of a black face, however, there were some yellow faces, as well as a spatter of passing references to Asia. There was a newspaper headline, 130,000 CHINESE LIVING IN TREES AS A RESULT OF FLOOD, in the first season of TAGS. In "Barney's Uniform," an episode during the fifth season, there was a Mr. Izamoto, a Japanese judo teacher in the next big town, Mount Pilot, who had one Charlie Chanish spoken line: "He no can cut it." Early in the seventh season, Floyd talked about The Mikado, a nineteenth-century comic opera and a symbol of Anglo-American "Oriental fever." And then there were a couple of references to the Chinese restaurant in Mount Pilot, where Mayberrians could get a Chinese dinner if they wanted to have a little gastronomical adventure beyond their usual pounded steak at Morelli's.

In the 209th episode, "Aunt Bee's Restaurant," TAGS finally did something substantial with America's endless curiosity about Asia, and the insulated world of Mayberry finally opened up and came into contact, however superficially, with China. The plotline is simple and comical, like all TAGS shows: Aunt Bee, whose only knowledge of China consists of a ham-loaf recipe she got out of the paper and a one-line tune she hums whenever she is in a jolly mood ("Chinatown, my Chinatown, when the lights are low"), decides to open a Chinese restaurant. What makes this episode fascinating, however, is not so much Aunt Bee's entrepreneurial venture as the appearance of the Chinese-born actor Keye Luke, as Charlie the cook. Luke was best known for his role

SIGN FOR MAYBERRY CAMPGROUND, MOUNT AIRY, NORTH CAROLINA

as Lee, Number One Son in Charlie Chan films. His cameo on this episode of *TAGS* breathed a whiff of "Oriental" air into the American rubecom, bringing some exotic flavors to a lily-white Southern town that seemed to live in blissful oblivion about external affairs and internal tensions.

My destination that day was Mayberry Campground, which sits on land that used to be part of Chang and Eng's farm, about five miles from downtown Mount Airy. Like his forefathers with a keen business instinct, Benny East, the twins' great-great-grandson, had turned his ancestral land into a campground and branded it with a familiar and most alluring name. On my earlier trip to Mount Airy, I had spotted the bucolic resort, sprawling across several hundred acres adjacent to the cemetery and the church I was visiting. This time, I planned to spend the night here, even though I brought no camping gear. Sensitive to the spirit of a place—call it *feng shui*, if you will—I was curious to know how it would feel to spend a night at the twins' old haunt.

Pulling in to the unpaved entrance, I saw a rolling green field bordered by trees. A few zigzagging gravel roads wove together narrow strips of parking spots for RVs. There were about a hundred of these gravel pads, where giant houses-on-wheels, proud symbols of leisure and consumption in postwar America, dotted the bucolic scene. Each one of these boxes of chrome and sheet metal dwarfed my Jeep, and I felt even more embarrassed for my lack of outdoors know-how after I parked and went into the office trailer near the entrance. Doubling as a gift shop, the office was presided over by a young woman in her early twenties, wearing a plain T-shirt and a friendly smile. Sitting behind her neatly ordered desk, she had just finished a phone call when I entered. She gave me a broad smile and introduced herself as Kali. A lovable husky snoozed quietly by her feet. I asked her whether I could camp there for the night.

"Sure. How big is your rig?"

Abashed, I told her that I only drove a Jeep. She looked surprised, staring at me as though I were pulling a prank on her. I went on to explain my plan of sleeping in my car, hoping she would just give me one of those parking spots.

"Those are for trailers," she said, impressing me with her firmness. Pondering for a minute, like the good manager she was, trying to solve a small problem, she told me that for $30 she could let me park for one night in an empty space right next to the trailer that has the only public restroom on site. I gladly took it, thanking her for being so considerate.

As she was quickly filling out the paperwork, I looked around the room, where T-shirts, coffee mugs, caps, postcards, and other souvenirs were displayed on shelves and tables. I asked her whether she was related to the twins.

"Yes, my dad still lives in that house there."

Earlier, I had noticed an old farmhouse standing on a corner of the campground, now visible through the office window. After I paid, she gave me a brochure containing a map and information about the facilities and rules: All parking spots, either pull-through or back-in, have hookups to electricity, water, sewer, cable TV, and wi-fi; the campground has picnic shelters, firepits, BBQ grills, playgrounds, two fishing holes, and a walking trail; quiet time is between 11 p.m. and 8 a.m., no firearms or fireworks allowed, and fishing is catch-and-release only, etc. It seemed like a well-managed resort, much in keeping with the way the twins had run their two large families.

Despite my curiosity, I was reluctant to ask Kali any more questions. Her illustrious ancestors, from the moment they had set foot in America in 1829, had stayed in the limelight of public attention, constantly on display as objects of curiosity. Millions of gawkers worldwide had flocked to exhibition halls, museums, ballrooms, parlors, pitched tents, or county fairgrounds to take a peek at the famous *lusus naturae*. The twins, even their daughters, as we have seen, had withstood probing gazes by all. After their retirement, local and national newspapers would regularly send reporters to knock on their doors for updates. Privacy was a rarity for the twins and their families. So I decided not to pry but just to get on with my camping plan, however absurdly impractical it seemed.

After moving my car into the designated space, I took a walk around the grounds. The sun, which dappled the surroundings like a child playing peekaboo, had just sunk behind the nipple-shaped Pilot Knob, a peak that had inspired the name "Mount Pilot" in *TAGS*. As the twilight waned, a brooding hush descended on the campground, as though some invisible hand had turned a knob on the projector and suddenly slowed the speed of a film. From the front of the office trailer, which sat on the highest ground and had a panoramic view of the tiered site, the gravel road dipped down a green slope and forked into four paths, each bearing a sign: Andy Taylor St., Barney Fife Blvd., Opie Taylor Ave., and, finally, Eng & Chang Way. I realized then that here, in this twenty-first-century RV park, two Mount Airy legends had been put on equal footing—yes, two strands of bona fide Americana woven, as unlikely as it seems, into one story.

I followed Opie's path, built of crushed granite and well trodden by big wheels. It took me past a small playground designed as an ancient sailing ship. The miniature masthead, gangway, and portholes reminded me of the *Sachem*, the Nantucket ship that had brought the twins from

Siam. It was during their four-month voyage on that ship, commanded by hard-shelled, Bible-thumping Captain Abel Coffin, that the twins, two green youths then, had first learned the strange language of English, the games of chess and checkers, and the undulations of a bizarrely Western world. Still on route, Captain Coffin, sounding like a character walking out of a Melville novel, shot off a missive, as we have seen, to his wife in Back Bay, Boston, announcing the arrival of "two Chinese boys," who he hoped would "prove profitable as a curiosity." That last word branded the twins like a hot iron, leaving a permanent mark and a legacy that still lingered in this park.

Under the crepuscular sky, whiffs of wood smoke wove their own ephemeral patterns. Some campers were cooking at grills, others walked their dogs on the grass, and others just sat and stared. In the "olden days," as often portrayed in *TAGS*, men would have lollygagged or whittled, amusing themselves with pocket knives. A group of elders were huddled inside a picnic shelter, watching a wood fire getting started in a stone pit. Being a stranger, I nodded to them and headed farther down the Opie road, which led me to a pond. Rimmed by wildflowers and weeds like thick eyelashes, the glassy lens of the water captured a megapixel image of the lush trees and the pastel-colored twilight. A fisherman in a red jacket sat on the other side of the pond, hiding behind tall grasses like a Taoist hermit. I had a sudden urge to throw a pebble or skip it across the water, perhaps in honor of Opie, but I was afraid to disturb the fisherman's dream of catching a silver carp or even a plain bass. These ponds, according to the brochure that Kali had given me, were well stocked with fish.

Just then, three ducks emerged out of nowhere, quacking, sashaying, and splashing into the water like kids in a backyard pool. They did not look like wild ducks, but on the grass near the water I found four newly laid eggs, soft pink like a baby's finger. Domesticated ducks do not lay eggs in the wild, so where did they come from? Whatever their provenance, I felt it was somewhat serendipitous that these ducks made an appearance while I was here at Chang and Eng's old estate. As described earlier, the twins, still in their early teens, had raised ducks and sold eggs to help their mother eke out a living. In fact, it was on a muggy afternoon in August 1824, after wrapping up the day's duck business and then cooling off in the muddy Meklong, that they were spotted by Robert Hunter, who would change their lives forever. Later, traveling on the open roads of America, the twins would log an entry in their account book for July 26, 1833: "Purchase of 3 wild ducks from Indian boys $0.50." Were they perhaps feeling nostalgic about their duck-raising days in Siam?

From the pond, I walked back to my car via Barney Fife Blvd., passing more RVs straggling by the wayside. These chrome-armored road warriors, ranging from twenty to forty-five feet long, were all emblazoned with impressive names: Regal, Winnebago, Airstream, Palazzo, Cheetah, Outback, Sabre, Sun Voyager, Freedom, and so on. No hippie's VW bus or love van, these recreational vehicles are babies of the American Dream, siblings to shining diners, bowling alleys with neon signs, and neatly organized trailer parks that emerged in the post-WWII era to assist Americans in their quest for the good life, to reach not for the top but for the solid middle. Machines of mobility, they are symbols of comfort and happiness through consumption.[2]

While growing up in a small town in China, I, in fact, had a fantasy of living in a house on wheels so that we would never have to change houses when we moved. Years later in America, I saw my childhood fantasy come alive in the shapes of those big rigs clipping down the roads at a brisk pace. But it did not take me long to figure out what trailers mean in American culture, even though I continued to feel fascinated whenever I found them lining up along highways like beached sea creatures, or hidden in the woods like pioneer log cabins, or hunkering down in the desert. As cultural historians have pointed out, even as trailers were initially offered as an entryway into the middle class and touted as a force for inclusion, they were also places where boundaries were drawn, whether over class, racial, ethnic, or generational divides.

Barney Fife Blvd. turned into Andy Taylor St., where the gravel road climbed to a higher tier and revealed some pull-through spots for even longer trailers. One big rig had just rolled in moments earlier, and the owner, an old man with a commanding belly, got busy setting up for the night. Although the twilight was fast fading, the man immediately pulled out the awning on the side of his trailer, as though to block off the cosmic rays that might descend during the night. In the next spot, another camper had set up his spall like a cozy backyard, a tent festooned with twinkly string lights and two lawn chairs facing a large-screen TV pulled miraculously out of the belly of the leviathan-on-wheels.

Andy Taylor St. ended near the campground entrance, which was now blocked by a tow truck. On the truck sat a police squad car, a replica of the one used in *TAGS* and driven around by Sheriff Andy and Deputy Barney. An antique Ford sedan from the 1960s, it sported a Mayberry Sheriff seal on the door and a then-fashionable whip antenna curling forward from the back. A tall and wiry man in his sixties, with a ponytail, was working under the hood of the squad car. Something in his manner, a kind of tenderness a parent would take with a newborn, made me believe that he had to be the proud owner of this cherished relic. A friend of his stood by, stroking his Fu Manchu beard and snickering, while two women watched. I chatted with the women, asking about the car.

"Yep, it's the real thang," one of them told me, pointing at the car with her half-burnt cigarette.

"What do you mean *real*?" I was confused.

"It's the same car," she began with a little impatience, but then she went on to explain that her man had gotten lucky finding one of the few remaining 1961 Ford Fairlane Town Sedans. He had painted and fixed it up like the "real" Mayberry Sheriff squad car. They planned to camp here first and then join the parade in the car over the weekend. I again regretted having to miss the parade, where the squad car would roll down Main Street, siren blaring and bluegrass music blasting.

When I got back to my car, it was dark, with only a half-moon hanging over the eastern hill like an emoji. It was too early to sleep, even though I was tired. I walked over to the deck in front of the office trailer and sat on a wooden bench, to relax a little. Under a clear night sky, the campground was quiet, with only a few shadows ghosting around, mostly campers going about their business in and out of their trailers, and some late dog walkers. Here and there, electronic glows from TV or computer screens were faintly visible through open windows or half-shut blinds. The Blue Ridge Mountains hulked in the far distance, like a ragged black curtain bejeweled with a few scattered lights. The invisible highway hummed with traffic, its rhythmic pulses occasionally disrupted by the roar of a big truck, like faint thunder. On this last day of summer, the Southern night had lost a bit of its dark opulence, though it was still faintly perfumed by scents of lilacs, pines, and wildflowers.

As I sat there musing, a white-haired woman emerged from the RV parked next to my car and approached me. After a friendly hello, she introduced herself as the night manager of the campground, having taken over after Kali went home. Well into retirement age, she and her husband, who was walking an old black dog, had been traveling in their RV from Maine since the previous winter. They were, in other words, "snowbirds," part of a population migrating southward seasonally or permanently to escape the colder climes of the North. This couple had picked up part-time jobs at trailer parks along their migration route in exchange for free camping. They had arrived here before summer, she said, before the heat wave last July hit this mountain area with an almost murderous intent. But they had stayed around because they liked it here. I asked her whether she knew about the history of this place. She said yes, and then she went on to tell me about Kali's family and the residents in that farmhouse down the road.

"They are very astute," she said.

When I asked her about the ducks, she told me that some campers had left them behind. Now they had become a nuisance, she said, because they would forage in trash cans and leave their droppings everywhere. I had thought about mentioning the twins' early life as duck farmers in Siam, but words got stuck inside of me, words like *reincarnation, karma,* and *soul.* Perhaps only someone like me, having pursued the twins' story for so long, would believe it to be good karma that, as I came to the end of my journey, I would encounter these wayward ducks, left here as though by design, roaming freely in the land of two duck fanciers who took the world by storm.

"You're here for the Mayberry Days, right?" she asked.

"No, I'm here for the twins."

She was taken aback.

When I asked her what she thought of the twins, she hesitated for a minute, trying to find the right answer.

"They're very different," she said.

Her careful choice of words, a polite euphemism, marked light years of distance from Captain Coffin's crude nomenclature, a commonplace assumption of that age about people like the twins—calling them freaks, monsters, jokes of nature, and so on. Over the years, these demeaning labels have slowly disappeared from our lexicon. But her remark on difference, though understandable, alerted me to what's troubling about the Myth of Mayberry, to the fact that in Mount Airy the Siamese Twins and Andy Griffith can coexist as a story about America. From the very beginning, Chang and Eng stood for what was abnormal, exotic, and extraordinary; they were the epitome of what Mayberry attempted to exclude. The Myth of Mayberry is built on kinship, on bond, and on the desire to stay put, if not to keep strangers out.

As Sherwood Anderson put it in *Poor White* (1920), a novel about small-town America characterized by homogeneity and xenophobia: "The people who lived in the towns were to each other like members of a great family. . . . Within the invisible circle and under the great roof every one knew his neighbor and was known to him." Or, as Gustavo Pérez Firmat rightly points out in his critique of *TAGS*, there remains no path to citizenship for outsiders in the Mayberry myth.[3] But Mount Airy, the inspiration for Mayberry, actually proved, though only for a matter of decades, otherwise. It was here that Chang and Eng, perhaps the most exotic "freaks" that America ever beheld, found a home. It was here, right in Mount Airy, that they got married, had offspring, and lived a semblance of a life like everyone else. In some strange ways, the story of Mayberry and that of Mount Airy, as two strands of the American identity, are still intertwined like that of the inseparable Siamese Twins.

In the wee hours of the next morning, I woke up in the backseat of the Jeep, shivering from cold. I had left open a crack in the window, and now the nippy mountain air crawled inside like something alive. Never having been a camper before, I crouched under a thin blanket and peeked out through the rear window.

The half-moon had crossed the apex of its nightly journey, caught in tall pines that soughed in the wind like the audible rushing of time. The highway continued to thrum like heartbeats. As I drifted in and out of slumber, some images of the previous day still hovered in my head like dream fragments, a mosaic of scenes both real and cinematic.

At some point, Floyd, that unvanquishable barber from *TAGS*, appeared like a phantom, squinting his almost Chinese-like eyes and speaking one of the most clichéd lines of what had bizarrely become my most favorite TV show, intoning, "It could only happen in America. . . ."

Acknowledgments

At the end of a book about human bonds, I wish to express my enormous gratitude to Bob Weil and Glenn Mott, two men with whom I have had the good fortune of building a bond of friendship. Ever since he became my editor at Norton, Bob has remained my inspiration and a *sui generis* "implied reader," who sets a high bar for all my writings. Having him as an editor should be the dream of every writer, and having him as a friend is a total blessing.

To call Glenn my agent is both a misnomer and, to quote Ezra Pound, a "correct naming." While our friendship started more than a quarter century ago in Alabama, Glenn, who has agented all my books for Norton, truly represents my interests in all aspects, both as a writer and as a human being.

Writing is a solitary job, but I have been blessed with wonderful friends and colleagues, who have given me encouragement, assistance, and camaraderie, including Marjorie Perloff, Charles Bernstein, Hank Lazer, Stephen Greenblatt, Jill Lepore, Harry Stecopoulos, Candace Waid, Rita Raley, and Evan Wender.

I also wish to thank the following people and institutions for having most ably and generously assisted me in accessing precious images and research materials: William Brown at the State Archives of North Carolina; Matthew Turi and Tim Hodgdon at the Wilson Special Collections Library, University of North Carolina at Chapel Hill; Dr. Annette Ayers, president of Surry County Historical Society in North Carolina; Elizabeth Williams-Clymer, Special Collections Librarian, Kenyon College; Heather Magaw at the Osher Map Library, University of Southern Maine; Special Collections Research Center, Syracuse University; and William L. Clements Library, University of Michigan.

It is my good luck to have again had as my copyeditor Kathleen Brandes, who has, as always, gone well beyond her call of duty and made this a much better book.

A generous fellowship from the John Simon Guggenheim Foundation enabled me to take a leave from my university in order to conduct research and writing for this book.

An earlier version of the prologue was published as a story in *The Iowa Review*. I thank the editor and the journal for permission to reprint the piece here.

The writing of this book coincided with the arrival of two new persons in my life, my wife JZ and our son Henry, who have both redefined my existence. In the same period, however, I also suffered a most painful loss, the sudden passing of my father, who had taught me to write when I was growing up in a small town in southeastern China. It seems that the universe has a strange way of evening out the scores.

Again, I have left for last my acknowledgment of the deepest bond, Isabelle and Ira, two tenacious kids who have now blossomed into vivacious young adults. They have given a special meaning to the title word, *inseparable*.

Notes

PROLOGUE: A GAME ON THE HIGH SEAS

1. *Official Guide and Album of the Cunard Steamship Company* (London: Sutton Sharpe and Co., 1878), p. 7.

2. *Passenger Lists of Vessels Arriving at New York, New York, 1820–1897.* Microfilm Publications M237, 675 rolls. Records of the US Customs Service, Record Group 36. National Archives (Washington, DC).

3. Sid Lipsey, "Cruise Nostalgia: Cunard Looks Back at 175 Years at Sea," Yahoo Travel. https://www.yahoo.com/travel/cruise-nostalgia-cunard-looks-back-c1427914909167/ photo-2-those-first-cruises-weren-t-exactly-super-luxurious-photo-1427914867608 .html (accessed 4/1/2015).

4. Charles Dickens, *American Notes for General Circulation*, ed. John S. Whitley and Arnold Goldman (New York: Penguin, 1972), p. 55.

5. Mark Twain, *Following the Equator* (New York: Ecco Press, 1992), vol. 1, p. 2.

6. *Official Guide and Album of the Cunard Steamship Company*, p. 105.

7. William DeWitt Hyde, ed., *Vocations,* Vol. 10 (Boston: Hall and Locke Company, 1911), pp. 247–50.

8. *Official Guide and Album of the Cunard Steamship Company*, pp. 18–20.

9. James W. Hale, *An Historical Account of the Siamese Twin Brothers, from Actual Observations* (New York: Elliott and Palmer, 1831), p. 9.

10. Edward Wilmot Blyden, "The Fifth President of the Republic of Liberia," in *African Repository* XLVI (1870), pp. 121–22.

11. Svend E. Holsoe, "A Portrait of a Black Midwestern Family during the Early Nineteenth Century: Edward James Roye and His Parents," in *Liberian Studies Journal* 3.1 (1970–71), pp. 41–52.

12. Tom W. Shick, *Behind the Promised Land: A History of Afro-American Settler Society in Nineteenth-Century Liberia* (Baltimore and London: Johns Hopkins University Press, 1977), pp. 3–4.

13. "The President of Liberia," in *New York Daily Tribune,* August 17, 1870, p. 3.

14. "Sunbeams," in *The Sun* (New York), November 14, 1870.

15. Claude A. Clegg III, *The Price of Liberty: African Americans and the Making of Liberia* (Chapel Hill and London: University of North Carolina Press, 2004), p. 5.

16. "The Siamese Twins," in *New York Times,* August 14, 1870.
17. "Chang and Eng," editorial in *Philadelphia Medical Times,* February 28, 1874.

CHAPTER 1. SIAM

1. R. Adey Moore, "An Early British Merchant in Bangkok," in *Journal of the Siam Society* XI (1914–1915), p. 21. W. S. Bristowe, "Robert Hunter in Siam," in *History Today* 24:2 (February 1974), p. 90.
2. David K. Wyatt, *Thailand: A Short History* (New Haven and London: Yale University Press, 1984), pp. 167–68.
3. Moore, pp. 22, 34. Bristowe, p. 90.
4. Kay Hunter, *Duet for a Lifetime: The Story of the Original Siamese Twins* (New York: Coward-McCann: 1964), p. 26.
5. Bristowe, p. 91.
6. Hunter, p. 26. Irving Wallace and Amy Wallace, *The Two: A Biography* (New York: Simon and Schuster, 1978), p. 35.

CHAPTER 2. THE CHINESE TWINS

1. Judge Jesse Franklin Graves, "The Siamese Twins as Told by Judge Jesse Franklin Graves," unpublished manuscript, North Carolina State Archives (Raleigh), n.d., p. 1 (hereafter, NCSA).
2. Wyatt, p. 166.
3. B. J. Terwiel, *A History of Modern Thailand, 1767–1942* (St. Lucia, Australia: University of Queensland Press, 1983), p. 110.
4. Rama II, King of Thailand, *Nang Loi: The Floating Maiden. A Recitation from an Episode of the Ramakien,* translated by Pensak Chagsuchinda (Lund, Sweden: Studentlitteratur, 1973), p. 30.
5. Terwiel, p. 123. John Crawfurd, *Journal of an Embassy to the Courts of Siam and Cochin China.* Oxford in Asia Historical Reprints (Kuala Lumpur: Oxford University Press, 1967), pp. 136–37.
6. William H. Pancoast, *Report of the Autopsy of the Siamese Twins: Together with Other Interesting Information Concerning Their Life* (Philadelphia: J. B. Lippincott, 1874), p. 2.
7. Wallace and Wallace, p. 17.
8. Terwiel, p. 114. G. William Skinner, *Chinese Society in Thailand: An Analytical History* (Ithaca, NY: Cornell University Press, 1957), pp. 1–68. Walter F. Vella, *Siam Under Rama III, 1824–1851* (Locust Valley, NY: J. J. Augustin, 1957), p. 27.
9. Hsieh Yu-jung, *Hsien-lo kuo-chih (Siam Gazetteer)* (Bangkok: Nan-hai tung-shun-she, 1949), p. 275.
10. Quoted in Sun Fang Si, *Die Entwicklung der chinesischen Kolonisation in Südasien (Nan-yang) nach chinesischen Quellen* (Jena, Germany, 1931), p. 15.
11. Wyatt, p. 145.
12. Skinner, p. 97.
13. Michael Smithies, ed., *Descriptions of Old Siam* (Kuala Lumpur: Oxford University Press, 1995), p. 58.

14. John Bowring, *The Kingdom and People of Siam; with a Narrative of the Mission to That Country in 1855* (London: John W. Parker and Son, 1857), p. 23.

15. Ibid., p. 24.

16. Charles Gutzlaff, *Journal of Three Voyages Along the Coast of China in 1831, 1832, 1833* (London: Frederick Westley and A. H. Davis, 1834), p. 53.

17. Edmund Roberts, *Embassy to the Eastern Courts of Cochin-China, Siam, and Muscat: in the U.S. Sloop-of-War Peacock, David Geisinger, Commander, during the Years 1832-3-4* (New York: Harper and Brothers, 1837), p. 73.

18. *Bangkok Calendar,* 1870, p. 90.

19. Skinner, p. 127.

20. Anna Leonowens, *The English Governess at the Siamese Court* (first published 1870; New York: Oxford University Press, 1988), p. 78. Contrary to her claim of pure British blood, Leonowens was born of a British officer and an Indian prostitute in Bombay, a secret she kept from King Mongkut and from the readers of her wildly popular and sensational autobiography.

21. Edmund Roberts and W. S. W. Ruschenberger, *Two Yankee Diplomats in 1830s Siam,* ed. Michael Smithies (Bangkok: Orchid Press, 2002), p. 86.

22. Wallace and Wallace, p. 22.

23. Anthony Farrington, ed., *Early Missionaries in Bangkok: The Journals of Tomlin, Gutzlaff and Abeel, 1828–1832* (Bangkok: White Lotus Press, 2001), p. 3.

CHAPTER 3. CHOLERA

1. Terwiel, pp. 110–11.

2. Crawfurd, p. 158.

3. Graves, p. 2.

4. Ibid., p. 7.

5. Archie Robertson, "Chang-Eng's American Heritage," *Life,* August 11, 1952, p. 72.

6. A report on CNN recently ranked Century Egg first on the list of "Most 'Revolting' Food I've Had," with a tagline running, "Century eggs—not as old as they sound, but they taste like it." "iReport: The Most 'Revolting' Food I've Had Is. . . ," June 28, 2011. http://travel/cnn.com/explorations/eat/ireport-most-disgusting-foods-world-053021 (accessed 4/10/2015).

7. Wyatt, pp. 112–18, 164. Bristowe, pp. 88–89. Gutzlaff, pp. 51–52. Moore, p. 34.

CHAPTER 4. THE KING AND US

1. Christine Quigley, *Conjoined Twins: An Historical, Biological and Ethical Issues Encyclopedia* (Jefferson, NC: McFarland & Company, 2003), pp. 46–47.

2. Ibid., p. 148.

3. Ibid., p. 90.

4. Moore, p. 21.

5. Graves, p. 7.

6. Smithies, p. 211.

7. Ibid., pp. 213–14.

CHAPTER 5. DEPARTURE

1. Moore, p. 34.
2. Smithies, p. 214.
3. Moore, p. 23.
4. Quoted in Moore, p. 24.
5. Karl Gutzlaff would later anglicize his first name to Charles.
6. Terwiel, pp. 133–34.
7. Gutzlaff, p. 71.
8. Terwiel, pp. 138–39.
9. Farrington, pp. 20, 21, 39–40.
10. Wallace and Wallace, p. 45.
11. Even though he dismissed the Chinese belief and practice regarding the lunar eclipse as pagan idiocy, Jacob Tomlin duly recorded in his missionary journals the events on March 20, 1829, as he witnessed them in Bangkok. See Farrington, pp. 46–47.
12. In March 1977, a short notice appeared in the classified ads section of the *Winston-Salem Journal*, advertising for sale a copy of the original agreement that had brought the Siamese Twins to America. After some negotiation, A. B. Clark, a professor at the University of Maine, a descendant of Abel Coffin and owner of the contract, donated the item to the Surry County Historical Society. See Roy Thompson, "Chang-Eng Pact Acquired," in *Winston-Salem Journal*, August 6, 1977.

CHAPTER 6. A CURIOSITY IN BOSTON

1. Cynthia Wu, *Chang and Eng Reconnected: The Original Siamese Twins in American Culture* (Philadelphia: Temple University Press, 2012), p. 1.
2. Abel Coffin, letter to Susan Coffin, June 28, 1829, NCSA.
3. Barbara M. Benedict, *Curiosity: A Cultural History of Early Modern Inquiry* (Chicago: University of Chicago Press, 2001), p. 1.
4. Herman Melville, *Moby-Dick; or, The Whale*, ed. Harrison Hayford, Hershel Parker, and G. Thomas Tanselle. Northwestern–Newberry Edition (Evanston, IL: Northwestern University Press and Newberry Library, 1988), p. 19.
5. Benedict, p. 248.
6. Leslie Fiedler, *Tyranny of the Normal: Essays on Bioethics, Theology and Myth* (Boston: David R. Godine, 1996), p. 151.
7. Fanny Trollope, *Domestic Manners of the Americans* (1832; reprint, Gloucester, UK: Alan Sutton, 1984), p. 150.
8. Alexis de Tocqueville, *Democracy in America*, ed. J. P. Mayer, trans. George Lawrence (New York: HarperCollins, 1988), p. 592.
9. William H. Herndon and Jesse W. Weik, *Life of Lincoln* (New York: 1896), vol. I, pp. 108–9.
10. Marquis James, *Andrew Jackson: The Border Captain* (Indianapolis: Grosset & Dunlap, 1933), p. 19.
11. Robert Bogdan, *Freak Show: Presenting Human Oddities for Amusement and Profit* (Chicago: University of Chicago Press, 1988), pp. 27–28.

12. Wallace and Wallace, p. 50.

13. Dickens, *American Notes*, p. 74.

14. *The Patriot* (Boston), August 17, 1829.

15. Rosemarie Garland Thomson, ed., *Freakery: Cultural Spectacles of the Extraordinary Body* (New York: New York University Press, 1996), pp. 1–3.

16. Edward Warren, *The Life of John Collins Warren: Compiled Chiefly from His Autobiography and Journals* (Boston: Ticknor and Fields, 1860), vol. 1, pp. 207–8.

17. Michel Foucault, *The Birth of the Clinic: An Archaeology of Medical Perception*, trans. A. M. Sheridan Smith (New York: Vintage Books, 1975), p. xii.

18. John Warren, "An Account of the Siamese Twin Brothers United Together from Their Birth," in *American Journal of the Medical Sciences* 5.9 (November 1829), p. 253.

19. John Warren, "The Siamese Brothers," in *Boston Medical and Surgical Journal* 2 (September 1829), p. 460.

20. Warren, "An Account," p. 255.

21. Warren, "The Siamese Brothers," p. 461.

22. Warren, "An Account," p. 255.

CHAPTER 7. THE MONSTER, OR NOT

1. Harold Kirker, "The Boston Exchange Coffee House," in *Old-Time New England*, vol. LII, 1961, pp. 11–13. Jack Quinan, "The Boston Exchange Coffee House," in *Journal of the Society of Architectural Historians* 38.3 (October 1979), pp. 256–62.

2. Wu, pp. 24–25.

3. Anonymous, "A Tour from Cincinnati to Boston, and Return, October 1829," *Flint's Western Review*, December 1829, reprinted in *Salem Gazette*, January 8, 1830.

4. John Kuo Wei Tchen, *New York before Chinatown: Orientalism and the Shaping of American Culture 1776–1882* (Baltimore: Johns Hopkins University Press, 1999), p. 100.

5. Leslie Fiedler, *Freaks: Myths and Images of the Secret Self* (New York: Simon and Schuster, 1978), p. 31.

6. Robert Bogdan, pp. 7, xi.

7. John C. Warren, "Some Account of the Siamese Boys, Lately Brought to Boston," in *Boston Daily Advertiser*, August 26, 1829.

8. *Boston Bulletin*, August 29, 1829.

9. *Baltimore Patriot*, September 3, 1829.

10. *Rhode Island American*, September 8, 1829.

11. Wallace and Wallace, p. 61.

12. "Double, Double, Toil and Trouble," reprinted in *Aurora & Pennsylvania Gazette*, September 8, 1829. Joseph Andrew Orser, *The Lives of Chang and Eng: Siam's Twins in Nineteenth-Century America* (Chapel Hill: University of North Carolina Press, 2014), p. 32.

13. Wu, p. 37.

14. "Double, Double, Toil and Trouble."

15. *Rhode Island American*, September 15, 1829. Orser, p. 34.

CHAPTER 8. GOTHAM CITY

1. Allan Nevins, ed., *The Diary of Philip Hone, 1828–1851* (New York: Dodd, Mead, 1936), p. 37.
2. Alexis de Tocqueville, *Letters from America*, ed. and trans. by Frederick Brown (New Haven: Yale University Press, 2010), p. 19.
3. Descriptions of New York City in 1831 in this chapter, unless otherwise indicated, are gathered from Philip Hone's diary; James Stuart, *Three Years in North America* (New York: J. & J. Harper, 1833); and David Minor, "New York Timeline," in *The Crooked Lake Review*, Fall 2007, January, February, and March 2008.
4. Dickens, *American Notes*, p. 133.
5. Minor, March 2008.
6. Nevins, pp. 12–13.
7. Robertson, p. 77.
8. Wallace and Wallace, pp. 88–89.
9. Melville, *Moby-Dick*, p. 320; Herman Melville, *The Confidence-Man: His Masquerade*, ed. Hershel Parker (New York: W. W. Norton, 1971), p. 93. Herman Melville, *Correspondence*, ed. Lynn Horth (Evanston, IL.: Northwestern University Press and the Newberry Library, 1993), p. 160; Herman Melville, *Billy Budd and Other Stories* (New York: Penguin Books, 1986), p. 327.
10. William S. W. Ruschenberger, *Narrative of a Voyage Round the World during the Years 1835, 36, and 37* (first published in 1838; Folkestone and London: Dawson of Pall Mall, 1970), vol. 1, pp. 40–41.
11. Hunter, pp. 43–45. Wallace and Wallace, pp. 64–65.
12. *Rhode Island American*, October 16, 1829.

CHAPTER 9. THE CITY OF BROTHERLY LOVE

1. Alexis de Tocqueville, *Letters from America*, p. 213. Trollope, p. 190. Dickens, *American Notes*, p. 145.
2. Russell F. Weigley, ed., *Philadelphia: A 300-Year History* (New York: W. W. Norton, 1982), p. 2.
3. Robert G. Lee, *Orientals: Asian Americans in Popular Culture* (Philadelphia: Temple University Press, 1999), p. 28. Charlotte Elizabeth Smith, "West Meets East: Exhibitions of Chinese Material Culture in Nineteenth-Century America" (MA thesis, University of Delaware, 1987), p. 8.
4. *Aurora and Pennsylvania Gazette*, October 9, 1829.
5. Richard Gordon, *The Alarming History of Medicine: Amusing Anecdotes from Hippocrates to Heart Transplants* (New York: St. Martin's Press, 1993), p. 132.
6. George B. Roberts, "Dr. Physick and His House," in *Pennsylvania Magazine of History and Biography* V (1881), p. 71.
7. Quoted in Wallace and Wallace, p. 69.

CHAPTER 10. KNOCKING AT THE GATE

1. Thomas de Quincey, *Confessions of an English Opium-Eater and Other Writings*, ed. Grevel Lindop (New York: Oxford University Press, 1998), pp. 73–74.
2. Ibid., pp. 56, 72.
3. Ibid., p. 73.
4. Susan Stewart, *On Longing: Narratives of the Miniature, the Gigantic, the Souvenir, the Collection* (Durham, NC: Duke University Press, 1993), p. 111.
5. Charles Harris, letter to William Davis, July 5, 1832, NCSA.
6. Peter Cunningham, *Handbook of London: Past and Present* (London: John Murray, 1850), p. 361.
7. Charles Dickens, *Bleak House* (1853; reprint, Boston: Houghton Mifflin, 1956), p. 1.
8. *The Times* (London), November 21, 1829, p. 2.
9. Hale, p. 12.
10. *The Times*, November 23, 1829, p. 2.
11. Michael P. Costeloe, "William Bullock and the Mexican Connection," in *Mexican Studies/Estudios Mexicanos* 22.2 (2006): pp. 275–78.
12. Jacob Korg, ed., *London in Dickens' Day* (Englewood Cliffs, NJ: Prentice-Hall, 1960), pp. 58–63.
13. *The Times*, November 25, 1829, p. 2.
14. Hale, p. 3.

CHAPTER 11. RACIAL FREAKS

1. Mikhail Bakhtin, *Rabelais and His World*, trans. Hélène Iswolsky (Bloomington: Indiana University Press, 1984), p. 27.
2. Henry Morley, *Memoirs of Bartholomew Fair* (London: Chatto and Windus, 1880), p. 246.
3. Paul Semonin, "Monsters in the Marketplace: The Exhibition of Human Oddities in Early Modern England," in Rosemarie Garland Thomson, pp. 69–70, 76–77.
4. Bakhtin, pp. 19–20.
5. Leonard Cassuto, "'What an object he would have made of me!': Tattooing and the Racial Freak in Melville's *Typee*," in Rosemarie Garland Thomson, pp. 235–42.
6. Quoted in Bogdan, p. 177.
7. *The Times*, November 26, 1829, p. 2.
8. Robertson, p. 77.
9. *The Times*, December 4, 1829, p. 3.
10. *The Times*, December 1, 1829, p. 4; December 4, p. 3; January 9, 1830, p. 4; November 25, 1829, p. 2.
11. George Buckley Bolton, "Statement of the Principal Circumstances Respecting the United Siamese Twins Now Exhibiting in London," in *Philosophical Transactions of the Royal Society of London* 120 (1830): p. 181.

12. Ibid., p. 182.
13. Ibid., pp. 178–79.
14. Ibid., pp. 185–86.
15. Ibid., pp. 182–83.
16. Elizabeth Grosz, "Intolerable Ambiguity: Freaks as/at the Limit," in Rosemarie Garland Thomson, pp. 64–65.
17. De Quincey, p. 83.

CHAPTER 12. SENTIMENTAL EDUCATION

1. Wallace and Wallace, p. 90. Orser, p. 90.
2. *The Times,* November 23, 1829, p. 2.
3. Bolton, pp. 184–85
4. Ibid., p. 185.
5. Susan Coffin, letter to her children, March 6, 1830, NCSA.
6. Abel Coffin, letter to his children, July 3, 1830, NCSA.
7. Abel Coffin, letter to his children, September 28, 1830, NCSA.
8. George Crabb, *A Dictionary of General Knowledge; or, An Explanation of Words and Things Connected with All the Arts and Sciences* (London: Thomas Tegg, 1830), pp. 175–76.
9. Hale, pp. 12–13.
10. Ibid., p. 9.
11. Susan Coffin, letter to her children, March 6, 1830, NCSA.
12. Abel Coffin, letter to his children, September 28, 1830, NCSA.

CHAPTER 13. THE GREAT ECLIPSE

1. Louis P. Masur, *1831: Year of Eclipse* (New York: Hill and Wang, 2001), pp. 3–6.
2. Kenneth S. Greenberg, ed., *The Confessions of Nat Turner and Related Documents* (Boston: Bedford Books, 1996), p. 46.
3. Susan Coffin, letter to her children, March 6, 1830, NCSA.
4. Abel Coffin, letter to Susan Coffin, January 8, 1831, NCSA.
5. Charles Harris, letter to William Davis, May 29, 1832, NCSA.
6. *Haverhill Gazette,* April 30, 1831.
7. Bayard Tuckerman, ed., *The Diary of Philip Hone, 1828–1851* (New York: Dodd, Mead, 1889), vol. 1, pp. 28–29. In the Hone diary edited by Allan Nevins (1936), the content of this entry is slightly different. See Nevins, pp. 37–38.
8. Nevins, p. 454.
9. Edgar Allan Poe, *Poetry, Tales, and Selected Essays* (New York: Library of America, 1984), pp. 329–30, 335, 908, 263.

CHAPTER 14. A SATIRICAL TALE

1. Leslie Mitchell, *Bulwer Lytton: The Rise and Fall of a Victorian Man of Letters* (London: Hambledon and London, 2003), pp. xv, 1.
2. *Berkshire Chronicle,* December 5, 1829.

3. Edward Bulwer Lytton, *The Siamese Twins: A Satirical Tale of the Times. With Other Poems* (New York: J & J Harper, 1831), p. 13. Subsequent Lytton citations in this chapter are from pp. 33, 76, 81, 144, and 220.

4. "Siamese Twins," in *Connecticut Mirror,* March 26, 1831, p. 3.

5. "Siamese," in *Eastern Argus Semi-Weekly,* May 6, 1831, p. 2.

CHAPTER 15. THE LYNNFIELD BATTLE

1. James Hale, letter to Susan Coffin, March 16, 1831, University of Michigan Library.

2. James Hale, letter to Susan Coffin, March 30, 1831, NCSA.

3. Ibid.

4. James Hale, letter to Susan Coffin, April 23, 1831, University of Michigan Library.

5. *Baltimore Patriot,* April 26, 1831.

6. *Connecticut Mirror,* June 25, 1831, p. 3.

7. *Salem Gazette,* August 2, 1831, p. 3.

8. Reprinted in *The New England Farmer* 9.47 (1831), p. 373.

9. *Essex Gazette,* August 6, 1831, p. 3.

10. *Salem Gazette,* August 5, 1831, p. 4.

11. *Salem Gazette,* August 16, 1831, p. 2.

12. *Baltimore Patriot,* August 20, 1831, p. 2.

13. For anti-Chinese violence in nineteenth-century America, see Yunte Huang, *Charlie Chan: The Untold Story of the Honorable Detective and His Rendezvous with American History* (New York: W. W. Norton, 2010), pp. 124–25.

14. *Baltimore Patriot,* August 20, 1831, p. 2.

15. Reprinted in *Eastern Argus Semi-Weekly,* September 9, 1831, p. 1.

16. Janet Gray, "Hannah F. Gould." http://www.lehigh.edu/~dek7/SSAWW/writGould Bio.htm (accessed 4/7/2016).

CHAPTER 16. AN INTIMATE REBELLION

1. Greenberg, p. 2. Subsequent Greenberg citations in this chapter are from pp. 7, 19, 46, 51, 57, and 106.

2. *The Liberator,* January 1, 1831.

3. *The Liberator,* September 3, 1831.

4. Masur, p. 30.

5. Ibid., p. 24.

CHAPTER 17. OLD DOMINION

1. Dickens, *American Notes,* pp. 236–37.

2. Tocqueville, *Letters from America,* p. 125.

3. Leo Damrosch, *Tocqueville's Discovery of America* (New York: Farrar, Straus and Giroux, 2010), p. 126.

4. Charles Harris, letter to William Davis, January 16, 1832, NCSA.

5. Charles Harris, letter to William Davis, December 28, 1831, NCSA.

6. Orser, p. 40.
7. Masur, p. 59.
8. Johann August Roebling, *Diary of My Journey from Muehlhausen in Thuringia via Bremen to the United States of North America in the Year 1831* (Trenton, NJ: Roebling Press, 1931), p. 117.
9. James Alexander, *Transatlantic Sketches* (1833; reprint, Charleston, SC: Nabu Press, 2010), p. 227.
10. Masur, pp. 38–39, 50–51.
11. Ibid., pp. 61–62.
12. Orser, p. 38.
13. Charles Harris, letter to William Davis, April 11, 1832, NCSA. Warren, "An Account," p. 253.
14. Orser, p. 41.
15. Charles Harris, letter to William Davis, December 28, 1831, NCSA.

CHAPTER 18. EMANCIPATION

1. Christopher Klein, "The Burning of Buffalo, 200 Years Ago," *History in the Headlines,* December 30, 2013, http://www.history.com/news/the-burning-of-buffalo-200-years-ago (accessed July 30, 2016).
2. Alexis de Tocqueville, *Journey to America*, trans. George Lawrence, ed. J. P. Mayer (Garden City, NY: Doubleday, 1971), pp. 129–30.
3. Tocqueville, *Letters from America*, p. 127.
4. Tocqueville, *Democracy in America*, p. 508.
5. Charles Harris, letter to William Davis, May 29, 1832, NCSA.

CHAPTER 19. A PARABLE

1. Chang and Eng Bunker, "An Account of Money Expended by Chang-Eng," Wilson Library, University of North Carolina at Chapel Hill (hereafter UNCCH); unless otherwise indicated, all subsequent information on the twins' expenses is drawn from this account book.
2. Masur, p. 63.
3. Graves, p. 10.
4. Masur, p. 66.
5. Paul E. Johnson, *A Shopkeeper's Millennium: Society and Revivals in Rochester, New York, 1815–1837* (New York: Hill and Wang, 1978), pp. 101–2.
6. Ibid., p. 115.
7. Ibid., pp. 114–15.
8. Charles Harris, letter to William Davis, January 22, 1832, NCSA.
9. Garth M. Rosell and Richard Dupuis, eds., *The Original Memoirs of Charles G. Finney* (Grand Rapids, MI: Zondervan, 1989), p. 325.
10. Quoted in Johnson, p. 5.
11. Charles Harris, letter to William Davis, July 5, 1832, NCSA.

12. Marc Shell, *Stutter* (Cambridge: Harvard University Press, 2006), p. 122.

13. Abel Coffin, letter to Susan Coffin, October 5, 1832, NCSA.

14. *New York Spectator*, October 26, 1837.

CHAPTER 20. AMERICA ON THE ROAD

1. Quoted in Jack Larkin, *The Reshaping of Everyday Life, 1790–1840* (New York: Harper Perennial, 1988), p. 204.

2. Ibid., p. 211.

3. Alexis de Tocqueville, *Voyage en Amérique*, in *Oeuvres* (Pléiade), vol. 1, p. 141; quoted in Damrosch, p. 64.

4. Damrosch, p. 133.

5. Richardson Wright, *Hawkers and Walkers in Early America: Strolling Peddlers, Preachers, Lawyers, Doctors, Players, and Others, from the Beginning to the Civil War* (Philadelphia: J. B. Lippincott Company, 1927), p. 27.

6. J. R. Dolan, *The Yankee Peddlers of Early America: An Affectionate History of Life and Commerce in the Developing Colonies and the Young Republic* (New York: Bramhall House, 1964), p. 242.

7. Wright, p. 23.

8. Dolan, p. 229.

9. Quoted in Wright, pp. 20–21.

10. Washington Irving, *Washington Irving's Sketch Book* (New York: Avenel Books, 1985), p. 74.

11. Nathaniel Hawthorne, *The American Notebooks*, ed. Randall Stewart (New Haven, CT: Yale University Press, 1932), p. 47.

12. Melville, *Moby-Dick*, pp. 19, 24.

13. Hawthorne, pp. 39, 43.

14. Wright, pp. 125–27.

15. Ibid., p. 127.

16. Marc McCutcheon, *Everyday Life in the 1800s* (Cincinnati, OH: Writer's Digest Books, 1993), p. 60.

17. I am grateful to Elizabeth Williams-Clymer, Special Collections Librarian at Kenyon College, for verifying the information regarding this donated book.

18. *United States' Telegraph*, April 17, 1832.

19. *Daily National Intelligencer*, September 11, 1832.

20. *Boston Investigator*, March 29, 1833.

21. David S. Reynolds, *Waking Giant: America in the Age of Jackson* (New York: Harper-Collins, 2008), p. 102.

22. Ibid., pp. 96–99.

23. *Daily National Intelligencer*, April 29, 1833.

24. *The Globe*, July 9, 1833. *New Hampshire Sentinel*, July 18, 1833.

25. Chang and Eng Bunker, "An Account of Money Received by Chang-Eng," UNCCH; unless otherwise indicated, all subsequent information on the twins' income from tours is drawn from this account book.

26. Reynolds, pp. 103–4.

27. Samuel Peter Orth, *A History of Cleveland, Ohio: Biographical* (Chicago and Cleveland: S. J. Clarke Publishing Co., 1910), vol. III, p. 855.

28. *Cleveland Advertiser,* July 5, 1833. *Lynchburg Virginian,* July 18, 1833.

29. *Elyria Atlas,* July 18, 1833. *Farmer's Cabinet,* August 9, 1833.

CHAPTER 21. THE DEEP SOUTH

1. Flannery O'Connor, *Mystery and Manners: Occasional Prose,* ed. Sally and Robert Fitzgerald (New York: Farrar, Straus and Giroux, 1970), pp. 44–45.

2. Ibid., p. 44.

3. Carl Carmer, *Stars Fell on Alabama* (1934; reprint, Tuscaloosa: University of Alabama Press, 2000), p. xxiv; W. J. Cash, *The Mind of the South* (1941; reprint, New York: Vintage Books, 1991), p. xlvii.

4. *The Athenian,* October 30, 1833. *Eastern Argus,* November 20, 1833. *Pittsfield Sun,* November 28, 1833.

5. *The Times,* December 18, 1833, p. 4.

6. *Daily Independent,* June 9, 1928. William Garrett, *Reminiscences of Public Men in Alabama: For Thirty Years, with an Appendix* (Atlanta: Plantation Publishing Company's Press, 1872), pp. 390–91.

7. F. Bret Harte, *The Heathen Chinee* (Chicago: Western News Company, 1870), p. 9.

8. Carmer, p. 104.

CHAPTER 22. HEAD BUMPS

1. Madeleine B. Stern, ed., *A Phrenological Dictionary of Nineteenth-Century Americans* (Westport, CT: Greenwood Press, 1982), p. 158.

2. John D. Davies, *Phrenology, Fad and Science: A 19th-Century American Crusade* (New Haven, CT: Yale University Press, 1955), p. 4.

3. George Combe, *The Constitution of Man, Considered in Relation to External Objects* (Boston: Carter and Hendee, 1829), pp. 102, 201.

4. Nathaniel Mackey, "Phrenological Whitman," in *Conjunctions* 29 (Fall 1997), p. 10.

5. Ralph L. Rusk, ed., *The Letters of Ralph Waldo Emerson* (New York: Columbia University Press, 1939), vol. 1, p. 291.

6. Davies, p. 13.

7. Nevins, pp. 71–72.

8. Davies, p. 32.

9. *American Phrenological Journal* 6 (1844), p. 23.

10. Mark Twain, *The Adventures of Tom Sawyer and The Adventures of Huckleberry Finn* (Everyman's Library, 1943), pp. 288–89.

11. Stern, p. 76.

12. Walt Whitman, *Complete Poetry and Selected Prose,* ed. James E. Miller Jr. (Boston: Houghton Mifflin, 1959), pp. 247, 124, 348.

13. Davies, p. 125.

14. Melville, *Moby-Dick*, pp. 345–47.

15. *Southern Literary Messenger* 2 (1835–36), p. 286.

16. "Edgar Allan Poe," *Phrenological Journal* XII (March 1850), pp. 87–89.

17. Reprinted in *The Scioto Gazette* (OH), July 22, 1835.

18. Francis Karwowski, "Giles Fonda Yates: The Forgotten Masonic Scholar." http://www.noveltysoft.com/demo/poj/who-was-giles-f-yates (accessed 6/9/2016).

19. Reprinted in *The Scioto Gazette* (OH), July 22, 1835.

20. Orson and Lorenzo Fowler, assisted by Samuel Kirkham, *Phrenology Proved, Illustrated, and Applied* (New York, 1837), pp. 322–23.

21. *Phrenological Journal* XIX, 48 (February 1854).

22. Mackey, p. 11.

23. George Finlayson, *The Mission to Siam and Hue 1821–1822* (first published 1826; Singapore: Oxford University Press, 1988), pp. 108–9, 230.

24. Roberts and Ruschenberger, pp. 174–75.

25. Ibid., p. 140.

26. See *Pennsylvania Inquirer*, April 10, 1838 and *Daily National Intelligencer*, May 1, 1838.

CHAPTER 23. WILKESBORO

1. Jennifer L. Peña and Laurie B. Hayes, *Wilkes County: A Brief History* (Charleston, SC: History Press, 2008), p. 17.

2. Federal Writers' Project, ed., *North Carolina: The WPA Guide to the Old North State* (Chapel Hill: University of North Carolina Press, 1939), pp. 408–9.

3. Federal Writers' Project, p. 408.

4. Shepherd Dugger, *Romance of the Siamese Twins . . . and Other Sketches* (Burnsville, NC: Edwards Printing Co., 1936), p. 8. Wallace and Wallace, pp. 158–59. Orser, p. 219.

5. Elisha Mitchell, *Diary of a Geological Tour by Dr. Elisha Mitchell in 1827 and 1828* (Chapel Hill: University of North Carolina Press, 1905), p. 18.

6. Ibid., p. 42.

7. *Times-Picayune*, December 25, 1838, p. 2.

8. Elisha Mitchell, p. 18.

9. "The Captives of the Amistad," in *Emancipator*, October 3, 1839.

10. Martin Crawford, *Ashe County's Civil War: Community and Society in the Appalachian South* (Charlottesville: University Press of Virginia, 2001), p. 65.

11. Ibid., pp. 18–19.

12. Ibid., p. 19.

13. Ibid., pp. 23, 35.

14. *North Carolina Standard*, October 16, 1861.

15. William E. Burton, letter to Edgar Allan Poe, July 4, 1839. http://www.eapoe.org/misc/letters/t3907040.htm (accessed May 22, 2016).

16. Linda C. Brinson, "The First Americans to Observe the 4th were Moravian Pacifists." http://www.thedailybeast.com/articles/2014/07/04/the-first-americans-to-observe-the-4th-were-moravian-pacifists.html (accessed July 4, 2016).

CHAPTER 24. TRAPHILL

1. Wilkes County Record of Deeds, vol. 23, p. 490, NCSA.
2. Robertson, p. 79.
3. Orser, p. 83.
4. Chang and Eng Bunker, sworn statement, October 12, 1839, NCSA.
5. Tchen, pp. 76, 231–32.
6. Lucy Cohen, *Chinese in the Post–Civil War South: A People without a History* (Baton Rouge: Louisiana State University Press, 1984), p. 3.
7. Orser, p. 82.
8. Wallace and Wallace, p. 166.
9. Peña and Hayes, p. 15.
10. *Newport Mercury,* November 16, 1839, p. 3. *Portsmouth Journal of Literature and Politics,* November 23, 1839, p. 1.
11. Chang and Eng Bunker, "General Store Account Book," UNCCH.
12. *Boston Transcript,* as quoted in *New Hampshire Patriot,* July 27, 1840, p. 3.
13. Quoted in Hunter, p. 80.

CHAPTER 25. A UNIVERSAL TRUTH

1. Jane Austen, *Pride and Prejudice,* ed. Claudia L. Johnson and Susan J. Wolfson (New York: Longman Publishers, 2003), p. 5.
2. *Carolina Watchman,* April 29, 1843. *Louisville Journal,* as quoted in *Milwaukee Sentinel,* May 27, 1843. *The Liberator,* May 12, 1843. *Greensborough Patriot,* May 6, 1843.
3. Graves, p. 14.
4. Ibid., p. 16.
5. "The Siamese Twins," *Biblical Recorder,* reprinted in *Raleigh Register,* May 24, 1848.
6. Dugger, pp. 9-10. Dugger might have been the last outsider to see the twins alive, when he visited them on January 12, 1874, four days before their death.
7. Graves, pp. 13–14.
8. Ibid., p. 16.
9. Orser, p. 86.
10. Martha Hodes, *White Women, Black Men: Illicit Sex in the Nineteenth-Century South* (New Haven, CT: Yale University Press, 1997), pp. 1–2, 39, 49.
11. Ibid., p. 3.
12. Graves, p. 17.
13. *Mobile Register,* as quoted in *Baltimore Patriot,* November 10, 1834, p. 2. *Pittsfield Sun,* December 11, 1834, p. 3. *New Hampshire Sentinel,* December 28, 1834, p. 4. *Portsmouth Journal of Literature and Politics,* December 24, 1836, p. 3. *New Hampshire Sentinel,* February 2, 1837, p. 4. *Times-Picayune,* June 9, 1838, p. 2.
14. Wallace and Wallace, p. 133.
15. James Hale, letter to Charles Harris, January (?), 1832, NCSA.
16. Dugger, p. 10.
17. Austen, pp. 208–9.
18. Graves, p. 15.

19. Ibid., p. 17.
20. Larkin, p. 269. Graves, p. 17.
21. Graves, pp. 19–20.
22. Burton Cohen, *The Wedding of the Siamese Twins* (New York: Dramatists Play Service, Inc., 1989), p. 23.
23. Graves, pp. 14–15.
24. Cohen, p. 23.
25. Graves, pp. 17–18.
26. Hunter, p. 83; Orser disputes this claim, pp. 94–95.
27. James Hale, letter to Charles Harris, May 12, 1843, NCSA.
28. Wilkes County Marriage Bonds and Licenses, NCSA.
29. Wallace and Wallace, pp. 167–68.
30. Wilkes County Superior Court Minutes, CR104.311.3, "Petitioned Court to Legally Adopt Name," 1844, NCSA.
31. Graves, pp. 18–19.

CHAPTER 26. FOURSOME

1. John S. Haller and Robin M. Haller, *The Physician and Sexuality in Victorian America* (New York: W. W. Norton, 1977), pp. 91, 92, 97, 104, 227.
2. Peter Gay, *Education of the Senses* (New York: Oxford University Press, 1984), p. 458.
3. John Humphrey Noyes, *Strange Cults and Utopias of 19th-Century America* (New York: Dover Publications, 1966; first published in 1870 as *History of American Socialisms*), p. 23.
4. Haller and Haller, p. 116.
5. Noyes, p. 25.
6. Orser, p. 99. "Recent Southern Scenes," in *Emancipator and Free American,* May 18, 1843. "Marriage Extraordinary," in *The Liberator,* May 12, 1843.
7. O'Connor, p. 40.
8. Alice Dreger, "The Sex Lives of Conjoined Twins," in *The Atlantic,* October 25, 2012. http://www.theatlantic.com/health/archive/2012/10/the-sex-lives-of-conjoined-twins/264095 (accessed 2/17/2016).
9. Wallace and Wallace, pp. 185–86.
10. Darin Strauss, *Chang and Eng: A Novel* (New York: Penguin, 2001), pp. 149–51.
11. Quoted in Wallace and Wallace, p. 186.
12. Daisy and Violet Hilton, "The Loves and Lives of the Hilton Sisters," in *Conjoined Twins in Black and White: The Lives of Millie-Christine McKoy and Daisy and Violet Hilton,* ed. Linda Frost (Madison: University of Wisconsin Press, 2009), p. 147.
13. Mark Twain, *The Tragedy of Pudd'nhead Wilson; and the Comedy, Those Extraordinary Twins* (New York: Oxford University Press, 1996), p. 311.
14. Ibid., pp. 328–29.
15. Sigmund Freud, "Sexuality in the Aetiology of the Neurosis," in *The Standard Edition of the Complete Psychoanalytical Writings of Sigmund Freud*, ed. James Strachey et al. (1953–1975), vol. III, p. 266.

16. Karen Tei Yamashita, "Siamese Twins and Mongoloids," in *Yellow Light: The Performance of Asian American Arts*, ed. Amy Ling (Philadelphia: Temple University Press, 1999), p. 135. Yamashita originally planned to write a novel based on Chang and Eng, but the project morphed into her award-winning novel, *I Hotel* (2010).

CHAPTER 27. MOUNT AIRY, OR MONTICELLO

1. Wu, pp. 163–65.
2. James Hale, letter to Charles Harris, July 27, 1843, NCSA.
3. Melville, *Moby-Dick*, p. 231.
4. Crawford, p. 2.
5. Graves, p. 22.
6. Melvin M. Miles, *Eng and Chang: From Siam to Surry* (self-published, CreateSpace, 2013), p. 65.
7. Evelyn Scales Thompson, *Around Surry County* (Charleston, SC: Arcadia Publishing, 2005), p. 14.
8. Graves, p. 23.
9. Orser, p. 127.
10. *Greensborough Patriot,* October 16, 1852.
11. *Greensborough Patriot,* October 30, 1852.
12. J. E. Johnson, "Siamese Twins," in *Mount Airy News,* January 3, 1956.
13. Ibid.
14. Wallace and Wallace, p. 193.
15. "The Siamese Twins at Home," in *Southerner,* reprinted in *Trumpet and Universalist Magazine,* November 2, 1850.
16. Tiya Miles, *The House on Diamond Hill: A Cherokee Plantation Story* (Chapel Hill: University of North Carolina Press, 2010), p. 87.
17. Hinton Rowan Helper, *The Land of Gold: Reality versus Fiction* (Baltimore, 1855), p. 75.
18. Lee, p. 42.
19. Ibid.
20. Helper, p. 71.
21. Ibid., p. 70.
22. Ibid., pp. 70, 55–56.
23. Wu, pp. 165–66.
24. Quoted in Wallace and Wallace, pp. 194–95.

CHAPTER 28. THE AGE OF HUMBUGS

1. See "Contract between Edmund H. Doty and Chang and Eng Bunker, 1849," UNCCH.
2. Herbert Asbury, *All Around the Town* (New York: Knopf, 1934). Joel Rose, *New York Sawed in Half: An Urban Historical* (New York: Bloomsbury, 2001).
3. Neil Harris, *Humbug: The Art of P. T. Barnum* (Boston: Little, Brown, 1973), p. 69.

4. Peter Ackroyd, *Poe: A Life Cut Short* (New York: Doubleday/Nan A. Talese, 2008), pp. 113–14.

5. M. R. Werner, *Barnum* (New York: Harcourt, Brace, 1923), p. 3.

6. Irving Wallace, *The Fabulous Showman: The Life and Times of P. T. Barnum* (New York: Knopf, 1959), p. 40. P. T. Barnum, *Struggles and Triumphs; or, Forty Years' Recollections* (Buffalo: Courier Company, 1883), p. 79.

7. Barnum, p. 53.

8. Ibid., p. 50.

9. Ibid., p. 56.

10. Ibid., p. 62.

11. Ibid., p. 83.

12. Ibid., pp. 89, 103.

13. Ibid., p. 119.

14. Ibid., p. 215.

15. Ibid., p. 107.

16. Nevins, p. 664.

17. *New York Tribune,* April 23, 1849.

18. *New Hampshire Patriot,* May 17, 1849. Wallace and Wallace, p. 216. *Pittsfield Sun,* July 26, 1849.

19. Barnum, p. 159.

20. Quoted in Wallace and Wallace, pp. 228–29.

21. Werner, pp. 230, 242.

22. "Movements of the Prince," in *New York Times,* October 15, 1860.

23. Lewis Hyde, *Trickster Makes This World: Mischief, Myth, and Art* (New York: Farrar, Straus and Giroux, 1998), p. 10.

24. Paul Radin, *The Trickster: A Study in American Indian Mythology* (New York: Schocken Books, 1972), p. xxiii.

25. Warwick Wadlington, *The Confidence Game in American Literature* (Princeton, NJ: Princeton University Press, 1975), pp. 9–10.

CHAPTER 29. MINSTREL FREAKS

1. "Some of *Uncle Sam*'s Passengers," in *Daily Evening Bulletin,* December 6, 1860.

2. Robert C. Toll, *Blacking Up: The Minstrel Show in Nineteenth-Century America* (New York: Oxford University Press, 1974), p. 31.

3. Lee, p. 34.

4. Huang, pp. 120–21.

5. Lee, pp. 32, 40–41.

6. Ibid., p. 32.

7. Frank B. Converse, *"Old Cremona" Songster* (New York, 1863), pp. 39, 63.

8. Mark Twain, *The Autobiography of Mark Twain* (New York: Harper and Row, 1959), p. 59.

9. Ibid.

10. Anthony J. Berret, "*Huckleberry Finn* and the Minstrel Show," in *American Studies* 27 (Fall 1986): pp. 37–49. W. T. Lhamon Jr., "Ebery Time I Wheel About I Jump Jim Crow: Cycles of Minstrel Transgression from Cool White to Vanilla Ice," in *Inside the Minstrel Mask: Readings in Nineteenth-Century Blackface Minstrelsy*, ed., Annemarie Bean, et al. (Middletown, CT: Wesleyan University Press, 1996), pp. 275–84. Eric Lott, *Love and Theft: Blackface Minstrelsy and the American Working Class* (New York: Oxford University Press, 1993), pp. 144–45.

11. Ralph Ellison, *Shadow and Act* (New York: Vintage, 1972), p. 50.

12. Mark Twain, "The Siamese Twins" (first published in 1869 as "Personal Habits of the Siamese Twins"), in *The Complete Humorous Sketches and Tales of Mark Twain*, ed. Charles Neider (Garden City, NY: Doubleday, 1961), pp. 280–83.

13. Twain, *Pudd'nhead Wilson*, pp. 315, xxxiii.

14. Sharon D. McCoy, "'The Trouble Begins at Eight': Mark Twain, the San Francisco Minstrels, and the Unsettling Legacy of Blackface Minstrelsy," in *American Literary Realism* 41.3 (Spring 2009): p. 245.

15. Paul Fatout, ed., *Mark Twain Speaking* (Iowa City: University of Iowa Press, 1976), p. 238.

16. Fatout, pp. 541–42; "Mark Twain and Twin Cheer New Year's Party," in *New York Times*, January 1, 1907.

17. *Daily Alta California*, December 15, 1860. *Sacramento Daily Union*, December 22, 1860.

18. Orser, p. 145.

19. Chang and Eng Bunker, letter to their families, December 10, 1860, UNCCH.

20. "The 'Union' in Danger," in *New York Tribune*, November 12, 1860.

21. *Baltimore American*, as quoted in *Fayetteville Observer*, April 8, 1861.

CHAPTER 30. SEEING THE ELEPHANT

1. William S. Powell, *North Carolina through Four Centuries* (Chapel Hill: University of North Carolina Press, 1989), p. 350. Crawford, p. 77.

2. Wallace and Wallace, pp. 189–90.

3. Graves, p. 25.

4. Orser, p. 152.

5. Crawford, pp. 105–6.

6. Ambrose Bierce, *Ambrose Bierce's Civil War*, ed. William McCann (New York: Wings Books, 1996), pp. 22–23.

7. Drew Gilpin Faust, *This Republic of Suffering: Death and the American Civil War* (New York: Knopf, 2008).

8. "Lincoln Rejects the King of Siam's Offer of Elephants." http://www.civilwar.org/education/history/primarysources/lincoln-rejects-the-king-of.html (accessed August 2, 2016).

9. "United States Civil War Soldiers Index, 1861–1865" (Washington, DC: National Archives and Records Administration, n.d.), roll 8. FHL microfilm 881,402.

10. Webb Garrison, *Civil War Curiosities: Strange Stories, Oddities, Events, and Coincidences* (Nashville, TN: Rutledge Hill Press, 1994), pp. 67, 72–73.

11. Ruthanne Lum McCunn, "The Numbers," in *Asians and Pacific Islanders and the Civil War*, ed. Carol A. Shively (Washington: Eastern National, 2015), p. 33.

12. For details about the fascinating story of Thomas Sylvanus, see Ruthanne Lum McCunn, *Chinese Yankee: A True Story from the Civil War* (San Francisco: Design Enterprise of San Francisco, 2014).

13. Shively, pp. 108–13. Jim Sundman, "A Soldier from Siam," in *Emerging Civil War*, March 8, 2012. https://emergingcivilwar.com/2012/03/08/a-soldier-from-siam (accessed August 5, 2016).

14. Stuart Heaver, "The Chinese Soldiers Who Fought in the American Civil War," in *South China Morning Post*, June 30, 2013. http://www.scmp.com/magazines/post-magazine/article/1270170/gettysburg-redress (accessed July 31, 2016).

15. Christopher Bunker, letter to Nannie Bunker, November 18, 1863, UNCCH.

16. Shively, p. 68.

17. Christopher Bunker, letter to family, October 12, 1864, UNCCH.

18. Shively, p. 70.

19. Thomas D. Perry, *Civil War Stories from Mount Airy and Surry County* (Ararat, VA: Laurel Hill Publishing, 2013), p. 119.

20. *The War of Rebellion: A Compilation of the Official Records of the Union and Confederate Armies* (Washington: 1880–1901), XLIX, Series I, Part. I, p. 616 (hereafter cited as *Official Records*).

21. H. K. Weand, "Our Last Campaign and Pursuit of Jeff Davis," in *History of the Fifteenth Pennsylvania Volunteer Cavalry*, ed. Charles H. Kirk (Philadelphia: Historical Committee of the Society of the Fifteenth Pennsylvania Cavalry, 1906), p. 492.

22. Ina Woestemeyer Van Noppen, *Stoneman's Last Raid* (Raleigh: North Carolina State College Print Shop, 1961), p. 1.

23. *Official Records*, Series I, XLIX, Part II, p. 112.

24. Perry, pp. 120–21. Van Noppen, p. 32. Orser, p. 153. John G. Barrett, *The Civil War in North Carolina* (Chapel Hill: University of North Carolina Press, 1963), p. 353.

25. Wallace and Wallace, p. 252.

26. Quoted in Orser, p. 153.

27. Barrett, p. 353.

CHAPTER 31. RECONSTRUCTION

1. John T. Trowbridge, *A Picture of the Desolated States and the Work of Restoration, 1865–1868* (Hartford, CT: L. Stebbins, 1868), p. 577.

2. *The Sun* (New York), December 10, 1870.

3. J. C. Shields, letter to Chang and Eng Bunker, December 10, 1870, UNCCH.

4. Wallace and Wallace, p. 256.

5. "Disastrous Fire," in *New York Times*, July 14, 1865.

6. Graves, p. 32.

7. Nannie Bunker, diary (unpaginated), NCSA; all subsequent quotes from her, unless otherwise indicated, are from her diary.

8. Barnum, p. 283.

9. Graves, p. 35.

10. James Simpson, "A Lecture on the Siamese Twins and Other Viable United Twins," in *British Medical Journal,* February 13, 1869.

CHAPTER 32. THE LAST RADIANCE OF THE SETTING SUN

1. "Chang and Eng," in *Philadelphia Medical Times,* February 19, 1874, p. 327.
2. William Linn Keese, *The Siamese Twins and Other Poems* (New York: E. W. Dayton, 1902), p. 7.
3. Hunter, p. 106.
4. Wallace and Wallace, p. 292.
5. Neider, p. 281.
6. Graves, p. 29.
7. Ibid., p. 39.
8. Wallace and Wallace, p. 286. Hunter, p. 100.
9. Charles Morrow Wilson, *Liberia: Black Africa in Microcosm* (New York: Harper & Row, 1971), pp. 76–77.
10. See Edward James Roye, "Letters from Colonists," in *African Repository* XXII (1847), p. 232.
11. Crabb, p. 222.
12. For the concept of the "gray zone," see Primo Levi, *The Drowned and the Saved,* trans. Raymond Rosenthal (New York: Vintage, 1989), pp. 36–69.
13. "Chang and Eng," in *Philadelphia Medical Times,* February 19, 1874.
14. Fatout, p. 278.
15. "Chang and Eng," in *Philadelphia Medical Times,* February 19, 1874, p. 328. *New York Times,* February 20, 1874, p. 8. *Daily News,* Raleigh, NC, January 21, 1874, p. 4.

CHAPTER 33. AFTERLIFE

1. Mary Roach, *Stiff: The Curious Lives of Human Cadavers* (New York: W. W. Norton, 2003), pp. 9–10.
2. Nannie Bunker, letter to Christopher Bunker, January 19, 1874, NCSA.
3. Roach, pp. 41–44.
4. Ibid., p. 46.
5. Edward Warren, *The Life of John Collins Warren, M.D.: Compiled Chiefly from His Autobiography and Journals* (Boston: Ticknor and Fields, 1860), vol. 2, pp. 412, 419–20.
6. Letter, Rozell, Horton, and Gray to Mrs. Chang and Eng Bunker, January 29, 1874, UNCCH.
7. "Death of the Siamese Twins," in *Charlotte Observer* (Charlotte, NC), January 28, 1874, p. 1.
8. "The Dead Twins," in *Morning Star* (Wilmington, NC), January 28, 1874, p. 3.
9. William H. Pancoast, "Report on the Surgical Consideration in Regard to the Propriety of an Operation for the Separation of Eng and Chang Bunker," in *Transactions of the College of Physicians of Philadelphia* (1875): pp. 150–51.
10. "Chang and Eng," in *Philadelphia Medical Times,* February 19, 1874, p. 329.

11. "The Dead Chang and Eng," in *Greensborough Patriot* (Greensboro, NC), February 4, 1874, p. 3. "The Twins," in *Daily News* (Raleigh, NC), February 26, 1874, p. 2.

12. "The Siamese Twins Autopsy," in *Daily News* (Raleigh, NC), February 20, 1874, p. 2.

13. "The Twins—Clear as Mud," in *Daily News* (Raleigh, NC), February 26, 1874, p. 4.

14. C. W. and S. D. Bunker, letter to Harrison Allen, April 1, 1874, UNCCH.

EPILOGUE: MAYBERRY, USA

1. Gustavo Pérez Firmat, *A Cuban in Mayberry: Looking Back at America's Hometown* (Austin: University of Texas Press, 2014), p. 16.

2. Andrew Hurley, *Diners, Bowling Alleys, and Trailer Parks: Chasing the American Dream in Postwar Consumer Culture* (New York: Basic Books, 2001), pp. 195–272.

3. Sherwood Anderson, *Poor White* (New York: New Directions, 1993), pp. 44–45. Pérez Firmat, p. 45.

Selected Bibliography

Ackroyd, Peter. *Poe: A Life Cut Short.* New York: Doubleday/Nan A. Talese, 2008.

Anderson, Sherwood. *Poor White.* New York: New Directions, 1993.

Asbury, Herbert. *All Around the Town.* New York: Knopf, 1934.

Bakhtin, Mikhail. *Rabelais and His World.* Translated by Hélène Iswolsky. Bloomington: Indiana University Press, 1984.

Barnum, P. T. *Struggles and Triumphs; or, Forty Years' Recollections.* Buffalo: Courier Company, 1883.

Barrett, John G. *The Civil War in North Carolina.* Chapel Hill: University of North Carolina Press, 1963.

Benedict, Barbara M. *Curiosity: A Cultural History of Early Modern Inquiry.* Chicago: University of Chicago Press, 2001.

Berret, Anthony J. "*Huckleberry Finn* and the Minstrel Show." *American Studies* 27 (Fall 1986): pp. 37–49.

Bierce, Ambrose. *Ambrose Bierce's Civil War.* Edited by William McCann. New York: Wings Books, 1996.

Blyden, Edward Wilmot. "The Fifth President of the Republic of Liberia." *African Repository* XLVI (1870).

Bogdan, Robert. *Freak Show: Presenting Human Oddities for Amusement and Profit.* Chicago: University of Chicago Press, 1988.

Bolton, George Buckley. "Statement of the Principal Circumstances Respecting the United Siamese Twins Now Exhibiting in London." *Philosophical Transactions of the Royal Society of London* 120 (1830).

Bowring, John. *The Kingdom and People of Siam; with a Narrative of the Mission to That Country in 1855.* London: John Parker and Son, 1857.

Bristowe, W. S. "Robert Hunter in Siam." *History Today* 24:2 (February 1974).

Carmer, Carl. *Stars Fell on Alabama.* 1934. Reprint, Tuscaloosa: University of Alabama Press, 2000.

Cash, W. J. *The Mind of the South.* 1941. Reprint, New York: Vintage Books, 1991.

Cassuto, Leonard. "'What an object he would have made of me!': Tattooing and the Racial Freak in Melville's *Typee.*" In *Freakery: Cultural Spectacles of the Extraordinary Body,* edited by Rosemarie Garland Thomson, pp. 235–42. New York: New York University Press, 1996.

Clark, J. C. D. *English Society 1688–1832: Ideology, Social Structure and Political Practice during the Ancien Régime.* London: Cambridge University Press, 2000.

Clegg, Claude A., III. *The Price of Liberty: African Americans and the Making of Liberia.* Chapel Hill and London: University of North Carolina Press, 2004.

Cohen, Burton. *The Wedding of the Siamese Twins.* New York: Dramatists Play Service, Inc., 1989.

Cohen, Lucy. *Chinese in the Post–Civil War South: A People without a History.* Baton Rouge: Louisiana State University Press, 1984.

Combe, George. *The Constitution of Man, Considered in Relation to External Objects.* Boston: Carter and Hendee, 1829.

Converse, Frank B. *"Old Cremona" Songster.* New York, 1863.

Costeloe, Michael P. "William Bullock and the Mexican Connection." *Mexican Studies/ Estudios Mexicanos* 22.2 (2006): pp. 275–78.

Crabb, George. *A Dictionary of General Knowledge; or, An Explanation of Words and Things Connected with All the Arts and Sciences.* London: Thomas Tegg, 1830.

Crawford, Martin. *Ashe County's Civil War: Community and Society in the Appalachian South.* Charlottesville: University Press of Virginia, 2001.

Crawfurd, John. *Journal of an Embassy to the Courts of Siam and Cochin China,* Oxford in Asia Historical Reprints. Kuala Lumpur, Malaysia: Oxford University Press, 1967.

Cunningham, Peter. *Handbook of London: Past and Present.* London: John Murray, 1850.

Damrosch, Leo. *Tocqueville's Discovery of America.* New York: Farrar, Straus and Giroux, 2010.

Davies, John D. *Phrenology, Fad and Science: A 19th-Century American Crusade.* New Haven: Yale University Press, 1955.

De Quincey, Thomas. *Confessions of an English Opium-Eater and Other Writings.* Edited by Grevel Lindop. New York: Oxford University Press, 1998.

Dickens, Charles. *American Notes for General Circulation.* Edited by John S. Whitley and Arnold Goldman. New York: Penguin, 1972.

Dolan, J. R. *The Yankee Peddlers of Early America: An Affectionate History of Life and Commerce in the Developing Colonies and the Young Republic.* New York: Bramhall House, 1964.

Dreger, Alice. "The Sex Lives of Conjoined Twins." *The Atlantic,* October 25, 2012. http://www.theatlantic.com/health/archive/2012/10/the-sex-lives-of-conjoined-twins/264095/ (accessed 2/17/2016).

Dugger, Shepherd. *Romance of the Siamese Twins and Other Sketches.* Burnsville, NC: Edwards Printing Co., 1936.

Dulles, Foster Rhea. *America Learns to Play: A History of Popular Recreation, 1607–1940.* New York: D. Appleton-Century, 1940.

Farrington, Anthony, ed. *Early Missionaries in Bangkok: The Journals of Tomlin, Gutzlaff and Abeel, 1828–1832.* Bangkok: White Lotus Press, 2001.

Fatout, Paul, ed. *Mark Twain Speaking.* Iowa City: University of Iowa Press, 1976.

Faust, Drew Gilpin. *This Republic of Suffering: Death and the American Civil War.* New York: Knopf, 2008.

Federal Writers' Project, ed. *North Carolina: The WPA Guide to the Old North State.* Chapel Hill: University of North Carolina Press, 1939.

Fiedler, Leslie. *Freaks: Myths and Images of the Secret Self.* New York: Simon and Schuster, 1978.

———. *Tyranny of the Normal: Essays on Bioethics, Theology and Myth.* Boston: David R. Godine, 1996.

Finlayson, George. *The Mission to Siam and Hue 1821–1822.* First published 1826; Singapore: Oxford University Press, 1988.

Foucault, Michel. *The Birth of the Clinic: An Archaeology of Medical Perception.* Translated by A. M. Sheridan Smith. New York: Vintage Books, 1975.

Fowler, Orson, and Lorenzo Fowler. *Phrenology Proved, Illustrated, and Applied.* New York, 1837.

Freud, Sigmund. "Sexuality in the Aetiology of the Neurosis," in *The Standard Edition of the Complete Psychoanalytical Writings of Sigmund Freud.* Edited by James Strachey et al. (1953–1975).

Garrett, William. *Reminiscences of Public Men in Alabama: For Thirty Years, with an Appendix.* Atlanta: Plantation Publishing Company's Press, 1872.

Garrison, Webb. *Civil War Curiosities: Strange Stories, Oddities, Events, and Coincidences.* Nashville: Rutledge Hill Press, 1994.

Gay, Peter. *Education of the Senses.* New York: Oxford University Press, 1984.

Gordon, Richard. *The Alarming History of Medicine: Amusing Anecdotes from Hippocrates to Heart Transplants.* New York: St. Martin's Press, 1993.

Graves, Jesse Franklin. "The Siamese Twins as Told by Judge Jesse Franklin Graves," unpublished manuscript, North Carolina State Archives, n.d.

Greenberg, Kenneth S., ed. *The Confessions of Nat Turner and Related Documents.* Boston: Bedford Books, 1996.

Grosz, Elizabeth. "Intolerable Ambiguity: Freaks as/at the Limit." In *Freakery: Cultural Spectacles of the Extraordinary Body,* edited by Rosemarie Garland Thomson. New York: New York University Press, 1996.

Gutzlaff, Charles [formerly Karl]. *Journal of Three Voyages Along the Coast of China in 1831, 1832, 1833.* London: Frederick Westley and A. H. Davis, 1834.

Hale, James W. *An Historical Account of the Siamese Twin Brothers, from Actual Observations.* New York: Elliott and Palmer, 1831.

Haller, John S., and Robin M. Haller. *The Physician and Sexuality in Victorian America.* New York: W. W. Norton, 1977.

Hawthorne, Nathaniel. *The American Notebooks.* Edited by Randall Stewart. New Haven, CT: Yale University Press, 1932.

Heaver, Stuart. "The Chinese Soldiers Who Fought in the American Civil War." *South China Morning Post,* June 30, 2013. http://www.scmp.com/magazines/post-magazine/article/1270170/gettysburg-redress (accessed July 31, 2016).

Helper, Hinton Rowan. *The Land of Gold: Reality versus Fiction.* Baltimore, 1855.

Herndon, William H., and Jesse W. Weik. *Life of Lincoln.* New York: 1896.

Hodes, Martha. *White Women, Black Men: Illicit Sex in the Nineteenth-Century South.* New Haven, CT: Yale University Press, 1997.

Holsoe, Svend E. "A Portrait of a Black Midwestern Family during the Early Nineteenth Century: Edward James Roye and His Parents." *Liberian Studies Journal* 3.1 (1970–71).

Hsieh, Yu-jung. *Hsien-lo kuo-chih (Siam Gazetteer).* Bangkok: Nan-hai tung-shun-she, 1949.

Huang, Yunte. *Charlie Chan: The Untold Story of the Honorable Detective and His Rendez-vous with American History.* New York: W. W. Norton, 2010.

Hunter, Kay. *Duet for a Lifetime: The Story of the Original Siamese Twins.* New York: Coward-McCann, 1964.

Hurley, Andrew. *Diners, Bowling Alleys, and Trailer Parks: Chasing the American Dream in Postwar Consumer Culture.* New York: Basic Books, 2001.

Hyde, Lewis. *Trickster Makes This World: Mischief, Myth, and Art.* New York: Farrar, Straus and Giroux, 1998.

Hyde, William DeWitt, ed. *Vocations.* Vol. 10. Boston: Hall and Locke, 1911.

Irving, Washington. *Washington Irving's Sketch Book.* New York: Avenel Books, 1985.

James, Marquis. *Andrew Jackson: The Border Captain.* Indianapolis: Grosset & Dunlap, 1933.

Johnson, Paul E. *A Shopkeeper's Millennium: Society and Revivals in Rochester, New York, 1815–1837.* New York: Hill and Wang, 1978.

Keese, William Linn. *The Siamese Twins and Other Poems.* New York: E. W. Dayton, 1902.

Kirker, Harold. "The Boston Exchange Coffee House." *Old-Time New England*, Vol. LII, 1961.

Korg, Jacob, ed. *London in Dickens' Day.* Englewood Cliffs, NJ: Prentice-Hall, 1960.

Kutzer, Jewell Mitchell. *Memories of Mayberry: A Nostalgic Look at Andy Griffith's Home-town, Mount Airy.* St. Augustine, FL: Dynamic Living Press, 2001.

Larkin, Jack. *The Reshaping of Everyday Life, 1790–1840.* New York: Harper Perennial, 1988.

Lee, Robert G. *Orientals: Asian Americans in Popular Culture.* Philadelphia: Temple University Press, 1999.

Leonowens, Anna. *The English Governess at the Siamese Court.* First published 1870; New York: Oxford University Press, 1988.

Levi, Primo. *The Drowned and the Saved.* Translated by Raymond Rosenthal. New York: Vintage, 1989.

Lott, Eric. *Love and Theft: Blackface Minstrelsy and the American Working Class.* New York: Oxford University Press, 1993.

Lytton, Edward Bulwer. *The Siamese Twins: A Satirical Tale of the Times. With Other Poems.* New York: J & J Harper, 1831.

Mackey, Nathaniel. "Phrenological Whitman." *Conjunctions* 29 (Fall 1997), p. 10.

Masur, Louis P. *1831: Year of Eclipse.* New York: Hill and Wang, 2001.

McCoy, Sharon D. "'The Trouble Begins at Eight': Mark Twain, the San Francisco Min-strels, and the Unsettling Legacy of Blackface Minstrelsy." *American Literary Realism* 41.3 (Spring 2009).

McCunn, Ruthanne Lum. *Chinese Yankee: A True Story from the Civil War.* San Francisco: Design Enterprise of San Francisco, 2014.

McCutcheon, Marc. *Everyday Life in the 1800s.* Cincinnati, OH: Writer's Digest Books, 1993.

Melville, Herman. *The Confidence-Man: His Masquerade.* Edited by Hershel Parker. New York: W. W. Norton, 1971.

———. *Moby-Dick.* Edited by Harrison Hayford, Hershel Parker, and G. Thomas Tan-selle. Northwestern–Newberry Edition. Evanston, IL: Northwestern University Press and Newberry Library, 1988.

Miles, Melvin M. *Eng and Chang: From Siam to Surry.* Self-published. CreateSpace, 2013.

Miles, Tiya. *The House on Diamond Hill: A Cherokee Plantation Story.* Chapel Hill: University of North Carolina Press, 2010.

Mitchell, Elisha. *Diary of a Geological Tour by Dr. Elisha Mitchell in 1827 and 1828.* Chapel Hill: University of North Carolina Press, 1905.

Mitchell, Leslie. *Bulwer Lytton: The Rise and Fall of a Victorian Man of Letters.* London: Hambledon and London, 2003.

Moore, R. Adey. "An Early British Merchant in Bangkok." *Journal of the Siam Society* XI (1914–1915).

Neider, Charles, ed. *The Complete Humorous Sketches and Tales of Mark Twain.* Garden City, NY: Doubleday, 1961.

Nevins, Allan, ed. *The Diary of Philip Hone, 1828–1851.* New York: Dodd, Mead, 1936.

Noyes, John Humphrey. *Strange Cults and Utopians of 19th-Century America.* 1870. New York: Dover Publications, 1966. First published in 1870 as *History of American Socialisms.*

O'Connor, Flannery. *Mystery and Manners: Occasional Prose.* Edited by Sally and Robert Fitzgerald. New York: Farrar, Straus and Giroux, 1970.

Official Guide and Album of the Cunard Steamship Company. London: Sutton Sharpe and Co., 1878.

Orser, Joseph Andrew. *The Lives of Chang and Eng: Siam's Twins in Nineteenth-Century America.* Chapel Hill: University of North Carolina Press, 2014.

Orth, Samuel Peter. *A History of Cleveland, Ohio: Biographical.* Chicago and Cleveland: S. J. Clarke Publishing, 1910.

Pancoast, William H. *Report of the Autopsy of the Siamese Twins: Together with Other Interesting Information Concerning Their Life.* Philadelphia: J. B. Lippincott, 1874.

Passenger Lists of Vessels Arriving at New York, New York, 1820–1897. Washington, DC: National Archives.

Peña, Jennifer L., and Laurie B. Hayes. *Wilkes County: A Brief History.* Charleston, SC: History Press, 2008.

Pérez Firmat, Gustavo. *A Cuban in Mayberry: Looking Back at America's Hometown.* Austin: University of Texas Press, 2014.

Perry, Thomas D. *Civil War Stories from Mount Airy and Surry County.* Ararat, VA: Laurel Hill Publishing, 2013.

Poe, Edgar Allan. *Poetry, Tales, and Selected Essays.* New York: Library of America, 1984.

Powell, William S. *North Carolina through Four Centuries.* Chapel Hill: University of North Carolina Press, 1989.

Quigley, Christine. *Conjoined Twins: An Historical, Biological and Ethical Issues Encyclopedia.* Jefferson, NC: McFarland & Company, 2003.

Quinan, Jack. "The Boston Exchange Coffee House." *Journal of the Society of Architectural Historians* 38:3 (October 1979).

Radin, Paul. *The Trickster: A Study in American Indian Mythology.* New York: Schocken Books, 1972.

Rama II, King of Thailand. *Nang Loi: The Floating Maiden. A Recitation from an Episode of the Ramakien.* Translated by Pensak Chagsuchinda (Lund, Sweden: Studentlitteratur, 1973).

Reynolds, David S. *Waking Giant: America in the Age of Jackson*. New York: HarperCollins, 2008.

Roach, Mary. *Stiff: The Curious Lives of Human Cadavers*. New York: W. W. Norton, 2003.

Roberts, Edmund. *Embassy to the Eastern Courts of Cochin-China, Siam, and Muscat; in the U.S. Sloop-of-War Peacock, David Geisinger, Commander, during the Years 1832–3–4*. New York: Harper and Brothers, 1837.

———, and W. S. W. Ruschenberger. *Two Yankee Diplomats in 1830s Siam*. Edited by Michael Smithies. Bangkok: Orchid Press, 2002.

Roberts, George B. "Dr. Physick and His House." *Pennsylvania Magazine of History and Biography* V (1881).

Roebling, Johann August. *Diary of My Journey from Muehlhausen in Thuringia via Bremen to the United States of North America in the Year 1831*. Trenton, NJ: Roebling Press, 1931.

Rosell, Garth M., and Richard A. G. Dupuis, eds. *The Original Memoirs of Charles G. Finney*. Grand Rapids, MI: Zondervan, 1989.

Roye, Edward James. "Letters from Colonists." *African Repository* XXII (1847).

Ruschenberger, William S. W. *Narrative of a Voyage Round the World during the Years 1835, 36, and 37*. 1838. Reprint, Folkestone and London: Dawson of Pall Mall, 1970.

Rusk, Ralph L., ed. *The Letters of Ralph Waldo Emerson*. New York: Columbia University Press, 1939.

Semonin, Paul. "Monsters in the Marketplace: The Exhibition of Human Oddities in Early Modern England." In *Freakery: Cultural Spectacles of the Extraordinary Body*, edited by Rosemarie Garland Thomson. New York: New York University Press, 1996.

Shell, Marc. *Stutter*. Cambridge: Harvard University Press, 2006.

Shick, Tom W. *Behold the Promised Land: A History of Afro-American Settler Society in Nineteenth-Century Liberia*. Baltimore and London: Johns Hopkins University Press, 1977.

Shively, Carol A., ed. *Asians and Pacific Islanders and the Civil War*. Washington, DC: Eastern National, 2015.

Simpson, James. "A Lecture on the Siamese Twins and Other Viable United Twins." *British Medical Journal*, February 13, 1869.

Skinner, G. William. *Chinese Society in Thailand: An Analytical History*. Ithaca, NY: Cornell University Press, 1957.

Smith, Charlotte Elizabeth. "West Meets East: Exhibitions of Chinese Material Culture in Nineteenth-Century America." MA thesis, University of Delaware, 1987.

Smithies, Michael, ed. *Descriptions of Old Siam*. Kuala Lumpur, Malaysia: Oxford University Press, 1995.

Stern, Madeleine B., ed. *A Phrenological Dictionary of Nineteenth-Century Americans*. Westport, CT: Greenwood Press, 1982.

Stewart, Susan. *On Longing: Narratives of the Miniature, the Gigantic, the Souvenir, the Collection*. Durham, NC: Duke University Press, 1993.

Strauss, Darin. *Chang and Eng: A Novel*. New York: Penguin, 2001.

Stuart, James. *Three Years in North America*. New York: J. & J. Harper, 1833.

Tchen, John Kuo Wei. *New York before Chinatown: Orientalism and the Shaping of American Culture, 1776–1882*. Baltimore: Johns Hopkins University Press, 1999.

Terwiel, B. J. *A History of Modern Thailand, 1767–1942.* St. Lucia, Australia: University of Queensland Press, 1983.

Thompson, Evelyn Scales. *Around Surry County.* Charleston, SC: Arcadia Publishing, 2005.

Thomson, Rosemarie Garland, ed. *Freakery: Cultural Spectacles of the Extraordinary Body.* New York: New York University Press, 1996.

Tocqueville, Alexis de. *Democracy in America.* Edited by J. P. Mayer, translated by George Lawrence. New York: HarperCollins, 1988.

———. *Journey to America.* Translated by George Lawrence, edited by J. P. Mayer. Garden City, NY: Doubleday, 1971.

———. *Letters from America.* Edited and translated by Frederick Brown. New Haven, CT: Yale University Press, 2010.

Toll, Robert C. *Blacking Up: The Minstrel Show in Nineteenth-Century America.* New York: Oxford University Press, 1974.

Trollope, Fanny. *Domestic Manners of the Americans.* 1832. Reprint, Gloucester, UK: Alan Sutton, 1984.

Trowbridge, John T. *A Picture of the Desolated States and the Work of Restoration, 1865–1868.* Hartford, CT: L. Stebbins, 1868.

Tuckerman, Bayard, ed. *The Diary of Philip Hone, 1828–1851.* New York: Dodd, Mead, 1889.

Twain, Mark. *The Autobiography of Mark Twain.* New York: Harper and Row, 1959.

———. *The Adventures of Huckleberry Finn.*

———. *Following the Equator.* New York: Ecco Press, 1992.

———. *The Tragedy of Pudd'nhead Wilson; and the Comedy, Those Extraordinary Twins.* New York: Oxford University Press, 1996.

Van Noppen, Ina Woestemeyer. *Stoneman's Last Raid.* Raleigh: North Carolina State College Print Shop, 1961.

Vella, Walter F. *Siam Under Rama III, 1824–1851.* Locust Valley, NY: J. J. Augustin, 1957.

Wadlington, Warwick. *The Confidence Game in American Literature.* Princeton, NJ: Princeton University Press, 1975.

Wallace, Irving. *The Fabulous Showman: The Life and Times of P. T. Barnum.* New York: Knopf, 1959.

———, and Amy Wallace. *The Two: A Biography.* New York: Simon and Schuster, 1978.

The War of Rebellion: A Compilation of the Official Records of the Union and Confederate Armies. Washington, DC: Government Printing Office, 1880–1901.

Warren, Edward. *The Life of John Collins Warren: Compiled Chiefly from His Autobiography and Journals.* Boston: Ticknor and Fields, 1860.

Warren, John. "An Account of the Siamese Twin Brothers United Together from Their Birth." *American Journal of the Medical Sciences* 5.9 (November 1829).

———. "The Siamese Brothers." *Boston Medical and Surgical Journal* 2 (September 1829).

———. "Some Account of the Siamese Boys, Lately Brought to Boston." *Boston Daily Advertiser,* August 26, 1829.

Weigley, Russell F., ed. *Philadelphia: A 300-Year History.* New York: W. W. Norton, 1982.

Werner, M. R. *Barnum.* New York: Harcourt, Brace, 1923.

Wilson, Charles Morrow. *Liberia: Black Africa in Microcosm*. New York: Harper & Row, 1971.

Wright, Richardson. *Hawkers and Walkers in Early America: Strolling Peddlers, Preachers, Lawyers, Doctors, Players, and Others, from the Beginning to the Civil War*. Philadelphia: J. B. Lippincott, 1927.

Wu, Cynthia. *Chang and Eng Reconnected: The Original Siamese Twins in American Culture*. Philadelphia: Temple University Press, 2012.

Wyatt, David K. *Thailand: A Short History*. New Haven and London: Yale University Press, 1984.

Yamashita, Karen Tei. "Siamese Twins and Mongoloids." In *Yellow Light: The Performance of Asian American Arts*, edited by Amy Ling. Philadelphia: Temple University Press, 1999.

Index

Note: Page numbers in *italics* refer to illustrations.

abolitionist movement, xv, 97, 122–24,
    128, 229, 247, 249
aborigines, 82
Adams, John, 177
Afong Moy "Chinese Lady," 83
Agassiz, Louis, 177
Age of Discovery, 41, 82
Alexander, Sir James, 127–28
Allen, Harrison, 322
American Colonization Society (ACS), xxii
American Museum, 260–62, 263, 264,
    267, 268, 270, 301
American Philosophical Society, 44
Anatomy Act (1832), 319–20
Anderson, Sherwood, 327, 346
Andrews, Thomas, 322
Andy Griffith Show, The, 189, 197, 327–47
Anglo-Burmese War (1824), 4
Anthony, Susan B., 177
Aristotle, 53
Arnold, Benedict, 149
Ashe, Samuel, 194
Astor, John Jacob, 177
Austen, Jane, *Pride and Prejudice,* 206,
    215–16, 217
Ayudhya Revolution (1688), 9, 18

Bacon, Francis, 101
Bakhtin, Mikhail, 80, 81
Bangkok, twins' travel to, 23–25, 26
Bank of the United States (BUS), 157–58
Barnum, P. T., 54, 256–67, 300–305
    and American Museum, 260–62, 263,
        264, 268, 301

and Chang and Eng, 137, 264–65,
    275, 300, 302–4, 313
and hoaxes, 48, 73, 100, 253, 259,
    265–67, 313
The Humbugs of the World, 258
and Tom Thumb, 40, *256,* 261–62, 302
Bartholomew Fair, 81, 82
Baugus, Robert J., 198
Baugus, Samuel, 207
Beaumont, Gustave, 126, 132–33
Beecher, Henry Ward, 173
Beecher, Lyman, 142
Benton, Rev. J. A., 269–70
Berrisford, James, xviii
Bibb, William Wyatt, 164
Biddenden Maids, 20, 84
Bierce, Ambrose, 286
Biggers, Earl Derr, 155
Birkbeck, George, 77
Black Hawk, 133, 159–61
Black Hawk War (1832), 147
body-snatching, 319–20, 321
Bogdan, Robert, 54
Bolívar, Simón, 6
Bolton, George Buckley, 85, 86–87, 90
Bonaparte, Napoleon, 40, 74, 77, 167
Boone, Daniel, 147, 188, 190, 200
Boone, Rev. William J., 200
Booth, John Wilkes, 177, 188, 325
Borden, Lizzie, 177
Boston:
    twins' arrival in, 39–40, 44–45
    twins' debut in, 51–55
Bower, George, 195

Bowring, Sir John, *The Kingdom and People of Siam,* 11
Bradley, Dan B., 12
Brady, Mathew, 300
British Isles, twins' tours to, 72–79, 80–87, 92–93, 99, 143, 302–5
Broadnax, William Henry, 128
Brodie, Sir Benjamin Collins, 77
Brooks, Joshua, 78–79
Brown, John, 177
Brown, Lydia Waters, 194–95
Browning, Elizabeth Barrett, 89
Buchanan, James, 287
Buffalo, New York, 131–33
Bullock, William, 77–78, 82
Bunker, Adelaide Yates, *301*
    after Chang's death, 318, 320–21, 322–23, 325
    children of, 237, 238, 284, 292
    marriage of Chang and, 216–24, 232, 236
Bunker, Albert, 300, 309
Bunker, Catherine, 213–14, 222
Bunker, Chang and Eng, *see* Chang and Eng
Bunker, Christopher Wren, xxiv, 263–64, 288, 291–93, 318, 325
Bunker, James, 309
Bunker, Josephine, 253
Bunker, Katherine, 253, 264, 302–5, 309
Bunker, Montgomery, 265
Bunker, Nannie, 302–4, 309, 318
Bunker, Patrick, 249, 264, 265, 300
Bunker, Sarah Yates, *301*, 316
    after Eng's death, 318, 320–21, 322–23, 325
    children of, 237, 238, 285
    marriage of Eng and, 216–24, 232, 236
Bunker, Stephen Decatur, xxiv, 293–94, 325
Bunker family, *298*
    and Aunt Grace, 236, 238, *239*, 241, 298
    reunion (2003), 235–38, 249–50
    and slavery, 249–51
    and tours, 253, 263–64, 275, 277–78, 302–5
    and twins' deaths, 320–23, 325
    see also Chang and Eng, children and descendents of
Burke, William, 60–61, 319
Burney, Henry, 19, 27
Burney Mission (1826), 9, 26–27, 74

Cahill, Thaddeus, 276
Calhoun, John, 157
California:
    gold rush in, 271, 277
    twins' tour in, 268–79
Calloway, James, 190
Capote, Truman, 119
Carlisle, Sir Anthony, 85
Carmer, Carl, 164, 167
Carmichael, Abner, 201, 204
Carnegie, Andrew, 177
Cash, W. J., 164
Céberet du Boullay, Claude, 11
Century (Thousand-Year) Eggs, 17–18
Chan, Charlie (fict.), 155, 328
Chang and Eng, 37, *52*, 70
    account book of, *95*, 154–56, 161, 165, 190, 193, 198, 203, 213
    aging of, 308–10, 311
    arrival in U.S., 39–43, 45
    autopsy of, 68, 182, 232, 249, 321–25
    and Barnum, 137, 264–65, 275, 300, 302–4, 313
    birth of, xxii, 6, 7
    as chess players, xviii–xix, xx, xxii, xxiv, xxv, 310
    children and descendents of, xxiii, xxiv, xxv, 235, 237, 238, 248, 249–50, 253, 262, *269*, 284–85, 292, *301*, 330, 336, 339
    and Civil War, xxiv, 284–85, 288, 291–94, 296, 297–300
    connecting cartilage of, xix, 5, 13–14, 45, 48–49, 68–69, 78, 83, 85, 322, 323–25
    contract with Hunter and Coffin, 33–35, *33*, 109, 130, 133–34
    critics of, 56, 244
    debut of, 51–55
    disagreements of, 306–9
    double wedding of, xxiii, xxv, 206, 220–24
    early years of, 11, 13–14
    earnings of, xxii–xxiv, 67, 162, 191, 284, 285, 297–99
    events after death of, 317–25
    and fame, 99, 157, 202, 270, 272
    family background of, 8–9
    final illness and death of, xxv–xxvi, 306, 308–9, 311, 313–16
    final performances of, 193–94, 195, 309–10

as freak of nature, xxii, 44, 45, 56, 58, 73, 76, 100, 112, 115, 212, 214, 219, 236, 244, 245, 265, 346
gravestone of, 334, *334*
homesickness of, 93, 109, 269–70
homestead of, *185*, 193, 197–205, 216, 217, 238, *307*
independence sought by, 130, 133–37, 139, 144–45
and Lynnfield Battle, 112–16, 179
married life of, 225–34, 248–49, 272
medical exams of, 46–50, 68–69, 76–79, 85–87, 129, 164–65, 172, 177, 180–81, 304–5, 319–20, 321–25
as merchants, 18, 26, 32, 140, 151, 203–4, 207
mother of (Nok), 6, 12–13, 17, 22, 32–33, 34, 312
names of, 8, 34, 214, 222–23
in North Carolina, xxii–xxiv, *185*, 187–92, 195–96, 207, 221
as performers, 54, 55, 61, 83, *84*, 198
and phrenology, 177, 178–83
possible separation of, 49, 69, 236, 263, 304, 315, 324
publicity about, 45–46, 51, 54–55, *57*, 69, 75–76, 79, 101, 110, 158, 178, 213, 242, 262–63, 272, 300, *301*
religious conjecture about, 55, 227–28
return to U.S., 94, 310
signatures of, *137*
and slaves, *see* slavery
studies of, 91–92, 140
Ti-eye, father of, 6, 13, 16–17, 304
on tour, xxiv–xxv, 22, 32, 44, 54–56, 61–65, 66–68, 72–79, 81–87, 92–93, 109–10, 112, 125–27, 130, 141–42, 143, 146–50, 154–59, 162, 163–69, 177–78, 198, 252–53, 261–65, 268–79, 299–305, 309–10
U.S. citizenship of, 199–202, 211, 223
and women, 89–90, 205, 206–21, 249
Charles II, king of England, 80
Chase, Salmon Portland, xxi
Cherokee Nation, 245
Cherokee Nation v. Georgia, 97, 100
Chinaman, use of term, 271
Chinese Siamese history, 9–13
cholera, 15–17, 98, 304
Christie, E. P., 270
Chulkhurst, Mary and Eliza, 20
Cigrange, Jacob, xvii
circuit court judges, 153–54

Civil War, U.S., xviii, 283–96
Asian men serving in, 288–94
and Chang and Eng, xxiv, 284–85, 288, 291–94, 296, 297–300
deaths in, xv, *281*, 283, 287
economic effects of, 285, 297–300
psychological effects of, xv, 286–87, 297
secession as prelude to, 147, 157, 277, 278–79, 283
twins as metaphor for, 278–79
Clanny, William Reid, 77
Clay, Henry, 147, 158, 284
Clemens, Samuel, *see* Twain, Mark
Cleveland, Benjamin, 187
Coffin, Abel:
and Chang and Eng, xxii, 32–35, 39–40, 44, 45, 49, 54, 72–73, 75, 76, 91, 93, 109, 123, 129, 133–36, 143–44, 262
death of, 145
and Hunter, 30–35
travels of, 98–99, 133, 135–36
twins' resentment of, 73, 99, 130, 143
Coffin, Susan, 73, 91, 93, 98–99, 108, 117, 125, 127, 130, 133–36, 139, 142–45
Cohen, Burton, *The Wedding of the Siamese Twins,* 218, 219, 235
Coleridge, Samuel Taylor, 71
Combe, George, 171, 173, 174
conjoined twins, 20–21, 49
autopsies of, 55
possible separation of, 69
Conscription Act (1862), 285
Converse, Frank B., 273
Cook, Capt. James, 77, 82
Cooper, Sir Astley, 77, 78, 319–20
Cooper, James Fenimore, 194
Crabb, George, *Dictionary of General Knowledge,* 91–92, 312
Crawford, Martin, 237
Crawfurd, John, 7, 9, 16, 18, 19, 181
Crockett, Davy, 147
Cunard Steamship Company, xix–xx
curiosities, use of term, 40–41, 48, 265
Curtis, John Harrison, 77
Cushing, William, 153
Czolgosz, Leon, 177

Dana, Richard Henry Jr., 63
Darwin, Charles, 53, 127
Davis, John D., 173

Davis, Warren R., 157
Davis, William, 135
Demopolis, Alabama, 167–69
de Quincey, Thomas, *Confessions of an English Opium-Eater,* 71–72, 82, 87–88, 237
Deslondes, Charles, 6
Desnouettes, Charles Lefebvre, 167, 168
Dickens, Charles, xvi, 41, 45, 59–60, 66, 74, 75, 77, 125–26
Diderot, Denis, *Encyclopedia,* 91, 92
Dobson, Bettie, 296
Dolan, J. R., 149
Doty, Edmund, 253, 262, 263
Douglass, Frederick, xix–xx, 177
Dreger, Alice, 229, 230, 231
Dugger, Shepherd M., 189–90, 208–9, 214
DuPont, George, 290
Dwight, Timothy, 149–50

Early, Jubal, 294
East, Benny, 339
Edison, Thomas A., 177
Edwards, Jonathan, 151
Edward VII, king of England, 265
Ellison, Ralph, 274
Emerson, Ralph Waldo, 171, 177, 271
Emmett, Dan, 43
Erie Canal, opening of, 131, 140
Ethridge, Brenda, 236, 238

Faust, Drew Gilpin, 286
Fiedler, Leslie, 11, 41, 53, 87, 332
Fifteenth Amendment (1870), 200
Finlayson, George, 181–82
Finney, Charles, 139, 140–41, 142, 144
Floyd, John, 121
Forrest, Emmett, 337
Foucault, Michel, 48
Fowler, Orson, 226, 300
Fowler brothers, 173–74, 176–82
Fox, Charley, 273
Franco-Prussian War, 309, 310
Frankenberry, Frank, 295
Franklin, Benjamin, 258
"freaks":
    born vs. "gaffed," 48
    conjoined twins, 20–21, 49, 73
    and curiosities, 40–41, 48, 265, 312–13
    hoaxes, 48, 253–56, 259
    and monsters, 53–54, 76, 80–81, 90, 94, 325
    mummy exhibition, 47
    Ourang Outangs, 111–12, 161

and phrenology, 174
    racial, 82–88, 112–16
    Southern writers on, 163, 168–69, 229
freak shows, xiii, 43–45, 46, 48, 49, 61, 69, 78, 80–81, 82, 84–85, 259, 272
Freud, Sigmund, 172, 233
Fugitive Slave Law (1850), 284

Gall, Franz Joseph, 170, 172, 176, 258
Gambill, Martin, 195
Gambill, Nancy, 203
Garfield, James A., 325
Garrison, William Lloyd, 97, 116, 122–24, 206, 229
Gates, Grace [Aunt], 236, 238, *239,* 241, 298
Gay, Peter, 227
George III, king of England, 77
George IV, king of England, 74
Germany, twins' tour in, 309–10
Gerry, Elbridge, 112–14
Gerry, Elbridge Thomas, 113–14
Gibson, Josh, 234, 336
Gilded Age, xvi
Gist, Christopher, 188
Gould, Hannah F., "To the Siamese Twins," 116
Graham, Sylvester, 226
Grant, Ulysses S., 294, 300
Graves, Judge Jesse Franklin, 17, 207, 209, 216–18, 239–40, 241, 284, 308, 330
Gray, Henry, *Gray's Anatomy,* 77
Gray, Thomas, 119
Great Awakenings, 60, 139, 140–41, 151, 178, 227, 228
Great Moon Hoax, 254–55
Greeley, Horace, 177
Griffith, Andy, *331*
    Andy Griffith Show, 189, 197, 327–47
    memorabilia of, 337
Grosz, Elizabeth, 87
Gutzlaff, Karl, 11–12, 28–30, 31
Gwyn, James, 201, 203

Hale, James:
    and Coffins, 98, 108, 125, 145
    publicity arranged by, 54–55, 110
    and tours, 73, 75, 92–93, 108–10, 117, 177
    as twins' manager, 54, 98, 133, 177
    and women, 214, 236
Halford, Henry, 77
Haller, John S. and Robin M., 225

Hare, William, 60, 319
Harley, Robert, 21
Harris, Charles:
  and Coffin correspondence, 126–27,
    133, 135–36
  marriage of, 198, 220
  and retirement, 193, 198–99
  and tours, 126–27, 142, 190
  and twins' accounts, 154, 166, 190, 203
  and twins' independence, 133, 135–36,
    144
  as twins' manager, 125, 129, 139, 166
  and twins' wedding, 220–21
Harris, Fanny, 198, 207, 213
Harrison, William Henry, 7
Harte, Bret, 272
Hattee (servant), 21
Hawthorne, Nathaniel, 150, 152, 177
Haynes, Milton, 233
Hearst, William Randolph, 301
Hefner, Hugh, 301
Helper, Hinton Rowan, 246–49, 271, 272
Hemings, Sally, 236, 249, 250
Henry I, king of England, 81
hermaphrodite, 87
Herschel, Sir John, 254
Heth, Joice, 73, 100, 259
Hilton, Violet and Daisy, 232–33
hoaxes, 48, 253–56, 259
Hobbes, Thomas, 40
Hodes, Martha, 211
Hollingsworth, Joseph, 315, 318, 321–22
Hollingsworth, William, 315, 321
Hone, Philip, 58, 59, 61, 100–101, 172,
    262
Honeywell, Martha Ann, 43–44
hoodlum, origin of the term, 115
Houston, John, 200
Hugo, Victor, 41
  The Hunchback of Notre Dame, 89, 90,
    94
human being, definition of, 87
Hume, David, 40
Hungarian Sisters, 21, 49, 311
Hunter, David, 291
Hunter, Kay, Duet for a Lifetime, 308
Hunter, Robert, 3–5, 19
  and Chang and Eng, xxii, 20, 21–22,
    26, 31–35, 39, 44, 45, 72–73, 76, 93,
    129, 144, 205
  and Coffin, 30–35
  ownership of twins sold by, 98
  in Siam, 4–5, 27–28, 29, 29, 30
Huntington, Collis Potter, 149

individual, use of term, 87
Industrial Revolution, 74
Ingalls, H. P., 300, 302
Irving, Washington, 150, 253

Jackson, Andrew, 41–42, 43, 147, 157–
    58, 159, 172, 177, 289
Jackson, Michael, 301
Jackson, Thomas J. "Stonewall," 294
Jackson, William, 265
Jacksonian democracy, 253
Jefferson, Thomas, xxi, xxiii, 177, 194,
    236, 249, 250
Johnson, Ebenezer, 132
Johnson, Hilary R. W., xxii
Jones, Tanya, 330

Keese, William Linn, 306–7
Keller, Helen, 177
Kellogg, John Harvey, 226
Keogh, Myles, 295
Khan, Genghis, 98
Kirkham, Samuel, 179
Know-Nothing party, 284

Larkin, Jack, 147
Layley, John, 91, 92
Lee, Robert E., 285, 300
Lee, Robert G., 247, 272
Leidy, Joseph, 322
Leonowens, Anna, 13, 27, 287
Levi, Primo, 238
Liberia, xxii, xxv, 310–11, 312
Lincoln, Abraham, 43, 133, 177, 264,
    300
  gift from king of Siam to, 287–88
  on judicial circuit, 154
  and secession/Civil War, 157, 278–79,
    283, 284, 288
Linnaeus, Carl, 53
Locock, Sir Charles, 77
London, Henry Armand, 300
London Missionary Society, 28–29
Ludd, Ned; Luddites, 6
Luke, Keye, 338–39
Lynn, Betty, 330
Lynnfield Battle, 112–16, 179
Lytton, Edward Bulwer-Lytton, 1st
    Baron, 101, 102–7
  The Siamese Twins, 103–6

Mackey, Nathaniel, 181
Madison, James, 113
Malloch, D. E., 9

Mallos, Jean-Baptiste Pallegoix, bishop
    of, 11
Maltacle, Modeste "Canadian Giant," 61
manifest destiny, 171–72
Mao Zedong, 117
Marsh, Peter, 198
Marshall, John, 97
Masur, Louis, 128, 140
Mayberry (fict.), 327–47
Mayberry Campground, 339–47, *339*
McCausland, John, 291, 292
McCunn, Ruthanne Lum, 289
medicine shows, 46, 47–48, 68–69, 78,
    111, 172
Meklong, Siam, 3–5, 6, 11
Melville, Herman, 99, 106, 258, 265, 274
    Billy Budd, 63
    The Confidence-Man, 62–63, 174
    Moby-Dick, 41, 62, 151, 176, 237
    Typee, 83
Miles, Melvin, 240
Minor, David, 60, 61
minstrel shows, 43, 270–77
Mitchell, Elisha, 191, 193, 194, 237
Mongkut, king of Siam, 13, 287–88
Mongkut, Prince (Siam), 4
Monroe, James, 311
Moore, Thomas, 156
Morley, Henry, 80, 81
Moss, Henry, 43–44
Mount Airy, North Carolina, 238, 244,
    252, 327, *331*
Mütter Museum, Philadelphia, 68,
    323–25

Nabokov, Vladimir, 40
Naturalization Act (1790), 200
Neale, Frederick Arthur, 27–28
Neill, John, 322
New York City, twins' tours in, 58–60,
    61–65, 261, 262–63
Nok (mother), 6, 12–13, 17, 22, 32–33,
    34, 312
Noyes, John Humphrey, 227–28
Nye, Edgar "Bill," 275

O'Connor, Flannery, 163, 169, 229
Ohly, Herman and Honersia, xviii
Opium Wars, 30, 72
Orser, Joseph, 129, 190, 198, 201, 229
Ourang Outangs, 111–12, 161

Palmyra, xv, xvi–xxv, *xxiii*, 310, 313
Pancoast, William H., 8, 231–32, 321,
    322, 323, 324

Peale, Charles Willson, 67, 72–73, 153,
    177
Peale, Rubens, 177
Peel, Sir Robert, 74
Penn, William, 66
Pérez Firmat, Gustavo, 337, 346
Perry, Thomas, 296
Phaulkon, Constant (Yeraki), 18–19
Philadelphia, twins' tours in, 66–69,
    109–10
Phra Nangklao, 4
Phraya Tak (Taksin), 10
phrenology, 170–83, 226, 258, 322
Physick, Philip Syng, 68, 69, 172
Poe, Edgar Allan, 101, 176, 196, 255
Pope, Alexander, 21, 311
Posey, Sidney C., 166, 238
Post, Marjorie Merriweather, 301
Prang, Louis, xvii–xviii
Prang, Rosa, xvii–xviii
Prather, Thomas F., 239, 242
Prendergast, George, 193, 198
Ptolemy I, 319

race:
    and citizenship, 211
    and freaks, 82–88, 115–16
    and harassment, 112–16
    "honorary whites," 211–12
    and immigration, 247, 271, 277
    and licensing fees, 128–29
    and minstrel shows, 270–77
    and miscegenation fears, xxiii, 211,
        220, 221, 248–49
    and phrenology, 181–82
    and sex, 237–38, 244, 249
    and slaves, *see* slavery
    U.S. hierarchy of, 146
Raffles, Sir Thomas Stamford, 15
Rama I, king of Siam, 10
Rama II, king of Siam, 4, 7, 15–16, 18
Rama III, king of Siam, 4, 22–25, 26, 27,
    31–32
Randolph, Thomas Jefferson, 127
Raoul, Nicolas, 167
Reconstruction, xv, 309
Revolutionary War, U.S., 42, 286
Reynolds, David S., 157
Rice, Thomas D., 43
Richardson, Jane, 238
Riley, James, 275
Roach, Mary, *Stiff*, 317–18, 319, 320
Roane, William Henry, 127
Roberts, Edmund, 12, 13, 19, 27
Robinson, Sophonia "Sophia," 89–90

Rochester, twins' tour in, 140–42
Roebling, Johann August, 127
Rogers, Will, 268
Roget, Peter Mark, 85–86
Roye, Edward James, xxi, xxii, xxv, 310–12, 313
Ruschenberger, William, 27, 181–83, 322
Rutherford, John, 82–83

Sachem, 35, 39–40, 39, 45
Scottish Brothers, 20, 84
Scovill, Caroline, 213
Scriblerus Club, 21
Sequoyah (Cherokee), 188
Shelley, Mary, Frankenstein, 53
Sherburne, Samuel, 143
Sherman, William Tecumseh, xv, 149, 290, 294
Shields, J. C., 299
Siam:
    cholera in, 15–17
    lunar eclipse (1829) in, 32, 98
    Protestant missionaries in, 28–29, 31
Siamese Connection, The (documentary), 234, 336
Siamese Twins:
    as Civil War metaphor, 278–79
    as freaks, 20–21, 49, 73
    and marriage, 216, 218, 232–33
    and sex, 232–34, 237
    as slaves, 129–30
    uses of the term, 65, 157, 265
    see also Chang and Eng
Simpson, Sir James, 305
Sink, Alex, 336
Sin Say, 200
Skinner, G. William, 13
Slack, David B., 56
Slatt, John H., xvii
slavery:
    and abolition, see abolitionist movement
    and Amistad, 193
    and black codes, 128
    and Bunker family, 249–51
    Chang and Eng as slave owners and traders, xxiii, xxiv, 204, 207, 236, 238–46, 239, 240, 249, 284, 297–98, 312
    and Cherokee Nation, 245
    and emancipation, 127, 128
    and free blacks, xxi, 128
    and Fugitive Slave Law, 284
    and Jefferson/Hemings story, 236, 249, 250

    and Middle Passage, xv
    uprisings, 6, 97–98, 117–24, 127–28, 193, 241
Slouka, Mark, 106
Snyder Act (1924), 200
solar eclipse, 97, 98, 118
Sparks, Rev. Colby, 219, 221
Speakman, Townsend, 68
Spicer, Hardin, 203
Sprague, Timothy, 47
Spurzheim, Johann Gaspar, 171, 172–73, 176
Stewart, Susan, 72
Stoneman, George, 294–96, 328
Stowe, Harriet Beecher, 146, 173
Strauss, Darin, 106
    Chang and Eng, 231
Supreme Court, U.S., 97, 99–100
Sutter, John, 271
Swift, Jonathan, 21
    Gulliver's Travels, 81
Sylvanus, Thomas (Ah Yee Way), 289–90

Tan Puying Sap, 19
Tarkington, Rockne, 338
Tchen, John, 200
Tecumseh, Chief, 7
Tennyson, Alfred, Lord, "Ulysses," 252
Terwiel, B. J., 16
Testerman, Morgan, 285
Thomas, Leigh, 77
Thoreau, Henry David, xvi
Thumb, "General" Tom, 40, 256, 261–62, 302
Tieu (Tian Cheng), 33, 34, 39, 73, 93
Ti-eye, 6, 13, 16–17, 304
Tocci, Giovanni and Giacomo, 233
Tocqueville, Alexis de, 42–43, 58, 66, 126, 132, 134, 147, 148
Toll, Robert C., 270
Tomlin, Jacob, 14, 28–29, 31
Tomney, John, 291
Trail of Tears, 97, 147
Traphill, 185, 197–205, 216, 221, 225, 238
Travis, Joseph, 118
tricksters, 265–67
Trollope, Fanny, 42, 66
Trump, Donald, 301
Turner, Nat, 97–98, 117–20, 125, 127–28, 130, 133, 241
Twain, Mark (Samuel Clemens), xvi, 41, 106, 174, 233, 273–77, 308, 311, 315–16

Van Buren, Martin, 157, 170, 195–96
Vanderbilt, Cornelius, 60, 177
Vann, James, 245
Verne, Jules, 255
Vico, Giambattista, 5, 317
Victorian Age, 225–28

Wales, Albert Edward, prince of, 265, 267
Wallace, Irving and Amy, *The Two*, 8, 190, 230–31, 296, 308
War of 1812, 131, 286, 289
Warren, John Collins, 46–50, 53, 54, 68, 69, 72, 78, 129, 172, 320
Washington, George, 43, 73, 110, 149, 188, 259
Watson, William, xvi
Wellar, Captain, 30
Wells, H. G., 255
Whitefield, George, 151
White Plains Baptist Church, 334–35, 335
Whitman, Walt, 174–76, 300
Wilkes, John, 188

Wilkesboro, North Carolina, 187–93, 333
Williams, John, 290–91
Willson, Meredith, *The Music Man,* 254
Wong Kong Chai, 200
Wordsworth, William, 81
Wright, Richardson, 149, 153
Wu, Cynthia, 236

Yamashita, Karen, 234
Yankee peddlers, 148–51, 265–67
Yates, Adelaide, 207–12
    marriage of Chang and, *see* Bunker, Adelaide Yates
Yates, David, 207, 212, 218, 219–21, 238
Yates, Giles Fonda, 178–80
Yates, Nancy, 218–19, 220
Yates, Sarah, 207–12
    marriage of Eng and, *see* Bunker, Sarah Yates

Zheng He, 9
Zhou Daguan, 9
Zimmerman, Simon Bolivar, 299–300
"Zip, the Monkey Man," 265